Control of Cartels
and Monopolies

STUDIES IN COMPARATIVE LAW

New York University

Institute of Comparative Law

French Administrative Law and the Common-Law World

The Code Napoleon and the Common-Law World

Procedure and Democracy

Trade Regulations Overseas

Control of Cartels and Monopolies

An International Comparison

by

Corwin D. Edwards

A Study in Comparative Law
Published under the Auspices of
The Institute of Comparative Law
New York University School of Law

OCEANA PUBLICATIONS, INC.
Dobbs Ferry, New York

1967

Library of Congress Catalog Card No. 67-10657

Manufactured in the United States of America

Table of Contents

Preface

This book analyzes and evaluates (a) the concepts and procedures that are common to a considerable number of the countries outside North America in which laws designed to curb cartels and monopoles exist and are seriously applied; and (b) the relevant concepts and procedures of the two international agencies that have made sustained efforts to control cartels and monopolies. It is based upon 18 months of field work sponsored by the Brookings Institution in 1959-60, during which I studied the laws of fourteen countries and of the two international agencies, and upon study of major subsequent developments, partly from documents and comments supplied by officials and friends abroad, and partly during an additional three months of work in Europe for the Department of State in the autumn of 1963.

These studies have resulted in two prior publications. The first, a 98-page pamphlet entitled *Cartelization in Western Europe*, was published by the United States Department of State in June 1964. It sets forth such information as I could obtain about the nature and number of European cartels, discusses the status of cartels both under European national laws and under the European Economic Community and the European Coal and Steel Community, and offers suggestions as to American foreign policy toward restrictive agreements.

The second, a book published in 1966 by Oceana Publications for the Institute of Comparative Law of New York University, is entitled *Trade Regulations Overseas: The National Laws*. It consists of thirteen monographs, each concerned with the legislative history, content, and application of the law of a particular country. The countries covered are Austria, Belgium, Denmark, France, Germany, Ireland, Japan, the Netherlands, New Zealand, Norway, Sweden, the Union of South Africa, and the United Kingdom. These countries, plus Finland, are the ones in which I did field work in 1959-60.

By early 1964, when the present book began to take form, twenty-two countries additional to the United States and Canada had enacted and seemed to be seriously applying laws designed to curb restrictive practices. Apart from the thirteen covered by the monograph mentioned above, they included Finland, which I studied briefly in 1960 when experience under its recently enacted law was too limited to justify a separate monograph; Argentina and Mexico, which had pre-war laws, but which I had been unable to include in my field trip; Israel and Colombia, in which laws were enacted in 1959, too late for those countries to be covered by the field trip; Brazil, Spain, and Switzerland, whose laws had been enacted in 1962 and

1963; and Australia, wnose long-dormant law had been revived in 1963-64. In the four of these countries last mentioned, experience with the application of the laws was not yet available.

The discussion of the national laws in this book is based primarily upon my thirteen monographs, supplemented by study of subsequent developments in the thirteen countries covered by them; but it seeks also to take account of the laws of Finland, Israel, Spain, and Switzerland. In Finland, I have done a limited amount of field work. I discussed Swiss law with Swiss officials and businessmen in the autumn of 1963, after the statute was enacted but before it took effect. I discussed the Israeli law with the official responsible for its administration during a visit he made to the United States while my study was in progress. I have thrice visited Spain, and have read the Spanish government's long explanation of its newly enacted law. Thus, I have at least a slender acquaintance with the background of the laws of these four countries. For the Latin American countries and for Australia I have only the texts of their statutes, unsupported by field study, by discussion with informed persons, or by knowledge of the relevant background. Hence I have not attempted to use the laws of these countries in this book, and the reader should not assume that my statements are relevant to Australian or Latin-American experience.

Trade Regulations Overseas: The National Laws contains footnotes as to sources of information. So far as what is said in this book consists of conclusions about or analyses of matter contained in that one, I have not repeated the citations; I have footnoted only such matters as the former book does not cover.

My debt to the Brookings Institution extends over all three of the publications mentioned herein. The Institution defrayed the cost of the field work in 1959-60, as well as much of the cost of preparing the manuscripts of the monographs in *Trade Regulations Overseas* and of this volume. That we eventually differed as to the proper length and scope of my writing does not diminish my debt. Without the Institution's assistance, neither the earlier publications nor this book would have been possible.

When *Cartelization in Western Europe* was written, the Department of State agreed that material originally intended for this book which was used in that pamphlet could be reused here. The appendix of this book is an extension of Part IIA 1 of *Cartelization in Western Europe*; but whereas the previous version was focused upon European laws about cartels, this appendix also covers other aspects of European restrictive practice laws, and includes information about four countries outside Europe. Though earlier versions of Chapters XV and XVI of this book were included as Parts IIB and C of *Cartelization in Western Europe*, what appears here is the result of substantial revision in the light of later information.

Part I

THE NATIONAL LAWS

Chapter I

The Burst of Post-war Legislation

The Status of Restrictions Under General Law. Where there is no special legislation about cartels and monopolies, the legal status of such business arrangements is determined by general principles of law. In countries whose institutions are derived from the Western European inheritance, the relevant parts of the law are those concerned with the right to enter into contracts, the right to associate with others, the right to choose one's occupation, and the right to be protected against unfair competition.

Freedom of contract was established during the 19th century or earlier, usually without special curbs upon restrictive agreements. At the beginning of the 20th century, (a) restrictive agreements could be enforced in court against recalcitrant participants; (b) legal remedies were available against outsiders who induced or contributed to the violation of such an agreement; and (c) parties to an agreement were not generally responsible for damage inflicted upon others by it. These rights and immunities were not absolute: Agreements that were contrary to public policy were void,[1] and participants in them were liable for damage done by their participation. In all countries this rule curbed agreements to engage in methods of competition that were recognized as unfair. In some, such as England, it also invalidated agreements that contained restrictions so sweeping as to be unreasonable; but since restrictions were considered reasonable if they served the business interests of the participants, this limitation did little more than exclude restriction that was purposeless or malicious. Agreements that were maliciously intended to injure others were vulnerable in suits brought by persons injured. But just as today an enterprise carries no general responsibility for the damaging impact of its fair competition upon its competitors, parties to a restrictive agreement, having no duty to compete, carried no general responsibility for the damaging impact of commercial collaboration that served their mutual interests. The limitations that were applicable to unfair conduct and malice had only a peripheral effect upon restrictive agreements. Enterprises could restrict themselves as their business interests made appropriate; they could restrict others within the wide limits set by concepts of fair conduct and public policy.

---

[1] This limitation later furnished a principle under which, by extending the conception of agreements contrary to public policy, cartels could be invalidated.

1

The right of association reinforced freedom of contract. This right, at first sometimes regarded as suitable for business but not for labor,[2] was extended during the 19th century to labor groups also, with explicit recognition of their rights to bargain collectively, to use concerted restriction as a bargaining weapon, and to impose some discipline upon their members. So far as these rights were not already possessed by business associations, the fact that they were recognized for labor groups was presumed, where there was no antitrust legislation, to imply their legitimacy for business groups also. In the United Kingdom and Ireland, for example, statutes enacted in 1870 and 1871 defined trade unions to include business groups as well as labor groups, and declared that a purpose to restrain trade did not render a trade union agreement void. By the period between the two World Wars, business associations in most countries not only possessed the right to exist but also the right to undertake restrictive activities on behalf of their members and, to an extent that varied from country to country, the right to regulate the conduct of their members and impose penalties upon members who violated their rules.

The right to choose one's occupation was not wholly consistent with the other two rights. Occupational freedom was generally in effect by the beginning of the 20th century, except as licensing requirements had circumscribed it for particular occupations. In some countries, e.g. France and Germany, it had statutory origin. By guaranteeing freedom to engage in business, such statutes afforded legal ground for challenge of concerted restrictions that excluded persons from fields of business activity. Persons who were excluded could obtain redress in the courts; and contracts the central purpose of which was exclusion were likely to be held invalid as contrary to public policy. It was not clear, however, whether or not the right to engage in business included the right to be free from restriction in the way one did business. In the early part of the 19th century, French courts were inclined to believe that freedom of occupation included freedom to compete. In a key decision in 1897 the German Supreme Court held that the legal guarantee of business freedom did not permit a wood pulp manufacturer to violate a cartel agreement by which a common sales agency was used to prevent "ruinous" competition. The court thought that contracts could temporarily limit business freedom provided they did not permanently destroy it.

Thus the interaction between the guarantees of freedom of contract and freedom of association and the guarantee of freedom of occupation led

---

[2] But in France a law against "coalitions", which forbade association by either business or labor, was mitigated by labor legislation before its application to business was altered.

courts to invalidate some kinds of contractual restrictions. Under general
legal principles, a rudimentary class of "bad" agreements was identified.
But business freedom, not the well-being of consumers, was the basis for
the identification.

By forbidding malicious efforts to destroy competitors, laws to prevent
unfair competition reinforced, in some countries, the right to choose and
exercise one's occupation. In certain other respects, however, some of these
laws tended to restrict competition. They not only forbade various unconscionable practices, such as misrepresentation of goods, but also treated
as unfair the aggressive price competition by which one seller might seriously inconvenience another. For example, conduct contrary to public
morals, which was forbidden by the Austian law of unfair competition, was
interpreted under that law to include destructive price-cutting (preis-
schleuderei).

The limited control of restrictive agreements that was provided by
general laws in the early years of this century was not reinforced by even
limited control of private monopoly. Though some countries—e.g., England
—had forbidden government grants of monopoly, the scale of industry and
trade had been so small that sustained control of the market by single
enterprises had not been possible except where it was supported by law.
When trade between localities was still small, local markets had been regulated by laws that condemned such activities as "engrossing," "forestalling,"
and "regrating,"[3] by which local supplies might be briefly monopolized.
These activities had been considered objectionable forms of conduct, akin
to fraud and unfair competition. No legal effort had been made to limit the
size and power of a business enterprise.

Restrictive Practice Laws Before the Second World War. Except in
North America,[4] laws designed to curb cartels and monopolies were rare
until after the Second World War. During the French Revolution, France
prohibited "coalitions" by which people sought to serve their "pretended
common interests." Shortly thereafter, it included in its penal code a provision against combinations to fix prices at noncompetitive levels. In 1884,
however, associations to protect business interests were authorized by
French law; and thereafter the prohibition of price-fixing was attenuated,
first by judicial interpretation and later, in 1926, by amendment of the

---

[3] *Engrossing* was attempting to corner a market; *forestalling* was buying before
others had opportunity to buy; *regrating* was buying for the purpose of reselling in
the same market.

[4] The original version of Canada's Combines Investigation Act was enacted in
1889, fourteen months before the American Sherman Act. For discussion of the evolution of the Canadian law, see Lloyd G. Reynolds, *The Control of Competition in
Canada,* Harvard University Press, 1940.

penal code. In Austria a law that was enacted in 1870 to control labor unions included a provision that made some business agreements unenforceable; and during the next sixty years it was successfully invoked from time to time in private lawsuits. A few other general laws were enacted but fell into disuse.[5] A few special situations became the subject of *ad hoc* legislation of varying scope.[6] Certain national constitutions condemned monopoly in general terms, and some countries enacted, but did little to apply, laws designed, on the model of the French penal code, to prevent speculative manipulation of markets by use of such devices as hoarding or cornering supplies.

Between the two World Wars, some countries undertook to curb restrictive agreements and the activities of associations engaged in restrictive practices (both of which will be here called cartels). Norway in the 1920's and Denmark in the 1930's required registration of restrictive agreements and gave to control boards the power to take corrective action against abuses. In each country, the policy survived the Second World War and became a basis for postwar legislation. From 1923 until the National Socialists took power, Germany applied a law for the correction of cartel abuses, and in 1930 extended it to forbid "uneconomic" price fixing. During the 1930's Bulgaria, Yugoslavia, and Rumania undertook to control restrictive agreements. All three countries set up public registers of cartels; and in addition, the Bulgarian and Yugoslavian laws empowered government officials to dissolve cartels or invalidate parts of restrictive agreements, and the Rumanian law subjected cartels to governmental surveillance and to control of their prices. In the 1920's South Africa authorized a government agency to give advice about the prevention of monopolies and restraints of trade, and provided for tariff adjustments in the light of the agency's reports. This measure was supplemented in the 1930's by a law, originally applied to gasoline but subsequently made applicable by proclamation to any commodity, under which certain restrictive activities became criminal offenses. In the 1920's Sweden provided for investigation of monopolies, but for no sub-

---

[5] The Dominican Republic included in its penal code in 1901 authority for the government to act against certain restrictive practices. (Codigo Penal de la Republica Dominicana, Santo Domingo, 1901.) In Australia a law enacted in 1906 contained provisions against monopolistic practices. (Australian Industries Preservation Act; see Commonwealth Acts 1901-1935, consolidated edition, Vol. III, pp. 2832-36, Canberra, 1936.)

[6] In New Zealand, for example, a law enacted in 1907 exempted flour, wheat, and certain types of agricultural implements from customs duties when their prices were raised above competitive levels; and in 1910 another law, applicable to food, coal, petroleum, and agricultural implements, forbade agreements for the control of demand or supply or prices and efforts to bring about boycotts or exclusive dealing. In South Africa, agreements in unreasonable restraint of the trade of a butcher were forbidden by the Cape Meat Trade Act of 1907.

sequent corrective action. In 1923 Argentina enacted a law against abuses by trusts. In 1934 Mexico prohibited monopoly (including arrangements to dictate prices) but provided for certain exceptions. In 1936 Portugal enacted a law to curb cartels, which still exists but has never been applied. Laws imitative of the French penal code were enacted in other countries. Constitutional provisions that prohibited private monopolies became more numerous, especially in Latin America, but often were not supported by legislation.[7]

But such beginnings were overshadowed during the 1930's by policies of another kind in some of the most powerful countries. Even before the great depression, mandatory cartels had been established occasionally by law—in Germany, for example, in the cases of potash, coal, and matches, and in the United Kingdom in the case of electric power. After the onset of the depression, more such cartels were approved *ad hoc*,[8] and business groupings with quasi-governmental powers were systematically authorized in several countries. Under the Fascists, Italy experimented with a "corporative" state in which many branches of industry were subjected to compulsory cartelization and others were allowed to establish voluntary cartels under government supervision. Under the Nazis, Germany first made cartels compulsory, then subordinated them to government direction through quasi-public bodies. In the United Kingdom, the government fostered quasi-public business organizations through which restrictions were applied by producers of cotton textiles, steel, and coal, and operators of ocean ships. In 1931 Japan authorized by law the cartelization of major and minor industries; and later, in mobilizing for war, made cartels general and compulsory under government control. During the depression, Belgium enacted a law by which cartel restrictions could be made binding upon non-participants. The Netherlands did likewise, but added provisions by which undesirable restrictions could be invalidated. Latvia authorized a public official to approve cartels, extend them by registration, and enforce their

---

[7] See Antitrust Developments in the Common Market, Hearings before the Subcommittee on Antitrust and Monopoly of the Senate Judiciary Committee, 88th Congress, First Session, pursuant to S. Res. 56, Part I, pp. 127-146. See also Antitrust Legislations of the World (as of 1960), Eibun-Horei-Sha, Tokyo, 1960; and Review of the Legal Aspects of Industrial Agreements by Henri Decugis, Robert E. Olds, and Siegfried Tschierschky, League of Nations Economic and Financial Section, 1930. In the early 1960's constitutional provisions not supported by legislation existed in Burma, Costa Rica, Dominican Republic, Equador, El Salvador, Guatemala, Haiti, Honduras, Indonesia, Nicaragua, Panama, Paraguay, Peru, Thailand, and Venezuela. Similar provisions were included in the constitutions of certain communist countries.

[8] In Germany, cartels for milk, beet sugar, starch, and barge shipping were made mandatory soon after the depression began. In France, cartel restrictions were made mandatory for sugar, shoes, potash, chicory, cod fishing, and herring fishing.

rules.[9] New Zealand undertook general licensing of business, set up quasi-public marketing organizations for agricultural products, and adopted legislation for quasi-public organization of industries generally. When the second World War began, restrictive business programs sponsored by governments were pervasive in Germany, Italy, and Japan, were broadly authorized by law in Belgium, the Netherlands, Latvia, and New Zealand, and were in effect in important industries in the United Kingdom and France.

Legislation After the Second World War. After the second World War, laws designed to curb cartels and monopolies burgeoned in Western Europe and in certain other countries whose institutions have been strongly influenced by Western Europe. Laws imposed upon Germany and Japan by military occupation were followed by similar domestic legislation. Norway and Denmark tightened their prewar laws. The Netherlands enacted a law similar to the prewar one, but used it to curb cartels instead of to encourage them. Laws intended to reduce restrictions by business were enacted for the first time or were given significant new scope in thirteen European countries and seven countries outside Europe. By subsequent, amendment the original legislation was strengthened in at least ten countries, and weakened in one.[10]

At the beginning of 1964, laws to curb restrictive practices covered North America; all of non-Communist Europe except Italy, Greece, and Turkey;[11] and seven other countries: Japan and New Zealand in the Far East; Israel in the Near East; Argentina, Colombia, and Brazil in Latin America; and South Africa. During 1964 a dormant Australian law was resuscitated. With the exception of Japan, the non-European countries were heirs to European institutions and cultural traditions.

International Collaboration. While the various national laws were developing, three separate arrangements for international action about restrictive business practices were established—in the European Coal and Steel Community in 1951, in the European Economic Community in 1957, and in the European Free Trade Association in 1959.

The Coal and Steel Community was designed to establish international control over the coal and steel industries of six countries—Germany, France, Italy, Belgium, the Netherlands, and Luxembourg—and thus to lay a basis for eventual political unification by creating an international market. The

---

[9] *Statute Concerning Community of Interest of Trade and Industrial Enterprises,* December 12, 1936.

[10] The sequence and scope of the post-war burst of legislation are traced in Appendix A.

[11] Portugal enacted a law in 1936; but, though the statute is still in force, it has never been applied.

treaty by which the Community was established contained broad prohibitions of restrictions, public and private, that were deemed incompatible with the purpose, and provided that the Community should assure the maintenance of normal conditions of competition.

The European Economic Community, covering the economies of the same six countries, except as to coal and steel and atomic energy,[12] was designed to create an area in which goods, capital, and persons could move freely across national boundaries, and to provide for the gradual harmonizing of national economic legislation. To this end, an international body was given authority to control commerce among the member states and activities that might affect such commerce. Its functions included not only prevention of governmental activities that might impair or distort commerce among the participating countries but also prevention of private restrictions having similar effects. Since the treaty contained provisions by which membership in the Community could be enlarged, its potential field was not limited to the six original members.

The European Free Trade Association, fostered by the United Kingdom as a counterweight to the European Economic Community, consisted of the United Kingdom, Austria, Denmark, Norway, Portugal, Sweden, and Switzerland. It established a customs union administered by a council representing the member states. The treaty that established it contained cautious provisions about restrictive practices by which these were recognized as matters for possible intergovernmental negotiation.[13] It provided that before the end of 1964 further action about restrictive practices should be considered.

It is noteworthy that both of the European communities (though not the Free Trade Association) provided for curbs upon restrictive practices more ambitious than those contained in the laws of the member countries. When the Coal and Steel Community was established, the laws promulgated by military occupation were still in effect in Germany, the Netherlands was applying a cartel decree issued by the Nazis during the war, and there were no effective laws to curb restrictive practices in France, Italy, Belgium, or Luxembourg. When the Economic Community was established, Germany, the Netherlands, and France had enacted laws to curb cartels, and the first two had provided for control of the abuses of dominant firms; but in each country the curbs were less comprehensive than those of the Community. In Italy, Belgium, and Luxembourg, there was no comparable domestic legislation. International collaboration not only supplemented national action but strengthened the policies that were applicable.

---

[12] A special international arrangement as to atomic energy was developed in a separate treaty.

[13] Convention of the European Free Trade Association, signed Nov. 19, 1959.

Reasons for the Postwar Legislation. The burst of legislation reflected a dual condition: First, those who might have opposed such laws had been weakened by the war and had not yet recovered their strength; second, for various reasons governments had come to think that control of cartels and monopolies was desirable.

The war had done much to weaken cartels, international and national. International cartels had been destroyed or crippled, not only by conflicting national loyalties, but also by embargoes upon trade and censorship of communications, and, in some instances, by government action. During the war important members of international and national cartels had lost substantial parts of their assets by bomb damage and by confiscation of their property in enemy countries. Wartime governmental controls of supplies and prices had superseded the programs of domestic cartels in all belligerent countries and in some countries economically dependent upon belligerents: Regulation in the public interest had replaced private restriction; and the bodies that made and administered decisions, though often composed partly of business men, usually had represented broader groups than single industries. By the end of the war, most international cartels had disappeared, or survived in vestigial form. In belligerent countries, most cartels had been transformed into subordinate administrators of government programs. In non-belligerent countries, their fortunes had varied with the degree of the country's economic involvement with belligerent states and with the extent to which the national economy had been subjected to emergency controls. Where these influences were important, the chief domestic cartels had been weakened; but numerous cartels had survived unscathed, particularly in minor industries and on a local scale. Elsewhere, prewar domestic cartelization had not been greatly affected.

In the period immediately after the war, cartels in Germany and Japan had been further weakened by repressive laws imposed by military occupation, and dominant enterprises in these countries had been subjected to dissolutions and reorganizations.

The reconstruction period was not suited to the rapid reestablishment of the prewar cartel system. Enterprises that had held key positions before the war were generally preoccupied with problems of reconstruction, dissolution, or reentry into foreign markets. Opportunities to trade had been changed greatly by the partition of Germany, the relocation of national boundaries, the transfer of Japan's colonies, the iron curtain across Europe, and the mass migrations that accompanied and followed the war. To cope with the changes and with problems of reconstruction, governments exercised extensive control over economic affairs, including quantitative limitations of foreign trade, exchange controls, subsidies, rationing, and price controls.

Though these controls were gradually reduced, some of them, particularly controls over prices, were still partially in effect in some countries at the close of the 1950's. The pervasive role of governments in the early postwar years left little room for private restrictions except as adjuncts to public control.

As government control diminished, efforts to reestablish private cartels were common. Three special conditions often enhanced the usual incentives toward cartelization. First, enterprises that had not been exposed to strong competition during the war desired to prevent entry into their fields of business by business men who needed substitutes for discontinued wartime activities, by demobilized soldiers, and by refugees. Second, as industries that had been sheltered by governmental trade barriers found themselves increasingly exposed to import competition, they sought to protect their home markets by erecting private barriers. They did this sometimes nationally, by concerted efforts to exclude foreign goods, and sometimes internationally, by efforts to agree with foreign enterprises upon reciprocal limitations of international competition. Third, trade associations, deprived of control functions they had exercised during the war, sought to devise new controls as means of retaining their membership and providing jobs for their staffs. Had these incentives been allowed full play, cartelization as pervasive as that before the war probably would have been restored.

For various reasons, however, governments viewed cartelization differently from before the war. First, they were better informed about cartel activities. From censorship of the mails and from disclosures in American congressional investigations and antitrust proceedings, they had obtained detailed information about many international restrictive arrangements; and this information had often tended to discredit the self-serving justifications offered to them by participants in the restrictions. As early as 1944, the British minister of reconstruction declared that, though cartels do not necessarily operate aaginst the public interest, "the power to do so is there."[14]

Where concern about the possible effects of cartelization resulted in postwar efforts to get more information, the information that was obtained provided a basis for subsequent enactment of stronger laws. In Sweden, mandatory registration of cartel agreements, undertaken in 1948, led to remedial legislation in 1953. In the United Kingdom, reports by an investigatory commission that was established in 1948 resulted in a law against restrictive agreements in 1956. In Denmark, a commission set up in 1949 prepared the ground for permanent postwar legislation in 1955.

Second, governments regarded control of cartels as a weapon against

---

[14] Paragraph 54 of the White Paper on Employment Policy; see *The Times* (London), May 27, 1944, p. 8.

postwar price increases. Reflecting major currents of postwar opinion, they desired to curtail or to terminate public price control; but they also desired to prevent price inflation, and found that when released from control prices usually rose. Though postwar price increases probably were due chiefly to such influences as inflation of currency and credit, shortage of equipment and consequent shortage of goods, the need for producers' goods in reconstruction, and the demand of consumers for goods that had not been available in wartime, governments believed that the effect of these influences on prices was enhanced by cartel price policies. This view was clearly expressed by the Dutch government in 1950, when prices were rising under the stimulus of the Korean War. The power of sellers was greater than that of buyers, the government thought; international competition had been greatly reduced by the war, business organizations were strong, restrictive measures had become common in wartime, and many business men had come to desire prices that afforded profit even to the least efficient. Public price control must not be replaced by private price control under which prices that had been maxima became minimum prices.

Where policy toward wages was closely related to prices, this attitude was peculiarly strong. In Norway, for example, postwar wage agreements provided that wages would be renegotiated if the cost of living rose above a level known as the red line. Desire to avoid an upward spiral of wages and prices was an important ground for Norwegian legislation that gave the government power both to control business agreements and to control prices and profits. These two types of control were regarded as alternatives: Where concerted restrictions were eliminated, price control was likely to end; where restrictive agreements were permitted, price control was used to safeguard the public.

Third, governments came to regard curbs upon cartelization as appropriate parts of postwar efforts to reduce barriers to international trade. Postwar programs to reduce tariffs and quantitative restrictions upon imports were of two types. One involved an effort to relax trade restrictions globally. Such an effort was unsuccessfully proposed in the draft charter for an International Trade Organization, and was later given effect in more modest form in the General Agreement on Tariffs and Trade. The second type consisted of efforts by groups of contiguous countries to eliminate restrictions upon trade among themselves. Such efforts resulted in the Benelux Economic Union, the European Coal and Steel Community, and the European Economic Community.

In both types of effort, the participating governments recognized that private agreements to restrict access to international markets could destroy much of the effect of public agreements to facilitate such access. Accordingly, curbs upon private restriction were considered logical corollaries of agreements to terminate public restriction. This view of control of cartels was formulated just after the war in negotiations over the draft charter for the proposed International Trade Organization; and one purpose of several of the earlier postwar national laws was to enable the government to curb cartels as might be necessary to give effect to that charter. Curbs upon private restriction were later incorporated in the treaties that established the European Coal and Steel Community and the European Economic Community. Belgium enacted a restrictive practice law, and Italy began to consider one, largely because membership in the European Economic Community imposed obligations upon both countries to prevent cartels from restricting trade in ways contrary to the treaty.

As national trade barriers were reduced, further incentives for policies unsympathetic to private restriction appeared. Greater exposure to foreign competition increased the possibility that restrictions which raised costs or prices or retarded improvements in products or processes would result in loss of sales and reduction of domestic employment. Fear of such consequences made governments more sharply aware of such restrictions and more willing to condemn them, and made business more willing to forego restrictions. If foreign enterprises were to have easier access to domestic markets, efforts to make domestic enterprises more capable of competing with foreigners seemed wise.

Fourth, governments and a growing part of the business community came to regard many restrictive arrangements as inconsistent with efforts to attain high levels of productivity. During the war they had been impressed by the productive achievements of the American economy. In the postwar period they were told by American government agencies that there was an intimate connection between American productivity and the intensity of competition in American industry. This statement was repeatedly endorsed in public reports by groups of business men who were sent to the United States to find out if American methods could be used to expedite European reconstruction.[15]

The view that competition was the road to efficiency was inconsistent with certain deeply rooted European attitudes: European socialists had argued that competition was wasteful and that efficiency was to be achieved by public planning and coordinated productive effort. The spokesmen of European cartels had often described cartel programs as means of "rationalizing" industry. Postwar European opinion attempted to reconcile the conflicting attitudes by assuming that there was some truth in each. French

---

[15] See, for example the reports of the Anglo-American Council on Productivity, 1949-1952.

law was designed to strike at agreements that hinder reductions of costs or prices, and to exempt agreements that improve or extend markets or ensure economic progress. German law was shaped to prohibit restrictive agreements that are likely to influence production or market supply, but to provide for exemption of various types of agreements, including those that increase efficiency or productivity. The laws of various other countries were based upon broad standards of public interest that could be interpreted to authorize whatever might be deemed desirable. But the view that some restrictive agreements promote efficiency did not impair the force of the postwar opinion that other restrictive agreements retard efficiency.

Fifth, governments became more receptive to policies based upon competition as postwar developments decreased the political attractiveness of collectivist prescriptions for economic problems. At the close of the war, it seemed possible that the trend in Western Europe and elsewhere would be toward nationalization of industry, central economic planning, and state trading. But this prospect soon changed. On the one hand, the communism of countries beyond the iron curtain was discredited as its inconsistency with democratic freedoms became manifest. On the other hand, the democratic socialism of Western Europe no longer seemed, even to socialists, a possible panacea; for socialist governments had found it necessary to use nationalization sparingly and had been able to undertake only a limited amount of central economic planning. It was evident that in democratic countries large parts of the economy would be privately administered through market mechanisms, whether or not governments were socialist. Private restrictions could no longer be regarded as transitional phenomena, conducive to socialism and shortly to be terminated thereby. Desiring to minimize restrictions in sectors of the economy that might be enduringly private, socialists showed new sympathy for competition. As competition became relatively immune from socialist attack, it became more attractive politically to non-socialists. Policies based upon competition tended to occupy a middleground between extremes of collectivization and cartelization. They became politically viable and sometimes even expedient.

The tendency of these various influences to result in governmental curbs upon private restrictive practices was strengthened by official advocacy and cultural borrowing. In the early postwar period, the United States exerted pressure for adoption of competitive policies by other countries. During the period in which Germany and Japan were under military occupation, it took the lead in imposing an antitrust policy upon these countries. In other countries, it exerted pressure against restrictive agreements through its policies in aid of reconstruction.[16] It was the principal

---

[16] See Corwin D. Edwards, Regulation of Monopolistic Cartelization, 14 Ohio State Law Journal 252.

advocate of a program against cartels as a part of the proposed International Trade Organization;[17] and after proposals to create that organization had failed, it renewed its advocacy of such a program through the Economic and Social Council of the United Nations.[18] It induced various countries to accept provisions against restrictive business practices as parts of bilateral treaties of friendship, navigation, and commerce.[19] American pressures were sporadic rather than sustained, and they diminished with time. Nevertheless, they had a significant influence.

Other intergovernmental influences appeared later. When the European Economic Community was organized, three of the members (Belgium, Italy, and Luxembourg) had no domestic law to curb restrictive practices. Pressure from the other three members of the Community played a substantial part in procuring enactment of the Belgian law, consideration of which had been dormant for nearly ten years, and in inducing the Italian government to consider legislation more actively. When South Africa enacted a law, the decision was preceded by a public report based upon study of laws and of major investigations in the United States, Germany, the United Kingdom, Canada, and the Scandinavian countries, the law then under consideration in France, and the writings of foreign economists. Similarly, legislation in New Zealand was preceded by study of foreign experience, particularly that of Sweden and the United Kingdom.

These various incentives, pressures, and interactions had cumulative effect. In the early postwar years, legislation appeared to be largely a reflection of American influence and a response to temporary problems of the postwar transition. By the close of the 1950's, this had ceased to be true. In many countries the law had been not only accepted but repeatedly strengthened. It had become an expression of national concern about enduring problems as to prices, barriers to trade, and relations between restriction and efficiency. The various national laws had become parts of a general trend, and countries such as Spain, initially uninfluenced, had been drawn in.

---

[17] Proposals for Expansion of World Trade and Employment, Publication 2411, Commercial Policy Series 79, U.S. Department of State, 1945.

[18] U.S. Proposes U.N. Action on Cartels, Department of State Bulletin, October 8, 1951, pp. 590-595.

[19] For example, Article XV of the Treaty of Friendship, Commerce, and Navigation with Ireland, signed January 21, 1950, 2 UST 785, T.I.A.S., 2155.

Chapter II

The Influence of the Cultural Inheritance

The legislation about cartels and monopolies that has been briefly described differs significantly in purpose, content, and spirit from the American antitrust laws. There are differences in attitudes toward private economic power, the grant of broad discretionary authority to governmental bodies, the place of morality in economic affairs, the importance of freedom of contract relative to freedom of trade, and the emphasis to be placed upon distributive justice as compared with enhanced productivity. These differences reflect dissimilarities in cultural, moral, and political history—that is, in the cultural inheritance. Cultural difference appears to be more significant than contemporary dissimilarity in economic structures, processes, and interests.

With the exception of Japan, the countries that now seek to curb restrictive practices have a common cultural inheritance. But in the United States ideas inherited from Europe were deprived of much of their authority by revolution, by conquest of the frontier, and by blending of immigrants whose national cultures had become somewhat dissimilar. In Europe these ideas evolved but retained considerable continuity; and in New Zealand, where settlers came from only one country and the ideological pattern was not similarly shaken by political revolution, more of the European inheritance was preserved. Latin America, however, drew its culture from Spain and Portugal, which had not participated fully in the evolution of countries beyond the Pyrenees; and its Latin inheritance was modified not only by revolution but also by influences derived from the indigenous population and from Africa, Northern Europe, and the United States.

The significance of the cultural inheritance can be best perceived in northern and western Continental Europe, where its influence is greatest. Though it has been more influential in New Zealand, and probably in South Africa, and perhaps even in Israel than in North America, this chapter will not attempt to evaluate its importance in the outlying areas into which European traditions were imported.

Contemporary policies toward restrictive practices in northwestern Continental Europe (and, to a lesser extent, in other countries that adhere closely to the European tradition) are significantly grounded in inherited ideas, and cannot be understood from mere examination of the postwar problems with which they are currently concerned.

Striking differences between European and American policies toward business restrictions are based upon different attitudes toward possession of power, private or public. The European legislation reflects little distrust of concentrated business power. In 1966 no European country except the United Kingdom authorized action to dissolve monopolistic enterprises or to prevent powerful enterprises from attaining more power by acquiring their competitors. Similarly, business associations and cartel agreements have not been considered objectionable as combinations that have excessive power. Monopolies and cartels alike have been subjected to controls intended to make their activities acceptable. The laws invoked for this purpose usually entrust broad discretion to government officials; and enterprises subject to the laws show little concern lest these officials exercise too much power. In the content of the laws and in the application thereof, power is accepted in a spirit that contrasts sharply with American distrust of both powerful business and powerful government.

In European society hierarchies of power have been accredited by history. The medieval mind accepted concentrated power as natural and right. Until the Reformation, the Church was a hierarchy of power under the Pope. In feudal societies, each vassal owed allegiance and loyalty to his superior; and such societies became relatively stable and orderly only as kings acquired power clearly superior to that of the greater nobles. Concentration of economic power was characteristic of such societies because feudal status was simultaneously political and economic. So far as concentrations of power appeared in the early stages of banking and trade, patterns of centralized authority were familiar and not likely to be challenged.

But concentration of power was not irresponsible; it was curbed by moral law. As the servant of God and the guardian of faith and morals, the Pope, through the Church, was expected to act in accord with the Divine will. Those who possessed secular power were expected to exercise it morally; and the greater the power, the greater the obligation. Even kings, though they ruled by Divine right, were subject to the discipline of the Church when they transgressed. Good rulers were a necessary requisite for a good society.

Applied to economic affairs, these views resulted in formulation by the Church of codes that were appropriate to the moral conduct of business. To charge interest was immoral. Goods were to be produced at just wages and sold at just prices. Compensation that did not enable a man to live in a way appropriate to the station in life in which God had placed him was not just. Competition was to be fair; and types of competition inconsistent with just wages, just prices, and just compensation for business activity were not fair. Correct functioning of an economy was not dependent upon the intensity of competition nor inconsistent with concentration of economic power; it depended upon good moral conduct in economic life. Though the ideas about what was fair changed with the passage of time, the changes did not eliminate the belief that to be fair was necessary and that what was fair could be ascertained.

This point of view contrasts sharply with the reliance upon the interplay of selfish motives in competitive markets that Adam Smith later made the cornerstone of economics. In the moral philosophy of Smith, private greed, when exercised in competitive markets, produced beneficial results, as though by the guidance of an invisible hand. Competition converted private vices into public virtues. From the earlier European point of view, this heresy would have been unintelligible. All of Catholic Europe and major parts of Protestant Europe still regard it as wholly or partly untrue. Moral attitudes continue to have a pervasive effect upon economic legislation.

Acceptance of concentrated power and belief that it must be morally exercised result in efforts, moral and if necessary legal, to correct the conduct of those who use power immorally. If the possessors of power are incorrigible, there are two possibilities: Either one may seek to transfer the power to those who will use it properly, or one may conclude, with Lord Acton, that all power corrupts, and hence may seek, like those who founded American society, to minimize concentrations of power.

In Europe ecclesiastical and political discontent at first resulted in transfers of power. After accusing the Catholic Church of intolerable abuse of power, leaders of the Reformation such as Luther and Calvin accomplished their schism, not by establishing independent congregational churches, but by setting up piously authoritarian religious bodies. When ecclesiastical control of temporal affairs was challenged, the solution was to transfer power to kings and sometimes also to bring religious matters under royal authority by making the king head of a royally established church. Later, when democratic movements challenged royal power, their emphasis was not upon reduction of the authority of the central government by more local autonomy or by bills of rights that circumscribed all governmental authority. Instead, they sought to reconstitute national governments in such a way as to make them more trustworthy. At intermediate stages in the process, governmental power was diffused by compromises in which kings shared their authority with representatives of the dissenting groups. The objective of the dissenters, however, was transfer of power, not diffusion of it. Where they were fully successful, royal power was replaced by the power of parliaments. Governmental authority continued to be centralized, with minimal curbs upon the discretion of those who possessed it. Exercise of it, however, was expected to be subject to moral obligations and responsive to popular sentiments.

Before the changes were completed, efforts to reduce governmental power appeared also. The developing business community became restive under the pervasive economic controls applied by governments, many of which were vestiges of a transition from feudal society. Kings had fostered the beginnings of trade and of manufacture by giving towns an autonomous status under which localities or local guilds legally made and applied regulations, charged fees for transportation of goods into local markets, controlled entry into occupations, and applied by regulation the contemporary standards of business morality. As trading areas became larger and more numerous, the accumulation of ill-supervised regulations, each reflecting local vested interests, had become obstacles to further development. To get rid of these impediments, business innovators urged that government regulation be drastically reduced. Their watchwords were *laissez faire, laissez passer,* that is, let people do things, let them move from place. Do not, in other words, maintain barriers to occupations, business decisions, and free movement from one local market to another. Adam Smith's writings furnished useful support in the effort to dismantle the edifice of economic control, not because they emphasized the role of competition, but because they condemned pervasive control as unnecessary and said that free business decisions would produce good results.

Since the relief sought was from restrictions imposed by a network of laws, not by private monopolies and cartels, the objectives of those who advocated freedom were freedom to arrange their affairs by private contract, to associate according to their own wishes, and to engage in such activities as they chose. At a rate that differed considerably from one part of Europe to another, the *laissez faire* movement resulted in legal changes that established freedom of contract, freedom of association, and freedom of occupation. Though much of the demand for these freedoms had been due to a desire to liberate trade, freedom of trade was not sharply defined as a right or as an objective. Trade was to be free in the sense that previous restrictions publicly applied were no longer to persist. A need to prevent private restriction was not yet apparent.

But the potentiality for developing significant private restriction was inherent in the new freedoms. Liberty to make private contracts included the right for competitors to make restrictive agreements. Liberty to form associations included the right to bring all competitors into a single organization, and to bind them to it by contracts under which they must conform to its collective decisions or suffer prescribed penalties. The latent inconsistency between freedom of contract and freedom of occupation, to which reference was made in Chapter 1, meant merely that where exercise of the two freedoms was incompatible, some authority must decide which must give way.

Upon a peaceful and stable continent, freedom of contract, of association, and of occupation might have done more than it actually did in Europe to reduce the economic role of national states. For European countries, however, war had been and was expected to be a recurrent experience; and between periods of armed conflict public policies were enduringly concerned with maneuvers for position and efforts to increase military strength. These preoccupations led to the establishment of relations between governments and their business enterprises similar to those that have become familiar in the United States during the period of so-called "cold war." Within each country, business and government were believed to have overriding common interests in the strength and security of the state. Governments sought to strengthen their business enterprises at the expense of enterprises in other countries by nationalistic economic policies. Business looked to government as a necessary protector. Since coherent leadership was requisite both to military power and to the mobilized economic strength upon which such power was increasingly dependent, governments attained primacy in guiding economic life, but did so in close consultation and collaboration with business leaders. Important contractual arrangements and business groupings were informally supervised by and supported by governments. Leaders in business and government became closely associated and often interchangeable.

During the 19th century, business power was challenged, but not because of the growth of cartels and monopolies. With increased division of labor and enlargement of the scale of enterprise, business undertakings had become stratified into classes of employers and employees. Unlike the journeymen who were their predecessors, the latter did not typically become, in time, independent craftsmen. Though the arrangements for their employment took the form of free contracts, they actually created an enduringly subordinate status for labor. Moreover, the level of wages and the terms of employment often aroused indignation both among workingmen and among others who sympathized with them. The idea of the just wage, revivified and reformulated, became the basis of a critique of capitalism. The relation between employers and wage-earners was said to be inherently immoral. The remedy suggested was that traditional in Europe—transfer of the power of employers into hands more trustworthy. In the countries where democracy had become most fully established, the critics of capitalism thought that the state was, or could be made, morally reliable and responsive to public desires. Hence they proposed that governments acquire business property, became the employers of labor, and manage enterprise for the public good. In countries in which the idea of a morally reliable and responsive government seemed more chimerical, the hope was to create and federate syndicates of workers that could become the new repositories of economic power.

In the development of the socialist critique of capitalism, distributive justice was the central theme. Concern about productivity played a minor part. From time to time capitalism was called wasteful as well as unjust. But not until the period between the two World Wars did socialists emphasize the belief that central economic planning might substantially enlarge the aggregate economic product.

In socialism there was also little or no place for concern about cartels and monopolies. Indeed, the tendency of socialism was to treat concentration of business power as desirable. In the immediate impact upon labor, socialists saw little to choose between competition and monopoly. A monopolist was likely to be a monopolist in buying labor. If so, he could pay as little as he chose. Competitors, vying with one another to reduce prices without lessening their profits, were likely to compete in reducing wages and worsening conditions of labor. Indeed, a benevolent monopolist might moderate his greed, but a benevolent competitor would be forced to forget his benevolence by his harder-hearted rivals. Hence there was no benefit in substituting competition for monopoly.

The eventual impact of monopoly, as socialists came to appraise it, was definitely preferable to that of competition. As big capitalists swallowed smaller ones, enterprises became larger and fewer; wage-earners became more numerous and capitalists fewer; larger segments of the business community were coordinated by administrative decisions instead of market bargains; and thus the eventual abolition of capitalism must become both more popular and more feasible.

As the socialist critique of capitalism penetrated the thinking of those who controlled powerful military states, it affected their economic policies. Socialist criticisms of the labor policies of business were consistent with moral tradition and were treated as, in large part, legitimate. Socialist belief that the state should be the instrument of reform was not objectionable. In an age of large standing armies or general conscription, military policy would be stronger if the laboring population, like the business community, came to look upon the state as the protector of its interests. For this purpose abolition of capitalism was not necessary; action against abuses of capitalism that affected workingmen would be sufficient. From such considerations emerged the modern welfare state, designed to promote distributive justice and to increase the security of low-income groups. Its general purposes and programs were accepted by most of the European business community, partly as a safeguard against revolutionary socialism and partly because business men were too dependent upon the stability and military strength of their governments to be recalcitrant.

The historical process that has been summarized above gave Europe characteristic attitudes that have been significant in the development of European policy toward business restrictions. These attitudes appear with different degrees of strength in different countries, are more evident in Continental Europe than in England, and are more evident in Europe than in overseas European communities. But regardless of differences in degree, they are strong enough to differ from characteristic attitudes in the United States. The following are among the most important:

1. *Emphasis upon moral obligation in economic affairs.* Though stronger where Catholicism is more prevalent, this emphasis exists also in Protestant countries. Impersonal institutional means for attaining satisfactory economic results do not win confidence. Though competition is considered desirable, its function is thought to consist largely in strengthening incentives to effort and thereby reinforcing one part of moral conduct. It is not accepted as an automatic selective device by which the fittest survive. Instead, forbearance in competition is regarded as a virtue and ruthlessness as a vice. Fair business conduct and fair prices are emphasized, and what a competitive market produces is not thought to be automatically fair. That what is fair can be identified and generally agreed upon is taken for granted.

2. *Emphasis upon distributive justice and equality of opportunity rather than productivity.* As used here, the term "distributive justice" is not applied to the relation between employers and employees but to the relations among business enterprises and between such enterprises and their customers. Public policy toward restrictions is focused upon fairness in dividing what the economy produces rather than enlargement of the product. Fairness as to prices, as to availability of supplies, and as to access to markets is the point of attention. This fairness has two aspects. First, it includes fairness between supplier and customer, both as to the height of prices and as to the availability of supplies. Second, it includes fairness between one supplier and another as to access to markets and as to discrimination in the terms of access. Though these goals are moral, they are usually described as economic. They are so in the sense that they identify fair conduct by the nature of the economic relationship that it establishes rather than by the motives of the participants. But they are not economic

in the sense that the preferred courses of action have been chosen because they yield the largest practicable aggregate economic product. In only one European country has enhancement of productivity been emphasized as the chief goal of policy toward restrictive practices.

3. *Acceptance of concentrated private economic power.* The existence of a powerful cartel or monopoly is not considered objectionable in itself. Instead, such aggregations of power are appraised according to their conduct. If they do nothing that calls forth condemnation, they are treated as harmless. If their behavior is not satisfactory, efforts are made to correct it. The incorrigible cartel may be subjected to close control or may be dissolved; the incorrigible enterprise may be subjected to close control, or, in some countries, deprived of the right to do business.

4. *Acceptance of broad discretionary governmental power.* Europeans entrust to single officials or to small groups not only ascertainment of facts and application of law but also formulation of the substantive content of law and even of the broad policy objectives that the law is expected to serve. Laws are deliberately phrased in broad language; but what is done under them is conceived as formulation of policy rather than enforcement of legal obligations. In a particular decision, the discretion of an official in a ministry or of a public board may be comparable in breadth to that exercised in the United States by the Supreme Court. Unlike the Supreme Court, the official or board is only loosely affected by precedents set in previous decisions. The curbs of publicity as to governmental acts, disclosure of the grounds for action, and rights of appeal differ greatly from one country to another but are generally less than in the United States.

5. *Grant of public power to representatives of private interests.* In some countries, representatives of private interests participate in the governmental bodies that make public decisions, or have a statutory right to give advice prior to decision. In these cases, the arrangement is not conceived as one for negotiation among private interests or between private interests and the government, but rather as one in which these private persons, possessing special knowledge and a special point of view, act in the public interest.

6. *Stress upon the importance of freedom of contract.* Though curbs upon restrictive business agreements are necessarily limitations of freedom of contract, concern about any limitation of contractual freedom is greater in Europe than in the United States. Efforts to obtain voluntary corrections by negotiation are carried further, and action to set aside objectionable restrictions tends not only to be narrower in scope but also to result in control that is of shorter duration. Corrective orders usually have time

limits, designed to preserve future contractual freedom. The permanent injunction is not European.

The fact that many of the countries with which this book is concerned are relatively small and homogeneous has reinforced some of these attitudes. In a small homogeneous country moral traditions are more compelling, and there is more consensus in political attitudes, than in a large country. Indeed, in some of the smaller countries the force of public opinion is so great that mere public disclosure of the nature of restrictive practices has had a considerable remedial effect. Emphasis upon fair dealing and equal opportunity tends to be greatest in a limited environment in which alternative opportunities are few and disparities of treatment are readily perceived. Citizens are less likely to be alarmed by broad governmental discretionary power when the officials who exercise it are their neighbors and share their basic attitudes. Concentration of private economic power is more acceptable where, since markets are too small to hold many competitors, an enterprise that occupies most of the field enjoys clearly discernible economies of scale. Emphasis upon morality, concern with standards of distributive fairness, breadth of governmental discretion, participation by private persons in governmental decisions, and acceptance of concentrations of economic power are greater in the smaller countries.

One of the peculiarities of European policies—reliance upon use of discretionary power—is also strengthened by the fact that most European governments are parliamentary. In a parliamentary system, heads of the executive establishment are drawn from the parliament, and reflect the attitudes that are dominant there. When serious disagreement develops between the parliament and the executive, the ministry is replaced or a new election alters the parliamentary majority. In such a system government officials act in a way consistent with prevalent political opinion; and when that opinion changes, executive decisions and laws can be altered without great difficulty. Thus the need to control officials by statutory curbs or judicial interpretations is diminished. Where the country is homogeneous, as is the case in most of the smaller countries, these political characteristics are reinforced by the fact that political parties, unlike those in large countries formed by federation, tend to have an ideological basis. Party politics consists not of compromises among factions and sectional interests that are similar in each party, but of conflict between rival ideas and attitudes. The views of the electorate obtain clearer political expression and more quickly modify the actions of government. The transparency of parliament as an institution by which general opinion influences policy increases the willingness of the society to allow public officials free rein.

Chapter III

The Broad Patterns of Control

By the beginning of 1964, more than 20 countries were engaged in serious efforts to control restrictive practices by law. In some countries, laws that expressed chiefly a desire to control prices were, to a limited extent, relevant to control of restrictive practices. In some countries laws that were clearly applicable to restrictive practices had never been used, had fallen into disuse, or were applied very seldom. If such instances are included, the number of countries engaged in legal control of restrictive practices appears larger; if not, it appears smaller. For the purposes of this book, the appropriate number is twenty-four. It includes the following countries:[1]

In North and Central America
    Canada
    Mexico
    the United States
In South America
    Argentina
    Brazil
    Colombia

In Europe
    Austria
    Belgium
    Denmark
    Finland
    France

---

[1] Portugal is omitted because, though a law enacted in 1936 still exists, it has never been applied.

The Australian law of 1906, as amended in 1909 and 1910, fell into disuse after 1913, partly because of doubts about constitutionality. After some of these doubts were allayed by a court decision in a private suit in 1963, the government instituted three cases in May, 1964. This fact, plus the fact that further legislation was then pending, has induced me to treat the law as effective rather than dormant. See Department of State Dispatch No. A-1011 from Canberra, June 12, 1964, and a speech by the acting Attorney-General, G. Freeth, in Australian Parliamentary Debates, December 6, 1962.

Germany
Ireland
the Netherlands
Norway
Spain
Sweden
Switzerland
the United Kingdom

Elsewhere
    Australia
    Israel
    Japan
    New Zealand
    Union of South Africa

This book is not concerned with the laws of the United States and Canada; and for reasons given in the preface, it also excludes discussion of the laws of the Latin-American countries and Australia. This chapter sets forth the more significant characteristics of the laws of the seventeen remaining countries.[2]

A. *The Scope of the Laws*

Substantive Scope. Restrictive agreements are the principal subject of the national laws that are covered in this book. Each of these laws contains provisions for control of such agreements. In most countries the parts of the statutes applicable to agreements have been more fully formulated than the parts that pertain to other subjects. In all countries except possibly Japan, Sweden, and Ireland,[3] restrictive agreements have received primary attention from those who apply the law.

In most countries, restrictive agreements have been broadly conceived. Control has been applied equally to explicit agreements and to collective activities carried on through trade associations. Not only formal contracts but also informal arrangements, collective recommendations, and even

---

[2] Appendix B contains a brief summary of the law of each of these countries.

[3] In Japan dissolution of great corporate combines was the matter of greatest concern during the period of military occupation. The limited recent application of the law has been concerned chiefly with price-fixing by trade associations and with unfair business practices, and the relative emphasis is not clear. In Sweden, control of cartels has been overshadowed in recent years by control of refusals to sell. In Ireland, control of individual and collective action has been consistently combined, with particular attention to terms of sale and channels of distribution.

parallel action have been treated as agreements. The British law provides, for example, that the term *agreement* covers arrangements not intended to be enforceable, and that a trade association's recommendations to its members shall be treated as if each member had agreed to comply with them. The Austrian law explicitly covers recommendations about prices if they are supported by "economic or social pressure" or are not expressly designated as non-compulsory. Even in the Netherlands, where the statute applies only to agreements and collective decisions to which civil law is applicable, an order in council can extend its application to unenforceable arrangements as well.

Some control of powerful single enterprises is also included in the laws of all 17 countries. In some countries, such as Germany, it takes the form of special provisions applicable to such firms, which may be supplemented by provisions applicable to particular types of restrictive practice by single enterprises whether powerful or not. In other countries, such as Belgium, the applicable legal concepts are so formulated that they pertain both to powerful firms and to restrictive agreements. In some countries provisions explicitly concerned with powerful firms are more recent, and in some countries more limited, than provisions concerned with restrictive agreements. They were adopted in Austria in 1962 and in France in 1963. In Finland they consist only of a requirement that predominant positions and restrictions by single firms must be reported on request. In Austria they consist only of a reporting requirement and of a provision that dominant firms may be subjected to comments about the effect of their activities.

In half of the countries or more the provisions applicable to powerful enterprises pertain to "dominant" firms.[4] The concept of dominance is often broader than the American concept of monopolization. It may include

---

[4] The laws of eight countries—Austria, Finland, France, Germany, the Netherlands, Norway, Spain, and Switzerland—refer to dominant firms or dominant or preponderant positions; but in Germany and Spain, unlike the other countries named, the underlying concept seems to be that of monopoly. Denmark (which applies control to enterprises that have a substantial influence in the market) and the United Kingdom (which applies control to enterprises that occupy one-third or more of the total field) use concepts similar in significance to the concept of dominance. In four countries no special concept is invoked for control of single firms because agreements and enterprises alike are subject to the law if they restrain competition (Sweden), bring about certain restrictive effects (South Africa), abuse economic power (Belgium), or are covered by rules and orders that set forth fair trading conditions (Ireland). Two countries, Israel and Japan, control or forbid "monopolies," but apply no general control to the conduct of dominant firms. In one country, New Zealand, a law applicable to various kinds of agreements and trade practices covers also complete or partial monopoly of supply. Only in the three countries last named does the control of powerful firms fail to cover oligopolistic enterprises. The German and Spanish laws are applicable both to monopolies and to oligopolies within which competition has become substantially non-existent.

firms that are part of an oligopoly, even though they compete with other oligopolists. It may include firms whose brands possess special prestige or firms that are significantly larger than their competitors, suppliers, or customers. It may include two or more firms in the same industry.

Except in Japan, in the United Kingdom beginning in 1965, and perhaps in New Zealand and South Africa, the laws applicable to powerful firms are concerned with the conduct of such enterprises, not with their power.[5] Possession of dominant power is not subject to challenge; neither, except in Japan and the United Kingdom, is enhancement of that power by merger.[6] But if the behavior of a dominant firm is objectionable, it may be subjected to corrective orders. In most countries these orders have to do with such matters as prices, terms, trade practices, and the availability of supplies. But in the United Kingdom, Japan, and South Africa they may not only alter business conduct but even dissolve an enterprise.

More than half of the countries under discussion provide that certain practices of single firms shall be forbidden or controlled, even where no dominant power is involved. Some of the provisions are so inclusive that they subject all business conduct to discretionary control. Irish law, for example, instructs a Fair Trade Commission to make rules of fair competition in the light of a list of unfair practices that covers, inter alia, acts that "in any other respect operate against the public interest or are not in accord with the principles of social justice." Similarly, Norwegian law prohibits "such middleman activities as are unnecessary and raise prices" and also prohibits sale "to buyers who are engaged in such activities."

Disregarding such blanket provisions—the stretch of which actually remains unused— one finds a few types of practice recurrently subject to prohibition or limitation. Significant among them are resale price maintenance by individual suppliers,[7] exaction of excessive or unauthorized

---

[5] Japanese law not only forbids monopoly but contains various provisions designed to curb concentration by mergers, by stockholding, and by interlocking directorates. Little use is made of these provisions. Since the occupation there have been two monopolization cases and five cases concerned with evasion of the provisions about concentration. There has been no case in either category since 1957. New Zealand authorizes corrective orders against partial or complete monopoly and against practices tending to monopoly, but has not yet invoked these parts of the law. South African law covers "situations" as well as activities, and authorizes dissolution as a possible remedy; but neither monopolization nor attempt to monopolize has yet been the subject of any action under the law.

[6] Though the German and Spanish laws require report of mergers if, after the merger, a stated percentage of the market is under a single control or a stated size has been attained, they authorize no subsequent repression or control.

[7] Denmark, Finland, France, Ireland, Japan, Norway, Sweden, the United Kingdom. Austria, Germany and New Zealand provide for some kind of control of resale price agreements between a single seller and his customers. The Netherlands forbids resale price maintenance by individual suppliers of designated commodities and restricts the methods by which other individual suppliers may enforce resale price contracts.

prices,[8] discrimination,[9] refusal to sell[10], coercion,[11] and use of tying arrangements in selling.[12]

The substantive provisions of the laws are supplemented, in some countries, by requirements that particular kinds of restriction be reported to the government and (in most cases) be publicly registered. General reporting of restrictive agreements is required in eight countries, in all but one of which the reports or summaries of them are made public.[13] In Germany, Spain, and Japan special types of agreement that are subject to approval or exemption are reported or publicly registered. Registration requirements extend to dominant firms in five countries.[14]

Exemptions. The scope of the various laws is modified by exemptions or possibilities for grant of discretionary exemption, which, from country to country, differ in nature and extent. Five kinds of exemptions are provided: First, particular segments of the national economy may be placed beyond the reach of the statute. This is frequently true of agriculture, and sometimes true of finance, transportation, natural monopolies, and the professions. Second, particular types of economic relationship may be exempted by law. In all countries this is true of collective bargaining between employers and employees. Third, particular types of enterprise may be exempted by law—e.g. cooperatives in Austria and Japan, state-operated enterprises in several countries. Fourth, statutory or discretionary exemption may be provided for particular types of restrictions: export agreements, import agreements, resale price maintenance, standardization arrangements, exclusive dealing, agreements about terms of sales or discounts, agreements restricting the use of patents or of unpatented technical knowledge. Fifth, discretionary exemptions may be authorized by which whatever restrictions may be deemed appropriate to particular situations can be used—restrictions designed to "rationalize" economic processes or to alleviate the economic distress that arises from temporary depressions or from substantial unbalance between demand and supply.

---

[8] Ireland, Japan, and Norway. New Zealand authorizes orders against payment of excessive royalties, commissions, or fees. France condemns certain speculative activities designed to raise prices artificially.

[9] France, Ireland, Japan; also Germany for dominant enterprises, firms maintaining resale prices, associations, and cartels; also the United Kingdom if more than one-third of total supply is involved.

[10] France, Ireland, Norway, and New Zealand. Germany applies a similar provision to sellers who fix resale prices. Japan sometimes interprets refusal to sell as boycott, and thus as an unfair business practice.

[11] Germany, Ireland, Japan.

[12] France, Ireland, Spain. In Japan tying has been defined by the Fair Trade Commission as an unfair business practice.

[13] Austria, Denmark, Finland, Israel, the Netherlands, Norway, Sweden, the United Kingdom.

[14] Austria, Denmark, Finland, Norway, Sweden.

Of the exemptions applicable to particular types of restriction, the most common are those for export agreements and for resale price maintenance by individual sellers. Of the exemptions applicable to particular types of situation, the most common are those for rationalization agreements.

Territorial Scope. In any national system of trade regulation, difficult questions arise as to the application of national law to situations that involve more than one country. There is need to decide whether or not the law applies a) to activities within the country by foreigners, b) to exports from the country, c) to activities abroad by the country's citizens that have effect within the country, d) to activities abroad by foreigners that have similar domestic effects, e) to activities abroad by citizens that have effects only abroad.

That national trade regulation applies to the activities of foreigners within the country has become axiomatic.[15] No similar consensus exists, however, as to the other points listed. The differences of national policy about claims of jurisdiction are sometimes expressed in statutes, decisions, and traditions that apply generally to all national laws and regulations. So far as this is true, they lie beyond the limits of this book. In some countries, however, the breadth of the application of restrictive practice laws is stated in the laws themselves, and is not necessarily the same as that of other statutes. The following comments will be limited to these cases.

Without exception, the national laws that are the subject of this book are concerned primarily with restriction of domestic markets. In the countries that set forth clearly the territorial limits of the statute, however, this concern is expressed by two different principles of jurisdiction.[16] Based on the first principle, the laws of the United Kingdom,[17] the Netherlands,

---

[15] In the colonial era, however, foreigners trading in some countries that were under foreign control were, to a large extent, subject not to local laws but to special laws imposed and administered by the foreign country.

[16] As to the ensuing discussion of asserted jurisdiction, cf. Corwin D. Edwards The Internationality of Economic Interests, 111 University of Pennsylvania Law Review 183, at 189-92.

[17] In the United Kingdom, two basic statutes invoke somewhat different principles of jurisdiction. Section 6(1) of the Restrictive Trade Agreements Act requires registration of agreements if two or more parties do business in the United Kingdom and two or more parties accept restrictions; and section 8(8) excludes from registration agreements in which restrictions apply wholly to export, to production abroad, to acquisition abroad of goods not to be used at home, and to supply abroad of goods not to be exported from the United Kingdom. Thus an agreement is registrable by which two or more firms outside the United Kingdom agree to restrict the amounts or prices of their shipments into the country, provided two or more British firms are parties to the agreement. The Monopolies Act, as amended, is applicable to exports of goods if arrangements that restrict competition in relation to exports are in effect or if, for any particular export market, arrangements that restrict competition in relation to supply from the United Kingdom or elsewhere are

and New Zealand[18] apply to persons doing business in the country, and the law of Finland to sale within the country. Based on the second principle, the laws of Germany, Denmark, and Spain apply to restrictive effects upon the country's domestic trade, regardless of the territorial locus of the restrictive acts or of the persons engaged in them.[19] Thus they invoke a concept of jurisdiction like that of the American antitrust laws. Presumably they can be applied to an agreement made abroad by foreigners if its purpose or effect is to restrict the domestic market. Swedish law partially invokes a similar principle by applying prohibitions to resale price maintenance and to bidding agreements where the resale, or the supply under the contract subject to bidding, takes place in Sweden.

Restrictions applicable to export trade are sometimes wholly exempt and sometimes subjected to more limited control. Finnish law contains an explicit exemption,[20] and Spanish law authorizes one.[21] Germany exempts export agreements that have no domestic restrictive effects, and authorizes exemption of those whose domestic restrictions are necessary to the effect abroad, but requires that both types of agreement be reported and the latter be publicly registered. Norway relieves export restrictions of the control applicable to domestic ones, but subjects them to supervision in order to counteract "conditions which may have a detrimental effect on Norwegian interests." The United Kingdom requires that export agreements be confidentially reported to the Board of Trade, and, where restrictions of competition in export markets are operative for at least one-third of the relevant goods produced in the United Kingdom, subjects such agreements

---

in effect, and if, in either situation, one third or more of the relevant goods produced in the United Kingdom is affected.

[18] Though the New Zealand law applies to persons carrying on business in New Zealand, it is explicitly made applicable (by Section 11) to agreements relating to sale or supply in New Zealand if any party carries on business there. Section 19(5) provides, however, that in such cases orders may be made only about the part of the activity that is being carried on in New Zealand.

[19] The German law (Section 98(2)) is applicable "to all restraints of competition effective in the area of applicability of this law, even if they result from acts done outside such area." The Danish statute is applicable (Section 2(1)) to enterprises and associations within trades in which competition is restricted in Denmark, and registration under it is required (Section 6) for agreements and enterprises that may exert a substantial influence in Danish markets. The Spanish law (Article 1(1)) forbids arrangements that restrict competition on the domestic market.

[20] It applies also to offers of Finnish shipping in the international cargo market.

[21] The prohibitions of the Spanish law apply only to restrictions of competition and abuses in the domestic market (see Sections 1 and 2). A tribunal has power, nevertheless, to exempt arrangements that foster exports if the restrictions do not have adverse effects on the domestic market and do not violate international treaties. The intention apparently is to authorize certain export arrangements that also involve restrictive domestic effects.

to possible investigations and corrective orders.[22] However, orders can apply to conduct outside the United Kingdom only in the case of British subjects, British corporations, and persons doing business in the United Kingdom.

Few laws contain special provisions about imports. Finland, however, exempts purchase for import; and Germany and Spain authorize exemption of import agreements that counteract an absence of competition among foreign suppliers.

Scarcely any effort is made in the laws to control participation by the nation's enterprises in restrictions that take effect in foreign countries. Specific exemptions are provided for such arrangements in the laws of Austria, Finland, the Netherlands, Norway, and the United Kingdom. Norway, however, provides for supervision to protect Norwegian interests. Japan alone forbids its enterprises to take part in international agreements that involve unreasonable restraints of trade or unfair practices.

B. *Central Concepts of the Laws*

Objectives. The clearest and strongest purposes of most of the laws are to keep prices down to levels regarded as reasonable and to protect businessmen from unreasonable interference with their opportunity to do business. A secondary purpose is to maintain stability in economic life and thus to protect people from changes so rapid as to be painful.

The standards of reasonableness that govern the pursuit of these objectives are usually derived from custom, cultural inheritance, and moral tradition rather than from economic analysis. Though maintenance of a substantial amount of competition is considered useful, it is a means, not an objective. The purpose in most countries is not to achieve or to approximate a self-operative economy, but to apply curbs to such conduct as is an obstacle to maintenance of standards of fairness.

Improvement in economic performance is desired, and competition is thought to be useful in bringing it about; but except in France it has a secondary place in policy toward restrictions. Moreover, though restrictions are often permitted as means to greater productivity, they are seldom repressed as obstacles to it unless they are also considered to be unfair.

Though in all of the countries under discussion the attitude just summarized is evident to an extent that contrasts with attitudes in the United States, it is present in different degrees in different countries. It is most conspicuous in Ireland, the Netherlands, Denmark, and Sweden; least so in Germany, the United Kingdom, New Zealand, and France. In New Zealand, though the law stresses reasonable prices, it has been applied by

---

[22] Monopolies and Restrictive Practices (Inquiry and Control) Act, 1948, and part three of the Restrictive Trade Practices Act, 1956.

a series of decisions that treat price fixing as inherently unreasonable. The main provisions of the German law are designed to establish a market economy as a means to good economic performance and as a requisite to political liberty; but numerous accessory provisions have other purposes and invoke standards of fairness similar to those of other countries. The French law is divided into two parts, of which one, concerned chiefly with fair prices and business opportunities, is systematically enforced, while the other, which, as interpreted, is an instrument to enhance productivity, has been applied capriciously. English law includes a rebuttable presumption against restrictive agreements, with leeway where restriction can result in lower prices; but as applied it is tolerant of restrictions by powerful single enterprises.

Concepts of Appropriate Control. The laws under discussion fall into two classes, based respectively upon what Europeans call the prohibition principle and the abuse principle. Countries that accept the prohibition principle regard restrictive agreements and monopolistic practices as typically objectionable. The grounds for this attitude differ, at least in emphasis, from one country to another. They include a) belief that one-sided formulation of prices and conditions of trade that are vital to both sides of the market is inherently unfair; b) belief that competition affords incentives and correctives that are ordinarily the best means to good economic performance; and c) belief that by destroying the diffusion of economic authority and well-being that are essential to democracy, cartelization and monopoly undermine political freedom. Decisions in New Zealand have emphasized the first belief; decisions and official reports in the United Kingdom the second; and official statements in Germany the third.

No country accepts the prohibition principle so consistently as to prohibit all restrictive agreements and monopolies or to rely wholly upon competition. Prohibition is applicable in some countries to restrictive agreements in general, in others to particular classes of agreements or of restrictive relationships, and in no country but Japan to monopolies. Under most prohibitions, however, exceptional circumstances are believed to justify exemption, either because they remove the harm that the restriction might otherwise do or because they make possible benefits from the restriction that outweigh the detrimental effects. Where circumstances are clear and their effects are thought to be uniform, the exemption is provided by statute; where not, authority to grant exemptions is delegated.

The other class of laws is inaccurately described by Europeans as an expression of the abuse principle. It includes statutes like the Belgian, under which the purpose is merely to apply correctives to agreements and to business practices that are thought to involve abuses of economic power.

However, it also includes statutes like the Dutch, under which, without prior presumptions, restrictive agreements and practices are evaluated case by case as to their bearing upon the public interest and are forbidden, amended, permitted, or even required, according to the conclusion reached. The second kind of law is obviously capable of more ambitious application than the first; but the two have been consistently commingled in public discussion. This confusion has arisen because (a) neither abuse nor the public interest has been clearly defined; (b) the public interest has been usually conceived in terms of standards of immediate fairness (departure from which would be abuse) rather than in terms of the long-run economic and political effects of restriction; and (c) lack of preconceptions about the desirability or undesirability of particular kinds of restriction has been common to both kinds of law.

So far as the "abuse" principle prevails, concepts of abuse and of the public interest are crucial to the practical effect of a law. Some statutes make no effort to define these terms, but entrust their meaning to those who decide each particular case. Other statutes grapple with the problem of definition by such phrases as distortion of the *normal* play of competition (Belgium), encouragement of *artificial* increase of prices (France), *unreasonable* prices or business conditions (Denmark), or interference with economic freedom (Belgium). Ireland provides a list of eleven practices, which are characterized as unfair when they are *unjust, unreasonable, without just cause or good reason, or contrary to the public interest*. In most instances, the relevant statutory language invokes standards of fairness or reasonableness rather than tests of economic effect. Standards similar in content are often invoked as a basis for exemptions in countries that apply the prohibition principle. Under such standards, the discretion of those who apply the law remains substantially unchecked by the statutory language.[23]

In practice, agreements contrary to the public interest and agreements that involve abuse of economic power have been conceived in substantially the same way. Under both concepts attention has centered primarily upon excessive prices and unreasonable denial of business opportunity. Prices have been regarded as excessive either because they had risen without obvious cause or because they were inexplicably higher than in other countries or because they exceeded costs by amounts regarded as abnormal and

---

[23] This is not true in the United Kingdom, Spain, or France; but the first two countries are among the few in which control is basically prohibitory, and the French statute, though in effect discretionary, employs prohibitory language that is not applied as written.

thus resulted in unusually high profits. Unreasonable denial of business opportunity has been found where goods were withheld from a would-be buyer or a particular class of buyers except for reasons regarded as proper; where, without similar proper reasons, particular buyers or classes thereof were subjected to discrimination in prices or in terms of sale; and where businessmen were prevented from engaging in lines of business for which they were considered qualified or from establishing such (not unreasonable) prices and undertaking such (not unfair) competition as they might wish.

In France similar concepts of fairness have been supplemented by strong belief that the public interest requires improvements of economic efficiency that can be achieved by specialization and other forms of "rationalization." Agreements have been approved on condition that they include such measures, and the concept of unfair discrimination has been so formulated as to encourage reduction of costs of distribution. Though ideas of efficiency play a minor role in the other countries, they have no similar central place in official policy toward restriction.

C. Methods of Applying Policy

Types of Control Used. Prohibition of restrictive agreements has a major place in the laws of only a few countries. German and Spanish laws prohibit restrictive agreements generally, subject to numerous types of exemption the authorization of which depends, for all exemptions in Spain and for some types of them in Germany upon the authority's discretion.[24] In Norway two royal decrees under a statute designed to be regulatory have applied general prohibitions to horizontal and vertical price fixing, subject to possibilities for exemption. In the United Kingdom collective resale price maintenance is categorically forbidden, resale price agreements by individual suppliers are forbidden subject to possible exemption, and other types of restrictive agreements are subject to a rebuttable adverse presumption under standards so tight that few such agreements are actually permissible. In New Zealand a statutory provision that authorizes orders against trade practices that unreasonably limit competition has been prohibitory in effect, since except in one case price-fixing covering most of a market has been interpreted as unreasonable. Though French law contains a sweeping prohibition of cartels, it is qualified by a sweeping exemption; and in practice cartels are treated as though they were not prohibited. Similarly, in Japan, though the law is prohibitory in language, it has been

---

[24] In Germany, unlike other countries that authorize discretionary exemption, full judicial review is available.

applied until recently with such laxity that its prohibitory effect has been uncertain.[25]

In the statutes of seven countries that do not use prohibition generally, particular types of restrictions are prohibited. Subject to possible exemptions, resale price maintenance by individual suppliers as well as by groups is forbidden in France, Sweden and the United Kingdom, and for certain designated classes of commodities in the Netherlands. Enforcement of such arrangements is forbidden in Denmark and Finland. Subject also to possible exemptions, collusion in bidding is forbidden in Sweden and Finland (and must be reported to the recipient of the bid in Norway). Discriminatory pricing and tying arrangements are forbidden in France. Refusal to sell is prohibited in France and may be prohibited in Norway. Subject to certain broad exemptions, Switzerland forbids boycotts and similar collective measures designed to keep independent enterprises from competing. Austria refuses to authorize agreements that include provisions for exclusive selling, exclusion of qualified persons from opportunity to sell, or imposition of restrictions upon the price or quantity of comparable goods not covered by the agreement.

A second method of control, used for restrictive agreements in Austria and Israel, consists in requiring that agreements be submitted for authorization by a designated agency before they take effect. In such a system, unapproved agreements are prohibited and civilly invalid; and any statutory conditions that are imposed upon approval constitute, in effect, a body of requirements and prohibitions applicable to all agreements for which approval is required. Apart from such specified conditions, the agency entrusted with authorization is free to apply its conception of the public interest, in the light of any guidance furnished by the statute. Austrian law, for example, provides that the agreement must appear justified from an overall economic viewpoint, with special attention to the interests of consumers, but with account taken of any possible major disadvantage to cartel members from disapproval of the registration.

More frequent than prohibitions or requirements for advance approval, however, are provisions under which some authority is authorized to conduct investigations and issue corrective orders against what it considers

---

[25] Prohibiting unreasonable restraint of trade, the law defines that term to include price fixing and various other types of restrictive agreement that cause a substantial restraint of competition contrary to the public interest. Though this language, adopted by amendment in 1953, may have been intended to becloud the prohibition that was explicit before the amendment, Japanese courts have not interpreted it as a substitution of the abuse principle for the prohibition principle. Laxity in Japan has consisted in infrequent use of this part of the statute. In the four and three-quarter years beginning in January 1958, no case involving it was instituted.

abusive or contrary to the public interest. Like orders by the Federal Trade Commission in the United States, such orders are then enforceable, either because violation of an order is a punishable offense or because powers of enforcement similar to American proceedings for contempt of court are available. Procedures of this general type are employed in nine countries.[26]

In most countries, informal processes of settlement are used, with or without statutory support, before corrective orders are issued; and punitive action is very seldom taken. In Germany, the United Kingdom, and the Netherlands, those who apply the statutes usually give opportunity for voluntary change in objectionable practices. In the United Kingdom reference of an agreement to the Restrictive Practices Court has sometimes been postponed upon assurance that the agreement was being terminated; and cases before the court in which restrictions were held to be unjustified have been usually concluded, not by an order, but by an undertaking that the restrictions would cease. In Japan, resort to a recommendation rather than an order is authorized by law. In France a decree authorizes the responsible minister to suggest a course of action before instituting punitive proceedings, and in practice he has done so instead of resorting to prosecution. In Denmark an order must be preceded by negotiations for a voluntary settlement. In Belgium initial action must consist of a verbal recommendation, followed if necessary by a written one; and orders are issued only by the King when those who receive the recommendation are recalcitrant. In Ireland a procedure for promulgation of unenforceable rules of conduct is employed more often than a procedure for investigation followed by orders; but if the rules are not obeyed, orders may replace them. In Sweden and Finland, where informality has been carried furthest, the statutory procedure consists of negotiations to remove the harmful effect of restrictive arrangements. If negotiation fails, the statutory remedy in Finland is temporary suspension of the agreement. In Sweden it is public report to the King, who thereupon has only the power, if a price is "obviously too high," to set a maximum price for not more than a year.

Where punitive provisions are available, the laws have had a considerable deterrent effect, so that the impact of the infrequent prosecutions has reached beyond the proceedings actually brought. The possibility of punitive proceedings has usually induced business groups to adjust their practices to the informally expressed wishes of the authorities. In the early stages of mandatory publicity for restrictions, such as is involved in re-

---

[26] Belgium, Denmark, France, Ireland, Netherlands, New Zealand, South Africa, Sweden, Switzerland. They are also used in Norway for restrictions other than price fixing. In New Zealand the effect of the procedure in price fixing cases has approximated that of prohibition.

quirements for public registration, similar but smaller deterrents and remedial effects have often appeared. Though corrective orders not supported by punitive power are less effective as deterrents, the fact that they are available has frequently enabled the authorities to obtain comparable corrective action by informal means. But where, as in Sweden, negotiation is not bolstered by effective power, negotiated settlements sometimes result in compromises that fall short of what the responsible authority considered appropriate.

The formal proceedings that develop under these laws differ considerably in most countries from proceedings under the American antitrust laws. Only under the laws of Germany, Japan, New Zealand, and possibly Spain, and parts of the laws of the United Kingdom and France, can a proceeding be conceived, even approximately, as one in which a designated authority applies statutory standards by prescribed procedures to determine whether or not certain defendants should be enjoined from or punished for violating the law. Even in these countries, such a description is not adequate; for except in one country, the authority has power not only to hold that no violation took place but also to alter the scope of the statute by granting exemptions; and in two countries it is authorized to apply its own conceptions of the public interest within certain statutory limitations.

In the other countries proceedings under the law do not resemble lawsuits. They are activities by which policy is formulated and applied by bodies that possess, through statutes or decrees, broad discretion to make policy. The procedures used are those regarded as appropriate either to lawmaking or to decisions by an administrative agency about the way in which a general line of policy shall be interpreted and applied in meeting a particular problem. In many respects they resemble American policy-making procedures rather than American procedures in law enforcement. These resemblances are conspicuous in a) ascertainment of facts; b) extent of publicity; c) nature and limits of rights of appeal; d) the role played by penalties; and e) use of advisory bodies representing private interests. In the last respect, however, some of the laws reach beyond any American analogy by entrusting to spokesmen for private interests not only advisory functions but also functions in making decisions.

Even the countries in which proceedings most resemble American lawsuits use procedures that, in some respects, appear to an American more appropriate to policy making than to judicial decision.

a) *Ascertainment of Facts.* Controversy about facts and about inference from facts plays a smaller part than in legal proceedings in the United States. In most countries corrective action begins with a substantial investigation, supported by mandatory powers, similar to the field investigations that precede American cases. Ascertainment of the facts during this period is facilitated in some countries by the fact that the entire content of restrictive agreements has been reported under reporting requirements; in some countries by the fact that investigation or decision rests with bodies that include businessmen (and sometimes labor leaders) likely to be familiar with, or to have acquaintances familiar with, the relevant field of business activity; and in all countries by the fact that restriction is likely to be considered less reprehensible than withholding or falsifying information. The important question about matters that are not subject to a prohibition is not the exact shading of the facts but the standards that are appropriate in deciding the bearing of the general state of facts upon the public interest.

Some of the procedures that result in decisions consist essentially in the preparation of a report based upon field investigations that include opportunity for interested persons to state their views. This is true in South Africa, where reports by the investigating authority include recommendations that may be accepted or rejected by the minister without formal hearings. A similar procedure is used in Ireland when orders rather than advisory rules are in prospect, and in the United Kingdom for proceedings concerned with restrictions other than those in registered agreements. In France, the results of a cartel investigation that included interviews with interested persons are reported to a commission which has power to hear these persons directly but seldom does so; and the commission's recommendations are then submitted to a minister who decides, without further formalities, whether to propose corrective changes or to institute prosecutions. In Belgium, too, an investigatory report is the chief basis for recommendations that can then become the basis for action. Defendants are heard, but the law gives the council that makes these recommendations discretion to decide whether or not it will hear complainants or others, and requires that the hearing be completed in one day.

In other countries facts are elicited by investigatory hearings that are often devoid of precautions that are customary in the United States to assure accuracy, completeness, and full light on controversial matters. In Denmark an authority has power to investigate by hearing, but interested persons obtain access to the evidence only after the decision is rendered. In the Netherlands persons who desire to be heard may submit requests, not to the ministry that makes decisions but to an advisory committee, and the latter has authority to terminate its hearing when it considers itself sufficiently informed. In Sweden and New Zealand a hearing consists essentially of comment by those who are being investigated upon a written report by an official who has made an investigation. In the United Kingdom (for restrictive agreements) and in Germany and Japan, procedures resemble those of American judicial proceedings.

Short-cuts in ascertaining the facts appear to be partly the cause and partly the result of a tendency for facts to become matters of general agreement, even in proceedings that in other respects are controversial. These short-cuts are major reasons for the fact that proceedings in all the countries under discussion are short and inexpensive as compared with similar proceedings in the United States.

In the United Kingdom and Austria, the role of economic evidence in litigation seems peculiar to an American. Because decisions about restrictive agreements by the British Restrictive Practices Court turn upon the question whether or not these agreements can be shown to produce certain benefits, and because claims of benefit usually involve comparison of existing conditions with those that would exist if the restriction were terminated, economic evidence is central in most of the cases. Economists present evidence in the farm of written opinions that compare existing conditions with a hypothetical alternative, and are subjected to cross examination on these opinions. They may say, for example, what they think the price would be in the absence of agreement, and conclude that the agreement does or does not give consumers the benefit of substantially lower prices.[27] To be qualified to express such an opinion, an economist need not be familiar with the particular industry either by experience or by research; his expertise is accepted if he is adequately trained in general economics. Economic theory unsupported by factual research is regarded as admissible. In some Austrian cases a similar attitude has been carried much further: Comparison of a static economic model with a cartel agreement has been set forth in certain decisions as an adequate basis for determining whether or not a cartel price was reasonable.

b) *Extent of Publicity.*   Proceedings in many of the countries involve much more secrecy than American proceedings. In South Africa and Ireland, hearings are not a part of the process by which investigatory reports are prepared. In Denmark, where corrective action begins with negotiation, there is no formal hearing, public or private. In the United Kingdom, preparation of reports by the Monopolies Commission (as distinguished from trial of cases involving restrictive agreements) may involve hearings, public or private, but the Commission has discretion to hold closed hearings or

---

[27] In the cement case, for example, the court accepted an economist's conclusion that, since the industry was expanding and prices of equipment had risen, prices of cement in the absence of the industry agreement would be not less than stated figures decidedly higher than the agreed prices.

to dispense with them entirely.[28] In France the Cartel Commission is not required to hold hearings, seldom does so, and never holds them publicly. In Belgium defendants in a proceeding must be heard privately, but the authority that formulates conclusions and recommendations decides whether or not to hear complainants or others and hears them privately if at all. In the Netherlands quasi-public boards representing business[29] must be heard by the advisory committee, not by the ministry that makes decisions, and persons interested are also heard at their request; but the committee may terminate the hearing "as soon as it considers itself sufficiently informed." In Switzerland the proceedings of the Cartel Commission are not public. In Norway procedure differs for specific corrective action and for issue of regulations. For the former, proceedings can be closed or open, at the authority's option, but are usually closed; and the right of participants to examine documents submitted by others is limited by provisions that technical processes must be kept confidential and that on request the authority can keep confidential such other information as it considers unnecessary to enable others to protect their interests. When regulations are under consideration, persons to be regulated must be allowed to "state their case" unless this is not feasible or would facilitate evasion of the regulation or reduce its effectiveness.

In some countries, however, public hearings are standard. This is true in the United Kingdom for judicial decisions about restrictive practices, in Japan for civil cases before the Commission and criminal proceedings before a court, in New Zealand for all proceedings under the law, and in Germany for judicial proceedings involving penalties and for proceedings by the Cartel Authority if any party desires an oral hearing. In Austria matters that are not informally settled by agreement between representatives of the business and labor groups that participate in decisions are argued before a cartel tribunal. In Sweden a public hearing inaugurates the negotiations that are central procedures of the law.

---

[28] The "extent, if any," of public hearing is determined by the Commission, and hearings are not in fact public. Persons substantially interested and bodies representing substantial numbers of persons have the right to submit written statements, and must be heard orally if they request it unless the Commission considers that this is not "reasonably necessary" or "reasonably practicable." As to all others, the Commission has authority to determine "the extent, if any," of their part in the investigation.

[29] These boards, established in 1950, are corporations of three types: commodity boards, vertically organized in a branch of industry; industrial boards, horizontally organized at one level of such a branch; and general industrial boards covering several related branches. They possess by law significant regulatory power, limited by a provision that their regulations shall not be impediments to fair competition. Their regulations must be approved by the Crown. In 1960 there were 15 commodity boards, more than 30 industrial boards, and 2 general industrial boards.

Some countries also limit disclosure of decisions about restrictive agreements and the findings that support these decisions. In Austria, decisions about registration of cartels are not available in a readily accessible form. In Ireland no explanatory statements are made public with the rules of fair competition. In the Netherlands decisions by the Ministry are disclosed only in summary form that does not identify the enterprises involved, and recommendations by the advisory committee have been disclosed only once. In France the advice of the Cartel Commission and the decisions of the Minister are disclosed only after long delay and are often too brief to provide information about the underlying facts and the grounds for decision. In Switzerland the government decides whether or not to publish the advice of the Cartel Commission, and what is published must not contain business secrets. In Belgium, if recommendations by the Minister are accepted, a minute summarizing them is sent to the complainants and the parties, but nothing is disclosed publicly except the fact that a settlement has been reached. However, if recalcitrance makes a formal decree necessary, the decree is published.

In the Netherlands, secrecy is at a maximum. Not only is publication of decisions limited to unrevealing summaries; in annual reports to Parliament the law requires that "facts on particular enterprises shall not be given in such a way that it is evident or can easily be concluded to what enterprises it relates," and that no mention shall be made of facts that "would needlessly damage any reasonable business interests." Even when orders by the Ministry are appealed to a court, the Minister is authorized by law to refuse for reasons to public interest to supply particular information or documents, and to stipulate that particular documents must not be disclosed to a party to the appeal. When he imposes such a restriction, the court is forbidden by law to read the restricted document unless other parties say that they do not object.

c) *Nature and Limits of Rights of Appeal.* Where broad discretion is entrusted to officials or commissions, review of its exercise is provided; but that review is not always judicial and is sometimes narrowly limited.[30] In Sweden and Belgium, where the power to issue orders is entrusted only to the King, review consists merely in his decision whether or not to act. In Ireland and under the British Monopolies Act, Ministerial orders must be approved by Parliamentary resolutions. In Finland, Germany, and Norway, discretionary administrative decisions are subject to review at higher

---

[30] Germany, the United Kingdom, and Japan authorize appeal to the courts analogous in breadth to similar action in the United States, and in New Zealand there is appeal to a designated judge. It is noteworthy that in the first three cases the law is basically prohibitory and that in New Zealand it consists of provisions for prohibitory orders that have been so interpreted as to minimize the discretionary aspect of the statute.

administrative levels, but in Germany subsequent broad review by the courts is available. In France recommendations by the Minister are informal substitutes for prosecution in court.

In Austria, Denmark, and South Africa, appeals are taken to special tribunals containing lay members and, in the Austrian case containing representatives of private interests. In Spain the tribunal's decisions in particular cases cannot be appealed except for lack of due process in proceedings in which penalties are imposed. In the Netherlands, though appeal to the courts is authorized, the law grants unlimited substantive discretion, and therefore grounds for appeal are limited to such matters as procedural and jurisdictional flaws, abuse of discretion, and conflict of laws.

d) *The Role Played by Penalties.* So far as legal proceedings are used in applying these laws, they are primarily civil rather than criminal. Penalties are available in the first instance only under the laws of Germany, France and Japan.[31] In other countries the function of penalties is to cope with those who withhold facts from the responsible authority or disobey an order issued by it.

Because until recently restrictive agreements were generally lawful and enforceable in the courts, and because an appreciable number of them still are, statutes that deprive such agreements of legal validity have a substantial impact from that fact alone. Disregard of unenforceable agreements by parties to them, and suits for damages or for injunctive relief by persons injured, have been considered major means of reform in some countries. Recognizing that civil proceedings by private persons may be inadequate, however, all states provide the possibility of public proceedings. In most countries, the law provides first for administrative action or for civil proceedings before tribunals, and contemplates that these shall be exhausted before any punitive proceeding is undertaken. Even where this is not formally required, it has become the norm of actual procedure. In practice, Japan nearly always resorts to civil orders or corrections by consent instead of the criminal prosecutions that are available as alternatives; in Germany informal correction is common and administrative fines are rare; and in France, though the part of law in which a cartel commission has an advisory role can be enforced by prosecution, formal recommendations that have the effect of orders are used by the Minister instead.[32]

---

[31] In Japan proceedings under the most important parts of the law may be either criminal or civil. In France, though criminal penalties are available for the entire law, a part of it is applied by recommendations for corrective action rather than by prosecution.

[32] The statement applies to types of concerted action as to which a statutory prohibition depends upon purpose and effect. Certain other prohibitions, applied chiefly to conduct by single firms, are enforced by prosecution. They cover fixation of minimum prices, refusal to sell, individual discrimination, and tying.

But though penalties are held in reserve rather than used initially, the penalties available are often drastic. In all countries they include fines, the upper limit of which is often substantial. In most countries they include imprisonment. In addition, particular countries provide for a) repayment or forfeiture of excess profits,[33] b) ineligibility for government contracts,[34] c) closure of an establishment,[35] d) dissolution of a trade association,[36] e) exclusion of a person or an enterprise from a field of business,[37] and f) punitive requirements that stockholdings be sold and there be no participation in mergers.[38]

e) *Use of Private Persons in Official Roles.* In more than half the countries, the law formally provides that private persons shall have a part in advice upon or formulation of public decisions. Three countries[39] give an advisory role to bodies composed wholly or partly of such persons, not only as to general matters of policy but also as to decisions in particular cases. Seven countries[40] entrust decisions in particular cases partly to representatives of private interests.

These bodies consist of from three to eighteen persons. Whether empowered to decide or only to advise, they characteristically include public officials and representatives of business. In seven of the nine countries they include spokesmen for consumer interests, in five countries for labor interests, in five countries for agriculture, in five countries persons chosen for knowledge of economics, and in four countries persons chosen for knowledge of law.[41]

---

[33] Austria, Denmark, Norway, Spain, Sweden.

[34] Japan.

[35] France.

[36] Denmark, Japan.

[37] Belgium, Norway. Under Japanese law a company official can be required to resign his post.

[38] Belgium. Japanese law also provides for divestiture of stock illegally held, but the provision is remedial, not punitive.

[39] The Netherlands, Spain, Switzerland.

[40] Austria, Denmark, Finland, France, Israel, Sweden, Switzerland. This listing omits instances in which laymen who did not retain their private posts are given official status. In the United Kingdom the court that makes decisions about agreements includes lay judges chosen for their knowledge or experience in industry, commerce, or public affairs, but, in practice, persons chosen have already retired from other employment. In South Africa a special court of appeal consists of a judge, an economist, and a person with experience in business, in cooperatives, or in engineering.

[41] The classification is only roughly indicative. Various persons on these bodies possess qualifications that might justify listing them in more than one category, but each has been attributed only to one. For example, an Israeli, treated here as a representative of consumers because he was so chosen, is a trade union official especially charged with consumer protection; and another Israeli, treated here as a businessman because he is a sales manager, is also a lecturer in economics.

In some instances the category into which a person officially falls does not

The business members of such bodies are expected to perform a dual function; first, to explain the nature and importance of any business interests affected by matters that come before the body for advice or decision, and second, to participate impartially in considering the bearing of these interests and all other relevant matters upon the public interest. They take full part in considering questions of general policy that arise, whether or not their companies or industries will be affected by the policy decisions. By law or by custom, a business member does not take part in recommendations or decisions about the practices or agreements of his own company. In Denmark, however, he may participate in preliminary discussions even in such cases, and is not disqualified from full participation in a case involving a trade association of which he is a member.

Since in France, Denmark, and the Netherlands the proceedings of the bodies that include representatives of business are secret, information about the way businessmen perform their dual role in these three countries is slight. Nothing is available for France, and only hearsay for the Netherlands and Denmark. In the Netherlands,[42] the members of the advisory committee (18 persons, including 6 businessmen) seldom have difficulty in agreeing upon the facts of a case. The committee often divides as to the bearing of the facts upon the public interest, but no information is available about whether or not business representatives stand together in such divisions. In Denmark,[43] where a 15-man authority includes 4 businessmen who represent respectively manufacturers, wholesalers, grocers, and handicrafts, one of the business representatives often supports the views of persons from his own segment of the economy who are involved in a case; but the four businessmen do not consistently vote together. Dissents by one business member are common, but dissents by four are rare.

In Austria, where the 3-man body that registers and thus permits a cartel consists of one representative of business, one of labor, and one judge, a decision is a bargain between conflicting interests, in which a public official can decide if agreement is not reached. But in addition to

indicate the true nature of his role. For example, the two persons selected in France for knowledge of economics are actually officials of banks, and the representatives of labor in Austria actually function as spokesmen for consumers. Where a person was appointed as a representative of a designated category, I have accepted the designation whether or not it seemed appropriate. Persons for whom an explicit type of qualification was not asserted have been allocated to categories that best fit their actual role. For example, the representation attributed to consumers in France is actually that of the state-owned railway system, which seeks to protect its interests as buyer.

Since I have not been able to ascertain the affiliations of two members of the Spanish Tribunal for the Protection of Competition, the figures given not only may be affected by dubious classifications but are also, in this particular, incomplete.

[42] Information from a member of the advisory committee.

[43] Information from a member of the Danish Monopoly Control Authority.

acting as advocate of the particular cartel, the representative of business exerts pressure upon the businessmen involved in a case to moderate restrictions sufficiently to enable him to induce the labor representative, or failing that, the judge, to accept them.

In Sweden the role of the business representatives on the Freedom of Commerce Board includes even less advocacy of particular business interests. The broad interest of Swedish business has consisted in assuring the success of the existing legal provisions for negotiated settlements, for fear that if a case in which negotiation has failed is publicly reported an effort will be made to enact a more drastic law. Hence the business men on the Board frequently concur with other members about the merits of a case, and frequently put pressure upon an enterprise or an industry to accept the Board's recommendations.

Chapter IV

Reporting and Registration

In some countries restrictive practice laws require that restrictive agreements and information about large enterprises be reported to the government. Where there are such requirements, there is usually provision that what is reported, or a summary of it, shall be placed in a register available to the public.

Reporting requirements are part of the law of eleven of the seventeen countries covered by this book.[1] From country to country, the scope of the requirement differs greatly, as indicated in the table.

Reporting of Agreements

The most common and most significant reporting requirements apply to restrictive agreements. Four different purposes underlie these requirements.

The first is to give information to the government about the nature and scope of restrictions. In some instances, e.g., in the Netherlands, the government has undertaken to regulate cartels with a professed attitude of neutrality, on the assumption that particular cartels may prove to be either desirable or undesirable. In other instances, e.g., in Finland, much of the initial purpose was to get information as a basis for the formulation of policy. The function of reporting, as seen by such governments, is to provide the knowledge from which a policy can be developed either toward cartels in general or toward particular cartels.

In other instances, standards and courses of action to be applied to restrictive agreements have been set forth in a statute. Reports serve to define precisely the field within which investigation and action pursuant to the statutory policy are appropriate and thus to facilitate application of the policy. This is broadly true in such countries as the United Kingdom, Denmark, and Norway. In Germany, where resale price agreements made by a single enterprise to cover its branded goods are authorized by law, the Cartel Authority is empowered to invalidate the contractual obligation to maintain resale prices where it finds abuse, probability of unduly high

---

[1] Austria, Denmark, Finland, Germany, Israel, Japan, the Netherlands, Norway, Spain, Sweden, the United Kingdom.

47

Scope of Reporting Requirements

What Must Be Reported	Austria	Denmark	Finland	Germany	Israel	Japan	Netherlands	Norway	Spain	Sweden	United Kingdom
Restrictive agreements											
all or nearly all	X	X	X		X		X	X		X	X
types subject to approval or exemption					X		X			X	
international agreements							X				
Dominant firms	X	X	X					X		X	
Mergers and related acquisitions					X[1]		X			X[1]	
Existing concentration											
Interlocking directorates							X				
Stockholdings by large non-financial											
companies							X				
Stockholdings over 10 percent by											
financial institutions							X				
Stockholdings over 10 percent in com-											
peting companies by others							X				
Trade associations							X				
Foreign firms or certain ties with foreign firms							X		X		

[1] Only if after the acquisition the firm would have 20 percent of the market or more in Germany, 30 percent or more in Spain.

prices, or probability of restricted production or sale. Exercise of this authority is facilitated by a requirement that such price agreements be filed with the authority, with full information about prices and margins. Until recently the information filed was not made public.

A second purpose is to diminish the number and the restrictiveness of restrictive agreements by exposing the terms of such agreements to public criticism. Whereas the first purpose could be served by secret reports (and in the Netherlands is actually served in this way), the second purpose requires that the agreement be made public by registration and that its contents be well publicized. To minimize criticism by consumers, by political adversaries, and by businessmen adversely affected, participants in restrictive agreements may abandon them or eliminate from them the restrictions that are least defensible. To curb agreements by public opinion is a secondary purpose of the registration requirements in the United Kingdom, Denmark, Norway, and Finland. Swedish cartel policy has relied heavily upon registration to produce such effects. The process has stimulated corrective action by trade groups, known in Sweden as self-sanitation.

The third purpose, to police exemptions, is significant in Germany, Japan, and Spain. The clearest example of it is in Germany, where horizontal restrictive agreements are made invalid by general rule and disregard of their invalidity is prohibited. The law exempts some classes of agreements and empowers the Cartel Authority or the Minister of Economics to exempt others under stated conditions. Provision is made that most classes of exempted agreements shall be included in a public register. Registration is required for (a) agreements designed to bring about a planned adjustment of capacity to demand after lasting decline in the latter; (b) agreements by which economic processes are rationalized in a way apt to increase efficiency; (c) agreements that promote or protect exports but also restrict domestic trade; (d) agreements concerning importation of goods for which there is little or no competition among suppliers; (e) agreements about terms of sale; (f) agreements about discounts and rebates for services; (g) standardization agreements; (h) agreements under exceptional circumstances that are thought by the Minister of Economics to justify restrictions of competition; and (i) certain kinds of agreements pertaining to public utilities and transportation. Resale price agreements between an individual supplier and his customers, which until 1965 were reported on a confidential basis, are now also subject to public registration. Moreover, agreements that restrict only export markets must be filed with the Cartel Authority, though they are not made public. The same is true of some agreements pertaining to transportation. In requiring that restrictive agreements be reported and that most of them be disclosed, the lawmakers evidently intended, first, to make sure that those who enjoy the exemptions do not include in their agreements restrictions not within the scope of the exemptions, and second, to subject those who grant exemptions to public criticism if they are unduly lenient.

The fourth purpose of reporting and registration is to serve as a means by which the content of restrictive agreements can be directly limited. Where this type of policy is followed, reported agreements are publicly registered and are given a different legal status from unregistered agreements. In Denmark, for example, an unreported agreement is legally invalid and unenforceable; and in Austria and Norway, not only is such an agreement unenforceable, but compliance with it is a violation of law. In avoiding handicaps such as these through registration, persons who make agreements must adjust them to the substantive requirements of the statute. Thus registration becomes a means of enforcing minor limits upon permissible restrictions, such as requirements that participants be authorized to withdraw or that agreements have a maximum time limit. In Norway, for example, the law provides that unless special approval is obtained restrictive agreements must have a time limit of a year (with possibility of renewal) or must authorize a participant to withdraw after notice covering a period not exceeding three months. Registration is a convenient device for making certain that such requirements are observed.

By establishing substantive limits upon what may be registered, requirements for registration thus become equivalent to explicit statutory prohibitions. The most ambitious use of registration in this way is to be found in the Austrian cartel law. An unregistered agreement is both invalid and unlawful. Entry into the register is to be granted if various conditions are met. One of these conditions is that the agreement shall not include any provision for exclusive selling or for exclusion of specified persons or groups from selling. Similarly, in the case of resale price agreements, registration may be authorized only if the resale margins correspond to, or are lower than, the usually granted margins. Such explicit requirements are superimposed upon a general provision by which the Cartel Tribunal is to register only agreements that appear to it to be justified from the point of view of the national economy, with special consideration to the interests of consumers. The registration requirement becomes both a means to forbid particular types of restriction and a means to apply a broad discretionary authority in determining what agreements are to be permitted.

The purposes that have been discussed above are not mutually exclusive. A desire for information underlies the reporting systems of all countries. Formal or informal use of the information to curb cartels is also general. Hope that publicity will discourage restriction is general except where, as in the Netherlands, the reports are not published, or, as in Germany, what is published covers only agreements that have been granted approval or exemption, or, as in Austria and Israel, the registration process is also the process of approving cartels. Where the law contains prohibitions qualified by provisions for exemption, reporting (with or without public registration) is often used as an aid in policing the exemptions. Reporting fits into cartel law as a device to get information, check restrictions by publicity, and facilitate the application of administrative or judicial control in accord with statutory or discretionary standards that fall short of complete prohibition.

Requirements that agreements be reported are not merely incidental aids in applying substantive provisions of the statutes. They involve, in themselves, substantial questions of policy and substantial administrative difficulties. These are clearest where the requirement for reports applies broadly to all or most of the agreements subject to the law's control. Accordingly, the discussion that ensues will apply, except as otherwise noted, to requirements of this kind.

Where mandatory reporting is used, decisions about the scope and application of the law must be formulated with precision at the outset. Under the Sherman Act in the United States, decisions whether or not the law applies to particular types of business, such as insurance, or to particular kinds of restriction, such as requirements contracts, can be made from time to time as test cases under broadly worded statutes are presented to the courts. A body of law thus grows clear by accretion. Whether or not the law's substantive provisions are precise and clear, a country that requires and registers reports must decide quickly and comprehensively who shall report and what shall be reported, and thus must provide, in law or in supplementary regulations, relatively detailed information as to the substantive scope of the statute and as to the economic field of its application. Some countries reduce the need to determine all such matters at the outset by providing that reports must be made only when demanded by the proper government agency. Major matters that must be decided will be discussed in the next few pages.

The Definition of Agreement. Where reporting is required, there are difficult problems in defining the scope of what must be reported. Agreement may be expressed in a variety of ways: written contracts intended to be enforceable at law, written memoranda of agreement in such form that they are not legally enforceable, unwritten understandings that may be explicit or vague, consistent uniformities of action supported by a feeling that to deviate from the pattern would be improper. The executive of a trade association may make a decision the effect of which is indistinguishable from that of an agreement among the members, and coordinated action by the members may follow. By covering few or many of these possibilities, a reporting requirement may be substantially restricted or expanded.

Aware of the problem, the countries in which agreements must be reported have differed in their solution of it. The Netherlands requires report of agreements that are legally binding and of decisions by trade associations that members are bound to obey, and provides that by order in council the requirement may be extended to written agreements that are not legally enforceable. The Danish requirement, by contrast, covers not only enforceable agreements but oral agreements and arrangements, however informal, including recommendations by trade associations that may effectively influence trade. In particular countries, the scope of reporting is limited to written documents with legal effect, extended to include less formal arrangements, further extended to cover the restrictive programs of trade associations, extended further still to include implied obligations, stretched further to include recommendations made effective through pressure, made broad enough to include what has become known in the United States as "conscious parallel action," and merged into a general requirement that business must supply such information about restrictions as the government may demand.

Where an effort is made to require that informal arrangements be reported, means to make them sufficiently definite for registration must usually be devised. The United Kingdom, for example, requires that if an agreement is unwritten a memorandum in writing must set forth its terms. Filing requirements are sometimes supplemented by requirements for filed explanatory statements. The duty to report is often reenforced by a broad duty to furnish information to the government on request, so that background information about informal agreements can be readily obtained.

Problems in defining the scope of the duty to report are common, both in the case of restrictions carried out through trade associations and in the case of informal agreements. When unwritten agreements are reduced to written form, there is often difficulty in achieving precision, and sometimes the parties disagree about the content of the agreement. Parties tend to submit histories of their activities rather than statements of their obligations.

The information from a trade association that is needed to disclose restrictive arrangements applied by it is often not clear. In the United Kingdom, the Registrar of Restrictive Trading Agreements sought to clarify the requirement as to such registrations (and as to other problems of registration) in a guide published in 1956. Using the example of a price list determined by a subcommittee of a price committee established under a trade association, he suggested that registration required the names of the members for whom the prices were prepared, the price list, the rules under which it was established, the constitution of the association, and a list of the members thereof.

Supplementary advice about all kinds of obligations to register is given by the British Registrar's office on request. By October 1959, more than

1,000 applicants had been advised, and nevertheless seventy agreements that had been voluntarily offered for registration had been rejected as not subject to it.

The Definition of Restriction. What must be reported depends not only upon the conception of agreement but also upon the statutory conception of a registrable restriction. In countries in which a register is designed to supply information, without implied condemnation of what is registered, the tendency is to define restriction broadly, if at all, and to entrust to some authority the power to determine whether or not the requirement for reporting is applicable in doubtful cases. In Denmark, for example, the agreements that must be reported are those that exert, or may be able to exert, a substantial influence on price, production, distribution, or transport conditions, throughout the country or in local market areas. Subject to possible appeal, the Danish authority decides whether or not particular agreements have these characteristics. Enterprises that make binding agreements are presumed to have the power to make them effective. In determining the influence of recommendations, great weight is attached to the proportion of total trade done by the parties to the recommendations. Other matters are also considered, such as the relative size and number of parties and of independents, the setting of particular agreements amid others, and the nature of the subject matter.

Similarly, in the Netherlands the agreements that must be registered are those that regulate economic competition between owners of enterprises. In Sweden, the obligation to report agreements is a part of a general duty to give information (a) about restraints of competition (whether in agreements or not) that relate to conditions of price, production, commerce, or transport in Sweden, and (b) about prices, revenues, costs, profits, and other conditions affecting price formation.

Open-end categories such as these can be applied partly because parties to an agreement who desire legal validity are likely to take the initiative in reporting it for registration. Nevertheless, such requirements are administrable chiefly because broad discretion is entrusted to an administrative authority to apply them in a way that leaves little or no room for judicial review. The authority charged to supervise reporting is empowered to determine what must be reported. In some countries its decisions can be appealed only on grounds of abuse of power; in others, though there is a broader right of appeal, nearly all such appeals are rejected. In Denmark, where the authority does not have the right to determine the substantive limits of the reporting requirement, controversy about them is frequent. While 173 new agreements were being registered in the four and one-half years to the close of 1959, the Danish authority decided seventy disputes about the obligation to register[2] and ordered registration in 55 of the cases. Eight of its decisions were appealed, and two of them overruled.

The law of the United Kingdom contrasts sharply with those of other countries in the care with which the field of reportable restriction is defined. The restrictions that make an agreement registrable in the United Kingdom are to be brought, sooner or later, before a court, where they will be invalidated unless the parties to them can show that they are in the public interest. Hence the registration requirement has been formulated with the precision that is appropriate to its use as a basis for later judicial action. Subject to various exemptions and exclusions, an agreement is registrable if two or more of the parties accept restrictions (that is, negative obligations) with respect to any of the following matters:

(a) prices to be charged, quoted, or paid for goods supplied, offered, or acquired, or for the application of any process of manufacture to goods;

(b) the terms or conditions on or subject to which goods are to be supplied or acquired or any such process is to be applied to goods;

(c) the quantities or descriptions of goods to be produced, supplied, or acquired;

(d) the processes of manufacture to be applied to any goods, or the quantities or descriptions of goods to which any such process is to be applied; or

(e) the persons or classes of persons to, for, or from whom, or the areas or places in or from which goods are to be supplied or acquired, or any such process applied.

Industrial Scope. In general, where the obligation to report is not confined to agreements subject to special kinds of exemption, it covers an economic field comparable in breadth to the scope of the field subject to the substantive provisions designed to curb restriction. It may be limited, as in the United Kingdom, to agreements among persons who produce or supply goods or apply processes of manufacture to goods.[3] It may, as in Sweden and the Netherlands, cover service enterprises also. It may, as in Norway, cover everyone engaged in business. It may or may not cover

---

[2] The figures pertain to registration both of agreements and of other registrable matters. No breakdown is available.

[3] The law of the United Kingdom lists, in detail, types of agreements that are exempt from reporting and types of provisions that shall not be considered in deciding whether or not the reporting requirement is applicable. Supplying goods and applying processes of manufacture are terms of art in British law: Leasing goods and constructing buildings are included, as well as such activities as cleaning oriental carpets and packing merchandise. Goods are defined in the law to include ships, aircraft, minerals, substances, and animals (including fish).

industries subject to close government regulation. In particular laws, provisions explicitly include or exclude leasing, licensing, dealing in securities, borrowing or lending, writing insurance, cooperative activities, patent agreements, trademark agreements, resale price maintenance, shipping agreements, and non-profit undertakings. In no country does the reporting requirement apply to agreements between employers and employees about wages and working conditions.

In the United Kingdom, there is a slight difference in scope between what must be reported and what can be controlled. Certain classes of agreements are exempt from reporting. But what must be reported (and registered) must contain the whole of an agreement; and if the exempted restrictions are reported as parts of a broader agreement that is registrable because of its other provisions, some of them are subject to decision by the Restrictive Practices Court, while others are specifically exempted from the Court's jurisdiction.

Territorial Scope. Reporting requirements, like substantive curbs, are focussed chiefly upon domestic markets. Two different principles of jurisdiction are invoked. In five countries that require general reporting[4] reporting is required if the agreement has effects within the country. In two such countries[5] it is required if participants do business within the country.

In two of the countries in which the duty to report depends upon domestic effects, the law makes clear that foreign firms must report and agreements made abroad must be reported.[6] In the laws of the other such countries, similar obligations are not explicitly set forth, but apparently are imposed in practice. In the two countries in which firms that do business there must report, the application of the reporting obligation to foreign firms and foreign agreements differs. Netherlands law provides exemption from the reporting requirement for restrictions applied abroad,[7] and authorizes other discretionary exemptions, but affords no special status to foreign enterprises that operate in the Netherlands nor to agreements concerning the Netherlands that are made elsewhere. It obligates all firms established in the Netherlands to inform the government, on request, what enterprises, to the best of their knowledge, are parties to a restrictive agreement. The United Kingdom requires reporting of agreements in which two or more participants do business in the United Kingdom, and in which two or more

---

[4] Austria, Denmark, Finland, Norway, Sweden.

[5] The Netherlands and the United Kingdom.

[6] The Austrian law is explicitly applicable to agreements concluded abroad to the extent that they are implemented in Austria. Representatives in Norway of foreign enterprises are required to report, on behalf of their foreign principals, agreements that regulate the Norwegian market.

[7] The statutory phrase is "regulations of competition outside of the Netherlands."

parties accept restrictions; but those who accept the restrictions need not be those whose domicile establishes the jurisdiction. Moreover, where reporting takes place, the full agreement must be supplied. Thus there is an obligation for firms that do business in the United Kingdom to report agreements to which they are parties even if restrictions applicable to the British market are accepted only by foreigners not established in the United Kingdom.

Export agreements are usually exempt from reporting. This is true explicitly or implicitly in Austria, Finland, the Netherlands, Norway, and Sweden. In Denmark such agreements are reported and publicly registered. In the United Kingdom, if they pertain only to exports they must be reported, but are not publicly registered. In Germany, if they restrict foreign markets only they are exempt from the general statutory prohibitions, and are reported confidentially; whereas if they involve collateral domestic restrictions, exemption, though possible, is not automatic, and the exempted agreements become public. In Spain, if they do not involve objectionable domestic restriction, they can be exempted, and, if so, must be publicly registered.

Import agreements are usually subject to reporting under the broad language of the reporting requirements. But Finland specifically exempts agreements about purchases in other countries destined for Finland provided the interests of Finnish consumers are not affected. In Germany and Spain, where import agreements may be exempted from general prohibitions, those that are approved must be publicly registered.

In countries in which the obligation to report applies to agreements that have domestic effects, there is automatic exemption for agreements that pertain only to foreign markets. In the United Kingdom and the Netherlands, where the obligation attaches to enterprises doing business in the country, specific exemption is provided for such agreements. But in Norway, though the general requirement does not cover agreements about foreign markets, the law contains an explicit provision by which the Norwegian authority is empowered to supervise participation in foreign arrangements by enterprises within the realm, and the king is empowered to make regulations for appropriate reporting. Norwegian law also provides that if the authority obtains knowledge of foreign restrictive business arrangements detrimental to Norwegian interests, it shall report the matter to the Ministry.

What Must be Reported. Without significant exception, reporting requirements call for the full texts of written agreements and for full reporting of the terms of unwritten agreements. Names of parties to each reported agreement are also always required. In several countries[8] additional in-

---

[8] Austria, Denmark, Finland, Norway, Sweden.

formation may be required, pertaining to such matters as how the agreement came into existence; the nature, volume, and proportion of business covered by it; the names of important non-participating enterprises; the conditions upon which enterprises will be permitted to join or withdraw; the way execution of the agreement is supervised; the means for settling disputes; the relation of the agreement to other agreements; and pertinent information about prices, costs, and profits. Where trade association activities are involved, associations may be required to furnish information about their purposes, structure, membership, rules, decisions, punitive powers, and affiliations. In all countries the obligation to report is supplemented by a grant of broad investigatory power to the government.

What Becomes Public.   The extent to which the reported information becomes public varies greatly from country to country. In the Netherlands, the reports are confidential, and even an appellate court may be denied full access to them. Indeed, the law provides that even in annual reports to the Parliament the facts about particular enterprises shall not be given in identified form and no mention shall be made of facts if the Ministry thinks that any reasonable business interest would be damaged thereby. Publication of facts is authorized, however, as a punitive measure, when the government thinks that an agreement is contrary to the public interest.

In the other countries that provide for general reporting, a public register discloses some or all of the facts. In five countries the full text of an agreement is usually public; in two, the public register also includes the supplementary information that was required; and in one it may include additional statements by the government.[9] In two countries the law provides for a public register consisting of summaries of agreements. In one of these, Finland, the summary has usually been accompanied by exhibits that provided full disclosure;[10] in the other, Austria, it has often consisted of unrevealing generalities.[11]

In Spain, where agreements are registered only if they are exempted from statutory prohibitions, the exempted agreements are public. In Germany, where reporting is similarly limited to exempted agreements, most classes of such agreements are public; but agreements that apply solely to exports are filed without public registration.

---

[9] Denmark, Israel, Norway, Sweden, and the United Kingdom. Supplementary information is included in Norway and Sweden; government comment in Norway.

[10] For the first 139 Finnish registrations, underlying documents were attached to the summary in all but four instances. Whatever is not disclosed in a Finnish registration must be kept confidential for 20 years unless the parties consent to its publication. Interested persons may appeal against the content of draft summaries. To April 1960, twelve appeals had been filed and rejected.

[11] The Austrian register is explicit as to dates, period of validity, names and addresses of participants, and names and addresses of organizations or agents that administer the agreement. Its summary of restrictions is often brief and uninformative.

Four countries[12] make exceptions to their general rules of full disclosure where, in the opinion of government officials,[13] disclosure would be inconsistent with the public interest or would unduly harm legitimate private interests. Such exceptions are infrequent. By early 1960 one Swedish agreement had been kept wholly secret; parts of 16 other Swedish agreements had been granted secrecy for stated periods of time; and 10 Danish agreements had been granted partial secrecy. The United Kingdom does not disclose the number of its secret registrations, but there is reason to believe that the figure is comparably small.

The Burden of Paperwork. In an effort to reduce the burden of reporting and of maintaining a public register, some countries have provided special rules applicable to multiple agreements. An example of such an agreement is a standard resale price contract made separately by a seller with each of his numerous distributors. Austrian law provides that, in the case of resale price agreements, the standard agreement shall be registered and the names of the last resellers need not be entered in the register. Germany follows a similar practice, but requires that a filing include attachments giving complete data about resale prices and trade margins and showing whether or not the dealer is bound to render special services to customers. Where the registration authority has power to determine the details of reporting and registration, as is usually the case, similar labor saving devices are frequently used.

Changes in agreements must be reported as they occur. The laws of most countries explicitly require this.[14] Reports of change can be numerous, for an agreement is altered not only when its terms are changed but also when there is any change in the identity or number of the parties to it. In the United Kingdom, where each change in terms or in parties must be reported, more than 2,000 documents reporting changes had been registered by October 6, 1959. But the burden of report may be even heavier. An agreement may be regarded as changed if there is a change in any price, discount, quota, or similar quantity that is specified in it or that, though not explicitly set forth in the agreement, is directly controlled by the terms thereof. In Denmark a new report must be made if there is a change in "prices, margins, quotas, etc." already reported. An extreme example of

---

12 Denmark, Israel, Sweden, the United Kingdom.

13 In Sweden such decisions are made by the King in Council; in Denmark, by the Ministry of Commerce; in the United Kingdom, by the Board of Trade.

14 In Sweden, though the law is silent about reports of changes, the authority is believed to have power to require such reports. It has sometimes included in its requests for agreements currently in force a further request for notice of all changes made during a short period, such as two years. However, the principal means by which the information has been kept reasonably current has been to renew the request for current agreements at intervals of two or three years.

the resulting burden upon those that receive reports is furnished by Germany, where, under a legal requirement that resale prices be reported, the Federal Cartel Office had on file on September 15, 1963, about 162,000 prices filed by 1,206 enterprises that fixed resale prices and almost 21,000 additional prices filed by 394 enterprises that recommended resale prices. British law seeks to minimize such burdens by authorizing the Registrar of Restrictive Trading Agreements to make regulations excluding from the reporting requirement details as to persons, prices, terms, or other matters that are material only in defining the application from time to time of continuing restrictions. In the absence of such regulations, the British reports of change would have exceeded greatly the 2,000 mentioned above.

In efforts to minimize the burden of reporting and the application of subsequent control to trivia, Norwegian law provides that unimportant agreements may be exempted from the obligation to report and British law provides that agreements without economic significance may be removed from the register. But when, as in the United Kingdom, the procedure for exemption includes safeguards designed to prevent misuse, use of it is a time-consuming process and hence does little to reduce official burdens. Removal of such an agreement from the British register requires recommendation by the Registrar, decision by the Board of Trade, and report of the action to Parliament. Early in 1960 the Registrar estimated that about 200 agreements should be examined as possibly appropriate for removal. By December 2, 1960, about 26 had been removed. Lack of economic significance had been interpreted to mean, not smallness in the amount of trade affected, but absence of types of restriction likely to be harmful. Agreements that had been removed involved such restrictions as a provision that a trade association's dues be based upon its members' turnover, a requirement that certain precautions be taken in bottling a toxic liquid, a provision recommending a minimum specification for a commodity, and provisions, accepted as satisfactory by the customers to whom they applied, for standard terms of sale and for methods of computing the charges involved in readjustment of contracts.

Inducements to Report Fully and Accurately. The most common method of assigning responsibility for supplying information is to make reporting a duty of each enterprise or association that participates in the agreement, but to provide that when an agreement has been reported by one participant the duty imposed upon the others shall lapse.[15] Ordinarily, the duty rests, either implicitly or by statute, upon responsible officials of each organization that is to report. In Austria, however, one requirement

---

[15] In Denmark, however, each person who is obligated to report must sign the report.

for registration is that the cartel appoint a responsible agent, and the duty to report is assigned by law to this agent.

Where reporting is mandatory, problems arise whether reports have been made for all agreements that are covered by the requirement and whether, for each particular agreement, information has been furnished completely and accurately. The probability of failure to report and of deceptive reporting is greater in some reporting systems than in others. Where an unreported agreement is legally invalid and unenforceable[16] and where compliance with the terms of an unreported agreement is a punishable offence,[17] full reporting is made probable by desire to give agreements legal validity. Countries where unreported agreements are invalid, as well as other countries that require reports, provide penalties for failure to report and for false reporting. In Norway and the United Kingdom the authority also has power to register such unreported agreements as come to its knowledge; and in the United Kingdom, persons believed to be parties to unreported agreements may be required to state whether or not this is so.

The extent of violation of reporting requirements is not known, but is thought to be small. In the United Kingdom, about 250 agreements previously unreported—roughly one-ninth of all reported agreements—had been obtained by the close of 1959 by requiring enterprises to state whether they were parties to agreements. However, the Registrar thought that failure to report had been deliberate in only a few cases. In Denmark investigations have shown that the register was not complete: For example, after the authority had required termination of a plate glass agreement, an informal agreement was substituted without report, but later was discovered by the authority. In Sweden, according to business informants, some agreements have not been reported. In Norway the only flagrant instance of failure to report that came to official notice was treated drastically. A price agreement among about seventy-five printers, which had been registered for many years, was supplemented in 1938 or earlier by an agreement under which, if a printer's customer invited bids upon the expiration of a printing contract or for additional work, the invited bidders would protect the original contractor by bidding at higher prices. The supplementary agreement remained secret and unregistered until about 1958. The Norwegian Broadcasting Corporation then invited bids, and a recipient of the invitation, though willing to submit an equal bid, refused to submit a higher one. Thereupon the original printer reduced his bid, but the lost the contract because the Broadcasting Corporation was not satisfied with the quality of

---

[16] Austria, Denmark, Norway; also Germany, so far as exemption from prohibitory provisions is conditioned upon report.

[17] Austria, Norway.

his work. His complaint led to a Parliamentary inquiry why the low bid was rejected, and this in turn to an investigation by the cartel authority. Though the printers' organization denied that there were any unregistered agreements, the secret one was found in its archives, with evidence of its use since 1938. Thereupon, in May 1959, the government prohibited all restrictive agreements in the printing industry. The Parliament unanimously approved the decision. Unsuccessful efforts were made to prosecute criminally some of the persons involved.

Much more common than failure to report is effort to frame agreements so that they look innocuous on the register or escape the registration requirement entirely. A frequent comment by the authorities of countries that use registration is that the language of agreements grows increasingly vague, general, and pious in tone. An agreement in the British motor trade illustrates this tendency. Provisions by which sellers clearly had undertaken to enforce resale prices had been altered prior to registration to make them ambiguous. The only sentence that clearly set forth what the Restrictive Practices Court later found to be the central purpose had been deleted from a draft and did not appear in the final version; and the parties contended before the court there there was no such purpose.

Avoidance of the obligation to register is also illustrated in a British case. Before the British law was enacted, Austin Motor Co. had been party to multipartite agreements with its distributors and dealers by which sales territories were allocated, exclusive dealing was required, purchase quotas were established, channels of distribution were partially allocated, functional discounts were specified, trade-in allowances were fixed, and resale prices were fixed for certain types of transactions. In the light of the new law, Austin substituted a series of bilateral vertical agreements for each multipartite one, without significant change in the substantive content of the arrangements. Though the Registrar sought to register these agreements, the court sustained Austin's contention that they fell within the exemptions provided by the British law for vertical bilateral agreements.

Similarly, since horizontal agreements to record sales prices by filing them in a common depository are not registrable in the United Kingdom, numerous British trade associations have substituted such programs for other more vulnerable arrangements.

Reports by Single Enterprises

Unlike restrictive agreements, business decisions and business activities by single firms cannot easily be deprived of legal validity. Norway, for example, where unreported restrictive agreements are invalid, applies no equivalent provision to reports by single enterprises. Programs as to such reports select, from the entire field of enterprises and business activities, certain kinds as to which reports are wanted, and rely upon mandatory provisions of law to obtain compliance with reporting requirements.

The four Scandinavian countries and Austria require reports by single enterprises. In Sweden and Finland such reports are intended to make the government as aware of restrictions by single enterprises as of restrictions by agreement, and thus to facilitate uniformity in controlling the two types of restriction. In the other three countries, where the duty to report rests on the dominance or substantial influence of the reporting enterprise, the purpose is to place the activities of such enterprises under special surveillance and thereby prevent so-called abuses of economic power. Inclusion in a public register sometimes subjects the included firm to special control. In Denmark, for example, firms in the register must not raise prices without prior governmental approval.

As to segments of the economy covered, provisions about report of changes, provisions for assuring compliance with the reporting requirement, and various other matters, requirements that single enterprises report are like requirements for report of restrictive agreements. The discussions that follows will cover only aspects in which significant differences appear.

Who Must Report. The reporting requirement in Sweden and Finland is the same in principle for single enterprises as for restrictive agreements: an entrepreneur must report, on request, information about his restraints of competition. Conduct, rather than dominance, is the basis for reporting, and hence a small enterprise may be required to report if it engages in restriction.

In the other countries, the reporting requirement rests on the power of the enterprise. In Denmark, enterprises may be required to report only if they may exert a substantial influence on prices, production, distribution, or transport. In evaluating the influence of an enterprise, the authorities consider such matters as proportion of volume of trade, the number of competitors, the importance of imports, the prestige of sellers' brands, the possibility of independent price policies, and the existence of sole agency arrangements. Since influence in a local market area is sufficient to subject a firm to the reporting requeriment, small Danish firms may be required to report. Austria and Norway define a powerful firm statistically: In Austria a dominant enterprise is one that possesses 30 percent or more of the market unless there are more than three firms there; if so, it is one that possesses a market share of at least 50 percent. In Norway, a single enterprise must report if it (plus other enterprises that it controls) "must be assumed to" produce or distribute at least one-fourth of the Norwegian total of any commodity or service. In practice, the scope of the Norwegian requirement is reduced by interpreting the term commodity or service to mean an entire class of commodities or services. The requirement is also made flexible by provisions that empower the authority to extend it to enterprises whose activities are so important as to need supervision, and to relieve from it enterprises whose activities are so unimportant that supervision is not needed.

In Finland power as well as restriction must be reported on request. Persons engaged in trade must report whether they possess exclusive rights or otherwise occupy *de facto* a position so dominant as to restrict competition.

What Must be Reported. The extent of reporting is more difficult to define for reports by single enterprises than for reports of agreements. Requirements show great diversity.

In Austria the law provides that a company must report its sales and its market share. In all four Scandinavian countries the appropriate authority has wide power to prescribe the content of reports by rule-making, by modifying the scope of what it calls for, or by demanding supplementary information. In Sweden, as in the case of restrictive agreements, the authority can call for facts about restraints of competition, prices, receipts, costs, profits, and other conditions affecting price formation. It is explicitly authorized to demand books of account, correspondence, and other documents. In Denmark the report-form covers the structure and scope of the firm, commodity fields in which the firm is influential, prices and discounts, contracts with distributors, exclusive arrangements, policies about resale prices, and participation in restrictive agreements. In Finland reports about power must cover the legal or other basis for the firm's special position, plus information about volume, turnover, extent of service rendered, and similar matters regarded as essential to determine the extent to which a special position has been attained. In Norway a report must contain corporate by-laws; a list of stockholders and their holdings; a statement of any foreign ownership; detail about interlocks with other firms by ownership of majority stock interests or interlocking directorates; detail about the nature and extent of business activities; connections with associations; texts of restrictive agreements to which the firm is a party; and a statement about such other matters as resale price maintenance, exclusive or preferential dealing, refusal to sell, classification of customers, rates of discount, and "other matters of importance."

What Becomes Public. In Austria the public register contains the name of the company and its market share. In three of the other four countries, the rule governing the disclosure of information supplied by single enterprises is the same as that applicable to agreements. In Finland, summaries prepared by the authority are placed in a public register, with attached documents, so far as the authority thinks publication appropriate, and subject to the right of interested persons to appeal to an administrative court. In Denmark and Norway, reports from single enterprises, like reports of agreements, are fully registered. In Sweden, however, where agreements are publicly registered, there is no provision for the registration of anything else except the by-laws, rules, and regulations of trade associations. But although the facts about restrictions by single enterprises are not publicly registered, considerable parts of what is reported become public in Swedish governmental reports. Moreover, since under the Swedish constitution documents held by public authorities are, in principle, open to the public (subject to a narrowly interpreted exception designed to protect information about particular enterprises), other parts of the reported information are disclosed by newspapers and magazines.

Reports of Acquisitions and of Concentration

Except in Japan, requirements that acquisitions be reported are initial expressions of concern about impairment of competition by structural changes in the economy, and may be forerunners of efforts to curb increases in the concentration of economic power. In Japan, this requirement and other requirements for reports about aspects of economic concentration were retained by the Japanese from a drastic law imposed during military occupation's effort to dissolve concentrations of Japanese economic power. Though some of the prohibitions to which the reports were relevant—notably that applicable to mergers—remain a part of Japanese law, application of them has become infrquent.

Japanese companies are required to make prior report of intention to participate in any merger, thus giving the Japanese authority an opportunity to object. The same prohibition and the same obligation of prior report attach to various other ways by which enterprises may be amalgamated, such as contracts to share profits and losses, or acquisition of all or a substantial part of a business by purchase or lease or by purchase of fixed assets or by a management contract.

Japanese law seeks also to prevent merger-like effects from the acquisition or holding of stock by corporations or others, from interlocks in corporate offices, and from the pervasive influence of financial institutions. Prohibitions are applicable to the first two types of relationship if substantial restraints of competition are probable, and Japanese financial companies are prohibited from holding more than 10 percent of the stock of any Japanese company. To aid in applying these prohibitions: (a) non-financial companies with assets exceeding 100 million yen must report annually their holdings of stock in other companies in Japan; (b) persons (natural or juridical) other than companies must report promptly if they come to own 10 percent or more of the stock of two or more competing companies; (c) officers and employees of companies must report promptly their interlocking directorates; (d) financial companies that conduct a securities business or obtain securities by enforcement of a lien must report and obtain prior approval if they intend to hold over 10 percent of the total issue for more than a year. Trade associations must also report promptly their formation, changes in their operation and their dissolution.

In the other two countries, reports are less comprehensive. They cover only mergers and closely related acquisitions. Germany requires report of business consolidations, whether in the form of merger, acquisition of plants or net assets, management contract, or stock purchase, after which the acquiring interest controls 25 percent or more of the voting stock. However, the requirement is applicable only if, after the acquisition, the acquirer has 20 percent or more of the market for a specific good or service or has more than 10,000 employees, 500 million marks of annual sales, or 1000 million marks of assets.[18] Report follows rather than precedes the acquisition. The German reports are not means for application of a policy of control; for the authority can do no more with them than summon the acquiring firm to an oral hearing and require it to submit a written statement.[19]

The provisions of the Spanish law that require report of acquisitions are like the German ones in their definition of the kinds of acquisitions covered and their requirement that report be subsequent to acquisition; but they apply only to acquisitions by firms that, after the transaction, have at least 30 percent of the national market. These reports are intended, presumably, to aid the Spanish authority in identifying enterprises that have a dominant position and are therefore subject to statutory prohibitions of abuse of such a position.

By use of the reports described above, the Japanese Fair Trade Commission has published data about economic concentration in Japan more comprehensive than that available for any other country. But though it has reported the extent of mergers it has taken very little action against them. Before the German law was amended, the German authority encountered difficulty in ascertaining market shares (and hence in requiring

---

[18] The provision became law in 1965. Previously report was required if after the acquisition the firm had 20 percent or more of the market for a commodity or commercial service.

[19] Apart from the German cartel law, the German Parliament established by resolution an inquiry into the extent of economic concentration in Germany, which was completed early in 1964.

report of the relevant consolidations) that was disproportionate to the usefulness of the mild requirements that could subsequently be applied. Since the Spanish law took effect at the beginning of 1964, experience with reports under it had not yet accumulated when this book was written.

Reports by Foreign Companies

The special reporting requirements that are applied in Norway and Japan to certain ties with foreign companies reflect fears of possible domination by powerful foreign interests. In Norway a report similar to those from dominant firms is required from any enterprise that is controlled by a foreign firm or by an association that includes foreign firms, if the controller "may be assumed to have" substantial influence on the prices of one or more commodities or services in one or more countries. Japan requires an annual report of stockholdings not only by large non-financial Japanese companies, but also by foreign firms regardless of their size.

The Significance of Registration

Where restrictions are publicly registered, as in most countries that have been discussed, the public registers contain varying amounts of information about the prevalence and kind of restrictions currently in effect. Changes in the register through time reflect change in the pattern and frequency of restriction, as affected both by government policy and by the other influences upon restrictive activity. Where dominant firms are required to register, varying amounts of information are also provided about the number and size of such firms, their interconnections, and changes in these matters. In countries where reports are received by the government but not registered, summary statistical data are published, either regularly, as in the Netherlands, or in special government reports, as in Japan. The reporting systems and public registers provide, therefore, valuable sources for either contemporary or historical studies of cartelization[20] and industrial concentration. In Norway the relevant records cover more than 40 years; in Denmark, more than 25 years; in Sweden and Japan somewhat more than 15 years. In other countries they cover briefer periods.[21]

---

[20] In a monograph for the Department of State in 1964, I summarized the numbers and kinds of cartels reported in the countries of Western Europe that require cartels to report. See Department of State Policy Research Study, *Cartelization in Western Europe* by Corwin D. Edwards, June, 1964 (hereafter called Edwards, Cartelization).

[21] Though in the Netherlands the German occupation imposed a reporting requirement by decree in 1941, and the Dutch government, operating under this decree after the war, began a partially successful effort to require reports in 1946, reporting under a Dutch statute did not begin until 1958, and the adequacy of the earlier reports is uncertain. No other reporting system began earlier than 1957.

The purpose of this book is not, however, to estimate the scope and trend of business restrictions. It is to analyze and appraise policies overseas that are intended to curb such restrictions.

For this purpose, too, the public registers and statistical reports provide considerable information. This information differs in character with differences in the function of the reporting system. Where reports to the government are incidental to government authorization of the restrictive activity that is reported, the public registers and statistical reports record the number and kinds of restrictions that have been officially sanctioned. Where reports to the government are required generally under a law that authorizes the government to curb restrictions, the record gives information relevant to appraisals of the focus and effectiveness of repressive governmental action and the extent to which restrictions have remained immune because of statutory limitations or governmental inaction. Appraisals of the national laws that appear in subsequent chapters are based partly upon these sources.

One purpose of the laws that provide for public registration is to reduce restriction by the force of public opinion. This purpose has been significant for reports of restrictive agreements rather than for reports by dominant firms or reports of acquisitions. Restrictive agreements existed before reporting requirements. As documents intended to be legally enforceable, they were usually explicit and clear in setting forth courses of action and limits upon competition, and frequently included provisions for harsh discipline of recalcitrant enterprises. Hence if they were made public their nature could be readily understood and often was likely to arouse indignation in persons adversely affected. Reports by dominant firms and reports of acquisitions, by contrast, were carefully prepared for the specific purpose of submittal to a government, and summarized structural relationships and operating policies the significance of which was not self-evident. Moreover, where there was public opinion adverse to restriction, it was focused upon relatively crude types of cartels designed to raise prices or foreclose business opportunities. Influenced by Catholic and socialist thought and by belief that European enterprise was typically too small for efficiency, it favored enlargement of enterprises and was not inclined to condemn the market activities of large firms.

Where there is a purpose to arouse public sentiment about restrictive agreements, provisions to register them necessarily have certain similar characteristics: (a) They cover all restrictive agreements except those explicitly made unlawful, not merely the agreements that the government is willing to approve. (b) They provide for public access to the full texts of agreements, not merely to summaries. (c) They make such access easy for any interested person. These characteristics are evident in the registration systems of four countries—Denmark, Norway, Sweden, and the United Kingdom. In the three Scandinavian countries, public awareness is also encouraged by publication of summaries of what the register contains, either in a small book covering the whole register or in a periodical that covers new registrations and significant changes in old ones.

In the other countries that require reports of agreements, the reports are secret or are disclosed in summary or cover only agreements that receive government approval.

When public registration of restrictive agreements is first undertaken, substantial numbers of agreements are likely to be terminated or reduced in restrictiveness. Since registration in Norway is more than 40 years old, information about its initial impact there is not readily available. In Denmark, the United Kingdom, and Sweden, however, the first impact of registration was similar.

Denmark began to register agreements in 1937. From that time until the outbreak of the European war in 1939, cancellation and amendment of restrictive agreements are reported to have been common, though details are not available.

The United Kingdom required registration of agreements in two installments, effective in February and December 1957. Under the British requirement, though agreements as they stood at the time the requirements were announced were to be supplied to the Registrar, only agreements existing on the effective dates of the requirements were to be made public. In the intervening periods many agreements were cancelled, and, according to the Registrar, about one-third of the agreements that remained and were publicly registered had been substantially modified. Subsequent to registration, the incentive to abandon restrictions consisted partly in publicity and partly in the fact that the legality of registered agreements was eventually to be decided by a special court, which ruled against restriction in most of the early cases that came before it. Though no penalties were applicable to enterprises that adhered to their restrictions until the court decided against them, abandonment of restrictions continued for some time after agreements became public. By the close of 1959, apart from restrictions terminated by adverse decisions by the court, 300 agreements had been cancelled, in 320 others all restrictions relevant to the statute had been deleted, 60 agreements had expired without renewal, and in about 60 more instances the Registrar had been notified of an intention to abandon the agreement. Restriction had been abandoned in roughly 44 percent of the important national agreements, including nearly half of those that had fixed selling prices. By June 30, 1961, apart from action by the court, nearly 450 agreements, additional to those already mentioned, had been either abandoned or stripped of relevant restrictions; by June 30, 1963, about 450 more; and by December 31, 1964, an additional 110. By the latter date, relevant restrictions had been terminated by the parties in 1635 instances, and about 75 agreements had expired without renewal.[22]

Sweden, which initiated registration in 1946, has placed more reliance upon publicity to curb restriction than any other country. Until 1953, Swedish cartel law contained no provisions to curb abuses; from 1953 to 1956 it placed reliance upon publicity supplemented by negotiations designed to reduce restrictions; and after 1956, upon the same procedures with an addition by which the king can fix maximum prices if prices are too high and negotiations have failed. After 1953, agreements were cancelled or modified not only voluntarily, to escape general adverse publicity, but also under pressure from business associations that hoped to avert enactment of a strong anti-cartel law by "self-sanitation." In particular instances these associations even instigated price competition against recalcitrant cartels. In 1956, after the Swedish law had taken definite form, the private groups ceased to exert similar pressure, but continued to recommend that private restrictions be modified in accord with recommendations by the negotiating body, the Freedom of Commerce Board, upon which they were represented.

Publicity for registered restrictions is provided in Sweden not only by the public register but also by an official bulletin that summarizes the contents of the register. About 2,000 copies of this bulletin are circulated, and free copies are furnished to newspapers, libraries, instructional centers, organizations for business research, and public officials. The larger newspapers, with about one-third of all Swedish newspaper circulation, often print stories based upon the bulletin or the register. Moreover, some of the restrictions are dramatized by public hearings that are conducted by the Freedom of Commerce Board prior to deciding whether or not it should negotiate for the termination or mitigation of these restrictions.

In this setting, substantial numbers of agreements have been cancelled. From 1947 through 1956, the annual rate of cancellations ranged from 10 to 23 percent of the total number of agreements[23] and in half of those years was above 15 percent. The percentage of cancellations to new agreements during the same decade ranged, with the first year omitted,

---

[22] Registrar of Restrictive Trading Agreements, Report for the period 1st July, 1961 to 30th June 1963, January 1964, cmnd 2246, p. 10. Press release by the Registrar, February 18, 1865.

[23] Cancellations in a year are here stated as percentages of the total number of registered agreements valid at the end of the previous year plus the total number of new registrations during the year.

from 37 percent to 144 percent. By the end of 1956, a total of 836 agreements had been cancelled. In addition substantial numbers of agreements were modified—by 1958 about 15 percent of all agreements, according to an estimate by the head of the cartel office of the manufacturers' association. By July 1, 1964, more than half of all registered agreements had been cancelled—1098 of a total of 2136.[24]

The importance of the cancellations and modifications evident in the British and Swedish statistics can be easily overestimated. The agreements that were most readily cancelled were those that were obsolete, inoperative, ineffective, or unimportant. Inclusion of these gives a bulge to the early figures. Of the remaining restrictions, the ones most subject to public pressure were likely to be those that clearly set forth restrictions that were clearly objectionable. So far as Swedish self-sanitation was not concerned with unimportant agreements, it centered upon such restrictions; and the significant voluntary cancellations and modifications in the United Kingdom probably had similar characteristics. In some instances, no doubt, such restrictions were terminated entirely or substantively changed for the better. There is reason to think that in other instances, such as the resale price agreement in the British motor trade mentioned above, modifications consisted in finding more obscure and decorous language to express the same restrictive program or in devising a less direct way to reach a similar restrictive result.

Action in good faith to eliminate the more objectionable restrictions results in a register in which restrictions are more modest. Successful action to disguise objectionable restrictions produces the same apparent result. Without detailed study of the operation of particular agreements, it is not possible to determine how much of the decrease in apparent restrictiveness in the public registers is due to each kind of change. That some substantial portion of it is due to camouflage is suggested by the fact that where systems of registration are oldest the currently registered provisions about restriction are often vague and ambiguous, and that they usually invoke purposes such as "rationalization," which are thought to have public approval.

The corrective pressures of public opinion diminish with time. The diminution is delayed while a series of court decisions provides new and relatively severe interpretations of the law, as during the first years under the British statute, or while self-sanitation is encouraged by risk that a more severe law will be enacted, as in Sweden before 1956. But a continued

---

24 OECD Expert Committee on Cartels, Reports of Developments in the Field of Restrictive Business Practices, 29th July 1965 (hereafter call OECD July 1965 Report), mimeographed, p. 22.

effect from public opinion depends upon the existence of such additional pressures. Otherwise what was shocking becomes familiar; public interest flags; and restrictions that have been public for some time are likely to be considered harmless because the government has taken no action against them.

Experience in the Scandinavian countries and in England supports this view. In Norway, where the public register is summarized in a printed book, the first edition, published in 1956, appeared in 30,000 copies and was distributed free. In 1957 a new summary was offered for sale for 6 crowns. Of 8,000 copies published, 2,000 were still unsold early in 1960. Supplements to this edition were published in 1958 in 4,000 copies and in 1959 in 3,000 copies. By 1960 news stories derived from the register were seldom published, and information from it was obtained annually by about 30 persons who sent inquiries by mail and about 40 persons, mostly lawyers and businessmen, who visited it. Both in Norway and in Denmark, persons familiar with the application of the law believe that the register now has little deterrent effect. That the original substantial effect in Sweden has diminished greatly is suggested by the fact that business associations ceased to press for self-sanitation after 1956, and by the related fact that cancellation of agreements became less frequent thereafter.[25] Whereas from 1948 to 1956 the agreements cancelled each year were never less than about 12 percent of the total number in effect in that year, the equivalent percentage in 1957 was 5, and from 1958 through 1962 it varied between slightly more than 3 percent and slightly less than 1.

A similar decline has become apparent in England. The British Registrar's report for the first half of 1961 noted that the rate at which agreements were being terminated was decreasing, and commented that "It is probable that those which will be ended so to speak at the blast of the trumpet have been disposed of." The increasing tenacity of the registered British agreements was probably due, however, not only to the diminishing effects of publicity, but also to the fact that though certain early decisions by the British court indicated the illegality of numerous similar agreements, certain recent decisions by the court had increased the hope of participants in the remaining agreements that their restrictions might be held to be lawful.

---

[25] The number of new registrations also declined, but less rapidly. As a percentage of new registrations, cancellations in 1957 were one percentage point higher in 1957 than in 1956; but during the next five years they averaged slightly less than 39 percent per year as compared with slightly more than 54 percent for the five years preceding 1956.

Chapter V

Horizontal Price Fixing

In countries that require reports of restrictive agreements, horizontal agreements to fix prices and other terms of sale are usually the most numerous of the types of restriction reported. Except as legal prohibitions have repressed such agreements, this is presumably true also for countries in which reports are not required.

Such agreements fall into three classes (1) agreements that establish specific prices or minimum prices or mark-ups, or set forth uniform methods by which participants shall compute their prices, or provide for consultation with competitors before prices are quoted; (2) agreements that, without fixing prices as such, establish uniformity about such matters as time of payment, cash discounts, surcharges for cost of transportation, method and place of delivery, guarantees, and various other terms of sale; (3) agreements that fix the nature and amount of discounts for amounts bought and for the distributive function of the buyer, and determine the conditions of eligibility for such discounts. Because these three classes of restriction raise different issues of policy and are often subjected to different degrees of public control, they will be discussed separately. This chapter is concerned with agreements about prices.

Since changes in prices and price relationships are the chief means by which a competitive economy adjusts itself to changing circumstances, price agreements limit competition at a crucial point. Governmental policies toward such agreements constitute the most significant indicators of the extent of reliance upon competition.

Direct Price Fixing

Varieties of Policy Toward Price Fixing. Three types of curbs upon price-fixing appear in the relevant legislation. One prohibits price agreements, but authorizes a specified agency to exempt particular agreements. A second empowers a specified agency to examine price agreements and to require change in or terminate those that involve abuses or operate contrary to the public interest. A third seeks to make sure that prices fixed by agreement will be reasonable by requiring that they be approved by the government or by empowering the government to fix price ceilings. Some countries apply more than one of these methods of control.

Prohibition of price agreements has a part in the laws of eight of the countries covered by this study; and in another country, New Zealand, a law not couched in prohibitory language has been usually but not invariably interpreted to have a prohibitory effect. For four of these nine countries, however, information about the interpretation and use of the law is not available, or the prohibition has a limited scope or an uncertain application or has not yet been tested.[1]

In the remaining five countries, the prohibition principle is more clearly expressed and applied. Germany includes horizontal price agreements in a general prohibition of agreements that are apt to influence production or markets by restraint of competition, but provides for several specific types of exemption.[2]

France makes it unlawful for any person to fix minimum prices, and also forbids concerted action that has the purpose or may have the effect of interfering with competition by hindering the reduction of costs or prices or by encouraging "artificial" price increases; but the latter prohibition, unlike the former, does not cover agreements that "improve and extend" markets or "ensure further economic progress" by rationalization and specialization. The first of the two prohibitions is thought to be clear, and is enforced in the courts; the second, regarded as ambiguous if not self-contradictory, is interpreted in accord with the recommendations of an advisory commission that includes private interests, and has been applied as though it merely provided for discretionary control. A Norwegian Royal

---

[1] In Sweden, only collusion in bidding is forbidden, while other types of price agreement are subject to a different policy. In Spain a law that became effective January 1, 1964, generally forbids agreements that have the purpose or effect of restricting competition; but its application to different kinds of agreements has not yet been made clear by applying it. In New Zealand, price agreements among sellers have been interpreted as inherently violative of a statutory prohibition of unreasonable reductions of competition unless there is considerable non-conformity by the parties or considerable independent competition; but in a 1962 decision, the appeal authority, approving an agreement on the ground that it was in the public interest, cast doubt upon the interpretation previously followed. Though New Zealand law also provides for action against agreements that unreasonably increase prices, costs, or profits, these provisions have remained unused, and cases have turned upon unreasonable reductions of competition. In South Africa, where price agreements contrary to the public interest can be terminated by government action, the board that administers the law has vacillated in successive decisions between the view that price-fixing is inherently contrary to the public interest and the view that the effect of price agreements upon that interest must be evaluated anew in each proceeding.

[2] The more important exemptions apply to export agreements, agreements that fix discounts or terms of sale, agreements indispensable to rationalization, import agreements covering goods not available under competitive conditions, agreements as to license of patents and other forms of intangible industrial property, agreements about air or water transportation, agreements for joint use of storage or processing facilities in agriculture, and certain types of agreements among public utilities.

decree, issued in 1960 under statutory authority to make price regulations, forbids price-fixing but provides for exemptions.[3] In the United Kingdom, a price agreement, like other restrictive agreements, is to be invalidated by a court unless the parties prove that (a) it provides one or more benefits enumerated in the statute and (b) the benefits are more important than the detrimental effect of restriction.[4] Though the various provisions for exemption have been often invoked, their use has not been sufficient to destroy the repressive impact of the sweeping prohibitions. In Japan price fixing is prohibited by two provisions: One forbids trade associations to restrict competition substantially; the other forbids price fixing by any entrepreneur.[5] Under the former provision one or two proceedings per year have been instituted. The latter remained unused from 1957 to 1963.

Discretionary action against price-fixing that is regarded as abusive or contrary to the public interest is provided for in the laws of nine of the countries covered by this study (inclusive of South Africa, where the statute has been intermittently interpreted as prohibitory). Discussion of the policies of three of these countries—Belgium, Israel, and Switzerland—is handicapped by lack of relevant information.[6] The other six countries, upon which this chapter's account of discretionary control will be based, apply such control in various ways. In Ireland, discretion has been so used that it usually results in prohibition. Price agreements are covered by the

---

[3] The decree exempts exports, agriculture, banking and insurance and joint sales organizations. It also empowers the Ministry of Wages and Prices to grant exemption to agreements that (a) are necessary for technical or commercial cooperation that reduces costs or improves products; (b) are necessary to prevent unfair methods of competition; or (c) are otherwise in accord with the public interest.

[4] The significant benefits are (a) specific and substantial benefits to consumers; (b) maintenance of the level of employment in the area; (c) maintenance of the trade's export volume and earnings; (d) counteraction of unfair terms imposed by dominant enterprises.

[5] The second provision forbids effecting an unreasonable restraint of trade, but unreasonable restraints, as defined elsewhere in the law, include concerted activities that fix prices "thereby causing, contrary to the public interest, a substantial restraint of competition."

[6] From the statutes and such supplementary information as is available, however, it seems probable that in two of these three countries control of price agreements will be relatively unimportant. In Switzerland, where the principal emphasis of the law is to curb boycotts and thus protect the right of an enterprise to compete if it wants to do so, agreements harmful to the public interest may be set aside; but the power to take such action is apparently intended for use only in exceptional circumstances. In Belgium, where the law provides only for governmental action to correct abuses, little information about the application of the statute is disclosed; but what is available indicates that thus far price agreements have received little attention. In contrast with these countries, Israel applies a law that seems likely to affect price agreements substantially: All restrictive agreements must receive prior sanction by the government in the light of the public interest. But information is not available to me to show how price agreements have been treated under this requirement.

general authority of a commission to issue fair trading rules and by the general authority of a Minister to prohibit specified agreements and to issue such other orders about restrictive practices as he thinks fit. Moreover, a statutory list of unfair trade practices, set forth for the commission's guidance, includes unjust enhancement of prices and unreasonable restraint of free and fair competition. In practice these discretionary provisions have been used to condemn horizontal price-fixing. With minor exceptions, such price-fixing has been defined as unfair in those fair trading rules that covered the subject;[7] and it has been prohibited by ministerial order in five out of six industries in which its existence has been officially reported.[8]

In the other countries, however, horizontal price agreements are not consistently forbidden. In the Netherlands, the relation of price agreements [and of other restrictions of competition] to the general interest is determined by the government, with discretion so broad that it can be used to prohibit such agreements, require their alteration, or require non-participants to conform to their terms. In South Africa, agreements that enhance or maintain prices and are not considered to be in the public interest may be terminated or altered, either by negotiation or by ministerial order; and of the first four industries investigated, two were allowed to continue price-fixing, though in reports about the other two the authorities said that price-fixing is inherently contrary to the public interest. In Austria, where an authority must decide whether or not each restrictive agreement is economically justified, the effect of agreements upon prices is the most significant consideration relevant to these decisions.[9] Apart from prohibiting agreements about bidding, as mentioned above, Swedish law covers other price agreements by provisions that a board shall negotiate to eliminate the harmful effects of restraints of competition and that, if such negotiations fail and an important price is obviously too high, the King may fix a maximum price for not more than one year. In Denmark, where prevention of "unreasonable" prices is the chief purpose of the law, the statute provides

---

[7] While condemning price-fixing in general, the fair trading rules for coal make an exception for collective action by importers in buying from government-controlled suppliers.

[8] Such orders were issued for radio sets, building materials, motor vehicles, groceries, and gasoline. In the case of proprietary medicines, the investigatory commission recommended that price-fixing by wholesalers be forbidden but approved the continuance of actual lists of suggested prices, and the Minister decided to issue no order. The original grocery order was modified in such a way that, in practice, price-fixing continues to be possible.

[9] The first version of the law authorized disapproval of agreements that would be likely to increase prices or prevent them from falling. By subsequent amendments, this provision was extended so that an agreement, to become valid, must be found to be justified from an overall economic viewpoint, with particular attention to the interest of consumers.

that where such prices exist an effort to alter them must be made by negotiation, but that, if negotiation fails, the authority may cancel or alter the relevant agreements, require changes in prices, or fix maximum prices.

Discretionary control of agreements may be supplemented by overt price control, either in restrictive practice laws or in other statutes.[10] In the Netherlands a price act, in effect since the War and revised in 1961, gives the government power to fix maximum prices. In South Africa the scope of price control under special legislation diminished steadily during the 1950's, but still covered 60 commodity classes in 1959; and regulations under the price law included a requirement that prices that were concertedly fixed must receive prior approval by the price controller. In Austria the recommendations of a price-wage commission, established informally in 1957, have been made effective by interpretations under which enterprises that set prices in excess of those recommended by the commission have violated the provisions of an anti-profiteering law. In Sweden, where control of restrictive practices is based chiefly on publicity and negotiation, the modest and as yet unused provision of the restrictive practice law by which the King may temporarily fix a maximum price is supplemented by a reporting statute under which all businessmen may be required to report prices and relevant related information; and the reports become the basis both for sustained surveillance over the price structure and for frequent published reports about prices and margins. In Denmark, the restrictive practice law not only authorizes corrective orders that fix maximum prices, but also requires that parties to any restrictive agreement shall obtain prior approval before increasing prices. These controls were supplemented during the early 1960's, first by a temporary freeze of prices and profits, and then by legislation under which investigations may be undertaken and maximum prices fixed not only where there are price agreements but also in the "grey area" in which, though restriction is not overtly present, competition appears to be ineffective.

In France, too, control of cartels appears in a setting of pervasive price control; but, as has been noted above, French policy toward restrictive agreements is a blend of prohibition and discretionary control.

Underlying the various curbs upon price-fixing are two sharply different attitudes about the kind of problem that horizontal price agreements create. Policies that generally prohibit price agreements conceive competition in price as the central characteristic of competitive markets, and rely upon competitive markets to provide a major part of the adjustments and

---

[10] Price control is also part of government policy in Norway and New Zealand, where price agreements have been prohibited. In these countries, the prohibitory rule was recently applied, and one of its purposes was to make possible less reliance upon direct control of prices.

incentives needed in the economy. From this point of view, price-fixing is usually contrary to the public interest because it makes prices rigid and unresponsive to economic forces and because it denies persons on the buyers' side of the market an effective voice in the terms of market transactions. In a New Zealand case, the Trade Practices and Prices Commission held:

> "Whether or not private price-fixing is in the public interest depends neither upon the purpose of the prices fixed nor upon the reasonableness of the prices fixed. . . . Buyers and sellers have an equal interest in fair prices. Whether either buyers or sellers act in concert to fix prices paid or charged, their joint action relieves them of competitive pressures such as still exist on the other side of the market. Thus it tends to establish prices favorable to the parties to the agreement. Though the goodwill and good sense of the participants may limit the bias inherent in such arrangements, the public interest cannot rely upon this. Neither can public authority constantly re-examine the prices privately established to ascertain whether or not, under the changing private decisions and the changing conditions of the market, they are kept continuously fair. Where government authority does not control prices, competition in prices is almost always needed as a continuing safeguard for the interests of all."[11]

In some countries, particularly Germany, the economic basis for reliance upon price competition is strongly re-enforced by belief that unless free markets provide the predominant means of economic organization there is no reliable structural basis for political freedom. Thus Eberhard Günther, President of the German Federal Cartel Office, speaking in 1960, described the German cartel law as "an economic counterpart to the political rights which are guaranteed in our Constitution," and continued, "We think that the act, guaranteeing a maximum of individual freedom for every member of the business community, is actually the explanation and the filling out of the human rights guaranteed in our Constitution in the economic field."[12]

In some of the countries that hold such views, the presumption against price-fixing is not applied to certain specified segments of the economy, such as agriculture, banking, insurance, or transportation by water. For

---

[11] Decision No. 3 of the Trade Practices and Prices Commission in the matter of an inquiry into an agreement or arrangement between members of the Wellington Fencing Materials Association in respect of wire netting, Sept. 7, 1959, mimeographed, pp. 5-6.

[12] Statement to the American Federal Bar Association, reproduced in the Association's 1960 Institute on Legal Aspects of the European Community, pp. 136-138.

the most part, these exempted sectors are subject to special statutory regulation or to laws providing subsidy and support.

In all of the countries that prohibit price-fixing, the presumption against it in the parts of the economy to which the prohibition applies can also be overcome under specified conditions, and exemption is then available. Particular types of price agreement are occasionally exempted by statute. More frequently, the conditions that are thought to justify exemption are set forth in the law, and an agency is authorized to grant exemption where these conditions are found. The grounds for exemption differ significantly from country to country.[13] Nevertheless, they appear to express recurrently several beliefs about proper limits for reliance upon competition: First, that, as expressions of economic nationalism, restrictive agreements can be useful to exporting countries in international trade when the detrimental effects occur in foreign countries; second, that domestic restrictions may be appropriately met by counter-restrictions; third, that restrictions can be useful cushions against painful readjustments due to changes in demand; and fourth, that particular restrictions can make positive contributions to economic efficiency, quality, and technical progress. But although these beliefs substantially qualify the general reliance upon competition that is the characteristic feature of policies that prohibit price agreements, they do not destroy it. Apart from arrangements as to export trade that do not restrict domestic markets, exempted agreements are regarded as exceptions, and a process of review is invoked to make sure that each exception is proper.[14]

The attitude that underlies policies that provide for discretionary

[13] The two most common types of provision for exemption cover agreements pertaining to export trade and "rationalization agreements," that is, agreements that are believed to reduce costs, improve the quality of products, or promote economic progress. A provision in the law of the United Kingdom by which agreements that benefit consumers may be authorized may be regarded as a more precise equivalent of the provisions of other countries about rationalization. The policies of one or more countries also provide for exemption as to (a) adjustment to enduring conditions of declining demand; (b) adjustment to substantial imbalance between supply and demand; (c) counteraction of absence of competition among suppliers of imported goods; (d) counteraction of unfair terms quoted by dominant enterprises; (e) agreements that are directed against unfair practices; (f) agreements that are necessary to maintain the general level of employment.

[14] The only instances that have come to my notice in which exemption is provided for a particular type of domestic agreement without provision for administrative review pertain to agreements on bidding specifications (but not bids) under German law and agreements for joint sale under a Norwegian royal decree. Germany tempers the character of administrative review according to the severity of the restriction: Some types of agreement require specific approval; others are valid unless there is governmental objection; for still others, approval is required unless specified conditions are found.

curbs upon price agreements is quite different. It is not concerned to preserve the economic functions of price competition. Instead, it rests upon belief that appropriate levels for prices and appropriate relationships among prices, costs, and profits can be ascertained and that these levels and relationships are sufficiently stable to provide a basis for public control. Its concern, therefore, is not to keep prices competitive but to keep them fair. Fairness is not a matter of the direction given to economic incentives and the effect upon reallocation of economic resources, but a matter of distributive justice, closely related to historical concepts of economic morality. If a price agreement results in fair prices, it can be allowed to continue. If it results in unfair prices, change in the prices is an alternative to termination of the agreement.

When control of price agreements is thus conceived, it differs from other forms of price control chiefly in that it is more selective and less precise. Since it need not be applied to prices set by individual enterprises, it covers substantially less ground than general price control. Where it is applied after agreed prices have been set rather than before, it puts less burden upon those who exercise the control. Since only what is demonstrably unfair need be curbed, even relatively rigid concepts of fairness leave more leeway for private action than can be left in prescribing fixed prices or price limits; and if concepts of fairness involve toleration of a range of permissible conduct, control can be correspondingly reduced in scope. If, however, a government wishes to rely upon price control, discretionary control of price agreements can be readily given an appropriate place therein, without the need to reconcile conflicting attitudes that is apparent where price control stands alongside reliance upon competitive price adjustments.

It is noteworthy that, in general, the larger countries that are covered by this study base their policies toward restrictive agreements upon prohibition, while most of the smaller ones apply discretionary curbs. Thus, though discretionary control is used in as many countries, prohibitory policies probably cover a larger total of trade. Nevertheless, the ensuing discussion of control of price-fixing will be concerned chiefly with discretionary control. There is no need to explain to American readers foreign thinking about price-fixing which closely resembles that supporting American policy. Discretionary curbs upon price-fixing, however, cannot be readily understood on the basis of American analogies. Hence they will be examined at some length.

Historical and environmental roots of discretionary control. Discretionary control designed to keep prices fair seems natural in Europe. To maintain fair prices was regarded for centuries by the Catholic Church as one of the important moral duties of businessmen; and after the Reformation this moral tradition continued on the Continent to influence both the Protestant and the Catholic churches. Distributive justice, conceived as requiring that prices be fairly related to wages, became during the last century an important goal of European socialist parties. That control of the level of prices involved broad discretion for public officials was not seriously disturbing since, for reasons discussed in Chapter 2, the view persisted that concentrated power is acceptable if it is in good hands.

It is noteworthy that in several countries where there are now broad prohibitions of price-fixing, these prohibitions succeeded previous discretionary control. The first German cartel law, in 1923, provided only for control of cartel abuses. Norwegian control of cartels, also initiated in the 1920's, rested upon control of abuse, supplemented by direct price control until the close of the 1950's. Even in France, where collusive action was forbidden by one of the laws of the French Revolution, laws prohibitory in wording were reduced by interpretation to controls designed to keep prices reasonable, and the current prohibitions that are applied as such are of postwar origin. The present law of the United Kingdom was also briefly preceded by a statute that merely provided for discretionary investigation of restrictions and discretionary action against them in the light of *ad hoc* findings about their effect upon the public interest. However, British control of world trade exposed the United Kingdom over a long period to such diverse cultural inflences that attitudes important on the European continent were not similarly influential in England.

Discretionary control of price-fixing has also seemed appropriate to many continental Europeans because of the prevalence of other restrictions, public and private, in continental economies. Restrictions upon freedom of entry into occupations, upon movement of goods, upon methods of production and distribution, and upon methods of doing business have been (and probably still are) substantially more prevalent than in the United States. The natural trading areas of Europe have been segmented by tariffs and other national barriers to trade. Within particular countries restrictions have taken the form not only of cartel agreements and trade union requirements, but also of public price control, rules as to business competence and apprenticeship, laws precluding various types of conduct as unfair, a miscellany of national and local regulations, and numerous local customs that had binding force. In comparison with American and British economies, continental European economies have been characterized by relative immobility of the factors of production and relative inflexibility of prices. Correction of their maladjustments by reallocation of resources and readjustment of relative prices has not seemed feasible. To envisage competition as a sufficient means to make an economy self-adjusting has been far more difficult amid such pervasive restrictions than it was amid the relatively fluid frontier conditions that shaped the United States or the relatively fluid alternatives that British control of world trade gave the United Kingdom.

In this contrast, there is no intention to deny that price rigidity and immobility of the factors of production are also visible in the United States. I believe that they are substantially less here than in Continental Europe; but whether or not this is so, they have not here, as in Europe, existed long enough to shape traditional attitudes toward economic policy. It is noteworthy, however, that in recent decades their existence has been cited in support of extensions of governmental control of economic life and in criticism of reliance upon competition. They have even evoked proposals that in concentrated industries prices be subjected to public review as to reasonableness.

Discretionary controls over price agreements have also appealed to Europeans because they involve smaller initial commitments about the nature and scope of ultimate policy than are involved in prohibitions. A country that undertakes control of restrictive agreements for the first time may hesitate to condemn outright a whole class of restrictions. By deciding that each restriction shall be considered in the light of the public interest, it can shape its policy gradually as experience accumulates. The United Kingdom, for example, applied such an experimental policy in 1948, replaced it as to most domestic restrictive agreements by a qualified prohibition in 1956, and still retains its experimental law for use about other types of restriction.

The Conception of Unreasonable Price-Fixing. In countries that curb price-fixing by discretionary control, the heart of the control usually consists in efforts to keep the fixed prices reasonable. This may be attempted by limiting the conditions under which price-fixing may take place, by directly or indirectly limiting the height of the price, or by eclectic use of both methods.

Dutch policy illustrates the first kind of limitation. Price-fixing is believed to be undesirable by the Dutch government in the absence of conditions that provide good reason for it. Official statements indicate that the principal relevant consideration is whether or not, in the absence of a price agreement, price competition would be "unduly" severe, and that unduly severe competition is defined as that which results in sale at or below cost by most of the competing enterprises. Agreements that convert maximum prices set by the government into minimum prices set by a cartel are condemned. In particular instances governmental decisions have terminated

Dutch price agreements because there was no reason to fear unduly severe results from competition; and the number of price agreements listed in governmental statistical summaries of the extent of cartelization has fallen significantly since 1955. However, either the government believes that the dangers of unduly severe competition are frequently present or it is often reluctant to forbid price agreements even though it thinks them unjustified; for on January 1, 1963, there were still 360 horizontal price agreements of national scope.

Direct or indirect limitation of the level of the fixed prices is much more common. Indirect safeguards against excessive prices have an important place both in the Netherlands and in Austria. In both countries governments have approved particular agreements because they thought that independent suppliers were important enough to keep prices reasonable. When the Dutch government permits price-fixing, it endeavors to make sure that opportunity remains for "economically justified competition." To this end, it regards agreements that bind each participant to compute his prices by an agreed formula based upon his own costs as more acceptable than agreements that apply a specific price or a minimum price to all enterprises. The tribunals that determine whether or not each Austrian cartel shall be permitted to register are similarly receptive to "calculation agreements;" and until 1962 the fact that under Austrian procedures each change in an agreed price was subject to registration, while changes in prices computed under a registered agreed formula were not, induced price-fixers to prefer calculation agreements to direct price-fixing.[15] Price-fixing has also been permitted in Austria because a) buyers as well as sellers were parties to the agreement; or b) the prices set by the agreement were so closely related to other prices that were subject to government control that no abuse was thought to be possible. In one Austrian case, the possibility of an unreasonable price was rejected by the authorities because the product was sold to business enterprises and its price constituted a negligible part of the total costs of the buyers.

When price fixing is permitted in the absence of conditions like those mentioned above that are thought to preclude excessive prices, governmental control is focussed directly upon the level of the resulting prices. In deciding whether or not prices are reasonable, the authorities use three tests: a) relation to prices elsewhere, usually in other countries; b) relation to costs, with resultant levels of profits compared with profits in other industries; c) relation to prices that would have existed if there had been no agreement.

Comparison with prices elsewhere has limited uses. When, for various reasons, the authorities have decided to authorize a price-fixing agreement,

---

[15] In 1962 an amendment to the law required calculation cartels also to report price changes.

the decision may be supported by a finding that domestic prices are as low or lower than in other countries. Such statements appear, for example, in South African reports approving price agreements for automobile tires and for imported liquor. When domestic prices are found to be higher than prices abroad, this fact may result in an investigation and in pointed requests for an explanation. In particular instances in which a foreign market is notoriously competitive, price comparisons may enable a country in which competition has been eliminated to estimate the degree of departure from competitive levels of prices. If a quota system has been used by a cartel as a necessary means to exclude foreign goods, this fact may be thought sufficient to prove that domestic prices are too high.

But international comparison of prices is not considered adequate as the sole test of reasonableness. A price that is higher than the prices of similar goods in other countries is not found to be unreasonable without supplementary consideration of possible differences in cost. If the prices of imported goods are higher than the prices of these same goods in other countries, the question is whether or not transportation costs and tariffs can plausibly account for the difference. If goods domestically produced are priced higher than their counterparts in other countries, producers or distributors may be asked why; but appraisal of their answers usually requires consideration of alleged differences in cost, quality, or both, and thus becomes an especially complicated instance of the determination of reasonableness by cost standards. Moreover, countries that are concerned about unreasonable prices recognize that if prices abroad were accepted as a sufficient test of reasonableness, unreasonable prices could be easily overlooked. The foreign price may be itself the unreasonable result of a price agreement, or, for many different reasons, foreign costs of production may be higher than domestic costs.

The standard of reasonableness applied in Denmark and the Netherlands is that prices should be not higher than cost plus a reasonable profit. Since costs and profits differ from one enterprise to another, use of such a test requires a decision as to whose costs and profits shall be used for comparison. Danish law provides that "regard shall be had to conditions in enterprises which are operated with comparable technical and commercial efficiency," and that when maximum prices are set as correctives they shall not be lower than such enterprises require. These provisions have been interpreted to mean that the costs relevant to reasonableness are those that are "normal" or characteristic of most enterprises, rather than those of high-cost enterprises or the average of costs both high and low. Exceptional profits for enterprises with exceptionally low costs are permitted, and the possibility of them is regarded as a desirable incentive. Moreover, to preserve incentives, the Danish authorities have attempted to apply long-run regulatory standards that permit prices to vary with the trend of relevant wages and the cost of raw materials.

Dutch policy demands that, if prices are fixed, room must be left for "economically justified competition." If a single uniform price is set, the costs relevant to its reasonableness are the average costs of the more efficient enterprises. To preclude low prices by low-cost suppliers or for limited service is considered improper; and agreements under which each enterprise uses it own costs in computing its prices are considered more acceptable than agreements that fix specific prices.

Use of a cost standard also requires decision about what costs are relevant. The available decisions are too few to provide information about all the questions that may arise, but they show the general attitudes of the authorities. Danish law provides explicitly that maximum prices must cover "necessary costs including depreciation allowances and remuneration for services in connection with the purchase or replacement, production, storage, marketing, and transport of the commodity, as well as a reasonable net profit, regard being had to the risk involved. . . ." Under this provision, replacement costs are accepted when prices have risen. Dutch law contains no formula for computation of costs and profits, but Dutch decisions have included various efforts to prevent cost-padding. Costs are conceived in the Netherlands as those of a fully employed enterprise, and costs based upon "structural under-employment" have been rejected. Inclusion of a wholesale margin in prices has been held to be improper where no wholesaler was employed. To treat entrepreneurial wages as costs has been permitted, but inclusion of entrepreneurial profits in costs has been considered improper.

In using costs and profits to test reasonableness, the Danish and Dutch authorities have encountered little difficulty in obtaining information about costs. In Denmark, for example, as few as from three to five manufacturing firms supply most of the national output of many products, so that numerous separate cost investigations are not often considered necessary. Firms, particularly small ones, that believe that their own costs are high usually desire to submit them, lest the maximum level of reasonableness be set too low. Cooperatives and chain stores are generally willing to supply data. In the ordinary case, an informal discussion between the government and members of the industry results in agreement about the kind and amount of the cost data to be made available. In the distributive trades, invoice costs are readily available, and the margins that are customary among small enterprises are regarded as adequate guides both to operating costs and to reasonable profits. There has been no indication that either the Danish or the Dutch authorities share the view prevalent among American economists familiar with cost accounting, that computations of so-called costs are not statements of fact but summaries by which the past expenditures of an enterprise are imputed to future conduct in ways consistent with predictions of the future and policy decisions about suitable ways to adjust to these predictions.[16]

The growing complexity of business activity has caused difficulties in Denmark, however, in appraising the data received from the larger diversified enterprises. Where a large portion of all costs is joint and much of it consists of computed overhead charges for fixed equipment or other capital investments, the Danish authorities have found problems of allocation troublesome. In most instances, accepting the cost allocations made by business enterprises, they have attempted to make sure that, in the light of total costs for all products, the total profit of the enterprise was reasonable, and that there was no important disparity in the contribution made by each product to that total profit. They have used these two tests without complete consistency. Applying the test of total profit where there were efforts to raise a particular price alleged to be too low, they have resisted price increases if profits as a whole were adequate. Applying the test of disparity where, under the customary cost allocations, a particular price appeared to be exceptionally profitable, they have subjected such prices to downward pressure. But so long as profits as a whole were reasonable, they have not

---

[16] Past expenditures are not "costs." Some of them are treated as mistakes and written off as losses. Some of them may be inflated in computing costs, in the light of increases, current or anticipated, in the subsequent prices of what has already been bought. Some of them are treated as current expenditures, some as capital expenditures. Capital expenditures are divided into annual increments, which may not be equal from year to year and which may be greater or less according to estimates of the duration of the usefulness of the capital asset. Expenditures are regarded sometimes as direct costs of particular activities, sometimes as joint or overhead costs; and the latter may be allocated to the various activities to which they pertain in several different ways: in proportion to particular direct costs such as those for labor or materials; in proportion to aggregate direct costs; in proportion to the time or other measure of physical use of the facilities provided by the costs; in proportion to revenue from sales; or in accord with the estimated capacity of each kind of activity to provide income that will bear the costs.

Accounting consists of a series of self-consistent conventional ways of recording and summarizing expenditures and incomes. Its original purposes were primarily a) to provide a check upon employees that would prevent dissipation of the owner's assets and b) to ascertain the total profit of the enterprise, so that assets would not be inadvertently dissipated by the owner. Its conventions as to the meaning of cost were originally developed for the latter purpose, and were therefore designed to overstate costs and understate net incomes. Modern cost accounting, designed as a guide to management, is relatively recent. Its conventions are somewhat warped by the conservatism appropriate to the original purposes. Moreover, they inevitably imply presumptions about the economic future and about the stability of business programs to cope with it that would seem uncertain if explicitly stated.

challenged such policies of charging what the traffic would bear as could be cloaked by allocation of most of the costs to the products that bore the highest prices.

Even these loose tests of reasonableness have been so burdensome that short-cuts have been used if possible. In particular instances in which gross profits were low as percentages of sales, this fact has been accepted as evidence that prices were reasonable, without effort to compute the cost of doing business and the profit on investment.

Where such standards of reasonableness are used, the amount of profit that may be included in a fixed price must be determined. Apart from the provision in the Danish law that if the government sets a maximum price it must include a reasonable profit, with regard given to risk, the statutes do not indicate what is reasonable.

By estimating reasonable prices on the basis of the costs of normal enterprises, as in Denmark, or the costs of relatively low-cost enterprises, as in the Netherlands, the Danish and Dutch policies both apply standards that may result in cartel prices too low to give high-cost enterprises a profit. Explicitly recognizing that under their standard an enterprise with unusually low costs may be guaranteed a profit by the cartel price, the Danish authorities regard this possibility as a useful contribution to business incentives; and in practice, the same types of possibility and incentive are inherent, though to a lesser degree, in Dutch policy. The two policies diverge, however, about the amount of profit that a cartel's price may guarantee to the firms whose costs are used as a standard of reasonableness. Dutch policy permits entrepreneurial wages to be included in costs, but regards an allowance for entrepreneurial profits as improper. Danish policy accepts cartel prices that provide "normal" rates of profit. Though some consideration is given by the Danish authorities to degree of risk and similar environmental conditions, a rule of thumb tends to be applied by which profits in excess of 10 percent of capital (including what has been borrowed) are suspect, and may be treated as excessive unless they are shown to be justified. The need for capital in an expanding industry is not considered by the Danish authorities a proper ground for special leniency in estimating a reasonable rate of profit.

c) The third standard of reasonableness—the level of price that would have prevailed in the absence of price-fixing—has been applied in Austria. As there used, it has been more lenient than the cost and profit standards of the Netherlands or Denmark.[17] The Austrian authorities have simplified

---

[17] The decisions available to me pertain to the period prior to December 1959, when my field work in Austria was completed. By that time the changes made in the law in 1958, which gave greater influence to the Vienna Labor Chamber, had taken

their task by considering only the general level of a cartel's prices, without regard to the prices and price relationships of the particular products covered by the cartel agreement. The latter, they have held, can be properly set in accord with what the traffic will bear.

The relation of the general level of a cartel's prices to the prices that would have existed if there had been no price-fixing has been estimated in Austria by using a theoretical model of a static competitive market. From such a model the authorities have inferred that under competition prices would cover the costs of marginal producers and that therefore cartel prices set at levels below the cost of the highest-cost producer must be reasonable. By such reasoning, a price agreement based upon weighted average costs was held to invoke a standard too low rather than too high; and in several agreements where prices were set high enough to provide profits for sub-marginal producers this fact was regarded as a proper recognition of the principle that superior competence can command a differential rent, like superior land. Consideration was not given to the question whether cartel agreements prevented types of competitive pressure by which, through time, high-cost producers might be eliminated and prices might be reduced to levels reflecting the costs of low-cost producers. Instead, one decision included the statement that even in the absence of a cartel the stronger enterprises probably would set prices at levels that enabled their weaker competitors to live.

The presence of excess capacity has not been regarded in Austria as inconsistent with use of this static theoretical model. The fact that costs and prices were computed to cover idle capacity was treated as unimportant in one case. In another case, in which producers sold in both domestic and export markets, preservation of the weaker firms was said to be proper unless there would still be excess capacity under the most favorable conditions for export that could be foreseen.

But use of the simple competitive model was reconciled with acceptance by the Austrian authorities of two-price systems in international trade. Several decisions concerned agreements under which domestic prices were set high enough to cover most of the overhead costs and provide most of the profits, while goods were exported, sometimes below "cost," at the lower prices prevailing in foreign markets. Such agreements were considered ac-

---

effect, but if they had modified the standards of reasonableness here discussed, it had been through informal action in preliminary discussions of cartel agreements and had left no record in the publicly available documents. In 1962, further changes in the law required special consideration of the interests of the ultimate consumer in deciding whether restrictive agreements were permissible. Information is not available to me to show whether or not, during the brief subsequent period, this requirement has altered the standards of reasonable price.

ceptable as means of facilitating exports needed for the national balance of payments. Indeed, preservation of high-cost capacity to serve the domestic market was held to be proper as a way of facilitating exports by enterprises that had lower costs.

The profits permissible in Austrian price-fixing were generously conceived, not only by use of the concept of a rent for ability, but in other ways derived from models of static economic theory. Interest on capital, including the owner's capital, was regarded as a cost. If the owners had obtained the capital at low rates—for example, from American funds made available for Austrian recovery after the War—use of the higher interest rate customary in ordinary transactions was considered proper. Similarly, where alternative investments were available that promised a return higher than customary interest, the authorities permitted the costs of capital to be computed as the opportunity cost of the foregone profit and were not troubled by the possibility that they might thus be allowing one cartel's high prices to justify the high prices of another. A charge for risk (other than the "basic entrepreneurial risk") was also held to be a part of cost; and in computing such charges it was permissible to ignore reductions of risk that had resulted from the cartel agreement. Cartel prices could be computed not only to cover such imputed costs but also to provide a reasonable profit; and where, as in the use of weighted average cost, the cost formula appeared to the authorities to be unduly modest, they were willing to offset the dificiency by accepting rates of profit that they regarded as somewhat too high.

Direct Governmental Price Control. As was indicated earlier in this chapter, discretionary control over price-fixing by cartels often appears in a setting of governmental price control. Most of the price-control activities of governments, though they provide safeguards against unreasonable prices and reflect a point of view similar to that underlying control of prices under restrictive practice laws, were undertaken in a broader context than that of private price agreements, and discussion of them is not part of the purpose of this book. In Denmark, however, systematic control of price increases is part of the cartel law and hence needs discussion here.

As enacted in 1955, the Danish Monopolies and Restrictive Practices Act contained a provision, originally intended to be temporary, by which no enterprise subject to the registration requirement that applied to all restrictive agreements and dominant firms could increase the price of a commodity named in a specified list of commodities unless it first obtained government approval of the increase. In 1957, this provision was made permanent, and its application was extended to all commodities. In 1960, after a vain effort by business to get the requirement repealed, the Danish authority was authorized to waive it when conditions were believed to warrant such action; but such waivers have not been numerous. Decisions as to approval of price increases under this provision have constituted about half the total number of actions about prices by the Danish authority. They have been preceded by consideration of cost information and have resulted in particular instances not only in approval or disapproval of the proposed increase, but also in authorization of only part of what was proposed.

The Economic Significance of Discretionary Price Control. In countries that apply the standards of reasonable price that have been summarized above, control of the price level cannot provide a full administrative equivalent for the protections that are expected from competition. Control can be used to lop off prices or profits that are conspicuously high, but can be neither precise enough nor pervasive enough to cope with smaller instances of exploitative pricing. Under the sustained inflationary pressures of the 1950's, control was used to prevent price increases that exceeded increases in cost; to prevent well-organized industries from taking full advantage of the opportunities afforded by increasing demand; and sometimes to make cartel price increases lag behind cost increases. Thus control helped retard inflationary upward spirals of prices and increased somewhat the availability of cartelized consumer goods to the poor. The direct effects were spotty; for the number of cases in which the authorities intervened to mitigate the results of price-fixing were not numerous. The indirect effect of the fact that such control could be used may have been greater, but its magnitude cannot be measured. Information is not available to show whether controlled cartel prices rose more or less rapidly than other prices.

That tolerance of cartelization discouraged appropriate reallocation of economic activity is a reasonable inference from the theory of competitive markets: So far as cartels increased prices beyond the competitive norms, they reduced purchases, yet also reduced the incentive for suppliers to divert effort to other types of production; so far as control kept prices below the competitive norms, it reduced the incentive to economize scarce goods. But however persuasive these propositions may be as theoretical abstractions, they cannot be supported by evidence. Their theoretical persuasiveness is appreciably reduced by the fact that both custom and assorted trade barriers, public and private, stood in the way of easy movement of business from industry to industry, and that public subsidies and public price-fixing did much to maintain patterns of consumption that were inconsistent with simple price incentives.

The types of discretionary control that were used during the 1950's were obviously inadequate to cope with the long-run problem of keeping prices fair. Controls were better suited to preventing price increases than to forcing price reductions. Though largely cost-oriented, they took levels of cost for granted and did not contain safeguards or incentives adequate to prevent costs from rising or to assure that the more efficient cartel members would make sustained efforts to reduce costs. The Dutch and Danish methods of control, unlike the Austrian, put some pressure upon high-cost enterprises and afforded some incentives to low-cost ones; but if the latter preferred a quiet life to a struggle for more profit, they could be adequately protected in that preference by permissible agreements. If they preferred to reduce costs, they could do so, to the enhancement of their profits; and since re-examination of the reasonableness of prices was infrequent, control was unlikely to translate cost reduction into price reduction for a considerable time. If the same methods of control were to continue to be used in a period of generally falling costs and prices, they would be unlikely to prevent cartel prices from lagging behind the decline.

In applying a standard of current reasonableness, the lawmakers and those who applied the law in these countries were more concerned with distributive justice than with the potentialities of better technology and improved economic organization as ways of reducing costs, improving products, and enhancing consumption. Indeed, the idea of a reasonable price is essentially static. It is not properly applicable to a world in which methods of production, the location of markets, the amount sold, and the character of products are all in flux. It can be plausibly applied to a world in which production is carried on by techniques that are slow to change; ownership is largely individual, so that business profits are closely related to the family incomes of businessmen; population changes slowly, either in amount or in location, so that at a given time the size and structure of markets can be taken for granted as constant; and as a result of stability in the foregoing conditions, there is little change in wages or standards of living. Under such circumstances, costs, outputs, and amounts sold would be relatively stable, and could properly be reflected in stable prices; and these stable relationships probably would come to be regarded as not only reasonable but also morally justified. It is easy to recognize in such a model of a static society a simplified version of historical economic relationships. These relationships did much to shape the cultural traditions that support discretionary policies designed to keep prices fair. What is difficult to understand is that these traditions have been so little shaken by the mass migrations and reshufflings of markets incident to two world wars, by the population explosion characteristic of the contemporary world, and by the technological and organizational revolution that surrounds us.

Chapter VI

Fixing Terms of Sale and Discounts

From the statistics of reported agreements in the countries that require reporting, it appears that restriction of terms of sale is more frequent than price-fixing. In some agreements such restrictions are ancillary to price-fixing, and have a primary purpose to prevent various forms of evasion of the price provisions—enlarged discounts, concessions in transportation charges, and the like. In other agreements, control of terms of sale is not accompanied by direct control of prices. Such forms of agreement may be adopted because the participants believe that if secret concessions can be stopped prices will be maintained without explicit agreement; because, being unable to agree on prices, participants have agreed as far as they can, in the hope that further agreement will develop later; or because participants, even if competitive in other respects, desire to avoid the particular types of competition that take the form of flexible and unpredictable terms of sale.

From the point of view of public policy, different issues are raised by the restrictions upon terms that are ancillary to price-fixing and the ones that are not. If price-fixing is permitted, some control of terms is probably appropriate, though supervision may be needed to prevent it from being discriminatory or unfair under the standards by which price-fixing itself is supervised. Where price-fixing is not permitted or does not take place, restrictions upon terms raise public problems that differ from those raised by fixation of prices. In the countries whose policies are the subject of this book, a difference in significance is implicitly recognized: Where control of terms is a part of price-fixing, attention centers on the latter, though when price-fixing is permitted the restrictions on terms may be amended in particular respects. But when price-fixing is forbidden, the decision does not automatically settle the question whether or not some restriction on terms should continue; and when restrictions on terms stand alone, they receive special consideration, usually more favorable than that accorded to a price-fixing agreement.

Information is not available to show how many of the reported restrictions upon terms are, and how many are not, ancillary to price-fixing. It seems probable that if the ones that accompany price-fixing were eliminated, the number remaining would be substantially smaller than the number of price-fixing restrictions, but would be large enough to be significant. Information is also unavailable to distinguish the restrictions on terms according to the motives of the participants, and thus to separate those that are undertaken in the hope of indirectly fixing prices from those that are undertaken for their own sake. In the countries under discussion, such analysis of motives is not attempted. Instead, agreements about terms that are not parts of price agreements are assumed to be desired for their own sake, and are evaluated accordingly. Through this assumption, a certain amount of indirect private control of prices is probably permitted; but this fact has little significance where widespread overt private price control is tolerated.

So far as restrictions on terms are desired for their own sake and not as contributions to present or future price-fixing, they raise policy issues and involve policy decisions that deserve special discussion. This chapter will be concerned with these restrictions.

Terms of sale are many, and agreements about them may be narrow or comprehensive. Hence agreements about terms of sale differ widely in scope. Separate consideration of restrictions upon each of the numerous terms, and of each possible combination of such restrictions, is not practicable within the limits of this book. Only certain broad categories will be covered.

Three classes of restrictions upon terms raise somewhat different questions of public policy. They are (a) agreements about such matters as place and method of delivery, responsibility for costs of transportation, responsibility for various risks (such as damage in transit), time and method of payment, cash discounts, return privileges, etc.; (b) agreements about discounts or rebates in which the amount of the allowance depends upon the recipient's aggregate purchases in a stated period of time from a group of sellers; (c) all other agreements about the size of discounts or rebates and the terms upon which they shall be granted. Hereafter the first class will be called agreements on terms of sale; the second, aggregated rebate agreements; and the third, discount agreements.

Though agreements of all three classes can be either horizontal or vertical and either multipartite or bipartite, the problems to be considered can be seen most clearly in the case of horizontal agreements. Vertical agreements about terms or discounts, by which these matters are determined for transactions between one seller and one or more of his customers, are unlikely to raise significant problems of competition unless the seller has a dominant position (such as is the subject of a later chapter). Vertical multipartite agreements, as particular forms of collective bargaining, do not present clearly the questions relevant to restrictive control of terms and discounts.

Terms of Sale. Agreements about terms of sale are widely regarded, in the countries here under discussion, as either harmless or useful. In most countries, though agreements on terms are numerous, they have not been subjected to government criticism or repressive action. In much of Europe,[1] particularly in the Netherlands, Austria, and Germany, official opinion regards them as possibly useful. In Austria this attitude is expressed in a legal provision[2] under which agreements that pertain only to terms of sale may be registered (and thereby permitted) without regard to the interval of time specified for registration of restrictive agreements generally. In Germany agreements about terms of sale that do not relate to prices or components of prices are exempted by law from the general prohibition of restrictive agreements, provided only that the affected suppliers and buyers have been heard by the participants, that any comments by the affected persons are filed with the agreements, and that the cartel authority has not objected to the agreement within three months because of abuse or of treaty violation.

The benefit that is expected to result from such agreements is enhancement of the "transparency" of the market. Agreements that establish uniform terms of sale are expected to make transactions more readily comparable, to increase the capacity of buyers to choose the most advantageous alternative, and thus, by deflecting competition from the terms of sale to price and quality, to make both competition and government control more effective as to these more important matters. The thinking is akin to that which leads certain American critics of packaging to argue that the practice of competing sellers in offering packages that differ slightly from one another in weight is an obstacle to effective competition.

Some Austrian decisions also reflect the belief that agreements about terms increase economic efficiency: An agreement by brewers not to grant various forms of aid and credit to retailers was regarded as an elimination of waste, and an agreement by cotton spinners to limit credit to customers was regarded as a means to increase the speed of turnover of goods and to diffuse the costs of carrying inventories among the firms that could most readily bear them.

European and American official attitudes differ markedly in the degree of their acceptance of agreements that restrict terms of sale. An agreement

---

[1] For the four non-European countries covered by this study, insufficient information is available to justify discussion of any of the three topics of this chapter. I have not studied the administration of the Israeli law. Until 1963 application of the Japanese law about all kinds of agreements was lax. No South African report available to me has separated consideration of terms of sale or of discounts from consideration of price-fixing. In the only relevant case in New Zealand, which concerned electric lamps, the authority required changes in a discount agreement but not termination of it; but peculiarities in the structure and legal status of the industry deprived the case of significance as an indication of general policy.

[2] Article 17 of the cartel law.

setting cash discounts at a low level would be unlikely to result in legal proceedings in the United States, because of a presumption that its effects upon market competition were negligible. But the American authorities do not share European complacency about certain other terms of sale, such as, for example, methods of computing and charging for transportation. They not only think that agreements by which sellers compute transportation charges from a basing point instead of from the point of shipment are indirect equivalents to price fixing, but also see in such arrangements distortions of market boundaries and of patterns of industrial location, by which cross-hauling is fostered and the cost of transportation is unnecessarily raised.[3]

The greater willingness of Europeans to permit agreement about terms of sale is partly but not wholly due to the fact that, in general, such agreements are less likely to have concealed purposes in Europe than in the United States. The more permissive policies of Europe toward price-fixing create less incentive for indirect action and subterfuge than the more repressive American policies. European authorities are therefore less inclined than their American counterparts to suspect that an agreement about terms is intended to do more than appears on the face of the document. If European curbs upon major kinds of restriction become less lenient, the differences in the behavior of business groups and in the attitude of the authorities are likely to become smaller.

European leniency toward agreements about terms is also partly due to the fact that in Europe there is less belief than in the United States that improvements in the functioning of markets may result from experiment with new ways of doing business, and more fear than in the United States that such experimentation may have unfortunate effects upon business stability.

But Europeans do not accept all kinds of agreement about terms. a) By legal requirement or by administrative decision, countries that are very tolerant of agreements about terms of sale define such agreements so that they do not include provisions that fix discounts or that indirectly fix prices. b) Terms that are thought to be unfair are disapproved. For example, the German authority rejected a provision by which customers who sustained damages were denied the right to compensation. Moreover, knowing that terms of sale can be used to discriminate against certain enterprises or classes of enterprise or to exclude them from the market, governments that permit agreements about terms intervene to prevent the agreements from

---

[3] See for example *Report of the Federal Trade Commission on Price Base Inquiry; The Basing-Point Formula and Cement Prices*, March, 1932, and *Federal Trade Commission v. Cement Institute*, et al. 333 U.S. 683 (1948).

being used in such ways. Denmark, for example, requires that terms be fairly and uniformly applied; and in most countries provisions setting forth the qualifications of an approved trader are examined as to their exclusionary effects, not treated as mere terms of sale. Similarly, governments are likely to take action where agreed terms clearly preclude important kinds of competition. In New Zealand, for example, the authority required building contractors to terminate an agreement that when bids for construction contracts were rejected no bidder would submit a re-bid for six months; and though it did not object to a provision by which bakers agreed to accept no returned bread, it rejected a provision in the same agreement by which they undertook not to deliver to the customers of other bakers.

Discount agreements. Though discount agreements in general (as distinguished from agreements about aggregated rebates) raise somewhat different issues, they, too, are often regarded favorably. This attitude reflects two opinions: first, that, like agreements about terms of sale, discount agreements simplify transactions and add to the transparency of the market; and second, that such agreements help to keep prices down. In the ideas about transparency, European thought about discount agreements adds nothing to the ideas discussed above about agreements as to terms of sale.

The belief that discount agreements reduce prices expresses assumptions about business behavior that would not be plausible in an American setting. In the absence of such an agreement, many Europeans assume, producers will compete by granting larger discounts, but, to prevent these discounts from reducing their own net receipts, will try to raise resale prices by the full amount of the increase in the discounts. Recipients of the larger discounts will not use them for increased price competition and thus pass them on to their customers, but instead will retain the full amount of the discount, enhance their margins, and resell at the proposed higher prices. Thus consumers will pay more and middlemen get more, while producers get no less. Though such an analysis is clearly wrong when price competition is vigorous at the successive levels of distribution, it is plausible where price agreements are common among both producers and distributors and where resale price maintenance is also a common practice. Policies that curb price-fixing are too recent and their effects are still too limited to have altered thinking based upon the assumption of pervasive restriction.

Most policies toward discount agreements show little trace of an interpretation, common in the United States, that the chief significance of systems of discount consists in their effect in fostering particular channels of distribution. In such American thinking, functional discounts make middlemen secure and enable them to sell to customers who buy large amounts for which middlemen's services are not clearly necessary. Discounts based upon the amount bought in a single transaction encourage direct purchases by large buyers, and thus tend to confine middlemen to sales to the smaller buyers. Discounts based upon volume bought during a period of time strengthen large buyers at the expense of small ones, and thus encourage concentration in the buying market. American political discussion of the control of discounts by the price discrimination law emphasizes such considerations. By contrast, few countries overseas are concerned about similar impacts. Such consideration of the desirability of discount structures as takes place centers upon the direct effect of discounts upon prices and margins, and is a part of the emphasis upon reasonable prices. So far as official concern is expressed about the effect of discount agreements upon the structure of distribution, it consists of desire to make sure that discrimination in discounts does not handicap unorthodox types of distributors who may reduce retail prices, particularly cooperatives, chain stores, and buying groups. Most governments take action against agreements by which such enterprises are denied discounts that are available to others.

The most clearly formulated and explicit of the discount policies has developed in France as a part of French law about discrimination. Interpretative circulars by the Ministry of Economic Affairs have indicated that price differentials among customers may not be based upon business functions (except so far as differences in the functions performed by the buyer result in different costs for the seller) but should consist basically of quantity discounts or volume discounts, which, in French opinion, typically reflect reductions in cost. Retailers should pay as little as wholesalers if they buy comparable amounts. The interpretations specifically say that competition between different functional classes of distributors is desirable. The underlying purpose is to keep retail prices down by preventing the supplier from compensating middlemen except for their services in reducing the cost of distribution.

Where discount agreements are permitted, precautions to prevent abuse of discounts are taken. As in the case of agreements about terms of sale, a major purpose of these precautions is to prevent discounts from being discriminatory or exclusionary. In German law, discount agreements are exempted from a general prohibition of restrictive agreements, but those making the agreement must have heard representatives of the levels of business to which the agreements reply and must have filed with the authorities the comments of these affected interests. Moreover, the discounts must represent genuine compensation for services and must not lead to unjustified differential treatment of others who render the same service. An agreement becomes valid only if the authority does not object to it within three months. Objection may be made either because the foregoing requirements have not been met or because the agreement has harmful effects on the flow of production or trade or on adequate supply to consumers, particularly by making entry into distribution more difficult.

In applying the exemption, the German authority has interpreted it as precluding discount cartels that foreclose competition. Therefore, when forms of competition other than competition in discounts are absent the authority objects to discount agreements as devices that eliminate the remaining competition.

Unlike France, most of the countries are indifferent to the basis upon which discounts are granted and do not set standards for the size of the discounts that are made available. They insist, however, that criteria as to eligibility for discounts must be clear and objective and that such criteria shall be uniformly applied, without arbitrary denial of discounts for no good reason. In Denmark and Sweden, agreements that discounts would be granted only to members of a trade association were modified under official pressure. In Norway, before discount agreements were generally forbidden (in 1960), parties to a discount agreement were permitted to deny a discount to a trader who lacked the experience specified in the agreement's requirements as to eligibility for discounts; but a provision in another agreement, by which a discount was denied to a book dealer on the ground that he did not own his own business, was held to be unreasonable.

In 1960 a Norwegian royal decree forbade not only horizontal price-fixing, but also fixation of discounts. In recommending the decree, the Norwegian Price Directorate said that fixation of discounts often confines distributive functions to members of associations, makes distributors' territories inflexible, obstructs direct sale to large buyers, and prevents producers from adopting the methods of distribution that are most appropriate for them. Norwegian cooperatives opposed the part of the draft decree that pertained to discounts on the ground that consumers were often benefitted by discount agreements; but the government decided that exemptions authorized in the decree were sufficient to protect desirable discount agreements and other types of agreements by which price calculations were simplified.

Aggregated rebates. Sellers in Europe sometimes agree that the discount or rebate they will accord to each of their customers shall vary with the aggregate purchases by the buyer from all participants in the agreement. The significant feature of such schemes, as seen by European governments, is the fact that the rebate is not available upon purchases that are made from non-members of the group. Because of this feature the provision penalizes a buyer who chooses to buy part of his requirements from independent sources. Thus it tends to divert trade from non-participating sellers. Though such an agreement also facilitates division of the buyer's purchases among the participants and tends to foster uniformity in the prices and discounts quoted by them, these aspects of the matter are given little attention.

Aggregated rebate schemes that rest upon the exclusionary principle that has been described should be distinguished from the aggregated discounts that are sometimes granted to buyers in the United States. Since under American law sellers may not agree on discounts, the aggregated discounts that appear in this country are typically the result of decisions by individual sellers. In the typical case, small sellers find difficulty in making sales to a large buyer because that buyer, by making his purchases wholly from a firm large enough to meet his full requirements, can obtain volume discounts from his supplier. Unable to induce such a large buyer to transfer all his purchases from the large supplier, and desirous of selling some part of the large buyer's requirements, small suppliers may undertake to meet the prices charged by their larger rivals. A convenient way to do this is to quote a volume discount the amount of which depends upon the buyer's aggregate purchases from all sellers. When aggregated discounts arise from the interaction of individual decisions by sellers engaged in this kind of rivalry, they do not confine the discount to purchases made from a selected group. Their tendency is not to exclude certain suppliers but to facilitate access to parts of the market by suppliers who might otherwise be unable to obtain it.

Because of the exclusionary aspects of European aggregated rebate schemes, governments often, but not uniformly, frown upon such agreements. The German authorities, for example, rejected aggregated rebate schemes under which purchases from non-participating sellers were excluded from the aggregates upon which rebates were computed, or were included only under discriminatory conditions. After some initial hesitancy, however, they permitted other types of aggregated rebate arrangements. New Zealand explicitly empowers its authorities to issue orders against aggregated rebate arrangements.

But what makes exclusionary aggregated rebates questionable to governments may make them desirable to business groups. In the autumn of 1963 the public registers of Sweden, Norway, and the United Kingdom showed a dozen or more such restrictions in each country. In the Netherlands similar restrictions were believed to be more numerous; but since the register there is not public and separate figures for aggregated rebate agreements are not published, exact information was not available.

Chapter VII

Vertical Price Fixing

Resale price maintenance is a practice by which suppliers of goods designate the prices at which goods they sell shall be resold by distributors. From the point of view of suppliers, the practice, if successfully applied, prevents price competition among their distributors that might result in the loss of some outlets to the market, or in diversion of the sales effort of some of their distributors to goods thought to be more profitable, or in pressure upon suppliers to maintain distributive margins by reducing their own selling prices. From the point of view of distributors, the practice protects them from price competition and thus provides stable markups. If resale price maintenance is uniform by all who supply a commodity, it eliminates price competition in the resale markets and fosters elimination of it in the suppliers' market. If different suppliers follow different resale price policies, each user of the practice thereby stabilizes the vertical and horizontal price relationships for his own product and thus isolates whatever problems he may encounter from the difference between his policy and the policies of his competitors. In either case, distributors escape price competition among themselves.

In spite of substantial differences in policy toward resale price maintenance from country to country, the countries here under study differ markedly from the United States in their attitudes toward this kind of restriction. American policy toward maintenance of resale prices is less severe than toward other restrictions upon prices. In the countries covered by this study, there is no similar relaxation of policy. In one group of countries restrictions upon resale prices are curbed more sharply than other restrictions. In a second group of countries such restrictions are fully subject to the law that governs restrictions generally. The United Kingdom, which for nearly ten years permitted resale price maintenance by individual suppliers, abandoned this policy in 1964. The Netherlands, which follows an eclectic policy toward horizontal price-fixing, forbade collective resale price maintenance in the same year, and also forbade individual resale price maintenance for designated groups of commodities that had been frequently subject to it. In Norway, which since 1957 has prohibited most resale price agreements but permitted individual suppliers to recommend resale prices,

101

serious consideration has been given to the desirability of a more severe policy than that currently applied.

Special severity toward resale price maintenance was an appropriate expression of the incentives that produced postwar restrictive practice legislation. Concern about rising costs of living, the relation of these to an inflationary spiral of prices and wages, and unrealized opportunities to reduce the cost of doing business resulted in special attention to restrictions upon retail prices of consumer goods. Price-cutting by cooperatives, chain stores, and other unorthodox types of retail distributors seemed not only a valuable means to low retail prices but also the result of improvements in distributive efficiency that reduced the costs of distribution. Programs of resale price maintenance had been designed primarily to prevent price-cutting at retail; and their principal targets had been the unorthodox types of low-price distributors already mentioned. Hence a major purpose of some of the new laws was either to prevent resale price maintenance or to subject to close public control the resale prices that were maintained.

In countries in which this purpose was strongest, all forms of resale price arrangements were subjected to special prohibition or control. In other countries, particularly larger countries with more sources of goods, collective resale price maintenance by groups of competitors was repressed but suppliers individually were allowed greater scope. Control of resale prices by individual suppliers was thought to be relatively harmless because competition by rival suppliers was expected to keep resale prices reasonable and because cooperatives and chain stores had private brands of goods that could counteract increases in the prices of manufacturers' brands.

As in the United States, curbs upon resale price maintenance often raised difficult questions of the relation between freedom of contract and occupational freedom. To prevent sellers and distributors from entering into resale price contracts that they desired to make was repugnant to belief in the former. To permit certain enterprises to designate the terms upon which other enterprises should sell was repugnant to belief in the latter. This conflict of values was resolved in some countries by focussing policy toward resale price maintenance, not upon contractual arrangements, but upon the coercive devices by which reluctant businessmen were forced to enter into such contracts or to comply with their terms.

Programs of resale price maintenance may take various forms, horizontal and vertical, collective and individual. Collective programs may be formulated in formal agreements or in less formal recommendations. Four types of collective agreements are evident overseas. They are as follows: (1) Sellers may agree among themselves upon specified actual or minimum resale prices or specified actual or minimum markups that the buyer shall add to his purchase prices in reselling; and may agree to enforce compliance with such prices or markups collectively by incorporating them in sales contracts enforceable in court and by concertedly refusing to sell, or refusing to grant customary discounts, to buyers who do not comply. (2) Sellers may agree that each individually will prescribe resale prices or markups for his products and will include them in his sales contracts, and that the entire group will use means of collective enforcement against any reseller who does not comply with the prices or markups specified by his supplier. (3) Buyers may agree upon a uniform resale price or markup that should be specified by their suppliers, and may undertake to boycott or otherwise discriminate against any supplier who does not require his distributors to resell as specified. (4) A group of sellers and a group of buyers, acting together, may agree upon resale prices or markups to be observed by the latter and enforced by the former. Any of these types of collaboration may be limited to informal recommendations instead of formal agreements, and compliance with the recommendations may be obtained by less drastic economic and social pressures.

Two types of resale price maintenance by individual suppliers are also evident. (5) A single supplier may agree with each of his distributors upon resale prices or markups to be observed in resale of goods bought from him, and may enforce the obligation in the courts or by refusal to sell or by denial of discounts. (6) An individual supplier may unilaterally specify resale prices or markups that he desires his distributors to observe. His announcements may be mere recommendations or may be given effect by withholding supplies or discounts from recalcitrant distributors.

The vertical extent of any of these programs may be more or less comprehensive: Though the supplier who fixes a resale price is usually the manufacturer, he may be a wholesaler or an importer. Resale prices may be fixed only for the first resale by the distributor who bought from the supplier. Usually, however, if more than one resale takes place, resale prices to be set for subsequent resellers are stipulated also, and the program covers prices all the way to the ultimate consumer. Where this is the case, intermediary distributors are expected to notify their customers about the stipulated resale prices and may be expected to help enforce compliance with these prices, under penalty of being themselves treated as recalcitrants.

The first four of these programs would be clearly unlawful under the American antitrust laws. Except where state laws authorize the program and Federal enabling acts have provided an exemption for resale price maintenance contracts that are permissible under state legislation, the fifth program would be also unlawful. Even the sixth program would be of dubious legality, since the courts might see in it either permissible discretion in selecting customers or coercive restraint of the trade of others.

Overseas, such programs differ in legality from country to country. Under general law, prior to the enactment of the restrictive practice laws, the first five programs probably would have been permissible and the sixth program would have been regarded as a simple exercise of business freedom. Where restrictive practice legislation contains no special provisions about resale prices, the five programs that involve concerted action are subject to general provisions about restrictive agreements, most of which make legality depend upon *ad hoc* application of standards that forbid abuse or damage to the public interest.

Where there is no special control of resale prices, the sixth program is subject to the rules that govern abuse of economic power and refusal to sell; and under these rules curbs are likely to be applicable if the supplier is a dominant firm, but not otherwise. In countries having laws that include special provisions about resale price maintenance, the legality of the various programs differs according to the content of these special provisions.

In ten of the countries covered by this study, the legal status of resale price maintenance is determined by explicit provisions that apply to some or all forms of it. In the other countries, and in these so far as such provisions do not reach, it is subject to the general provisions of law relevant to restrictive arrangements.

The following table indicates the resulting legal status of resale price maintenance in the various countries. In it an X designates a provision explicitly pertaining to resale price maintenance; an O indicates the effect of a general provision of the law.

Four kinds of policy are expressed in the provisions that are summarized in this table. The first seeks to prohibit resale price arrangements, with or without exemptions in particular cases. This policy is expressed in the prohibitory legislation applicable in nine countries to resale price maintenance involving concerted action among suppliers, and in seven of these countries to resale price maintenance by individual suppliers.[1] By forbidding enforcement of resale prices, the second policy distinguishes between coercive and voluntary resale price arrangements and permits such schemes if they are maintained willingly.[2] This policy is applied by Denmark

---

[1] In the Netherlands, however, the prohibition as to individual suppliers covers only designated kinds of goods.

[2] Swiss law forbids enforcement of resale price arrangements only if their substance is not shown to be unobjectionable. Dutch law as to resale price maintenance by individual suppliers of the commodities for which it is permissible forbids use of private sanctions but permits resort to judicial enforcement.

Legal Status of Resale Price Maintenance

	Austria	Belgium	Denmark	Finland	France	Germany	Ireland	Israel	Japan	Netherlands	New Zealand	Norway	South Africa	Spain	Sweden	Switzerland	United Kingdom
Arrangements Including More Than One Supplier																	
Prohibition																	
Agreements unlawful, without exemption						X			O[1]	X							
Agreements unlawful, with provision for exemptions				X[5]	X							X		O	X[5]		
Enforcement unlawful																	X
Enforcement unlawful, with provision for exemptions			X		X							X				O[2]	
Recommendations unlawful, with provision for exemptions				X[5]	O[3]	O[4]						X			X[5]		X
Prior approval required, terms limited	X																
Supervision or limitation imposed																	
Discretionary prohibition or limitation authorized		O[7]	O					O			O		O		O		O
Registration required for agreements (public)	O		O	O				O				O			O		O
Registration required for agreements (confidential)										O							
Limits imposed on prices and/or margins	X											O					
Control of changes in quality imposed	X																
Duration of agreements limited	X																
Rules and orders for particular industries applicable							O[6]										
Arrangements including only one supplier																	
Prohibition																	
Agreements unlawful for designated categories of goods										X							
Agreements unlawful if they involve private sanctions or third party policing										X							
Agreements unlawful, with provision for exemptions				X[5]	X[3]				O[1]			X		O	X[5]		X

	Austria	Belgium	Denmark	Finland	France	Germany	Ireland	Israel	Japan	Netherlands	New Zealand	Norway	South Africa	Spain	Sweden	Switzerland	United Kingdom
Enforcement unlawful, with provision for exemptions			X	X⁵	X³							X				O⁷	X
Recommendations unlawful with provision for exemptions					X³										X⁵		
Recommendation unlawful if supported by pressure												X					
Recommendation unlawful unless accompanied by notice of right to disregard					X⁵							X			X⁵		
Prior approval required, terms limited	X																
Supervision or limitation imposed																	
Discretionary prohibition or limitation authorized for agreements	O⁷	O	X		X		O			O	O		O		O		
Discretionary prohibition or limitation authorized for recommendations					X⁵		X					X					
Registration required for agreements (public)	O		O		X		O								O		
Registration required for agreements (confidential)										O							
Registration required for recommendations (public)	X						X										
Limits imposed on prices and/or margins	X												O				
Control of changes of quality imposed	X																
Duration of agreement limited	X																
Rules and orders for particular industries applicable							O⁶										
Statutory exemption from general prohibition for commodities to be designated									X								

¹ Under Japanese law an entrepreneur may not engage in unreasonable restraints of trade or employ unfair business practices. In a list of unfair practices intended to be generally applicable, the Japanese Fair Trade Commission has included trading on conditions that restrict the other party in relation to third parties. What is forbidden to individuals is presumably unlawful also when it is the result of agreement. Though

to concerted and individual resale price maintenance alike. The third policy exposes a resale price arrangement to prohibitory or corrective action when the authorities think that it is contrary to the public interest because of excessive prices, abusive conduct, or any other objectionable characteristic. This policy is expressed in special provisions covering concerted resale price maintenance in Austria, individual resale price maintenance or resale price recommendations in Austria, Finland, and Germany, and recommendations in Norway. It is also expressed in the general provisions of law that are applicable to concerted resale price maintenance in seven countries and to individual resale price maintenance in seven.[3] The fourth policy subjects resale price arrangements to special limitations that are intended to make abuse of it more difficult and easier to correct. This policy is expressed in the provisions that require registration of agreements or recommendations, impose control upon prices or quality, or limit the duration of agreements.

The way in which the fourth policy can take effect is illustrated by the law of Austria. Like restrictive agreements generally, resale price agreements in Austria must be submitted for registration[4] and are registrable only if, with special attention to the interest of consumers, they appear to be economically justifiable. But additional requirements apply to them. Resale

the law contains an exemption for resale price maintenance, this applies only to contracts by individual suppliers as to commodities designated by the Fair Trade Commission.

[2] Switzerland's prohibition of discriminatory and coercive action carries an exemption applicable to enforcement of resale price maintenance, but only if the prices are reasonable and the arrangement is necessary to assure quality or service.

[3] The explicit prohibition covers any form of minimum price fixation, collective or individual. It is applicable to individual resale price recommendations. A collective recommendation would be appraised as a cartel, and thus would be subject to prohibition and possibility of exemption, depending upon its effects.

[4] Evasion of the law by recommendations is forbidden, subject to exceptions for recommendations explicitly defined as non-binding, not supported by pressure, applicable only to members of an association, and intended to promote competition with large or similar enterprises.

[5] The provision is applicable to requirements, and thus does not authorize invalidation of voluntary resale price contracts. It is also applicable to recommendations but only if they do not include a statement that they may be disregarded.

[6] These rules and orders include some directed against all resale price maintenance, some limiting it to recommendations, and some permitting it.

[7] The provision is applicable only to firms that possess substantial economic power. For Switzerland, note 2 above is also applicable.

[3] In the Netherlands these provisions are applicable only to individual resale price maintenance for products for which it is not forbidden.

[4] In 1958 the law was amended to require that recommendations, including those about resale prices, must be registered as cartels if they are supported by economic or social pressure and if they are not accompanied by explicit notice that they are not binding.

prices must be stated explicitly and must be accompanied by detailed descriptions of the commodities to which they apply. Prices and margins must be the same as or lower than those customary for the kind of goods they cover, and must be subjected to examination as to whether or not, though customary, they are excessive. Change in the properties of the goods to which the resale prices apply may not be made without prior notice nor without a finding by the cartel tribunal that no deterioration in quality is involved. Parties to the agreement must be allowed to withdraw earlier, and with less prior notice, than is authorized by law for other kinds of agreement. Thus the statute attempts to provide special protection for consumers as to price and quality and special opportunity for dissatisfied participants in the agreements to recover their independence of action quickly.

Where special provisions of law apply to resale price maintenance, they usually repress it more severely than other restrictive practices, particularly when it involves collective action by two or more suppliers. This is true in nine countries. The laws of eight countries contain prohibitions applicable to concerted resale price maintenance that are stronger than the provisions of the same law that are concerned with most other types of restrictive agreements. The law of an additional country imposes stronger discretionary controls upon such concert of action than upon other types of agreements. In six of the eight countries where there are special prohibitions, individual resale price maintenance is subject to similar prohibitions; in one of the remaining two it is prohibited for designated types of commodities. In three countries the law is reenforced by rules designed to prevent resale price recommendations from becoming coercive.

Only three countries, Japan, Germany, and Switzerland, relax their general rules of law in the case of resale price maintenance. Japan does so only for individual suppliers of goods designated as appropriate by the authorities. Switzerland does so only if resale prices are reasonable and the arrangement is necessary to assure good quality or good service.

Application of the Laws

In applying the rules against restrictive agreements to resale price maintenance, most of the countries that do not have special resale price provisions make no distinction between resale price agreements made by a single supplier and collective resale price agreements. Agreements by an individual supplier can be forbidden on grounds of public interest or abuse in New Zealand and South Africa and also in the Netherlands for the commodities for which they are not wholly forbidden. They can be exempted from a general prohibition in Spain; like other agreements they can be explicitly permitted in Israel; and rules of fair competition can be applied to them in Ireland. In Belgium and Switzerland, however, curbs can be applied to resale price maintenance by single suppliers only when the suppliers possess dominant power, and resale price arrangements by lesser firms are not subject to the law. In practice, Ireland has usually but not invariably condemned both collective and individual control of resale prices, and New Zealand and South Africa have given it very little attention. Information about the practice of Belgium and Israel is not available, and the laws of Spain and Switzerland are too recent to have afforded experience.

Application of the policies that are explicitly concerned with resale price control has greatly reduced the number of collective binding resale price arrangements. Even if exemption is permissible, most applications for it are rejected. In Germany no collective resale price fixing is permitted. In the United Kingdom and France, collective resale price fixing has not been authorized, though in France individual exemptions permit resale price maintenance for 24 different manufacturers of luxury perfumes and cosmetics and thus covers most of the industry. In Norway, three commodities have been exempted from the general prohibition, of which two—books and scrap iron sold to wholesalers—were still subject to resale price control in 1963. In Denmark in 1963 the only collective arrangement exempted from the prohibition was that for books. In Sweden only four resale price agreements, including those for individual suppliers, were found among nearly 500 registered agreements analyzed in September 1963.[5] In Austria, though resale price agreements could be made and registered, the limitations upon them made them so unattractive that even before 1958, when these limitations were tightened, only a few had been registered—for television, radios, photographic supplies, bicycles, a kind of umbrella frame, and a brand of cosmetics. For Finland and Japan, information is not available; but similar results were not to be expected there, for until revised in 1964 Finnish law contained only an authorization to forbid resale price maintenance in particular cases, and until recently the whole of the Japanese law about restrictive agreements had been laxly applied.

In the countries that have sought such a result, a smaller but striking reduction has also taken place in resale price maintenance by single enterprises. To the close of 1963 France had exempted agreements by numerous makers of luxury perfumes and cosmetics,[6] but only eight such arrange-

---

[5] The analysis covered all currently effective agreements for manufacture and trade contained in the Swedish cartel registers except agreements as to local manufacture and retail agreements in towns of less than 50,000 population.

[6] Though as many as 80 were exempted, only 24 exemptions were in effect in June 1965.

ments by other suppliers. To late 1963 Norway had exempted two publishers who were not parties to the collective book agreement, as well as sale of methylated alcohol (for technical use) by the state alcohol monopoly. In 1959 fourteen exemptions were in effect in Denmark. Exemptions for single firms in Sweden and registrations of agreements by single firms in Austria are included in the meager totals given for these countries above. In Japan, to mid-1964, exemption had been applied to eleven commodities.

The grounds upon which resale price maintenance has been permitted in the countries in which policy generally condemns it throw light upon the standards that are deemed to justify it in exceptional cases. A matter of primary concern is the level of prices to consumers. Denmark granted exemptions to a few suppliers whose prices or markups were lower than those of their competitors. Ireland authorized resale price maintenance for cigarettes to counteract a severe price war, and, in condemning the practice in various other trades, stipulated that a supplier could withhold goods from distributors who sold below purchase price or advertised the supplier's recommended resale price adjacent to their own lower prices. In one Irish report, resale price maintenance by a single supplier was held to be harmless because other suppliers who did not prescribe resale prices deprived the isolated effort to do so of any significant restrictive effect.

Resale price maintenance was permitted by Denmark in other instances because excise taxes upon sales to consumers made a stable and predictable resale price desirable. One exemption was granted by Norway for a similar reason. Denmark also granted an exemption because buying organizations as well as a dominant seller thought that inducements for users of a seasonally useful product to buy it in the off-season and store it for later use could best be maintained if seasonal price variations were fixed and predictable. In New Zealand and South Africa, control of resale prices has been considered a logical corollary of horizontal price fixing, to be condemned or approved as was consistent with the decision about the horizontal arrangement.

In the Scandinavian countries, collective resale price maintenance for books has been approved as a part of a broader program that is considered to be of cultural value. Long-standing arrangements between publishers and book dealers provide that each dealer will keep in stock, for not less than a year after publication, one or more copies of every book published in the country. Since the practice involves inventories of books that sell slowly, maintenance of the resale prices of best-sellers has been thought to be necessary to enable booksellers to carry the inventory costs. In Sweden, however, investigation of the book industry recently led the authority to conclude that slow-moving books were not actually distributed to stores, that the burden of selling them was relatively light, that the distribution structure of the book trade was unduly rigid, and that resale price maintenance for books would be terminated after a transitional period.[7]

The clearest public formulation of standards for authorization of resale price control appeared in a French government circular issued in 1960. It read as follows:

"The products of the enterprise must be technically of unquestioned quality, which in most cases presupposes a trademark, patent, or working license. The enterprise must also be able to prove . . . that its products reach the consumer at the lowest possible price and that this price, moreover, is at a low competitive level. In general, the right to fix prices can be granted, under this standard, only to enterprises that are leaders in their field, competing in this way to spur the others in the same line of business. . . . Account may also be taken of the fact that the enterprise imposed prices before the 1953 decree and of such secondary considerations as the prestige of a brand, the reputation of the maker, the care attending the launching of new products, the luxurious nature of the product, etc."

Use of this standard is illustrated by an exemption (no longer in effect) that was granted in France in 1960 to a producer of casseroles. He had reduced the general level of prices by from 30 to 35 percent, had improved productivity, and by such means had come to produce more than 500,000 of the 600,000 casseroles sold. Retail price reductions of about 7½ percent accompanied the exemption, and thereby saved the consumer, the government thought, five times what could have been saved by shopping for bargains. In granting the exemption the government stipulated that discounts of not more than 6 percent from the retail price must be permitted in order to maintain the margin of competition indispensable to progress.

In most countries, administration of the prohibitions or curbs upon resale price maintenance has not resulted in many corrective proceedings. Action, often informal, has been necessary from time to time to prevent illegal enforcement of resale prices by boycott (England) or by refusal to sell (France, Sweden); to see to it that a recommendation is accompanied by an explicit statement of its non-binding nature (Sweden); or to prevent resale prices from being set at levels regarded as excessive (the Netherlands). Only in Germany, however, has enforcement of the law resulted in numerous proceedings.

The exemption for individual resale price maintenance in the German law stipulates that the goods covered must be publications or trademarked

---

[7] Decision of the Freedom of Commerce Board concerning an application of the Swedish Publishers' Association for continued exemption from the prohibition of resale price maintenance in regard to the trade in books, Stockholm, March 17, 1965.

articles, that the latter must be in competition with other similar goods, and that the supplier must guarantee maintenance or improvement of their quality. Contracts must be filed and are subject to official invalidation if abused. To avoid invalidation, contracts are often modified to conform to official views. By interpretation of the statute, resale prices must be actual prices, not mere minima or maxima, and recommendations, though permissible if filed, must be accompanied by clear statements that they are not binding. In the four years to the close of 1961, administration of these provisions had resulted in 440 proceedings, of which 168 were closed without action, 52 resulted in voluntary correction, 23 resulted in orders, and the rest were pending at the beginning of 1962. These figures constituted 60 percent of all enforcement proceedings, 71 percent of all cases settled by voluntary correction, and all but two of the cases decided by formal order during the period. Contracts were invalidated because the necessary competition with other products was found to be precluded by restrictive agreement or non-existent in the light of reiterated simultaneous price increases. The scope of the resale price control permissible under a trademark was repeatedly decided, with permission for such control by plant breeders, producers of semi-processed goods, and producers of a major component of the price-fixed article, but with denial of control over theater admission fees by owners of moving-picture films. In certain cases, the extent to which a resale price contract can fix terms of sale or prevent grant of discounts was decided. In other cases, abuse was found in collective enforcement of individual contracts; in sale of the same product by the supplier, unbranded, for less than the contract price; in direct sale of the branded product by the supplier for less than that price; and in regional differentiation of resale prices without reasonable justification. That the resale price was excessive was inferred in one case from the fact that free deals and extra discounts were being used to sell a large inventory. Presumably these decisions do not exhaust the problems that inhere in efforts to apply the test of abuse to the maintenance of resale prices. By the end of March 1965 agreements for 663 articles had been invalidated.[8]

The nature of the changes incident to prohibition of resale price agreements in Norway was made clear in official reports. In 1957, when the prohibitory decree was issued, 105 collective resale price arrangements and 25 instances of resale price maintenance by dominant firms were on the Norwegian register. An official study made the previous year had estimated that, including dominant firms, nearly 700 individual suppliers undertook some form of resale price maintenance, in 181 cases through binding agreements and in at least 330 cases by announcing resale prices without telling

---

[8] OECD July 1965 Report, op. cit., p. 18.

distributors that they were not binding. Five months after the decree, 91 of the registered agreements had been terminated. Some were not replaced; some gave way to individual non-binding recommendations; and some were replaced by horizontal agreements on prices among suppliers or dealers (still lawful in 1957, but generally forbidden in 1960 by another decree). In 24 instances, dominant firms had converted binding arrangements to advisory ones. By early 1959, about 100 collective agreements had been terminated, and nearly 1,000 individual schemes had been either terminated or changed.

In Germany, where resale price fixing by single enterprises has been authorized in the restrictive practice law, and in the United Kingdom, where similar vertical price-fixing was permitted until 1964, such arrangements continued to be numerous. At the close of March 1965 resale price contracts by 1169 German suppliers covered nearly 166,000 filed prices, and resale price recommendations by 867 suppliers covered over 51,000 more.[9] Such agreements were not registered in the United Kingdom, and no reliable estimate of their number is available. But in two articles British economists estimated, respectively, that 23 per cent and 25 per cent of total consumer personal expenditures in 1960 (including expenditures for services) were subject to resale price control. Since an earlier official estimate for 1938 concluded that resale price maintenance was then in effect for about 30 per cent of private expenditures for goods (excluding services), these estimates justify doubt that resale price maintenance had become less prevalent since the 1930's.

The principal result of the repression of enforceable resale price agreements has been resort to informal recommendations. In most countries such recommendations are not controlled, sometimes because recommendations, as distinguished from agreements, arrangements, and practices, fall outside the scope of the law;[10] sometimes because, though the law may possibly cover them, the authorities have paid no attention to relationships so informal;[11] and sometimes because, by seeking to control only the enforcement of resale prices, the law clearly leaves room for unenforced expressions of views.[12] In some countries recommendations about resale prices are permitted by law or excluded from legal control on condition that they state explicitly that they are not binding and that lower prices or margins are permitted. This is true for both collective and individual recommendations

---

9 Ibid.

10 This is clearly true in the Netherlands and probably true in Belgium, Israel, New Zealand, Spain, and Switzerland. It is true in the United Kingdom for recommendations by individual suppliers.

11 This is true in Ireland, Japan, and South Africa.

12 This is true in Denmark, Sweden, and Finland.

in Austria, Sweden and Finland, and for individual recommendations in Norway; but a recommendation may be prohibited by the Austrian and Norwegian authorities if pressure is applied to support it or if it results in excessive margins or prices. In Germany, by judicial interpretation, individual resale price recommendations are permitted if filed with the cartel authority. Norway and Germany prohibit collective resale price recommendations.[13] Thus (except in the case of collective recommendations in two countries) business enterprises can suggest appropriate resale prices provided they make clear that the suggestions are only advisory and provided they do not use economic or social pressure when the advice is rejected. That informal resale price recommendations have become prevalent is indicated by the comments of informed persons in various countries, but facts about the present scope of the practice are not publicly available.

In France, where the law forbids recommendations as to actual or minimum resale prices, another device has been used. With government encouragement, various suppliers have announced maximum resale prices that may not be exceeded. Though in business circles such an announcement has been called a way out for a manufacturer who wishes to fix distributors' prices, statements by the government do not show concern lest such an announcement be a mere verbal mask for designation of a price to which all distributors will conform. Instead, maximum price announcements are thought to lead to discounting by distributors, and thus to have fostered competition in retail markets.

Substitution of price recommendations for enforced price agreements appears to have made little change in the maintenance of resale prices designated by suppliers. In Austria in late 1959 some price competition in retail sales of chocolate had become apparent, but most retail prices were being maintained at suggested levels. In Norway the Price Directorate estimated in 1962 that suggested retail prices were followed 95 percent of the time; and it considered seriously whether it should not forbid all resale price recommendations. In France, according to an unofficial estimate, a tendency for prices to increase was counteracted in 1958, and reductions of from 4 to 5 per cent took place in the retail prices of biscuits, soap, and certain major household appliances.

In the countries that have tolerated resale price contracts, this permissive policy does not appear to be firmly established. As a result of a study undertaken by the Board of Trade in 1960, the United Kingdom changed its law in 1964 to forbid resale price maintenance by individual suppliers. Previously it had permitted such resale price maintenance; indeed, it had authorized individual suppliers to enforce resale price contracts

---

[13] The German prohibition is qualified.

not only against distributors who were parties thereto, but also against subsequent distributors who had notice of the contracts. By the Resale Prices Act of 1964, however, agreements by individual suppliers for maintenance of resale prices were made unlawful, as well as the withholding of supplies and the imposition of discriminatory terms of sale for failure to maintain resale prices. Refusal to sell to persons who used similar goods as loss-leaders was given statutory exemption. The prohibited acts were not subjected to criminal penalties. Instead, the prohibited contracts became legally void, conformity to the law became a statutory duty, and those who did not conform were subjected to civil proceedings by the government and exposed to possible suits by persons damaged by the violation. Suppliers, their trade associations, and the Registrar of Restrictive Trading Agreements were authorized to apply to the Restrictive Practices Court for exemption. The court was empowered to grant exemption if, in its opinion, without maintenance of minimum resale prices various results detrimental to consumers would appear—substantial reduction of the quality or variety of goods; substantial reduction of the number of retail establishments selling them; long-run increase in prices; conditions dangerous to health; substantial reduction of the necessary services—and if such detriments would outweigh the detrimental effect of resale price maintenance.

In 1960 the Netherlands referred to a quasi-official advisory committee the question whether either collective or individual control of resale prices should be prohibited. In 1963 the committee submitted advice in which all participants opposed collective refusal to sell as a way of enforcing resale prices; a minority opposed all resale price maintenance in the belief that it raised prices; a second group desired to forbid collective, but not individual, resale price maintenance; and a third group, which approved individual resale price control as a means to orderly markets, regarded collective similar action as too unimportant to be generally forbidden. In 1964 three Dutch orders in council invalidated (and thus forbade) (a) all collective resale price maintenance; (b) individual resale price maintenance for designated classes of commodities unless the resale price did not exceed purchase price; and (c) individual resale price maintenance for all other commodities if the arrangement included private sanctions or entrusted detection or suit for non-compliance to third parties.[14] The designated commodities were those in the sale of which resale price maintenance had been most prevalent.

---

[14] Orders in Council of April 1 and August 31, 1964 (see Staatsblad Nos. 110, 352, and 353). The designated classes of commodities were radio and television sets, record players, tape recorders, electric refrigerators, toasters, mixers, vacuum cleaners, washing machines, centrifuges, flat irons, dry-shavers, hair dryers, passenger automobiles, cameras, photo or film projectors, and phonograph records.

A more repressive policy toward resale price maintenance has also been considered in Germany. The German government first recommended to the Bundestag that individual resale price control be forbidden; and when no action resulted, recommended in 1964 that the confidential register of resale price agreements become public and that resale prices be regarded as obviously too high if they were not actually maintained or if the supplier made sales at lower prices. These changes took effect by amendment of the law in 1965.[15]

---

[15] Gesetz zur Änderung des Gesetzes gegen Wettbewerbsbeschränkungen, Sept. 15, 1965.

Chapter VIII

Collective Restrictions of Other Types

Although the most common types of restrictive agreement in the seventeen countries here discussed are those concerned with prices and terms of sale, other kinds of restriction are also numerous. For six European countries in which restrictive agreements are reported to the government, the list below sets forth the more significant of these types of reported arrangement and the minimum aggregate number of agreements that provided for each type in 1963.[1]

1. Fixation of quotas of sale or purchase, or allocation of types of goods, territories, customers, orders, or bids—538 agreements.

2. Determination of the number, status, or qualifications of persons with whom to deal or to whom to grant customary terms of trade—375 agreements.

3. Joint production or sale or purchase or pooling of profits and losses—292 agreements.

4. Limitation of the character, variety, proportion, quality, or specifications of goods—181 agreements.

5. Exchange of information about such matters as prices, bids, costs, orders, or sales—159 agreements.

6. Sharing of legal rights under patents or trademarks, or of technological information—37 agreements.

7. Limitation of productive capacity or of amounts produced or offered for sale—16 agreements.

8. Limitation of methods of production—7 agreements.

Not all such arrangements are subject to substantive action or even

---

[1] The countries are the United Kingdom, Germany, the Netherlands, Denmark, Sweden, and Norway. The numbers are derived from analysis of cartel registers or from government statistics. They should be regarded as minima for several reasons: a) Agreements that pertain solely to foreign markets are not included. b) So far as information permitted, agreements pertaining to manufacture for local markets, handicraft manufacture, and retail trade in small towns were excluded from the analysis. c) For each country the figures omit types of restriction and segments of the economy that are not subject to that country's reporting requirements. This omission is particularly large in the case of the fifth and sixth types of arrangements, since significant exemptions are applicable to patent agreements and to agreements to exchange information. d) For one country some of the figures relevant to the second type of restriction are not available. See Corwin D. Edwards, *Cartelization in Western Europe*, op. cit., pp. 4-6, 8-24.

to reporting under the laws of the countries covered by this book. Exchange of information and exchange of patent rights are almost immune from control. Exchange of market information or cost information lies beyond the scope of the cartel laws in the United Kingdom, Belgium, and the Netherlands.[2] In other countries, in which the agreements that are subject to control are those with a purpose or effect of restriction, the authorities have not seen a restrictive purpose or effect in such exchanges. Similarly, arrangements to share patents are exempt under the cartel laws of Germany, the United Kingdom, Japan, Israel, and South Africa; agreements to share unpatented technology are also exempted under the laws of the first two of these countries;[3] and agreements of both kinds are viewed favorably by the authorities under the laws of countries that do not exempt them. One should bear in mind, however, that in various countries the patent laws contain provisions for compulsory licensing that diminish the potential restrictive effects of patents and of agreements about patents.[4]

No explicit immunity is granted by law to the other kinds of restriction listed above. For the most part, agreements involving them are subject to the general provisions of the applicable laws. In some laws, however, specific mention of some of these restrictions is made in definitions of restriction, lists of practices subject to control, or provisions that set forth the generally applicable rules of control or prohibition.

This is true in the following instances:

Limitation of capacity (or investment)—Israel, Japan, South Africa, Spain

Limitation of amounts produced or sold—Israel, Japan, New Zealand, South Africa, Spain, the United Kingdom

Limitation of methods of production—Israel, Japan, South Africa, the United Kingdom

---

[2] Belgian law covers only abuse of economic power; Netherlands law only agreements that explicitly regulate competition. In the United Kingdom, the Restrictive Trade Practices Act is applicable only to agreements that have restrictions with a specified substantive content, though other kinds of agreements might be subjected to investigations and corrective orders under the Monopolies Act if they cover more than one-third of the supply or processing of a category of goods.

[3] In Germany the exemption is applicable to restrictions permissible under patent law (generously defined) but includes a prohibition of restrictions that reach beyond the scope of the patent privilege unless the cartel authority approves them. In the United Kingdom, though such agreements are exempt from the Restrictive Trade Practices Act, they remain subject to investigations and corrective orders under the Monopolies Act if they involve more than one-third of the supply or processing of a category of goods.

[4] This is true in the United Kingdom if the patent results in various unreasonable burdens upon others; in France, the Netherlands, Denmark, Sweden, and Norway if the patent is kept unreasonably out of use; and in Germany under certain narrowly defined conditions.

Allocation of territories—Ireland, Spain, New Zealand
Allocation of types of goods—Spain
Restriction of the number of persons with whom to deal—Japan, New
   Zealand
Restriction of the type of persons with whom to deal—Ireland, Israel,
   New Zealand, South Africa, the United Kingdom

Some of the listed restrictions are subject to special statutory standards. Austria, France, and Norway apply special prohibitions to restrictions that limit the number, status, or qualifications of traders. Switzerland applies special prohibitions to boycotts.

Restrictive agreements of the types that are here under discussion may be exempted under the general provisions for exemption contained in the various national laws. In addition, several countries provide for special kinds of exemption applicable to restrictions of particular relevant types. These provisions are summarized below:

Restrictions upon capacity
   In case of lasting shrinkage of demand—Germany
   In case of depression—Japan

Restrictions upon amounts produced or sold
   In case of depression—Japan
   In case of excess capacity or shrinkage of demand—Spain

Restrictions upon productive methods
   For purposes of rationalization—Japan

Allocations of types of goods to be supplied
   For purposes of rationalization—Germany

Joint sale or purchase
   For purposes of rationalization—Germany

Limitation of the variety of goods
   For purposes of rationalization—Japan

Standardization of goods—Germany, United Kingdom

In spite of the various exemptions, non-exempt agreements of the kinds mentioned have been common. Those that involved exclusion from business, refusal to deal, or discrimination have aroused concern and have been important subjects of public policy. Those that could be regarded favorably as means to efficiency and progress have been approved, but sometimes modified to safeguard their beneficial effects. For the most part, the other restrictions have been ignored by the authorities; and when considered they often have been treated cursorily, while attention was focused chiefly upon other restrictions with which they were associated. The few cases in which they have been discussed contain only fragmentary developments of relevant policy.

The eight classes of agreement listed at the beginning of this chapter will be discussed in three chapters—this one and two later ones concerned respectively with rationalization and with exclusions and discriminations. Exchange of cost information and exchange of patents or of unpatented technology, so far as they have been involved in proceedings at all, have been considered in a context of rationalization and will be discussed in that context. Because of the same focus in public policies toward standardization, allocation of types of goods, and joint production or sale or purchase, these restrictions will also be discussed in the chapter on rationalization. That chapter will also cover the less common instances in which rationalization has been regarded as the central issue in considering quotas of sale or purchase, allocation of territory, limitation of capacity or supply, and limitation of productive methods.

A few of the issues that have arisen about restriction of the number, status, and qualifications of traders will also be examined in discussing rationalization; and the others, because they are common to restrictions applied by agreement and restrictions imposed by dominant firms, will be examined in a separate chapter concerned with exclusion and discrimination by restrictions originating in either way.

The other kinds of restriction will be the subject of this chapter so far as it appears from the available records that there have been significant applications of law and that the policy applied has involved other matters than rationalization. Since no available records indicate that action has been taken about restrictions that limit the character, variety, proportion, or quality of goods, these will not be discussed. The remaining relevant kinds of restriction are limitation of capacity or supply; limitation of methods of production; fixation of quotas of sale or purchase; and allocation of territories, customers, orders, or bids.

Restriction of Capacity. Cases involving restriction of capacity have been extremely rare. Restrictions of this kind appear to be relatively infrequent; and in most countries they have left no public record except in a context of rationalization. In an Austrian case the deciding authority said that cartel provisions by which increase of excess capacity is prevented serve the consumer's interest; in another it regarded agreement to rebuild war-damaged plants as an unwise enhancement of competition that lay beyond its reach under the statute; and in a third it thought that elimination of high-cost producers probably would reduce prices but that consumers should not be protected by means excessively damaging to employees.

During the first four years of the German law, no agreement involving reduction of capacity was approved under the provision that permits such restrictions to meet a long-run decline in demand. Instead, a quota agreement among producers of shoe accessories was disapproved because it contained no such provision. No record of a relevant proceeding in any of the other countries is available to me.

Restriction of Operation. Cases involving restriction of the amount produced or sold have been similarly infrequent. In Japan the Fair Trade Commission reported in 1957 its belief that eight cartels were limiting production, but in 1962 had not yet undertaken a proceeding against any of them. Its failure to act was probably related to the fact that similar restrictions of output were repeatedly given effect for various commodities under recommendations addressed to each producer by the Japanese Ministry of International Trade and Industry. During a recession in 1957-58, the Commission also repeatedly authorized restrictive agreements under the statutory provision about depressions. By the close of 1963 it had granted a total of eight exemptions of this kind; but none was still in effect.

A case in Denmark and a case in South Africa are the only ones of which records are available to me in which agreements to restrict output were treated as contrary to public policy. In a South African report on builders' supplies, programs of restriction of output were condemned; and corrections were subsequently negotiated. In the Danish case eight producers of canned and frozen peas, who together provided about 75 percent of the total supply, had agreed to refrain from selling one-third of their stock and to plant no more than 70 percent of the average acreage they had cultivated during the previous three years. They hoped to sell their surplus stock later after using a sales campaign to increase demand. Believing that the program would reduce competitive incentives to balance production with demand, that the sales campaign was likely to increase costs without balancing the market, and that a long-run increase of prices was a probable result, the Danish authority instituted negotiations that led to termination of the agreement.

Allocations and Quotas. Proceedings concerned with quotas and allocations have been more numerous; particularly in France, where the majority of cartel cases have involved such restrictions. The French authorities have regarded quotas as objectionable on two grounds, first that they tend to maintain prices by preserving high-cost competitors, and second, that payments to firms that do not sell their full quotas by firms that exceed their quotas are likely to have cost-raising effects that are reflected in prices. Believing that quotas are often associated with rationalization, the French government has permitted quota cartels in spite of these objections, but has insisted that quota schemes be revised to provide flexibility, enable low-cost producers to attain greater market shares, limit the size of compensatory payments, and eliminate payments for closed establishments.

Though few Dutch cases have involved allocations, they have made Dutch policy clear. In considering an agreement by which producers of sauerkraut had fixed total production and allocated shares of it, the government said that such an agreement could be accepted if total supply was not less than the demand reasonably to be expected and if each producer had opportunity to increase his share of the market. These requirements had not been met; and the participants chose to terminate the agreement rather than attempt to meet them. In considering an arrangement by which owners of space in an isolated shopping center had undertaken in long-term contracts not to engage in competing lines of business, the government held that, though such restrictions might be acceptable to cope with the initial risk of a new location, their continuance was an unreasonable impediment to the adjustment of distribution to the changing needs of the community. Hence the agreement was annulled. In considering an agreement by which consumers of milk were allocated to the nearest dairy and quotas of sale were established, with provision for compensatory payments, the government objected to the removal of competitive protection of the consumer as to price and quality, and also objected to the scheme's impairment of incentives to increase sales, keep prices low, and provide good service. In the belief that the scheme had important potential value for rationalization, it attempted to minimize these defects by requiring that a limited number of suppliers must remain available to each consumer and that the provisions for compensatory payments among participants must be modified to preserve incentives.

Austrian policy toward quotas and allocations has been permissive. Whether or not quota cartels are capable of raising prices has been regarded as an open question. In one case such a result was found to be impossible. In another the deciding authority held that quotas reduced prices by enabling producers to make more of their sales near their plants. Until 1958 the opinion of the authority was that the division of quotas among participants concerned only the parties and therefore was not ground for disapproval if participants were satisfied. Amendments of the law that took effect in that year included a provision, however, that treated quotas as matters important for public policy.

In the United Kingdom, reports by the Monopolies Commission have treated domestic quotas and allocations as objectionable in every report but one in which they were discussed. In a report about the production of insulin, however, approving a cooperative arrangement to buy ox-glands abroad, the Commission regarded allocation of the purchases among the participants as an appropriate corollary. In a report on matches, the Commission noted that foreign markets were allocated between the dominant British producer and the foreign producer that controlled the British one; but seeing no probability that British exports would be larger without the allocation, it did not think that the public interest was damaged thereby.

In Ireland, though quotas and allocations have not been involved in formal reports and Ministerial orders, thirteen of the first twenty-one sets of fair trading rules promulgated by the Fair Trade Commission—all that included any reference to allocation—contained rules against allocation of territories. Under the South African law only one of the first five reports had any relation to allocation and in it agreements that included such schemes for cast iron pipe and salt-glazed pipe were condemned.

In Denmark and Sweden, the only available cases indicate greater leniency. In the Danish case, the two producers of steel conduit for electric wiring allocated customer groups, and the one of them to which a wholesaler's association was allotted agreed with the association upon quotas for its members. The latter agreement was cancelled as a result of objections by the Danish authority, but the former remained in effect.

In three Swedish cases of which I have record, quota systems or allocations of territory were at issue. Informal corrective action was obtained by the authorities in two, respectively concerned with soda manufacture and the importation of Dutch flower bulbs. No harmful effect was found in the third, concerned with allocation of territory by beverage manufacturers; for the authority thought that prices were not affected and transportation costs were reduced.

In summary, policy toward quotas and allocations has ranged, in the relatively few actions that have dealt with such restrictions, from consistent opposition in Ireland to consistent permission in Austria. The authorities have condemned such arrangements in the United Kingdom, with few exceptions, and in France, with many. Isolated instances of similar condemnation have appeared in South Africa, Denmark, and Sweden; isolated instances of permission in Denmark, Sweden, and the Netherlands. In the Netherlands quota schemes must provide for enough supply to meet estimated demand. Both in the Netherlands and in France, any form of allocation is objectionable unless it allows opportunity for individual suppliers to qualify for larger shares of the market and retains some incentive for them to try to do so.

In general, the ground upon which the more permissive countries tolerate allocation is belief that it may contribute to greater efficiency and to reductions of cost. This is true not only in countries such as France, where the belief is part of a general policy that approves "rationalization," but also in isolated cases in other countries where no general formulation of policy about rationalization is apparent. The basis for belief in the beneficial effects of such restrictions will be discussed below in the chapter on rationalization.

Chapter IX

Rationalization

Most of the governments covered by this study believe that some cartels are desirable as means to enhance the efficiency and social usefulness of economic activity. In countries that prohibit restrictive agreements, the law provides that cartels having effects of this kind shall be exempt from the prohibitions otherwise applicable. In countries that evaluate cartels through discretionary decisions about their impact upon the public interest, a finding that a cartel contributes to efficiency and progress is likely to be decisive ground for approving it.

The cartels that are believed to contribute to good economic performance are of various kinds. They are identified, not by the types of restrictions that they apply, but by the economic effects that they produce. These effects are thought to include: a) reductions in the cost of doing business, achieved by better economic organization, b) improvement of technology by research and by exchange of information, c) enhancement of the quality or reliability of goods, and d) assurance of greater stability in operation. Some types of agreements are believed to contribute to such results because the restrictions that they apply are considered inherently useful. In most countries, standardization agreements, agreements to exchange information about technology and methods of production, and agreements to engage in joint research are regarded as desirable. In some countries, general approval is given also to specialization agreements (that is, agreements to allocate types of product that will be produced) and to agreements designed to require that members of a trade possess qualifications of skill and experience that are considered reasonable. But other types of agreements also are thought to have, in some instances, good effects. Under particular circumstances they may include agreements to allocate customers or trading areas; to accept quotas of sale or production; to buy, sell, or produce jointly; to limit or reduce productive capacity; and to fix prices. Whatever the type of agreement, it may be authorized if it is thought to have desirable economic consequences.

Belief in the constructive possibilities of cartelization has been fostered in Europe by the fact that existing economic organization could not be viewed as a self-adjusting competitive economy. Remnants of medieval regulation of trade, nationalistic restrictions against foreigners, controls

125

incident to the rise of welfare states, and private cartelization constituted pervasive obstacles to competition. Public and private obstacles were interlaced. To cope with particular defects in economic performance by rational programs of control has seemed easier than to do so by competition.

Belief that cartels may improve economic performance has also been fostered in Europe by widespread acceptance of the socialist critique of capitalism. European socialists have not accepted the prevalent American opinion that competition results in efficiency. Instead, they have thought that competition encourages impairment of the quality of goods, payment of pittance wages, wasteful and uncoordinated duplication of effort, and instabilities that result in recurrent waves of unemployment of men and capital equipment. Such views have been more persuasive in Europe than in the United States; for whereas the American industrial revolution appeared in a relatively fluid environment, the industrial revolution in Europe was accompanied by the many stresses incident to the crumbling of inherited handicraft skills and institutions and of the relatively stable economies of local markets. Disliking many aspects of economic change and attributing important parts of them to competition, European socialists saw little reason to prefer competitive capitalism to monopoly capitalism; and non-socialists, accepting socialist views about the impact of competition, were encouraged to regard cartels in the way that their ancestors had regarded guilds, as potentially useful means of attack upon economic disorder.

Postwar efforts at comprehensive economic planning by Western European governments have reinforced the willingness of these governments to approve cartels as means of rationalization. Central plans must be executed in large part by private enterprises; consistency with these plans constitutes a standard by which private business activities can be appraised; and if the programs of private associations can be made consistent with the plans, control is much easier than if the role of each enterprise must be separately considered. Rationalization cartels may plausibly be regarded as aids in public planning.

The Meaning of Rationalization

No clear and generally agreed terminology has evolved for use in making favorable appraisals of cartel restrictions. The term *rationalization,* current in Europe before legislative efforts to curb cartels became common, was used in the 1920's in various senses, ranging from avoidance of waste and enhancement of productivity to maintenance of prices and enhancement of profits by monopolistic methods.[1] When applied after the second World

---

[1] See Franz Segelmann, "Zum Begriff, 'Rationalisierung Wirtschaftlicher Vorgänge,' in ¶ 5, Abs. 2 GWB," 14 *Wirtschaft und Wettbewerb* 3 at 3-4.

War to the control of cartels, it had no precise content. The monopolistic connotations of the terms as employed in the 1920's were discarded, and the meaning was limited to types of economic performance that were thought to benefit the community. But the term might cover all contributions to good economic performance or only a part of such contributions. It has been used differently in different countries. In the German law, rationalization is a broad concept, and specialization is a particular way of achieving rationalization. The French law refers to rationalization *and* specialization, as though these were alternative ways of contributing to a general result defined as economic progress. Similar diversities of concept are evident in decisions in other countries. For simplicity's sake, the following discussion will treat rationalization as a generic term, applicable to all restrictive arrangements to which a contribution to good economic performance is attributed. Particular kinds of rationalization will be distinguished by appropriate descriptive terminology, such as standardization, joint sale, or specialization.

Thus used, rationalization is a term of appraisal rather than description. It expresses a conclusion that a cartel is desirable on economic grounds. Diversity in willingness to see rationalization in particular cartel activities is therefore as great as difference of opinion about the effects of cartel restrictions upon economic performance. The discretion of those who apply exemptions based upon rationalization is correspondingly large. Their task includes determination of the probable consequences of a restrictive arrangement, appraisal of each of the various anticipated results in the light of standards derived either from a statute or from their interpretation of the public interest, and balance of good consequences against bad. The practical significance of a policy that authorizes "rationalization cartels" depends upon the nature of the forecasts, the standards of evaluation used, and the attitudes of those who use them.

The Legal Status of Rationalization

In most countries no explicit statutory standards are applied to rationalization cartels. Instead, such cartels, like others, are subject to provisions that apply to agreements standards such as harmful effect, abuse of power, unreasonableness of prices or costs, unfairness, or the public interest.[2] Under such laws, rationalization cartels escape repressive action because they are thought to lack the effects on prices, costs, productivity, the interest of competitors or consumers, or the public interest which the statute is intended to curb.

Where rationalization cartels are subject to no special provisions of

---

[2] This is true in eleven countries—Austria, Belgium, Denmark, Ireland, Israel, the Netherlands, New Zealand, Norway, South Africa, Sweden, Switzerland.

law, cases sometimes arise in which restrictive agreements are deemed reasonable or consistent with the public interest primarily because they are thought to contribute to good economic performance. These cases appear to be less frequent in the countries that do not specifically exempt rationalization cartels than in those that do; but when they arise, the situations and appraisals they present do not often differ from those in the countries where such cartels are exempted. This chapter will be concerned primarily with the countries in which rationalization cartels are given a special legal status, but will note occasional instances in which cases in other countries constitute unusually clear examples of rationalization policy.

Standards for evaluating reationalization cartels are set forth in broad statutory language in the laws of five countries.[3] Under Spanish law a tribunal for the protection of competition is empowered, after hearing interested parties, to approve restrictive agreements if they improve the supply or distribution of goods or services or foster technical or economic progress and contain only restrictions essential to the result, provided a substantial part of the benefit goes to the consumer. This provision is so recent that experience of its use is not available.[4]

Under French law, the statutory prohibition of cartels does not apply to restrictive agreements if the participants can prove that the effect of these agreements is "to improve and extend the market for their products or to ensure further economic progress by means of rationalization and specialization." This language has been interpreted to cover all good aspects of cartels, and no effort has been made to assign the burden of proof to the cartel. Similarly, the law's general prohibition of cartels that may interfere with competition by hindering the reduction of costs or prices or encouraging the artificial increase of prices has been interpreted merely as a mandate to consider all bad aspects of cartels. Instead of applying the prohibition except where a claim of exemption is made and proved, the French authorities have interpreted the statute as though it merely directed them to use discretionary power to decide what cartels are contrary to the public interest. Whether or not a claim of exemption had been made, and whether or not proof had been offered in support of the claim, they have appraised the advantages and disadvantages of each cartel that came under their consideration, but have emphasized matters they thought relevant to rationalization. When no clear conclusion seemed to emerge, they have granted probationary periods during which the effect of a cartel could be made clear. In some cases in which the evidence indicated no ground for exemption,

---

    3 France, Germany, Japan, the United Kingdom, and Spain.
    4 Law Against Restrictions of Competition, Article 5 (1). See Boletin Official del Estado, No. 175, of July 23, 1963, pp. 11148 ff.

they have refrained from prohibiting the cartel, and instead have granted a period of time during which the cartel might qualify for exemption by instituting types of rationalization which they recommended. In a few instances, finding that the cartel was already exempt, they nevertheless have indicated that additional measures of rationalization were necessary if the exemption was to continue. In effect, they have interpreted their task as one of promoting rationalization rather than preventing restriction, and have used the prohibition in the law as a means of pressure upon French business to that end.

Because of this peculiarity of the application of the French law, policy toward rationalization is more important in France than elsewhere. In both Germany and the United Kingdom, rationalization constitutes only one of several bases for exemption; claims of rationalization are examined in relatively few cases; and only a part of policy toward cartels is at stake when policy toward rationalization is determined. In France, however, rationalization has come to include all grounds for leniency toward cartels, and the question of leniency is considered in every cartel proceeding.

Under German law, rationalization is one of several grounds for exempting a cartel from the law's prohibitions. Different types of rationalization cartels can obtain exemption by different procedures and under different standards of evaluation. The differentiation apparently reflects the varying degrees of promise and danger that the Bundestag saw in particular kinds of restriction. Agreements that establish specifications of services or breakdowns of prices to be used in some kinds of bidding,[5] but do not fix prices or elements of prices, are automatically exempt, though they must be filed with the Cartel Authority. Agreements that are concerned exclusively with "uniform application of standards and types"—that is, with standardization or simplification of goods—are legally valid if they are reported and if the comments of a rationalization body are attached.[6] Other types of rationalization cartels fall into three groups: (a) rationalization cartels in general, which must be approved by the Cartel Authority if, by restrictions reasonable in relation to the effect, they are "apt to raise substantially the efficiency or productivity of participating enterprises from a technical, economic, or organizational point of view, and to improve thereby the satisfaction of demand"; (b) specialization cartels, which are valid unless disapproved in three months because the parties have not shown that their

---

[5] These involve bidding for goods or services that "can be made only on the basis of descriptions which do not lend themselves to a qualitative examination at the time the contract is awarded." See Act against Restraints of Competition of 27 July 1957, Section 5 (4).

[6] In 1965 amendment of the law deprived the Cartel Authority of power to disapprove such agreements.

purpose was rationalization and that market competition is not "excluded";[7] and (c) cartels involving joint purchase or sale or price fixing, which the Cartel Authority has discretion to approve if the same effects on efficiency or productivity are probable, if the rationalization is in the public interest, if the restraints are reasonable in relation to the effect, and if the purpose cannot be achieved by other means. These standards express a presumption that standardization and simplification are desirable, that various other kinds of rationalization are desirable if their restrictions are functionally appropriate, that specialization agreements are desirable but only if there is residual competition, and that joint purchase, joint sale, and price fixing are too dangerous to be accepted unless their results are clearly useful to the public and are not otherwise attainable.

Under Japanese law special provisions apply to concerted activity in limiting technology, kinds of products, and the use or purchase of by-products when such activity is particularly necessary to promote technology, improve quality, reduce costs, increase efficiency, or otherwise rationalize enterprise. Such concerted action may be approved if it does not involve unfair practices, is not unduly discriminatory, gives reasonable opportunity for enterprises to participate and withdraw, does not unduly hurt the interests of consumers or non-participating enterprises, and (if the arrangement includes specialization) does not unduly concentrate the production of the products affected. Cartels approved in accord with these provisions existed in 1959 for 14 types of products. There were, however, other possibilities for lawful rationalization; for provisions concerned with rationalization are included in some of the laws by which substantial segments of the Japanese economy have been exempted from the cartel law. The clearest case appears in temporary legislation applicable to industries producing machinery: The statutes direct a Minister to prepare rationalization plans as to capacity, new facilities, disposal of obsolete facilities, and improvement of technology and efficiency. They authorize him, so far as necessary for rationalization, to instruct producers of machinery to act together in buying parts or raw materials, restricting technology, limiting kinds of machines, and (where limitation of kind is difficult) limiting the number of machines made or the types of equipment used in making machines.

Unlike the other countries that apply special rules to rationalization cartels, Japan has not done so to make exception to a generally accepted policy that is more severe. The drastic anti-cartel policy applied in the law that was enacted during the post-war military occupation of Japan has

---

[7] Prior to amendment of this law in 1965, such agreements were subject to approval, and a probable effect of substantial increase of efficiency or productivity was to be shown.

been twice relaxed by amendment of the statute, and additional weakening amendments have been strongly advocated by the government and by much of the business community. Further relaxation has been provided by a large number of special laws exempting various segments of Japanese industry for reasons that often express a basic purpose to curb competition as dangerous or undesirable. The anticartel provisions that remain legally applicable have not been often enforced. Japanese willingness to approve rationalization cartels is one manifestation of vacillation and enduring controversy as to the proper goals of Japanese public policy. For this reason, Japanese experience with rationalization offers little that is applicable to countries in which the purposes of the law are more solidly established.

Under British law, rationalization is exempted indirectly. No standard of efficiency or productivity is directly set forth, but provision is made that a restrictive agreement may be permitted if it produces certain specified desirable results. One of the results specified is benefit to consumers. Parties to an agreement may show that, in the absence of the agreement, users of the goods would be deprived of specific and substantial benefits resulting from the restriction. Benefits to users that are claimed by parties to agreements often include improvements of the quality or reliability of goods or reductions of prices based upon reductions of cost or of risk. Thus they cover much of what might be called rationalization in Germany or France. In British procedure, the burden of proof is upon parties to the agreement, and if they fail to prove that the agreement produces one or more of the specified desirable results, the agreement is unlawful. If a relevant desirable result is proved, the British court must then weigh the importance of the benefit against the detrimental effects of restriction, and, if it considers the benefit sufficiently important, may permit the agreement to continue.

The character of policy under which rationalization cartels enjoy a special status can be best understood by examining the policies of England, Germany, and France, countries in which rationalization has played a significant part in government action, and in which, unlike Japan, the general direction of cartel policy is not beclouded.

Procedures in Considering Claims of Rationalization

As a result of differences in standards, in procedure, and in underlying attitudes, the different methods of exempting rationalization cartels employed in England, Germany, and France have produced substantially different results in spite of similarity in the concepts of rationalization that are applied. In England, legal pleading results in precise formulation of the claims about rationalization; use of adversary proceedings before judges subjects both evidence and lines of reasoning to close scrutiny; the necessity of the restriction as a means to achieve the beneficial result must be made clear; public hearings and public judicial opinions expose evidence and decisions to public criticism; and since cartels have the burden of proof, the agreement is condemned if what is submitted is inconclusive. With benefit from rationalization clearly defined as benefit to users of goods and with judicial procedures used to test the claims of benefit, most such claims have been rejected. Moreover, when a benefit is proved the court must still decide whether or not it is worth its cost in restriction. Approval of rationalization cartels is thus surrounded by safeguards. However, approval is not accompanied by reporting requirements or other provisions for recurrently determining whether or not the beneficial effects continue to be visible. The furthest the British court has gone in this direction is to state in certain cases that any substantial alteration of the prices of cartelized products will be regarded as a change in circumstances sufficient to justify an application to the court to reconsider the decision.

Under British procedure, assertions that restrictions benefit consumers have been rejected far more often than they have been accepted. Such benefit was alleged in 24 of the 27 cartel cases that had been decided by the end of July 1963. In only six of these cases did the evidence show to the court's satisfaction that there was a clear, direct, and significant benefit. Apart from one case, in which the approved restriction consisted of a specification of minimum quality, these cases all involved price fixing, which was approved either because beneficial consequences were believed to result from it or because it was regarded as a necessary corollary to other beneficial activities, such as exchange of technical information.

In Germany, the control is less severe. The law does not place the burden of proof clearly on the cartel. It does not clearly require that improvements in efficiency or productivity must be shown to benefit consumers. That the restriction is indispensable to the beneficial effect must be determined only in the case of certain severe types of restriction, whereas for other types only the reasonableness of the restriction in relation to the effect need be found. Similarly, an evaluation of the benefit against the harmful effect of the restriction in the light of the public interest is required only for the more severe kinds of restriction, whereas for others only the existence of residual competition need be found, and for still others the desirability of the result is presumed by the statute. However, issues are clearly formulated in public hearings and decided in published decisions; and in practice the cartel authority has insisted that where rationalization is claimed there must be proof that the restrictions that it is supposed to justify are clearly and directly relevant to it. Few German claims of rationalization have been rejected. However, approval usually has been conditioned upon requirements that periodic reports be filed by the cartel showing measures of rationalization and their effects, as well as prices, realizations, and profits. Through these reports the Cartel Authority seeks to obtain assurance of the continued reality of an alleged rationalization and to ascertain whether or not the consumer continues to obtain benefits from it.

Most of the rationalization agreements considered under German law have established joint sales agencies that involved sale at agreed prices and discounts. In rare instances, price fixing has accompanied a different kind of rationalization. During the first four years of the law, until the close of 1961, decisions were made about 20 rationalization cartels that undertook joint sale or purchase or price fixing. Of these, 16 were approved and 4 disapproved. Only three other rationalization cartels were approved, of which two were agreements for standardization.

Decisions under French law have been devoid of procedural safeguards. The evidence underlying decisions is not publicly disclosed, nor do proponents and opponents of a cartel confront each other. The Cartel Commission which, though formally defined as advisory, has a decisive role, acts in camera; and its recommendations to the Minister of Economic Affairs are too brief to set forth either its reasoning or the evidence upon which it relied. For a year or more after the decision, a recommendation and the Minister's subsequent action are confidential from all but members of the cartel. Then recommendations and decisions are released to the public in batches, along with a brief summary report by the Commission. The scale of the eventual disclosure is indicated by the latest such release. In February 1964, thirty-two pages of the French official journal contained a summary report for the years 1960, 1961, and 1962, plus Commission reports and Ministerial decisions in the 17 cases decided during those three years. From documentation so scanty, an observer can discover what types of restriction have been regarded as means of rationalization, but usually cannot ascertain the nature of the evidence nor the reasoning that supported the decision.

Though the brief reports of French cases do not set forth clearly all the restrictions relevant to each case, they make clear that quota schemes have been the most significant and frequent forms of restriction and that decisions have centered upon the question whether such schemes have promoted specialization, concentration, standardization, investment, and the penetration of foreign markets.

What has been published indicates that the connection between restriction and beneficial result is conceived and tested more loosely in France than in Germany or the United Kingdom. In some cases, claims of rationalization were rejected because the restrictions that were under examination were unconnected with the improvements that were alleged to justify them. In other cases, similar claims were deemed to be exaggerated because the improvements were partially due to environmental factors. However, where restrictions were held to have fostered rationalization, the connection was not necessarily direct and clear. It sometimes consisted in creation of an atmosphere of mutual confidence in which rationalization was more likely to be undertaken, or in provision of economic security that might increase the willingness to rationalize. In one case "a certain stability of domestic markets" was deemed to facilitate collective export activities and the adoption of new technology. In another, quotas were said to have reduced producers' fears of the risks of specialization and thus to have "promoted, without being the basis of" arrangements favorable to economic progress.

Accepting such loose relationships, French decisions have treated rationalization as ground for restriction without consistent effort to eliminate the irrelevant restrictions. Instead of disentangling a cartel's restrictive activities and rejecting those that are unconnected with rationalization, or that, though connected, are not necessary to it, some decisions have evaluated a cartel as a whole and approved it if adequate rationalization was found.

Moreover, conclusions about whether or not rationalization was achieved appear to have rested in France upon preconceptions that standardization, specialization, and concentration are generally desirable, without test of the validity of these preconceptions in the circumstances of the particular case. The Commission seems to have assumed that further specialization and concentration are desirable whether productive units in an industry are large or small. Regardless of the structure of the industry before it, it apparently approved all developments in such directions and consistently urged further action along similar lines. However, in most cases its decisions in favor of a cartel have included provisions by which the situation is to be reexamined after an interval of a few years.

The peculiarities of the French decisions appear to be diminishing. The latest report by the French Commission, issued in February 1964, covers 17 cases decided in the years 1960-62. Decisions as to rationalization in these cases were less permissive than in the 20 cases previously reported: Termination of restrictions was recommended more often, and loose connections between restriction and rationalization were given less weight. The summary report that accompanied the reports of the cases contains what amounts to a statement of policy in the form of a summary of bad and good aspects of cartelization that were noted in decisions during the period. Though this statement still expresses the belief that a quota system may be the only way to assure enterprises the short-run security and stability of markets that will remove their hesitation to make important investments or to take risks in export markets, the Commission indicates that it regards such considerations as irrelevant where fixed capital is not important and technical necessities are not compelling.[8] The beneficial features of cartels noted during the three year period are listed as: a) results in developing production and increasing exports, or harmonious growth of a new industry; b) progress in productivity, whether achieved by shutting down certain productive units and concentrating enterprises, by reducing transportation costs and rationalizing distribution, by reducing general costs such as those for invoicing, by staggering orders so as to reduce the costs of seasonal fluctuation, or by other reductions of costs and prices; c) efforts, though limited, to specialize; d) development of services for research, information, and advertising; and e) strict control of the quality of products. But the Commission remarks that it has refused to regard cartels as justified when the good results are due to conditions foreign to the cartel or could have been achieved without restrictive practices, and when benefits, particularly as to price, have not reached consumers or the general economy.[9]

If one may assume that French decisions henceforward will express the views thus summarized, the policies of France, Germany, and the United Kingdom toward rationalization will show considerable similarity. Clear and direct connection between restriction and the beneficial result will be required except in the case of certain French industries in which, because of heavy fixed capital or other special features, restriction need only provide the stability and confidence that make rationalization possible. Restrictions will be accepted only so far as they are indispensable to rationalization except in Germany, where restrictions other than joint sale or purchase or price fixing need not be indispensable but only reasonably relevant. Benefit will have to be shown to the consumer in England, and to the consumer or the public interest in France, whereas in Germany similar public benefits will need to be shown only for schemes that include joint sale, joint purchase, or price fixing. Advantages and disadvantages will be balanced in the light of the public interest in England, and in German schemes for joint purchase or joint sale or price fixing, but not for lesser German restrictions nor consistently in France. Burdens of proof will rest clearly upon the cartel in England, nominally but not actually so in France, and actually but not nominally so in Germany. Subsequent review to make certain that the justification for the cartel still exists will be a matter of routine in Germany, a common recurrent practice in France, and non-existent in England. The

---

[8] Commission Technique des Ententes, Rapport au Ministre Chargé des Affaires Economiques pour les Années 1960, 1961, et 1962, Journaux Officiels. Paris, 1964 (hereafter called Commission's 1964 Report), p. 5.

[9] *Ibid*, p. 6.

weaknesses of the German policy will lie in the standards built into the law; those of the British policy in the lack of provision for periodic review of the effects of decisions; those of the French policy in continued receptiveness to certain loose claims of need for security or confidence, in preconceptions about the universal usefulness of specialization and concentration, and in procedures which expose the claims that restrictions are necessary for beneficial results neither to rigorous requirements of proof nor to vigorous public criticism.

Types of Rationalization

The cases in which governments have attributed rationalization to cartels have shown wide variety, partly due to peculiarities of national law and policy, and partly due to peculiarities in types of restriction and in environmental conditions in different countries. These cases may be analyzed, however, in an effort to ascertain from them the conditions under which restrictive agreements are believed to contribute to good economic performance, the kinds of restriction that are expected to have this beneficial result, and the way in which the result is believed to come about. What follows is an attempt at such an analysis. For clarity, comparisons with American attitudes are introduced.

The clearest and most persuasive cases are those in which reductions in cost are said to be derived from restrictive agreements. The cost reductions are attributed to such means as eliminating duplicate activities or duplicate facilities, reducing the distance to which goods are transported, shortening periods during which equipment is partly idle, attaining a more economical scale of operation, eliminating high-cost transactions or high-cost commodities, eliminating incompetent producers, and adapting investments more closely to demand.

Avoiding Duplication. Avoidance of duplication is one way to reduce costs. In distributive trades in which the delivery routes of different sellers pass along the same streets or otherwise overlap, costs can be reduced by eliminating duplicated deliveries. One way of doing this is allocation of customers. A striking instance of the possibility appeared in the milk trade in the Netherlands. Retailers sought to rationalize deliveries of milk by allocating customers to the nearest supplier, establishing quotas, and compensating sellers who surrendered business to their competitors. Where the plan was adopted, costs were reduced by 20 per cent or more. Fearing that incentive to maintain quality and keep prices reasonable would be unduly impaired, the government required that the arrangement be modified so that every consumer could have access to at least three retailers and so that the payments for transfer of business would not destroy the incentive to increase sales. The modified plan was adopted by retailers in about 200 Dutch towns, and has been repeatedly mentioned by Dutch officials as an example of useful cartelization.

That true economies are sometimes attainable by allocation of customers is evident. As in the Netherlands, it would often be possible in such instances to attain most of them and yet to preserve some competition for business by making more than one source of supply available to buyers. As in the Netherlands, however, such a program would necessitate governmental control over the character of the allocation program and governmental surveillance over the operation of it. The price of more economical distribution would be an increase of regulation, and the degree both of economy and of protection for the consumer would depend upon the skill with which these two goals were sought by the regulators.

Avoidance of duplication is sometimes sought by restrictions upon the number of distributors who will be admitted to a trade. Most restrictions of this kind are applied by individual sellers in relation to their own distributors, and therefore take the form either of vertical contracts or of restrictive policies in selecting customers. When they appear in this guise, governments sometimes are more concerned to prevent inequitable refusal to sell than to foster rationalization. Nevertheless, most governments, though anxious to assure the opportunity of distributors to buy, permit restricted distribution where it is thought to promote rationalization: France, for example, interprets its law against refusal to sell so that it does not prohibit exclusive dealing arrangements that are precise, reciprocal, and applicable throughout the seller's entire market. Under Irish fair trading rules, limitation of the number of agencies for the sale of footwear is authorized on the ground that more outlets would increase costs without increasing sales.

There are also instances in which horizontal agreements are used to limit the number of distributors. The most common appear to be collective agreements by which minimum volumes of sale are established as conditions of eligibility for receipt of wholesale or retail discounts. In Norway, such a restriction was applicable to wholesale discounts for insulated cable and lead conduit, and decisions in applying the restriction were entrusted to a committee containing a majority of wholesalers. When a wholesaler in North Norway protested against a decision by which he was denied a discount, the Norwegian Price Council sustained the restriction on the ground that if discounts were given for smaller volumes there would be too many wholesalers, smaller deliveries, and higher costs.

Rationalization agreements of this kind are approved in a setting in which governments set limits upon individual as well as collective refusals to sell. European prevention of discriminatory refusal to sell is like American prevention of price discrimination in that it requires government to undertake much more control of the marketing process than would be necessary to keep markets currently competitive. A policy that imposes general obligations to sell must be evaluated in the light of its effect upon the number of distributive outlets, and can properly be limited by a purpose to prevent that number from becoming excessive. Suitable limitation of the number of distributors can then be sought either by authorizing individual enterprises to refuse to sell under given circumstances or by permitting agreements involving similar refusals.

Where producers are permitted to determine the nature and number of their distributors, an uneconomic proliferation of distributors is less likely than it is where the government imposes an obligation to sell. Individual suppliers usually will try to avoid duplication that raise costs. Nevertheless, in fields such as the retail distribution of gasoline in certain localities, competition sometimes takes the form of multiplication of distributive outlets in a struggle for volume. Under these conditions, agreement to reduce the number of outlets could reduce the expense of distribution. But collective private action to deny certain distributors the opportunity to stay in business would be intolerable unless standards of equal treatment and fair dealing were enforced by the state. Moreover, the state would need to make sure that economy was not carried so far as to impose undue inconvenience upon buyers. Thus such programs, like those for allocation of customers, necessitate regulation of the scope and character of the restriction and surveillance of its execution. To most Americans, an uneconomic proliferation of distributive outlets is a symptom of insufficient price competition; and the appropriate remedy is not additional restriction under enhanced governmental supervision, but elimination of price-maintaining arrangements and encouragement of vigorous price competition that leaves no room for wasteful duplication of outlets.

Assuring Competence.   Restrictions designed to assure the competence of business enterprises are approved in some countries. Where this is done, these restrictions are carefully distinguished from other restrictions that are thought to impose unreasonable limitations upon access to a field of business activity. The point of view has been thus expressed by an official of the Dutch Ministry of Economic Affairs:

"Such agreements have never been accepted if they aimed at establishing a closed shop or at eliminating undesirable forms of enterprise (e.g. multiple shop companies, cooperative stores). On the other hand, certain standards of commercial knowledge, professional ability, solvency, stock-in-trade, equipment and administration set for entrance are deemed admissible in so far as they do not exceed what is required to guarantee a rational conduct of business."[10]

The agreements to which the quoted passage refers consist of regulations governing the admissibility of enterprises to a trade association. In the Netherlands, such regulations may control the right to do business; for vertical agreements by which an association undertakes to trade exclusively with an association of suppliers or distributors are common, and instead of forbidding such agreements the Dutch government insists that all qualified traders must be admitted to associations.

Norway's policy toward refusals to sell contains a similar tolerance for restrictions that establish standards of competence. Refusals to deal or to grant discounts, whether by groups of enterprises or by single firms, are forbidden if they are considered unreasonable; but associations as well as individuals are allowed to formulate and apply reasonable requirements as to the training, experience, facilities, and capital of those with whom they deal. In the paint industry special discounts are available to stores that possess six specified qualifications. When the industry's discount committee denied a special discount to a store on the ground that the proprietor did not have the requisite five years of experience, the Norwegian authorities sanctioned the decision, but recommended that the discount be granted after the proprietor had had "some further practice."

In Ireland, where much of the work of the Fair Trade Commission consists in making rules against restrictions upon admission to a trade, certain restrictions have been accepted as aids to rationalization. In promulgating rules for the light bulb industry that impose an obligation to supply retailers, the Commission included an exception designed to allow manufacturers to refuse orders for quantities too small for efficiency. Though the Commission frowned upon private rules for the motor vehicle trade that established minimum qualifications, it promulgated its own substitute rules. These made it an unfair practice to sell motor vehicles or replacement parts to any reseller other than a motor trader or a person engaged mainly in repairing or reconditioning motor cars. They provided that to be a motor trader a business must meet certain minimum qualifications as to premises, equipment, and workforce. Thus they reserved the retail sale of new cars and replacement parts for garages equipped to make certain types of repairs. Gasoline filling stations not attached to garages, for example, could not qualify to sell tires.

---

[10] J. F. H. Wijsen, *Developments in Cartel Legislation and Cartel Policy in the Netherlands*, mimeographed, undated, pp. 6-8. Mr. Wijsen was Director for Industrial Organization in the Ministry of Economic Affairs.

Rationalization by control of standards for admission to a trade has two peculiarities. First, competition is not regarded as sufficient to weed out the ill-trained, incompetent, or ill-equipped. In the interest of competent performance, entry into the trade is made difficult. Second, the standards of competence that govern entry, though subject to government surveillance for reasonableness in substance and methods of application and to possible changes by government order, may be privately formulated and applied. It is possible that by limiting opportunity such an arrangement reduces the number of subsequent bankruptcies and the net waste of social capital. It probably also excludes people with unusual types of experience and skill, who might be more likely to innovate than persons with the customary training.

Similar quasi-private control over access to an occupation is exercised in the United States in the case of certain professions, such as the practice of medicine or law. Such learned professions are supposedly guided by motives that are not solely or even primarily commercial. Their skills are regarded as too complex to be readily appraised by the purchasers of their services. The user of medical or legal service is thought to have such need to be well served that the gradual elimination of unfit practitioners as experience of their performance accumulates is deemed an insufficient safeguard of the user's interest. In the countries here under discussion, private control of admission appears in occupations that are commercial rather than professional, that call for simple types of competence that simple people can appraise, and that involve no comparably severe risk of loss if the buyer buys unwisely. Such private control probably is based more upon the persistence of the traditions of the craft guilds than upon analyses of relevant economic considerations.

Eliminating Other Kinds of Waste. In an occasional case, agreement to eliminate excessive sales expense or some other kind of wasteful practice is authorized as rationalization. In Austria, registration (and hence legal authorization) was granted to an agreement among six brewers by which they were forbidden to grant their customers loans, gifts, rebates, discounts from market prices, and various other forms of concession, and were to divide new business in proportion to old. Finding that the prices from which such allowances and concessions were computed were competitive market prices, the Austrian Cartel Commission had no statutory ground for disapproval;[11] but accounts of the case make clear that the agreement was thought to be a contribution to efficiency, because competition in granting

---

[11] Approval was not necessarily implied by authorization. At the time of this decision, Austrian law instructed the Cartel Commission to allow registration if certain conditions were met, and favorable decisions said that the cartel was "not disapproved."

such concessions had gone to excessive lengths. Indeed, one brewer was said to have consolidated a customer's good will, at a time when that customer was having marital difficulties, by falsely acknowledging that he was father of the customer's illegitimate child.

Doing Business Jointly. Joint activity is commonly regarded as a source of economy and is often permitted for this reason, particularly in Germany. In some instances, for example cartels among Parisian flour mills and among French producers of handle bars for bicycles, a single agency is used by cartel members to send out bills and collect accounts. In other instances, as in French superphosphate and German potash, lime, and iron barrels, members of a cartel use a joint selling agency or a joint buying agency.

The economies attributed to joint conduct of business include, but are not limited to, avoidance of duplication. In joint billing and collection, losses from bad accounts may be reduced. In joint purchase, the larger joint orders may qualify for larger discounts, may benefit from lower transportation rates, and may give bargaining power that can result in special price concessions, expedited service, or other advantages. In joint sale, directly competitive selling expenses may be avoided, collective advertising and other forms of collective promotion may enlarge aggregate sales, inventory costs may be reduced through use of a collective inventory, credit terms may be tightened without loss of sales to a competitor, delivery periods may be shortened, and transportation expenses may be reduced by use of pool cars or by making deliveries from the nearest source. Market information may be improved, and consequently production by the participants may be adapted more suitably to changes in demand. Where there are long lines of varied products, individual producers can cease to produce items that they sell rarely and have difficulty in making. If supply is irregular, the sales agency can apportion orders to fit fluctuating production schedules. If demand is irregular, the agency can guide producers in allocating their resources among different kinds of products and can allocate orders to take account of idle capacity or to maintain agreed quotas. Some of these advantages are greatest where long lines of product are sold under conditions of widely fluctuating demand or of frequently changing ability to produce. Several joint sales agencies in Germany have operated under such conditions.

Though some of the advantages of joint sale that are mentioned above supplement one another, some of them are mutually inconsistent alternatives. For example, inventory savings incident to maintenance of a central inventory cannot readily accompany savings in transportation costs incident to placement of each order with the nearest producer. Nevertheless, a cumulation of advantages often inheres in joint selling. Some of these are not true reductions of economic cost, since they involve offsetting disadvantages for others. The bargaining advantages by which joint buyers obtain a special discount, for example, may merely benefit them at the expense of their supplier and their competitors. But some true reductions of cost are evident in joint purchase and sale; and impressed by these, governments concerned with rationalization have not undertaken the formidable task of disentangling bargaining advantages from true economies. Particularly, they appear to have presumed that reductions of purchase prices are economically desirable unless the wages paid by suppliers are thereby reduced.

A limited acceptance of joint purchase and sale in the interest of economy appears in the policies of the United States. Consumers cooperatives and cooperatives of producers in fields characterized by small productive units, such as agriculture and fishing, are encouraged by special legislation. The activities of joint buying organizations are usually regarded as non-restrictive. Collaboration by members of voluntary food chains and similar organizations in some types of selling activity, such as branding and advertising, is treated as non-restrictive. However, except in the case of certain producers' cooperatives that enjoy legislative exemption from the antitrust laws, such joint activities must be voluntary, with freedom to participate or withdraw, must not involve control of the market, and must stop short of major types of restriction such as price-fixing,[12] division of the market, or agreed reduction of business activity.

Allocating Business. Savings in transportation cost similar to those that may be achieved by joint selling are sometimes attributed to allocations of territory or of the amount of business, on the ground that shipments are shorter if each seller is confined to the area contiguous to him. The Swedish Freedom of Commerce Board saw such an advantage in allocation of territory by beverage manufacturers, thought that the arrangement had no harmful effect since competitors were not injured and prices were not affected, and did not attempt to terminate it. In Austria, the sales quotas of the carbonic acid cartel were believed by the Cartel Commission to have reduced transportation costs.

---

[12] In 1963 the Federal Trade Commission issued an advisory opinion to the effect that collaborative advertising of prices is a violation of law. This action resulted in a hearing by the Small Business Committee of the House of Representatives, at which the Assistant Attorney General in charge of the Antitrust Division of the Department of Justice testified that the practice did not, in itself, violate the Sherman Act, and the Chairman of the Federal Trade Commission testified that no legal proceedings against the practice were contemplated by the Commission. In reporting the matter, the Committee called attention to the fact that the Federal Trade Commission Act instructs the Commission to act when a proceeding appears to it to be in the interest of the public. The Committee made clear its own view that such a proceeding would tend to suppress rather than to foster competition. See FTC Advisory Opinion on Joint Ads, House Report No. 699, 88th Congress, 1st Session, August 22, 1963.

Conducting Research Jointly and Exchanging Information. Improvement of techniques of production is even more prominent in European thinking about rationalization than elimination of duplicate activities. An obvious means to improvement is research, followed by diffusion of the resulting technology. Accordingly, restrictions by which such research or diffusion may be encouraged are regarded as contributions to rationalization. Agreements to conduct research jointly are not thought to be open to question. The value of agreements to exchange technical information is taken for granted. Where such arrangements exist, price-fixing is likely to be accepted as a safeguard without which the technical cooperation would not be practicable. The British Restrictive Practices Court decided that there was advantage to users of magnets in the magnet association's central research, exchange of technology, and patent pooling, and that without a minimum price agreement these activities would not continue. Similarly, the British Monopolies Commission reported favorably on the price agreement among metal window manufacturers because the agreement included exchanges of cost information that resulted in reduced costs and in reduced prices based upon the cost reductions. In the Commission's opinion, the agreement exposed the less efficient manufacturers to part of the pressure that would result from full price competition, yet gave them an "opportunity to catch up with the more efficient." Subsequently, the Trade Practices Court found that the price agreement was necessary to the exchange of cost information and of technical information, which reduced both costs and prices and thereby enabled the participants to compete more effectively with an independent large producer whose output was equal to their combined output.

Agreements to conduct research jointly are considered non-restrictive under American law if all enterprises that desire to participate can do so on equal terms, or if, though rights to participate are not available, persons excluded from one research agreement can readily join another or undertake research for themselves. Conduct of joint research necessitates little significant restriction. Participants undertake to provide facilities and personnel in agreed amounts during stated periods of time to work on agreed projects. They agree that the results of the research shall be available to all of them either equally or on terms that compensate their unequal contributions. They have no need to agree that they will abstain from independent research on other projects. They seldom need to exclude persons who desire to take part; but if such exclusion appears, public authority need intervene only where exclusion is likely to mean such lack of research opportunity as to involve probable ineffectiveness for the excluded enterprise as a competitor.

American policy does not treat a research agreement as justification

for general price fixing or other forms of restrictive commercial collaboration. American experience under this policy seems to show that such commercial restrictions are not necessary as incentives for joint research. Collaborative research is readily undertaken where it appears likely to afford
significant technological results and where research by individual enterprises appears to be less convenient.

But joint research may produce patentable inventions, and may thus
raise problems as to the relation between the antitrust laws and the patent
laws which are unlike the problems involved in the forms of rationalization
that are not concerned with rights to industrial property. Where there is a
pool of patents jointly owned by participants in a research agreement, the
pool is likely to convey power to restrict competition much greater than
would be afforded by the individual patents under diffused ownership and
competitive management. Restrictions accomplished by use of this additional
power do not enjoy immunity from the American antitrust laws as an
exercise of patent rights. Restrictive patent pooling is severely curbed by
American law, and to the extent that research agreements are based upon
desire to create and use such a restrictive pool, they are thus discouraged.
Research by individual enterprises is so common, by relatively small firms
as well as large ones, that the effect of such discouragement upon the rate of
technological progress is probably slight.

Agreements to exchange existing technology are considered non-restrictive under American law if they are open to all and are not made an excuse
for commercial restrictions. Such agreements actually exist; the conspicuous
case is a technological agreement among automobile manufacturers. In such
an agreement, it is permissible to provide for reasonable compensating payments when the technological contribution of the participants is unequal.

But technological exchange is not accepted as a justification for agreements not to compete. The latter remain subject to the American antitrust
laws, as modified by the patent laws. Under the patent laws, a patentee has
broad rights to impose commercial restrictions upon a licensee's use of the
licensed patent; but patent licenses may not be used to restrict activities
not covered by the patent, and neither patentees nor licensees may use
interrelated licenses as a cloak for prohibited horizontal agreements. Businessmen have often asserted that technological exchanges are reduced by
this limitation. In effect, they argue that comprehensive and enduring technological collaboration among competitors is prevented, and that it offers
possibilities greater than can be realized by a succession of unrelated patent
licenses. Antitrust cases that have involved such sustained collaboration
have shown clearly that the accompanying commercial restrictions were
often severely restrictive, but neither they nor other available sources of

specific information show the effect of prohibiting such restrictive arrangements upon the level of technology. However, the level of American technology has not visibly lagged in comparison with that in countries where such collaboration is permitted.

Allocating lines of product. Specialization agreements—that is, agreements among competitors to allocate types of goods—are regarded by the French Cartel Commission as obvious means to better methods of production. This relationship is apparently conceived as axiomatic; for the Commission has neither explained it nor indicated that its existence depends upon particular circumstances. The desire to foster specialization apparently rests upon the view that unspecialized producers do not achieve economies of scale. Indeed, specialization and concentration are often coupled as kindred concepts in French decisions.

This simple analysis is not persuasive. That enlargement of the scale of operations of an unspecialized producer by specialization will result in economies is obviously true if the amount of each product made by the producer is too small to permit desirable specialization of the labor force or to justify the purchase of specialized equipment that is necessary for efficiency. A worker who must shift from one kind of operation to another probably would be more efficient if he were specialized. When a labor force is too small for each man to be assigned a single task, a larger work force will permit more specialization of labor. When a routine task needs repetition often enough, a machine can do it more quickly and precisely than a man. If the scale of operations increases to the point at which more routine tasks require numerous repetitions, the degree of mechanization can be increased. If the scale increases still more, some machines that have been converted from time to time to different tasks can be used more economically because their production runs are longer and time lost in conversion is reduced. On a still larger scale of operation, convertible machines can be replaced by permanently specialized machines. At various stages in the process of growth, processes of inspection and supervision can be made more specialized; and some of them can be mechanized.

But the foregoing does not mean that under all conditions more specialization necessarily increases efficiency. The relatively simple kinds of specialization possible for men and machine tools reach their maximum with modest amounts of production, and further increases in size involves merely a duplication of the specialized units. Since possibilities of sale are limited, not only by total demand but also by distance and other difficulties of access to markets, a producer of a single type of product may be unable to grow large enough to attain the maximum possible economies of scale. His business may be too small to justify use of the most efficient power-generating equipment, or mechanization of processes of inspection, or full sub-division of supervisory tasks. Economies of scale in activities above the level of immediate productive activity may be attainable only if several different products are made by the same establishment. Though the smallest establishments may become more efficient if they become more specialized, this result decreases in probability with increase in the size of the establishment. Above levels of size that differ from industry to industry, the probabilities are that operating economies have been fully achieved and that any unrealized managerial or organizational economies can be attained most readily by kinds of diversification that do not destroy functional coherence.[13]

Moreover, some aspects of specialization are unfavorable to efficiency and economy. Fluctuations in demand are more likely to impose fluctuating production and recurrent idle capacity upon the highly specialized producer than upon his more diversified neighbors. The appearance of new substitutes and change in the tastes of buyers are more likely to find him without alternatives. The specialized equipment and specialized skills that were sources of economy in producing a single product become obstacles to easy adaptation to a changing environment. Nor is the specialized plant necessarily the most capable of producing the ideas necessary to preserve its own efficiency. Specialization is better suited to efficient use of a well-understood technology than it is to formulation and use of new methods in a developing technology. New ideas are stimulated by variety of experience and variety of contact. Specialization can readily become routine; and routine, stagnation.

The French published reports and decisions contain no indication that difficulties in determining the relative weight to be given to these complex considerations have troubled the French Commission, nor, indeed, that the conclusion that specialization is desirable has been reached in each case by examining the facts of that case. The Commission's endorsement of specialization was applied without differentiation to the numerous small producers of electric lamps that competed with the large Philips concern; to the flat glass industry, where there were only four producers; and to the production of identical products by the foremost two of the three French producers of malleable iron fittings. In some cases the Commission has recommended and the Minister has decided that quota cartels should be approved on the ground that, by providing security and mutual confidence, they resulted in specialization. In other cases, on the Commission's recom-

---

13 Economies are more probable from diversification that uses the same kinds of technology, equipment, and market channels than from diversification that brings together unrelated types of goods.

mendation, cartels that had not fostered specialization have been told to specialize. In the insulated wire and cable industry, which was mentioned above, more specialization, as well as joint research, was demanded during the cartel's probationary period. In a case involving railway switch points, the Minister adopted the Commission's recommendation that producers not be prosecuted for collusive bidding provided they undertook to specialize to reduce costs and prices. In a case concerning producers of bicycle rims and handlebars, members of the cartel were told both to discontinue certain restrictions and to undertake programs of specialization and simplification. In a case concerning copper alloys, the agreement was found to be exempt under the law, but the decision to this effect said that the exemption could only continue if additional efforts to specialize were made.

In the bicycle parts case one of the restrictions that was not terminated was a discount agreement under which buyers received volume discounts based upon their aggregate purchases from all participating sellers. The Minister evaluated this provision by considering, not whether it might hamper independents in selling, but whether it would promote or retard specialization. He thought that it might either promote specialization by encouraging buyers to divide their purchases rationally among specialized producers or else retard it by encouraging them to buy one product from several sellers. Accordingly, he instructed the cartel to withhold the discount from buyers who bought an unimportant product from more than one seller or an important one from more than two. He asked the cartel to submit proof within two years that the discount agreement did not artificially preserve small producers.

In such efforts to foster specialization, the French authorities showed no concern lest the number of producers be unduly concentrated. In the bicycle parts case, the Minister asked the cartel to try to reduce the number of producers of handle bars to fewer than the existing seven. In the case concerning pitchforks and hay hooks, the Commission recorded with approval the fact that the number of producers of most types had been reduced to one or two.

Though specialization cartels have had a negligible place under German cartel law, the German authorities apparently regard them with favor. In July, 1963, the Federal Cartel Office relaxed its procedures in an effort to encourage such cartels. It announced that specialization cartels would benefit from prima facie presumptions: a) that such cartels promote efficiency, and b) that, except where market domination is created or enhanced by the cartel, the restriction involved in specializing is appropriately related to the resulting rationalization. The Office also said that it expected that decisions about specialization cartels would ordinarily be made within three months from the date of application for approval. In 1965 amendment of the law reduced the safeguards in the proceedings by which such cartels can obtain legal exemption.[14]

Though, like Europeans, Americans presume that specialization often enhances efficiency, they also presume that under the pressures of competition enterprises will individually undertake such specialization as is desirable. Europeans who favor specialization cartels reject this view. When asked why an enterprise that has opportunities to reduce costs by specialization will refrain from doing so unless it can be party to a specialization agreement, they answer that the would-be specialist is usually unwilling to risk his business future upon one type of product if he knows that others also will make it. To be persuasive, this evaluation must rest upon belief that the economies of specialization are not great, or that the producer achieving them is either unwilling or unable because of cartel practices to use price-competition based upon his lower costs to make sure that he sells his specialty, or that buyers prefer to buy from non-specialists. Of these beliefs, those who think that specialization requires agreement usually accept the latter. They say that a seller must offer a full line of goods and that he can do so only if, through a specialization agreement, members of the industry have undertaken to sell their specialties to one another and thus to make offer of a full line feasible. When asked whether a specialist who desired to offer a full line could not fill out his line by purchases from other enterprises, either currently or under long-term contracts, without requiring those enterprises to agree to refrain from making or selling his specialty, they express doubt. Such possibilities are not vivid in their minds, and such practices are not common in the business world around them. So long as European governments are willing to pay for specialization by permitting restriction, nobody will be likely to offer it to them unrestricted.

Simplifying and Standardizing Goods. Simplification, standardization, and improvement of quality have been recurrent themes in the consideration of rationalization cartels, but in the majority of cases reference to them has been too cursory to make clear either the nature of the improvement that the cartel made or the reason for thinking that a restrictive agreement was an appropriate means. Where there was simplification—that is, agreement to reduce the number of different varieties of a particu-

---

[14] Previously such agreements required explicit approval, which was to be granted if (a) a substantial increase of efficiency or productivity was probable; (b) the rationalization was adequate to justify the restriction; and (c) market competition was not excluded. Under the amendment, such agreements are valid unless disapproved within three months and disapproval is authorized unless the participants show that their purpose is rationalization and that competition is not eliminated.

lar kind of goods—it presumably was approved as a contribution to efficiency because it reduced the diversity of a producer's operations in a way similar to specialization. So far as this is true, the questions raised by simplification are also similar, with one exception: Whereas a specialization program does not necessarily reduce the variety of goods available to the buyer, a simplification program is intended to do so. Hence there is a danger that the interests of buyers will be inadequately considered. Under British law, the benefit of an agreement to users must be proved in court. German law includes a more modest precaution by which affected persons and organizations that promote rationalization must be heard, their comments must be made available to the Cartel Authority, and objection by the authority on grounds of abuse can invalidate the cartel. No analogous provision appears in the French statute, and the published decisions do not indicate that the French Commission is sensitive to the possibility.

British law provides that in deciding whether an agreement must be registered (and thus subjected to judicial review) no account shall be taken of undertakings to observe standards of dimension, design, or quality approved by the British Standards Association. No special treatment is provided for other types of standardization and simplification.

Under the laws of France and Germany, standardization has not been significantly separated from simplification. In its ordinary meaning, standardization consists in agreement to produce goods to predetermined specifications, of which there may be only one or a larger number. Such an agreement may merely involve elimination of minor undesired variations in items successively produced. If so, it cannot properly be called simplification. However, a standardization agreement may eliminate some of the variation in goods that certain producers deliberately provided and certain buyers chose to buy. If so, it involves simplification as well as standardization. Both are considered under the same standards and procedures and receive equal approval as means toward lower costs, without apparent effort to differentiate them. In some of the French decisions, achievements in "normalization" are thought to have resulted from the security provided by quota cartels, and are treated as subsidiary reasons for approving these cartels. Cartels are also urged to undertake more such work. In the bicycle parts case, the Minister warned the cartel that if the number of types of rims was not reduced within two years he would abolish the cartel. No French case has involved simplification and standardization without other accompanying types of rationalization. Among the German cases during the first four years, two involved standardization without other restrictions, and one involved simplification accompanied by price fixing. In the latter, makers of iron barrels agreed to reduce the number of types and agreed upon surcharges to be levied for the types least often purchased. The agreement was approved.

Improving Quality. Improvement of quality is another recurrent theme in decisions about rationalization cartels. So far as standardization eliminates undesirable minor differences in what are supposedly units of the same goods, it automatically improves quality. However, the decisions cover somewhat more than this. A British blanket agreement included a specification of minimum quality as well as various restrictions on price. In eliminating the latter, the British court approved continued agreement on the minimum specification as useful to buyers. But an effort to disentangle arrangements about quality from other restrictions has appeared only in this case. A report by the British Monopolies Commission endorsed a price agreement for linoleum partly on the ground that it helped to maintain quality. In treating improvement of quality as one of the reasons for approving certain quota cartels, the French commission has not asserted that the improvement was the result of the restriction. Instead, in some decisions it has seemed to regard improvements of quality, along with reductions of prices and vigorous promotion of exports, as contributions to good performance that should be suitably rewarded by permitting a cartel to adopt profitable restrictions, whether or not these restrictions are necessary to the performance in question. It has examined the changes through time in quality, prices, and export position, and if it concluded that satisfactory performance in such respects was due to the initiative of the cartel, it has approved the cartel's restrictive program without considering whether or not performance as good or even better could be attained in a less restrictive way.

Adapting Capacity to Demand. Adaptation of capacity to demand by restrictive agreement has been approved in several countries. The Austrian appellate commission said in the yeast and farm tool cases that prevention of excess capacity by a cartel serves the interest of consumers. Under Japanese temporary legislation, a Minister was empowered to prepare a rationalization plan for manufacture of machinery, with provisions as to capacity, new facilities, improvement of technology, and disposal of obsolete equipment; and thereafter to order manufacturers to act together in accord with this plan in buying equipment, in restricting technology, and in limiting the kind, and if necessary the number, of machines. In France, after the rehabilitation of war-damaged railway rolling stock, facilities for repair of railway cars were excessive. An impartial person appointed by the repairmen's association designated eleven firms as enterprises to be shut down. The French government's railway monopoly then withheld repair orders from these firms. Rejecting a complaint by one of the excluded enterprises, the Minister, on the French Commission recommendation, held that concentration of this work would distribute orders better both geographically and technically, would improve the market, and would further economic progress. The Commission said that the railways could protect themselves if necessary by inviting more bidders. A private suit by the complainant, however, resulted in an award of damages from the association, which had acted beyond the limits of its by-laws.

Stabilizing Operations. Apart from the relatively explicit types of action to improve performance that are discussed above, the decisions about rationalization contain general references to such broad results as stabilization of demand or of production and coordination of investment. Restrictions are said to have produced stability and thereby to have regularized production or purchases or both, to have enhanced the capacity of suppliers to provide service, to have reduced prices, and to have permitted better investment planning. The French decisions, in which such statements are frequent, afford no indication of the process by which such results are supposed to have been achieved and no indication why similar lines of argument should not be used to attribute benefits to restriction in substantially every case. The argument has been more clearly and persuasively set forth elsewhere in four instances—decisions on cement and books in the United Kingdom, a decision on books in New Zealand, and a decision on tires in South Africa. In each of these instances, a price agreement was said to have rationalizing effects. In the usage of some countries— e.g. Germany—the term rationalization is applied only where unit costs are reduced, and cannot be extended to cover the effects of price fixing, however beneficial these may be. Regardless of niceties of nomenclature, however, the nature of the effect reported will be briefly noted here. For tires in South Africa, it was encouragement of quality competition, as a result of which the quality of South African tires became unusually good.[15] For books in both England and New Zealand, it consisted in provision of profits on fast-moving best-sellers that permitted the maintenance of a large inventory of slow-moving classics and technical books in bookshops and that preserved an adequate number of book dealers. For cement it was provision of a degree of security and stability in an expanding industry that enabled producers to finance expansion without raising prices to the level that replacement costs of equipment and market costs of funds would have required under price competition.

---

[15] In a British report on linoleum, common prices were said to have had a similar effect of promoting quality competition, but various modifications and safeguards were recommended to cope with restrictive effects. See Monopolies and Restrictive Practices Commission, *Report on the Supply of Linoleum*, August 2, 1956, pp. 53-67.

Appraisal. Some kinds of agreement that are permitted in Europe as aids to rationalization are permitted in the United States as devoid of forbidden restraints of trade; and some others are permitted in a form stripped of the restraints that accompany them in Europe. In this range of agreements American policy sanctions rationalization agreements, but, unlike European policy, insists that they take a form not conducive to significant impairments of market competition.

Under the American Sherman Act the so-called rule of reason accepts the lawfulness of restrictions that are merely incidental and ancillary to non-restrictive agreements. The classic case of lawful ancillary restriction is an undertaking by one who sells a business to refrain from immediately entering into competition with the buyers in adjacent premises.

European rationalization, however, includes much more than ancillary restrictions. Price-fixing, allocation of goods, quota systems, and joint purchase or sale may all be accepted either as direct aids to good performance or as inducements to participate in other programs that are believed to provide such aid. In some countries substantial restrictions such as these are justified by the belief that they provide a climate of cooperation in which useful concerted activities flourish. In some countries there is inadequate proof of benefits, inadequate proof that the relevant restrictions are necessary to the benefits, or inadequate provision for reconsideration in the light of experience. Some types of benefit supposedly derived from restriction, such as specialization of output or exclusion of the incompetent, probably would be provided more effectively by vigorous competition. Existing rationalization policies include much that is ill-devised.

But some governments review claims of rationalization carefully and still accept them, and some types of restrictive agreement seem to be sources of true economy. Appraisal of this portion of governmental policy toward rationalization must rest on several questions: a) Whether or not the alleged benefits exist and are significant; b) whether or not the restrictive means are necessary to the beneficial result; c) whether or not the adverse effects of restriction outweigh the benefits; and d) whether or not, in the application of such a policy, significant side-effects are encountered.

There can be no reasonable doubt that some rationalization agreements reduce economic costs. This is true of agreements such as those for Dutch milk, by which the overlapping of delivery routes is reduced and the average distance of delivery is shortened. It is also true of agreements by which meaningless minor variations in products are eliminated and of agreements that reduce the amount of expenditure upon competitive advertising or competitive selling.

The three examples just given represent three different kinds of economy. In the first, illustrated by Dutch milk, physical activity that is functionally unnecessary is eliminated, with consequent saving for everybody concerned. As in the Netherlands, the result can be achieved by allocation of territory or some similar device that partly shields the participants from competition. However, since the participants benefit even if competition is preserved, less restrictive means of attaining the economy can be devised if the more restrictive ones are prevented. In certain American large cities, for example, department stores that encountered expense from duplicate deliveries have organized joint delivery services that carry packages from all participating stores in the same trucks and thus eliminate unnecessary haulage without impairing competition in selling. Similarly, unnecessary duplication of such ancillary services as accounting is often avoided by use of independent accountants that perform the service for numerous firms and are compensated by fees. Where restrictions are thought to be justified by functional economies and hence are permitted, these non-restrictive alternatives are unlikely to flourish.

The second type of economy, illustrated by agreements to standardize or simplify products, consists essentially in eliminating obstacles to the achievement of economies of scale. Differences in successive units of the same goods are inconsistent with the economies of the machine process, both for the producer and for the buyer who uses his purchase to achieve exact results. Provision of a wide variety of goods that meet different specifications is also costly, but only to the extent that the amounts of the variant goods are too small to justify use of specialized equipment in supplying them. The economies of standardization and simplification are obvious. The question relevant to them is the importance that should be attached to the desire of some buyers for the varieties of goods that such a program eliminates. If the programs are developed and applied by groups of sellers, they may be excessively restrictive. If they are developed by organizations adequately representative of both buyers and sellers, the risk of excess is substantially reduced.

Savings that rest upon economies of scale can be attained not only by agreements that facilitate mechanization, but also by agreements under which several enterprises, individually too small for economical action, act together on a more appropriate scale. For example, a joint buying agreement may make possible purchase in carloads, or an agreement for joint research may make possible the use of more expensive research equipment.

Such economies should be clearly distinguished from mere bargaining advantages, with which they are often commingled. By enhancing the bargaining power of the associated buyers, a buying agreement may enable them to buy at lower prices. But if so, the net cost of producing and distributing the goods is not reduced, as in the case of true economies; instead, the sellers lose what the buyers gain. Whether or not this is desirable depends upon such considerations as the previous relative bargaining power of the groups affected and the previous desirability or undesirability of the relative prices and incomes involved. Whereas true economies are clearly beneficial, no similar blanket endorsement is possible for shifts of bargaining power.

Agreements that afford true economies through joint action do so only up to the point at which adequate economies of scale are achieved. An agreement that covers enough business to provide the relevant economies does not become more useful by covering still more business. Opportunities for such savings are numerous, therefore, only where the scale of enterprise is generally too small for efficiency.

In such a setting of unduly small business, agreement and growth both offer prospects of economies of scale. The economies attainable by growth are likely to be larger and more reliable than those attainable by agreement. Nevertheless, agreements are likely to seem more attractive, because they can be had without a competitive struggle in which, as successful enterprises become larger and fewer, the less successful ones are eliminated. The possibility of restrictive agreement for economy's sake is thus likely to retard appropriate changes in the scale of business organization, and to diminish the competitiveness of the process by which economies are attained.

Nevertheless, even where enterprises are of appropriate size, some agreements are still likely to be sources of conomy. Particular activities, such as research, may require a scale greater than that suitable to the principal activities of firms in the relevant field. Where this is true, agreement can provide economy even for enterprises that are big enough to be generally efficient.

The third type of economy, illustrated by agreements to reduce competitive advertising, consists in reducing the costs of competition by reducing the intensity of competitive selling. A private-enterprise economy necessarily includes not only activities by which goods are produced and distributed—activities that would continue to be necessary even if the economy were collectively managed—but also activities by which each member of the society struggles to maintain or improve his place among the others. In such a struggle, any one of the rivals merely counteracts the others if he merely matches their efforts, but may gain advantage if he outdoes them. As in the competitive armament of rival national states, the scope and cost of the rivalry tend to increase. Agreements to reduce such activities and expenditures can be a source of economy. They may involve not only limitation of advertising but also other reductions of sales effort, ranging all the way to joint sale at agreed prices.

To eliminate rivalry in selling is, of course, to eliminate competition. But it does not follow that every reduction of rivalry in selling is an impairment of competition. A particular agreement to limit advertising may leave ample scope for all functionally useful information and persuasion. A particular arrangement for joint sale may cover so little of the total supply that it does not affect the quality of competition among suppliers. But these are likely to be unusual cases. More commonly, reduction of rivalry in selling results in reduction of competition. It simultaneously involves true economies and changes in bargaining advantages.

Governmental willingness to permit activities that have such mixed effects depends upon the degree of reliance placed upon competition as a regulator of markets. In a competitive society, economies in selling that are inconsistent with competition must be foregone, whereas in a society that relies upon public price control or other public action to curb bargaining advantages no such abstention is necessary.

It does not follow, however, that greater reliance upon competition means greater waste. Rivalry to obtain favorable decisions from government is expensive too. It involves similar problems of escalation. It may convert a government into a weathervane that responds to the pressures upon it but has no direction of its own. Moreover, a government that applies administrative control to replace competition incurs the cost of that control and imposes upon business the costs that are necessitated by acceptance of governmental surveillance. If the publicly applied safeguards are inadequate, there are additional costs to the economy from functionally irrelevant restriction. These wastes and costs can be formidable. The American policy of competition rests, in considerable part, upon belief that they are likely to be greater than the wastes of competition and that the likelihood increases as the role of competition diminishes.

Chapter X

Exclusions and Discriminations

Restrictions designed to handicap particular enterprises or classes of enterprises or to exclude them from opportunity to do business are more consistently condemned by public policy in the countries that curb restrictive practices than any other type of restriction.

As Europe emerged from the Middle Ages, restrictions on the right to engage in occupations were widely administered by guilds or governments. Apprenticeship and tests of skill were required in handicraft production and in many kinds of shopkeeping. Itinerant merchants were widely subject to some equivalent of licensing. The purposes of such regulations were partly to assure the competence and trustworthiness of those engaged in an occupation and partly to protect the trade by limiting the number of entrants and by bringing each newcomer under the disciplinary control of those already established. As business evolved, most of these restrictions were broken, partly by the rise of new centers of activity where the older local regulations were not operative and partly by laws that established freedom of occupation. The changes by which occupational freedom was established were indispensable to the rise of the factory system and of modern methods of distributing manufactured products. By the time that factory production had become prevalent, occupational freedom and opportunity had won the support of the more powerful segments of business.

The legal basis for occupational freedom is recent. In most European countries the laws that established it were enacted less than two centuries ago. In some countries they provided for exceptions when passed, and were followed by reversions toward occupational licensing. For example, the Austrian law of 1800 that authorized unlicensed entry into trades contained significant exceptions, which were greatly enlarged by more than fifty subsequent amendments. The depression of the 1930's, in particular, resulted in various legal restrictions upon entry into business, some of which persisted thereafter; and the Nazis abolished occupational freedom in both Germany and Austria. In spite of such aberrations, however, freedom of occupation was to post-war Western Europe a valued norm of economic life, rooted in pre-war traditions and to be preserved except where there was clear reason to limit it. Public restrictions upon that freedom were often controversial; private ones were suspect when they reached further than public ones.

Economic and political developments immediately after the Second World War strengthened the desire of governments to support freedom of occupation. Because of demobilization and the mass migration of refugees, exceptional numbers of people were seeking to establish themselves in new business activities or in new places. Groups that were already established often saw the newcomers as threats to their own economic security and sought to exclude them; but governments saw an overriding need to enable the newcomers to become self-supporting as rapidly as possible. Under conditions of rapid change, new types of business enterprises appeared, particularly in distribution, and met resistance from older types; but governments, desiring to keep prices down, thought that some of these innovations gave promise of doing so, and therefore encouraged them. Thus traditions of freedom of occupation were reenforced, and private restrictions upon that freedom were widely condemned.

Types of Legal Control. Governmental efforts to safeguard entry into business and access to markets took several forms. They included action against collective boycott; action to forbid or limit collective establishment of conditions for membership in a trade; action to forbid or limit refusal to sell or to buy; action to limit the right of trade associations to exclude applicants; action against invidious discrimination in prices, discounts, or the terms of sale; and action against exclusive dealing and tying arrangements. In some countries, particular relevant policies were made applicable only to agreements or only to the practices of dominant firms; in others, they were applied to individual conduct by any enterprise.

Curbs upon exclusion and discrimination were sometimes made explicit in national laws and sometimes derived from interpretation of general provisions about restrictive practices. The countries whose laws have no explicit provisions against particular exclusionary or discriminatory practices do not, however, ignore them. So far as such practices are not subject to explicit statutory provisions, they are regarded in most countries as matters of concern under the provisions by which abuses of economic power and restrictive agreements or practices that are contrary to the public interest are forbidden or limited. In a few countries, such as Denmark, the Netherlands and the United Kingdom, an intention to apply such broad statutory provisions to exclusion and discrimination is made evident by listing among available correctives the power to order specified firms to supply specified buyers on customary terms.[1] In the United Kingdom corrective

---

[1] Danish law contains such a provision. Dutch law applies a similar provision to abuse of dominant positions. In the United Kingdom similar orders may be issued against firms subject to the Monopolies Act.

orders against price discrimination and other forms of preference have also
been authorized since 1965, but only against firms subject to the Monopolies
Act. In other countries, e.g. Sweden, exclusion and discrimination receive
major attention under provisions that have no special application to such
practices.

The Purposes of Exclusion.   Private control over access to a trade
can have various restrictive purposes. It may be used (a) to limit the total
number of traders and to make sure that new entrants are so located that
their competition with already established firms is minimized; (b) to exclude from the trade cooperatives, chain stores, mail order houses, firms
that do a combined wholesale-retail business, and other unorthodox types of
enterprise; (c) to exclude persons who are thought likely to cut prices or
otherwise engage in types of competition that are disliked; (d) to exclude
firms that lack experience, capital, or suitable equipment, or that do not
intend to offer the full services that are customary; (e) to exclude persons
whose record or reputation indicates that they are dishonest or engage in
illegal or unfair practices.

Though any of these purposes may be served, alone or in combination
with others, some of the more restrictive ones are often served indirectly.
A desire to limit numbers may take the form of a requirement that experience
be long and capital large. An effort to exclude the unorthodox may be concealed in a requirement that entrants possess experience or facilities that are
suited only to orthodox ways of doing business.

Reciprocal Collective Exclusive Dealing.   Several devices for limiting
entry to a field of business have been curbed under the restrictive practice
laws. The most effective are reciprocal exclusive dealing agreements between associations at successive vertical stages of economic activity. By
such an agreement members of a suppliers' association undertake to sell
only to members of a distributors' or users' association, and the latter undertake to buy only from the former. By excluding a firm from membership, either association can deprive it of opportunity to trade with members
of the other association and thus deny it access to the part of the market
controlled by those members. Requirements for membership in the association thus become conditions for admission to much or all of the market,
and the power to expel a member becomes a weapon so formidable as to
assure conformity by members to the restrictive programs of the associations. Such arrangements are so clearly objectionable under the laws of
most countries that formal cases involving them seldom arise, and where
there is such an arrangement it is likely to be condemned.

In the Netherlands, however, reciprocal exclusive agreements are permitted provided that membership in the participating associations is open
to all traders who meet standards for admission that the government re-

gards as reasonable, and provided that the power that such an arrangement gives the associations is not used to support restrictions regarded by the government as objectionable. Nothing inherently objectionable is seen in "reasonable" admission requirements nor in collective exclusionary action against firms that do not choose to join the association and participate in its permitted restrictive programs.

Approved Lists. A more common way to exclude newcomers is for members of a trade to agree to deal only with persons named on an approved list. Arrangements of this kind necessitate a procedure for approval under which applicants can be accepted or rejected. In some of the schemes, approval depends upon the opinion of participants about whether or not there is place for an increased number of traders. In others, such considerations are not raised, but standards of eligibility are applied. These standards may be vague or specific, and may be invoked capriciously or consistently. Under them, applicants may be excluded because of their morality or reputation, their unorthodox methods of doing business, or their lack of experience, training, capital, or facilities. Since approval may be withdrawn, the possibility of withdrawing it may become a disciplinary weapon by which approved firms can be required to accept restrictions imposed by the group that grants approval.

In some schemes the standards are raised from time to time, so that newcomers are made ineligible even though their qualifications are equal to those of firms already approved. Some schemes are applied leniently, excluding few applicants; others result in exclusion of a large percentage of all who desire admission.

Programs of this kind usually have been condemned if they applied numerical limits to the number of traders, if they excluded unorthodox types of business, if they were used as weapons against price cutters, and if standards of eligibility were thought to be excessively high.

Where use of approved lists has been permitted, the authorities have required that the standards of eligibility be objectively stated and applied. Such vague criteria as good business reputation have been considered unacceptable. Committees that consider applications for approval have sometimes been required to include non-members of the trade, and their decisions against applicants have sometimes been subjected to possible appeal either to a public authority or to a supposedly impartial private body. Standards of skill, equipment, or capital have been accepted only if they were thought to set reasonable minima. In occupations where minimum qualifications were required by law, private groups have not been allowed to impose more restrictive qualifications.

An example will serve to illustrate the degree of permissiveness in a government policy that authorizes some restrictions on membership in a trade. In Ireland prior to 1956, approved lists of retailers, repairers, wholesalers, factors and manufacturers of components and repair parts were maintained by the Irish motor trade. To qualify for approval, an applicant was required to maintain prices, refrain from selling to unapproved traders, and possess certain qualifications. A retailer was required to possess at least specified amounts of floor-space and equipment and to carry an adequate stock of parts. The requisite floor-space exceeded that of many retailers who were already on the approved list. Factors and wholesalers were required to possess stated amounts of floor-space and capital, to use salesmen and to abstain from retailing or selling from vans; and wholesalers were also required to have an exclusive agency for some component or replacement part of a motor vehicle. Manufacturers of components and parts were required to have stated amounts of floor-space, to sell under their own brands only, to abstain from all other business except the motor trade, and (if they did not make all of the goods that bore their brands) to possess a stated amount of capital. In 1956 an order abolished the approved lists and thus eliminated all of these restrictions. However, requests by the trade for minimum standards of entry into retailing were subsequently accepted on the ground that traders equipped for service should not be exposed to competition from others not so equipped. In 1959 rules issued by the Irish Fair Trade Commission made it unfair to supply for resale motor vehicles and replacement parts to anyone but a motor trader. A motor trader was defined as one who operated a service garage and had (a) ground floor space for repairs and service, (b) a mechanic, and (c) a specified small amount of equipment. The definition was applicable impartially to new entrants and to existing traders. Thus a low and non-discriminatory barrier to operation in the trade replaced a high one; but the low one had government support, and still prevented anyone from retailing motor vehicles or replacement parts unless he operated a service garage.

Agreement about Choice of Customers. Standards of eligibility similar to those discussed above are sometimes applied in less elaborate form. Without resort to an approved list or to formal consideration of applications, members of an industry may agree to sell only to specified types of buyers and may formulate definitions of each type. Similarly, without formal agreement for reciprocal exclusive dealing, a trade association may decide to admit to membership only firms with specified characteristics or qualifications, and thus may deprive excluded persons not only of the association's services but also of opportunities to trade with enterprises that prefer to deal with accredited firms. Such schemes lack the precision of those that include approved lists. Nevertheless, they may be effective in excluding or handicapping particular classes of enterprise such as cooperatives, chain stores, limited-price variety stores, and similar easily identified enterprises. In considering them, governments have applied criteria similar to those applicable to approved lists. Almost invariably they have objected to collective refusals to sell to unorthodox types of enterprises. Less consistently, they have subjected exclusion from a trade association to review, and have insisted on admission of firms they thought improperly excluded. Some countries, however, have permitted agreements to refrain from selling to persons supposedly unqualified by lack of suitable experience, resources, or volume of business, particularly if they thought that sale to such persons would raise costs of distribution. Similarly, some countries have permitted trade associations to exclude from membership persons in the trade who did not meet qualifications regarded as reasonable. In the Netherlands, agreements that limit the total number of traders may be permitted if the limitation is not considered "undue."

In Norway, during a period of four years (1954-1957), concerted refusals to sell were permitted in 17 cases, forbidden in 18. For example, a wholesaler and installer of insulated cable and rubber-covered lead conduit in North Norway was denied wholesale status because he did not buy the minimum volume required by an agreement. His appeal to the Norwegian Price Council was rejected on the ground that the specified minimum was not excessive and that without it there would be too many wholesalers, smaller deliveries, and higher distribution costs. Similarly, a Norwegian association of dealers in musical instruments was allowed to exclude a dealer because he lacked the five years of experience in the trade that were required by the association's by-laws.

Boycotts. Boycotts—that is, punitive collective refusals to sell—are condemned in most countries on the ground that they impair business freedom. Where there is a grievance against a buyer for breach of obligations, sellers are generally expected to resort to legal proceedings or, at most, to individual refusal to sell. In the Netherlands and Switzerland, however, a limited role for boycotts is considered legitimate. The Netherlands regards them as proper if their purpose is to enforce restrictions that the government believes to be substantively reasonable. In a statute that invalidates boycotts generally and exposes them to private suits, Switzerland specifically provides that they shall be permissible if they serve purposes such as protection of fair competition, giving effect to cartel arrangements in foreign markets, giving effect to resale price maintenance that is needed to protect quality or skill, or supporting reasonable technical or professional requirements or desirable industrial structure.[2]

---

[2] Law Concerning Cartels and Similar Organizations, Dec. 20, 1962, Articles 4-5.

Individual Refusal to Sell. Nearly two-thirds of the laws, unlike similar American legislation, place substantial limitations upon the right of single firms to refuse to deal with others. In six countries these limitations are applicable to all firms, whether powerful or not, by explicit statutory provisions or by interpretation of general statutory language.[3] In five more countries, provision is made for possible orders against refusals to sell in the provisions of law that are applicable to powerful firms.[4]

In the United States each seller has a right to select his own customers unless (a) his action is part of a scheme to acquire or maintain an unlawful monopoly or is otherwise ancillary to a forbidden restraint of trade, or (b) he is engaged in one of the few lines of business that, being "affected with a public interest," are obligated to serve all comers without discrimination.[5] This policy rests on presumptions that competition will discourage refusals to sell and will enable persons rejected by one seller to buy from another. Tolerating considerable amounts of restriction and often possessing fewer market alternatives, most of the countries here under discussion are less able to rely upon these presumptions. Instead they impose curbs upon refusal to sell.

Control of refusals to sell by any individual enterprise is a major purpose of policy in five countries—France, Denmark, Norway, Sweden, and Ireland. It is also undertaken seriously in Germany with respect to dominant firms and firms that fix resale prices. In France refusal to sell to any applicant whose request is made in good faith and has no abnormal character is categorically forbidden by law. In Norway the Price Council has statutory authority to forbid any enterprise to refuse to sell to any other or to a consumer; and since what may be forbidden is refusal of business connections, the provision also covers refusal to buy. Provisions that

---

[3] France forbids refusal to sell where the request has no abnormal character and is made in good faith. New Zealand authorizes orders against unjustifiable refusal to sell. Norway authorizes orders against refusal to have business connections where the refusal would be detrimental to the public interest or would unreasonably affect the firm refused. Irish rules of fair competition characteristically include provisions against refusal to sell. In Sweden and Denmark, cases involving refusal to sell are prominent among those to which the general discretionary language of the statute is applied.

[4] The Swiss law makes refusal to sell by dominant firms a practice for which injured firms may collect damages (Articles 3, 4, 6). The German law forbids dominant firms to hinder other enterprises unfairly or to treat them differently without justification (Section 26(2)). The Dutch law (Section 24, 1b (2)) and the British Monopolies Act (Section 10 (2) (c)) authorize orders that require powerful firms to sell specified goods to specified persons. The Belgian law authorizes official recommendations (which, if ignored, may be converted into royal orders) against abuses of economic power, of which refusal to sell may be one.

[5] Recently enacted civil rights legislation forbids certain places of public accommodation to discriminate against customers on grounds of race or color, even if in other respects they have no general obligation to serve.

are applicable to all types of restriction are used in Sweden primarily, and in Denmark substantially, to control refusals to sell. In Ireland provisions about obligations to sell or to abstain from refusing to do so are prominent among the rules of fair trading issued by the Fair Trade Commission and the orders issued by the Minister of Industry and Commerce. In Germany dominant enterprises and firms that fix resale prices are forbidden by statute to treat other enterprises differently unless there are facts that justify the difference.

Definition of refusal to sell is not important in the countries in which discretion as to control of it is inherent in the form of the legal provisions. In France, however, there was need to interpret the statutory prohibition precisely. Refusal to sell has been officially interpreted there to include offer of goods that do not have the seller's trade mark; offer of semi-finished goods when raw materials were requested; and offer of goods under unusual terms of sale. A French seller is not guilty of refusal to sell if he cannot get goods to sell or if, in periods of shortage, he first honors prior commitments or holds the customary reserve stock; but he must accept orders in sequence, without favoring regular customers. While he may choose to sell only in quantities that are appropriate to his way of doing business (e.g., wholesale quantities), he may not refuse buyers who offer to purchase those quantities (e.g., chain stores, cooperatives, or large retailers). Thus he may not select customers on the basis of their functional characteristics as distributors.

Since in France the buyer's lack of good faith or the abnormality of the type of requested purchase justifies a refusal to sell, the meaning of these terms has been interpreted also. Because of the buyer's bad faith, a seller may refuse to sell to a customer who wants the goods to pirate their design or to disparage them, or who resells them as loss leaders, or to sell except for cash to a customer who does not pay his bills. Because the transaction would be abnormal, a seller may refuse to sell in quantities that are peculiarly large or small, or to customers who lack the appropriate technical or commercial qualifications, or to customers who do not normally deal in similar goods and have not take appropriate measures to be able to do so effectively. Certain exclusive dealing arrangements which will be described below are also permissible.

In many respects, but not all, discretionary control of refusal to sell in the other four countries results in standards similar to those of France. In the Scandinavian countries, refusal to sell may be permitted if the rejected buyer has adequate access to the goods from other sources. In Ireland, since the applicable rules are formulated anew for each industry, they differ considerably in detail. In general, however, where refusal to sell would cause substantial difficulty for the rejected buyer, public policies in these countries condemn it if it is based upon the fact that the buyer is not a member of a trade association, is a new enterprise, is a cooperative, chain store, or mail order house, or is otherwise unorthodox. Refusal to sell may not be used as a weapon to discipline price cutters nor to control the buyer's selection of his own customers. It may not be undertaken to placate the buyer's competitors nor to limit competition by limiting the total number of buyers. It may not become a means of discriminating arbitrarily among customers who are similar.

Grounds upon which refusal to sell may be permitted are also similar in many respects to those in France. They include the buyer's bad character or criminal record; his use of unfair practices such as misrepresentation, sale of loss leaders, or sale below cost; his bad credit standing or failure to pay his bills; the unsuitability of his kind of business for the relevant goods; and the smallness of his order.

In two respects, however, these policies contrast with French policy. First, a large role is played by refusal to sell to unqualified buyers. In the Scandinavian countries and Germany, and to a lesser extent in Ireland, buyers may be rejected because they are deficient as to premises, capital, stock of goods, rate of turnover of goods, training, or length of experience. These standards of qualification must be impartially applied and may not be clearly excessive; but in practice they permit sellers to assert that buyers are not qualified for reasons that would not be acceptable in France. For example, the French authorities look with suspicion upon refusal to sell to dealers who do not carry a specified stock of goods and are likely to condemn such a refusal unless the stock is clearly necessary to performance of the distributive function.

Second, sellers are allowed more discretion than in France in their efforts to reduce costs of distribution. Whereas France requires sale to all distributors who buy normal quantities, the other countries permit limitation of the number of outlets to avoid increased cost, provided the method used does not discriminate between new and old customers and is otherwise non-discriminatory. More tolerance is also shown for decision to sell only to wholesalers. In Ireland, for example, sellers are often explicitly granted the option of selling only to wholesalers, only to retailers, or to both. In Germany refusals to sell incident to selection of distribution channels are permissible. Sellers may decide to sell only to specified functional groups such as wholesalers, to use specialized or unspecialized distributors, or to offer a full line to some distributors while offering only limited lines to others.

Discrimination is permitted by the German authorities when it consists in different treatment of different types of distributor, though it is not permitted in dealings with distributors of the same type.

Exclusive Dealing Contracts. Exclusive dealing involves two possible types of restriction. The seller may sell to a single buyer, or to a single one in each locality; or the buyer may buy only from a single supplier. An exclusive dealing arrangement may involve either type of restriction or both.

In most countries, contracts for exclusive sale are subject to no special policy, but have the same status as other types of refusal to sell. In France, however, some kinds of exclusive selling are permitted by interpretation of the provision that lets sellers refuse abnormal purchases. Sellers who are vertically integrated and sellers who deliver their entire output to a single buyer need not sell to others. A seller may sell exclusively to one outlet in each market provided (a) he uses such methods consistently everywhere he sells; (b) the contracts give each buyer a clearly defined territory and are otherwise precise; (c) each buyer is obligated to sell no competitor's goods; and (d) the goods are of high quality or their sale requires technical knowledge. These criteria of legality appear to have been chosen in an effort to permit ordinary exclusive dealing without impairing the protection that the law affords against refusals to sell that are intended to enforce resale price maintenance or to discriminate against chain stores.

Though, except in French situations that involve reciprocal exclusive dealing, little attention has been given to requirements that customers buy exclusively from a single seller, the few available cases suggest that when the restriction is imposed by a dominant firm it is likely to be condemned. A dominant Danish manufacturer of vacuum cleaners was ordered to terminate such a requirement on the ground that it prevented competitors from dealing with the majority of the retailers, deprived retailers of the right to carry an assortment, and made comparison of competing goods by consumers more difficult.

Tying. Little attention has been given to tying arrangements. In France the law prohibits sale of goods conditioned upon the acquisition of other goods.[6] In Germany and Spain, tying arrangements are abuses when imposed by dominant firms. In Ireland tying is forbidden in fair trading rules applicable to various industries. The available information contains nothing significant about the use of these provisions.

Discrimination in Prices and Terms of Sale. Denial of customary discounts, or any analogous discrimination, is, in effect, refusal to sell. This fact is generally recognized in applying the laws concerned with access to

---

[6] This provision is directed at full-line forcing and similar practices. It does not forbid requirements contracts, but these are limited to 10 years by a law enacted in 1943.

markets. The Norwegian law explicitly provides that "It is deemed to constitute a refusal when one party is willing to have business connections only on terms which the Council considers to be unreasonable or unusual." The laws of other countries, though less explicit, are similarly interpreted. The foregoing discussion of refusal to sell, collective or individual, applies also to discrimination in prices, discounts, and terms of sale.

Nevertheless, the statutes or rules of seven of the countries explicitly forbid some kinds of discrimination or authorize limits upon them. In three countries, France, Ireland, and Japan, the relevant provisions apply to all enterprises, large or small. In the other four countries, Germany, the United Kingdom, Spain, and Switzerland, they are applicable only to dominant firms and to discrimination by agreement and (in the case of Germany) to enterprises engaged in resale price maintenance. The chief purpose of these provisions is to reenforce curbs upon refusals to sell. Accordingly, the primary use of them is to prevent discrimination against individual enterprises by arbitrary deviations from generally applicable schedules of prices, discounts, or terms of sale.

France, Germany, and Ireland, however, use concepts of discrimination that also have broader significance. France, where control goes furthest, forbids habitual application of discriminatory conditions of sale or discriminatory price increases which are not warranted by equivalent cost increases. Since under French law two acts constitute a habit, the rule is far-reaching. It has been interpreted to require that differentials in prices shall consist primarily of volume discounts (which are believed to reflect differences in cost), and that functional discounts shall be limited to deviations from volume discounts by which economies derived from the services of distributors are recognized. It precludes discounts based merely on the buyers' status in the distributive trades, and requires that mass buyers be treated approximately as well as wholesalers. However, it has been interpreted to permit special price reductions designed to meet a competitor's prices, to offset the higher costs of resale in thin rural markets, to recognize fidelity in buying, or to attract new customers.

Germany approaches discrimination more permissively. It not only permits volume discounts, but also readily permits price differentials between distributors who perform different functions or occupy different places in the structure of distribution. The discrimination that it seeks to prevent is different treatment of customers who not only buy similar quantities but also are functionally the same.

The various Irish rules and orders express an attitude more like the German than the French. They permit volume discounts, functional discounts, and combinations of the two, as well as initial special discounts to new enterprises and discounts based upon the timing of the order or the payment. They are intended to prevent invidious treatment of particular buyers or of such unorthodox types of buyers as the cooperatives.

Summary. Policies toward exclusion and discrimination show considerable resemblance and are in some respects severe. They seek to keep markets open for independent enterprises, newcomers, cooperatives, chain stores, mail order houses, and various other kinds of unorthodox enterprise. They seek to prevent exclusion and discrimination from being used as disciplinary weapons against firms that cut prices or compete vigorously, but permit such discipline to be applied, more often individually than collectively, against firms that use competitive practices that are generally regarded as unfair. They condemn refusals by which the number of enterprises is limited to reduce competition, but may permit similar limitations that appear to reduce costs of distribution. They generally permit efforts to exclude enterprises that are not considered to possess adequate experience, facilities, and capital; but they seek to keep standards of qualifications objective and reasonable and application of such standards non-discriminatory. In general, they are concerned with discrimination primarily as an indirect way of refusing to sell; envisage it, therefore, as discrimination against particular buyers; and do not search out discrimination that may be concealed in orderly discount structures or uniformly applied terms of sale.

They differ in certain important respects: (a) whether they are applicable only to agreements, or also to dominant firms, or generally to all firms; (b) how far, particularly in the case of single sellers, they permit use of refusal to sell and of discounts as means to select channels of distribution; (c) whether they envisage discrimination as different treatment of buyers generally, thus tending to preclude functional discounts, or as different treatment within a functional group, thus tending to permit such discounts. In addition, France gives special immunity to reciprocal exclusive dealing systematically undertaken by individual suppliers; and unlike the other countries, the Netherlands and Switzerland consistently tolerate collective punitive action designed to force reluctant enterprises to accept restrictive arrangements that these countries do not find substantively objectionable.

In comparison with the United States, these countries treat collective exclusion and discrimination more leniently, though they apply controls intended to eliminate the greater restrictive effects. They also make a much less ambitious effort to protect buyers from systematic, as distinguished from invidiously individual, price discrimination. Envisaging discrimination as a danger to the newcomer and the unorthodox, they protect chain stores instead of curbing them by attacks upon their buying advantages. On the other hand, their policies toward exclusionary practices are generally applicable to dominant firms, and in some countries to all firms; and thus they curb restrictions, particularly refusals of supply, which, being neither concerted nor designed to create or maintain a monopoly, are not within the scope of the American law. Whether, on balance, exclusionary practices are repressed more fully in the United States than in Europe is problematical. The answer depends chiefly upon the relative importance that should be attached to collective restriction, toward which Europe is more lenient, and oligopolistic restriction, toward which it is less so.

Chapter XI

Coercion and Discipline

Restrictive agreements frequently give rise to controversies among persons who are parties to them or who desire to be. On the one hand, firms that wish to participate may be excluded. On the other, firms whose participation is necessary to success may refuse to take part or, after joining, may covertly flout their agreed obligations.

To cope with the latter two difficulties, the parties to agreements often use threats or coercive devices to bring reluctant firms into agreements and to force participants to comply. An agreement sometimes includes provision for formal enforcement by private means, to supplement or replace whatever enforcement is possible through courts of law. Private enforcement may rely on such penalties as discrimination, boycott, or other forms of concerted retaliatory action; assessment of monetary penalties or of estimated damages; forfeit of collateral that was deposited to guarantee compliance; or expulsion from the group. Discipline may be applied by arbitral processes set forth in the agreement or by privately established tribunals used instead of the courts.

So far as restrictive agreements are permitted, therefore, problems of public policy may arise, not only about their effect upon those against whom the restrictions are directed but also about rights to participate, rights to refuse or cease to do so, and disregard by participants of the obligations they have accepted.

In some countries, such as South Africa, neither the law nor experience under it has brought such problems to focus. In other countries, such as France, the law precludes many of the common disciplinary activities of cartels by broadly prohibiting discriminations and refusals to sell; but available records show little evidence that other kinds of disciplinary action have aroused public concern.[1] In five countries, however, the statutes include provisions explicitly designed to cope with the disciplinary problems that arise in connection with cartel membership and conformity to cartel agreements. These countries are Austria, the Netherlands, and Switzerland, in which the statutes applicable to cartels are broadly permissive; Norway, in which the similar permissiveness prevails except for price agreements; and

---

[1] French quota cartels have involved penalties and bonuses that have been regarded as objectionable, but the ground for the objection has been, not that private discipline was imposed, but that the charges tended to raise costs and thus raise prices.

171

Germany, in which a generally prohibitory policy includes exceptions that authorize considerable numbers of cartels. In a sixth country, New Zealand, exclusion from a trade association can be subjected to public review. In several more countries particular type of disciplinary actions are subject to control under general provisions of law.

In the Netherlands, Switzerland, and Austria, the applicable legal concepts rest on the assumption that private coercive pressures are permissible within appropriate limits. Swiss law, in forbidding boycotts generally, sets forth circumstances in which they will be considered appropriate. Dutch law is applied to boycotts and collective exclusive dealing on the theory that such devices are permissible if they are used for acceptable purposes. Austrian law defines as cartels, and thus recognizes the possibility of registering as permissible, associations that achieve their purposes through economic or social pressure. By contrast, the Norwegian and German laws contain nothing that implies the legitimacy of private coercion, and the German law contains prohibitions applicable to threats, coercion, inducements to block deliveries or purchases, and unfair hindrance of other enterprises.

The Right to Participate. In four countries a right to participate is afforded by law or governmental policy. The right exists, however, only as to the more formally organized groups or agreements. In New Zealand, orders may be issued against unjustified exclusion from a trade association if competition is unduly reduced thereby; but in the only two proceedings that dealt with such matters before the close of 1963, the authority refused to require that the excluded firm be admitted. In Germany and Norway firms that are denied membership in a trade association may appeal to a governmental authority from that decision; and in Norway the authority may also consider such exclusions on its own initiative. In Germany, admission may be ordered if the exclusion was factually unjustified and discriminatory and unfairly prejudices the capacity of the excluded firm to compete. In Norway admission may be ordered if the exclusion is considered unfair or contrary to the public interest.

During the first four years under the German law four orders were issued requiring that an applicant be admitted to an association, and in five more instances the association admitted the complainant before the government's investigation was finished. During the six years ending November 1, 1959, four cases involving exclusion from membership were considered by the Norwegian authority. In one the association had merely applied a rule about qualification for membership that was regarded as reasonable, and hence no action was taken. In the three others, admission of the excluded firm was ordered. In one of these cases, the association had acted arbitrarily to exclude a firm that had a record as a price cutter; in one, the excluded firm had been deprived of access to facilities that were necessary to economical operation; and in one, the standard for admission that had been applied was considered unreasonable, since it required that the manager of a retail book business be also the principal owner.

Though Dutch law contains no formal provision for review of exclusions from membership, in practice the Dutch authorities place greater emphasis upon admission than do the Germans and the Norwegians. Collective vertical agreements for exclusive dealing are common in the Netherlands, and are not considered objectionable by the authorities. The government insists, however, that the right to participate be open to all applicants for admission who meet what the government considers reasonable standards of qualification.

The Right to Avoid Participating. In four countries the law includes some kind of provision designed to relieve reluctant participants of obligation to conform to restrictive arrangements. Some of these provisions limit the scope or applicability of restrictive contracts; others empower participants to ask a public official to do so in a particular instance for good reason. The nature of the provisions appears in the following table.

Provisions that Protect Abstention or Withdrawal from Restrictive Agreements

Type of Provision	Austria	Germany	Norway	Switzerland
No restriction is binding unless accepted in writing				X
Participant may ask government to cancel agreement as unjustified	X			
Participants are given right to withdraw				
By limit of duration of agreement to one year unless agreement authorizes withdrawal on 3 month's notice			X	
By statutory right to withdraw after specified periods with specified advance notice	X			
By statutory right to withdraw at any time for adequate reason	X	X		
When authorized by judge on equitable grounds				X

Three purposes are served by these provisions. First, restrictions are made potentially more flexible by giving each participant opportunity to insist that they be modified or cancelled when changing circumstances make such action appropriate. Second, participants are enabled to safeguard themselves by abstention or withdrawal when they find a restriction so inappropriate to their business situation that conformity to it would entail heavy losses. Third, participants who experience discriminatory treatment by those who administer the agreement are enabled to protect themselves by withdrawal.

Protection from Unreasonable Disciplinary Action. As has already been indicated, the substantive law of various countries contains safeguards against practices that often have coercive or punitive effects, and thus not only protects the general public from cartels and dominant firms but also may be used to protect participants in cartels from harsh discipline. The following table lists types of coercive or punitive action that are subject to legal control.

Type of Practice Curbed	Belgium	Denmark	Finland	France	Germany	Ireland	Japan	Netherlands	New Zealand	Norway	Sweden	Switzerland	United Kingdom
Abuse of economic power or dominant position	X				X			X					
Coercion or threats					X		X						
Refusals to sell or to deal		X		X					X	X	X		
Boycott												X	
Unjust restriction of supply or orders							X						
Unreasonable conditions for supply							X						
Inducement to block deliveries					X								
Discrimination or preference	X			X		X	X		X	X	X		
Unfair hindrance of third parties					X		X						
Enforcement of resale price agreements	X	X	X									X	X

Such provisions are presumably available against a cartel that attempts to force unwilling firms to join or that disciplines members in ways that are forbidden by law or that the national authority considers unreasonable. Thus far, however, their use for such a purpose appears to have been very slight.

More specific protections are available in the five countries whose laws deal explicitly with problems of cartel discipline. One country, Austria, imposes criminal penalties upon anyone who exerts "unfair economic pressure" to induce a firm to join a cartel.[2] Similarly, the German authority regards as abuse any arrangement by which a cartel is so intertwined with a trade association that membership in the association compels membership in the cartel.

All five countries seek to control the discipline applied by cartels to their members. Such control has two aspects: imposition of rules designed to assure fair processes in deciding controversies and imposition of safeguards against excessive punishment.

The most ambitious attempt to apply standards of fair procedure has appeared in the Netherlands. After various correctives had been found necessary in cases involving particular cartels, the Minister of Economics issued a blanket order in July 1962 under which all cartel provisions for private enforcement were made invalid so far as they were inconsistant with requirements set forth in the order. These requirements attempted to impose upon private courts principles of action similar to those in public courts. They specified that defendants must be told the changes against them, must be heard, must be allowed to present witnesses and to hear opposing witnesses, must have access to pertinent documents, and must be allowed to employ counsel; that decisions adverse to defendants must contain the facts as to the offense, the evidence relied upon, and the rule that was violated; that penalties must be fully stated; that decisions open to appeal must not be enforceable before the appellate decision unless made by a body with a majority of non-members of the trade or made subject to stay by a non-member chairman of the appellate body; and that the body making final decisions must contain a majority of non-members of the trade.

In Austria and Switzerland, safeguards against arbitrary enforcement take the form of provisions that authorize resort to courts of law. Austrian cartel law, by amendment in 1962, specifies that disputes under cartel agreements may be taken to court by any party involved, even if the cartel agreement provides that they shall be settled by arbitration.[3] Swiss cartel law provides that agreements are void if they do not authorize every party to bring complaints before a court. It makes exception, however, for agreements that include persons resident abroad and provide for resort to an international arbitral body.[4]

Some control of private penalties exists under the laws of Austria, Germany, the Netherlands, and Norway. The Netherlands blanket order mentioned above includes provisions that where penalties are to be fixed in

---

[2] Article 40 a.
[3] Article 49
[4] Article 15

decisions the penalties applicable shall be stated as maxima, so that deciding bodies have discretion to impose less, and that costs to be borne by defendants shall be determined by the final deciding body. The German law provides that if collateral has been deposited it may be disposed of only after the Cartel Authority has given permission, and that permission shall be denied if the disposal would unfairly restrict the depositor's freedom of action or would harm him by unjustified discrimination.[5] The Austrian law, as amended in 1962, provides that if violators of a cartel agreement are punished by refusals to deliver or by cancellation of contracts, the courts may invalidate such penalties wholly or partially or may replace them by administrative fines.[6] Norwegian law authorizes the authorities to reduce or cancel private penalties of any kind if enforcement of them would be contrary to the public interest or would produce unreasonable effects upon the firm penalized.[7]

In establishing procedural requirements for systems of private enforcement, the Netherlands evidently modified substantially the existing methods of various cartels. Norway and Germany have specifically corrected a few abusive exclusions from membership, and the Netherlands probably has corrected more. However, the principal impact of the types of control discussed in this chapter has been preventative rather than corrective. Rights to withdraw can be exercised where they are legally available. Where rights to participate are clear, they are seldom challenged. Rights to resort to the ordinary courts and rights to obtain review of arbitrary or execessive penalties induce greater regard for the interest of defendants in private proceedings, and thus afford informal correctives without resort to formal action. Where the treatment of cartel members and potential members is thus safeguarded, the safeguards involve little administrative burden and may be effective even if little or no formal use is made of them.

It is noteworthy, however, that the available safeguards are incomplete. In the majority of the seventeen countries here under study, protection of the potential and actual participants in an agreement is not provided by law, or exists only against coercion that takes a specified form, or depends upon interpretation and use of such broad phrases as abuse of power. Even among the five countries that have sought to cope with such problems explicitly, not all protect the right to join, not all protect the right to refuse to join, not all offer protection against arbitrary procedure, and not all provide for limitation or review of private penalties. To an appreciable extent, the cartel member, like the outsider, is incompletely safeguarded against concerted attack.

---

[5] Section 14
[6] Article 36 b
[7] Section 40

Chapter XII

Dominant Firms

Although the laws of the seventeen countries covered by this study are concerned primarily with restrictive agreements, all of them apply some degree of control to the activities of powerful single enterprises. There is great diversity both in the extent of the control and in the means by which it is applied.

Control of dominant firms is more limited, less vigorously applied, less uniform in method, and in some countries more recent than control of cartels. In most countries, relatively slight attention has been given to this matter both in statutes and in the frequency of use of statutory provisions.

That this should be so was almost inevitable. In most countries, when the laws were enacted, large enterprises were relatively new and few. Their growth had been accompanied by changes in technology and in methods of doing business many of which had contributed to efficiency and some of which had visibly resulted in lower prices. This fact had induced not only the lay public but also economic and political experts to assume that the growth of large enterprise was typically both due to and indispensable to the attainment of a high level of productivity; and this belief was more plausible than it is in the United States because in the narrow national markets of countries with smaller populations, more of the bigness of the large firms was clearly attributable to the bigness of their plants, which presumably reflected economies of scale. Moreover, the restrictions that were applied by large enterprises individually were easier to conceal than those that resulted from cartelization; and their concealment was sometimes facilitated by a more tender regard by the government for the privacy of information about business than exists in the United States. The restrictions that became known were those that could not be concealed—e.g. refusals to sell and tying arrangements—and those that bore directly upon the well-being of particular business enterprises as buyers—e.g. arbitrary imposition of higher prices or harsher terms upon one purchasing enterprise than were regularly available to its competitors.

In Austria and France, laws about dominant firms came later than laws about cartels. Austrian law contained no provisions about them until 1962, though cartel legislation had been in effect since 1951. In France refusals to sell, discrimination, tying arrangements, and resale price maintenance were forbidden as early as 1953 when cartel control began; but these practices were forbidden to all firms, not merely to dominant ones. Not until 1963 were the restrictive practices of dominant firms brought under general control.

In other countries, control of dominant firms did not lag behind control of cartels. Laws provided for it in the United Kingdom in 1948, in Sweden, Norway, and Ireland in 1953, in Denmark and South Africa in 1955, in Germany in 1957, in the Netherlands and Finland in 1958, in Israel in 1959, in Belgium in 1960, and in Spain and Switzerland in 1963. In 1953, Japan, amending a law that had been reluctantly enacted during the military occupation, retained a considerable part of the provisions of the previous law that had been relevant to large firms.

Types of Control

Methods of controlling dominant firms are less uniform than methods of controlling cartels. The measures used are of several kinds: a) provisions about abuse or about restriction contrary to the public interest which, in some countries, are equally applicable to agreements and to the practices of particular firms, whether powerful or not; b) provisions about particular types of business practice, applicable to all firms, whether powerful or not; c) provisions applicable equally to dominant firms and restrictive agreements, but not applicable generally to firms or business practices; d) special provisions concerned with dominant firms, dominant positions, or monopolies, designed to curb the conduct of powerful enterprises or to prohibit monopolization; and e) provisions about mergers and other means of concentrating economic power, designed to provide information about such arrangements or to discourage or limit them. In some countries two or more of these types of control are applied.

In Ireland, Sweden, and South Africa, general provisions of law about abuse or restriction apply equally to agreements and to the activities of single firms. Ireland authorizes rules and orders that establish fair methods of competition for particular fields of economic activity. Sweden provides for negotiations to remove the harmful effects of restraints of competition, however these restraints may arise. South Africa authorizes corrective orders against monopolistic conditions that have effects contrary to the public interest, and defines monopolistic conditions to include not only agreements but also practices, acts, omissions to act, and situations that may have restrictive effects. Under all three statutes, procedures are undertaken without effort to distinguish sharply between collective and individual action nor between dominant enterprises and other enterprises. Nevertheless, in Ireland and South Africa, though apparently not in Sweden, the power of an enterprise may be considered relevant to the effect of its activities, and proceedings under the general law may thus have a special impact upon the conduct of powerful firms. Indeed, the orders authorized by South African law may not only prohibit conduct but also require dissolution of a corporation.

In eight countries,[1] some kind of limitation is explicitly applied by law to particular kinds of restrictive practice by single enterprises, whether or not these enterprises are powerful; and in a ninth country, Ireland, rules and orders issued under the law mentioned above consist typically in prohibitions or limitations of particular kinds of conduct. The practices thus explicitly curbed in two or more countries include refusal to sell,[2] discrimination,[3] tying,[4] coercion,[5] setting excessive prices or increasing prices,[6] resale price maintenance,[7] and sale through unnecessary middlemen.[8] Some of these practices could not be undertaken by a single enterprise unless it had substantial power. Others are subjected, in some countries but not in all, to control only if they have harmful effects that would be unlikely to appear unless a large part of the available supply were subject to the practice. In large part, therefore, these controls are focussed upon powerful firms.

Provisions applicable both to dominant firms and to restrictive agreements, but not to all firms, are included in the laws of three countries. Belgium seeks to correct abuses of economic power, whether the power is derived from agreement or from a single company's dominance. In France the activities of monopolies and "manifest concentrations of economic power" that may hinder the functioning of markets are subject, like cartel agreements, to prohibition or correction after an evaluation of their good and bad aspects.[9] In Switzerland single enterprises that control or substantially influence markets are subjected, as "cartel-like organizations," to provisions

---

[1] Denmark, Finland, France, Germany, Japan, New Zealand, Norway, Sweden.

[2] France, Ireland, New Zealand, Norway, Japan.

[3] France, Ireland, Japan.

[4] France, Ireland, Japan.

[5] Germany, Ireland, Japan, Norway.

[6] Ireland, Japan, Norway.

[7] Denmark, Finland, France, Ireland, Japan, the Netherlands, Norway, Sweden, United Kingdom. In addition, the laws of Austria, Germany, and New Zealand provide for control of resale price agreements entered into by a single supplier.

[8] Ireland, Norway.

[9] The wording of the law forbids what may interfere with full competition by hindering the reduction of costs or prices or by encouraging price increases, unless improvement and extension of markets or ensurance of economic progress by rationalization and specialization is proved. In practice, this statutory language has been treated as a mandate to evaluate all good and bad aspects of a cartel without regard to the limits of the statutory language. See Appendix B, discussion of the French law.

that a) forbid cartels to exclude independent enterprises from markets by boycott, discrimination, or destructive price-cutting except in specified situations and b) subject them to investigation and to judicial orders forbidding activities found to be contrary to the public interest.[10]

In eleven countries, special provisions of law are applicable to powerful firms, either instead of provisions that apply to others or in addition to such provisions. The extent of the explicit control to which powerful firms are subject to these countries differs greatly, however, from one country to another. In three countries[11] it consists merely of an obligation to report and register: in five countries,[12] of correction of practices that may be considered objectionable; in one country,[13] of possible termination of monopoly or practices that tend to bring about monopoly; in two countries,[14] of statutory prohibition of monopolization or of broad categories of monopolistic practice.

The control that is applicable to powerful firms is the combined effect of these special provisions and the other types of provisions already mentioned. Its full extent is shown in the following table.

Provisions concerned with means by which economic power is concentrated are included in the laws of only four countries. In Germany and Spain they consist merely in reporting requirements applicable to acquisitions that involve large firms.[15] In the United Kingdom they provide for control of mergers.[16] In Japan they include not only requirements for several kinds of reports but also provisions intended to set limits to various forms of economic concentration. These a) prohibit holding companies; b) where there probably would be substantial restraint of competition, prohibit stock acquisitions and stockholdings (both corporate and personal), interlocking directorships and officerships, mergers, asset acquisitions, management contracts, and arrangements to share profits and losses; and c) limit stockholdings by a financial company to not more than 10 per cent of the issued stock of the corporation whose stock is held.

As appears in the following table, the substantive controls that pertain to powerful enterprises consist almost wholly of correctives applicable to

---

[10] For a listing of these situations, see the discussion of the Swiss law in Appendix B.

[11] Austria, Denmark, and Finland. In Austria the law authorizes a quasi-public body to make reports about the effects of a registered firm's power. In Denmark, registration subjects a powerful firm to an obligation, also applicable to cartels, that the government's consent must be obtained before increasing prices.

[12] Germany, Israel, the Netherlands, Spain, the United Kingdom.

[13] New Zealand.

[14] Japan, Spain.

[15] German law provides that a report may be followed by an oral hearing or a request for a written statement, but conveys no corrective powers to the authority.

[16] These provisions were adopted in 1965 by enactment of a new law.

Country

Type of Control	Austria	Belgium	Denmark	Finland	France	Germany	Ireland	Israel	Japan	Netherlands	New Zealand	Norway	South Africa	Spain	Sweden	Switzerland	United Kingdom
Reporting and registration required	X[1]			X								X					
Conduct may be altered by order or negotiation																	
Under provisions of broad scope					X		X	X		X			X		X		X
Under provisions concerned with																	
Prices or price increases			X			X	X										
Coercion							X										
Resale price maintenance	X[3]			X		X	X		X		X[3]						
Refusal to sell							X				X	X[2]					
Discrimination							X										
Tying						X	X										
Sale to unnecessary middleman							X										
Conduct wholly or partly forbidden																	
Excessive prices										X	X						
Limitation of production, development, or investment													X				
Hindrance of third parties						X											
Coercion						X											
Unfair destruction of competitors										X		X					
Destructive price cutting															X		
Resale price maintenance		X		X												X	
Refusal to sell				X												X	X
Unfair hindrance to other party to transaction																	
Discrimination						X											
Tying						X											
Sale to unnecessary middleman														X			
Practices leading to monopoly may be terminated													X				
Monopoly may be terminated											X[4]		X				X[5]
Monopolization forbidden									X								

[1] A quasi-public body may report on effects of a firm's power.

[2] The order may cover any form of refusal of business connections, and hence can apply to refusal to buy.

[3] The provision applies to resale price maintenance by vertical agreement.

[4] New Zealand law clearly authorizes orders that terminate or control practices that tend to bring about complete or partial monopoly of supply. The language appears to define complete or partial monopoly as itself a practice and thus to authorize similar orders terminating a monopoly or imposing conditions upon its continuance. In early 1965 no case involving the relevant provision had yet been decided.

[5] Since 1965 orders for dissolution, divorcement, or divestiture have been authorized for matters subject to reference to the Monopolies Commission.

business conduct. No law, except that of Japan,[17] rests upon a presumption against concentration of economic power, nor contains provisions limiting the growth of large enterprises by acquisition of assets. No law, except those of Japan and the United Kingdom, provides for control of mergers. Except in Japan, the United Kingdom, South Africa, and possibly New Zealand, no law contemplates dissolution or divestiture as a means of action. Elsewhere the purpose of the statutes is to eliminate objectionable behavior by powerful enterprises, and the means is to issue orders that require changes in that behavior. An authority is usually given broad descretion to decide whether or not particular conduct is to be prevented and, if so, what correctives are to be applied.

The Concept of Power

A notable characteristic of policies toward powerful enterprise in these countries is that the power that makes the conduct of such firms subject to control is often more broadly conceived than in the American concept of monopoly. The laws that are explicitly concerned with powerful enterprise display four distinct concepts of power. One, illustrated by New Zealand, covers "complete or partial monopoly" in the country or in any part of it. A second, illustrated by Denmark, covers any enterprise that "may be able to exert a substantial influence on price, production, distribution, or transport conditions," either nationally or in local market areas. A third, illustrated by the United Kingdom, covers any firm that controls a stated share of supply or processing in the national market or in a substantial part of it. A fourth, illustrated by Israel, covers supply or acquisition by one person to an extent exceeding that designated by a minister as monopolistic for the particular commodity or service, nationally or in a particular area. These four concepts will be called respectively, a) monopoly, b) dominant influence, c) dominant share, and d) monopoly by variable definition.

Israel is the only country that relies upon the idea of monopoly by variable definition. The laws of Austria, Norway, and the United Kingdom use definitions of dominant share—one-third of supply in the nation or a substantial part of it in the United Kingdom; one-fourth of supply in the nation in Norway; and 30 per cent or 50 per cent of the market in Austria, depending on whether the number of competing firms does or does not

---

[17] In general the relevant provisions of the Japanese law were retained from a law enacted during the Occupation that expressed a desire to de-concentrate Japanese industry. They are applied laxly and should not be interpreted as equivalent in effect to provisions similarly worded in American law. Moreover, it is noteworthy that monopolization (which is prohibited) is defined in the law as activity excluding or controlling other entrepreneurs thereby causing substantial restraint contrary to the public interest. Conduct rather than market power is the statutory test.

exceed three. In the other ten countries whose statutes explicitly apply to powerful enterprise, ambiguities of language and absence of interpretative decisions sometimes leave uncertainties as to whether the law is intended to cover only monopoly or to extend to dominant influence. In these instances, classification must be tentative. In four of the ten countries[18] the intent is clearly to cover only monopoly. In two[19] is is clearly to cover dominant influence. In four,[20] though the scope of the statute is not clear, the probable intent is to cover dominant influence.

The idea of dominant influence is akin to that of dominant share in that it may apply to more than one firm in an industry. A dominantly influential firm need not possess a monopoly either in the whole country or in a part of it. In determining whether or not a firm has such influence, the authorities consider not only its share of the market, but also its relative share as compared with those with whom it deals or competes and its aggregate financial size as compared with other firms in the same general segment of the economy. They may also consider intangibles such as the prestige of its brands. In Denmark a firm has been required to register as a dominant enterprise even though it controlled no more than 15 per cent of the market.

It is noteworthy that the concept of dominance can be applied not only to single firms but also to groups of firms. An enterprise is usually conceived as including subsidiaries and, in some countries, as including also firms in which it holds a substantial stock interest or with which it has multiple interlocking directorates. But the concept of group dominance reaches further. In France, dominance may be attributed to a group of enterprises. In the Netherlands "a dominant position" may be held by an association or by the parties to an agreement. In Belgium "economic power" may be possessed by bodies acting in concert. In Germany and Spain, two or more enterprises may be considered dominant if there is no substantial competition between them and if jointly they encounter no substantial competition from others. In the United Kingdom two or more firms may be subject to the provisions that apply to powerful enterprises if, whether voluntarily or not, they so conduct their respective affairs as in any way to prevent or restrict competition.

In the countries that use concepts of dominant influence or dominant share, as well as in the three countries (Ireland, Sweden, and South Africa) that apply universally applicable concepts of abuse or of restriction contrary to the public interest, a showing that monopoly exists or is intended

---

[18] Germany, Japan, New Zealand, Spain.
[19] Denmark, France.
[20] Belgium, Finland, the Netherlands, Switzerland.

is not requisite to such corrective governmental action as the law contemplates. Policy often applies to all powerful firms, even if they compete with one another.

By covering the conduct of oligopolists, policies toward dominant firms apply directly to some kinds of behavior by large enterprises that cannot be readily challenged under the American antitrust laws. In the United States price discrimination, exclusive dealing and tying arrangements, corporate acquisitions, and interlocking directorates are subject to explicit statutory controls under the Clayton Act, and any business conduct is unlawful if it is found to be unfair under the Federal Trade Commission Act. Invoking in the Clayton Act tests of the probable effect of the conduct and in the Federal Trade Commission Act a flexible test of unfairness, these two American laws are conceptually akin to the foreign legislation, though their application is narrower. So far as the practices of large enterprises do not fall into the specified categories, they can be challenged under the American antitrust laws only if they are the result of agreement or if they arise from possession of, or effort to achieve, monopoly power. Discriminatory refusals to sell and perverse price policies, such as have repeatedly been alleged by Congressional committees in investigating oligopolistic industries, are not clearly subject to American law, but fall within the scope of most of the foreign laws here under discussion.

Tests of Abuse or Public Interest

Statutory concepts of abuse or of public interest that are invoked in provisions about dominant firms are often undefined, so that they merely delegate to some authority discretion to determine the field to which corrective action is applicable. The Netherlands seeks to prevent consequences that "conflict with the general interest." The French law applies to activities that have the purpose or potential effect of hampering the normal functioning of markets. Germany authorizes action against any abuse, but does not define abuse.[21] Ireland lists eleven types of practice as unfair, but only where their use is unreasonable, unjust, contrary to the public interest, or without just cause. Belgium sees abuse where the public interest is prejudiced by practices that distort or restrict the normal play of competition or that interfere either with the freedom of producers, distributors, or consumers or with the development of production or trade. Similarly broad provisions set forth the statutory standards of appraisal in Denmark, Norway, Sweden, Switzerland, and South Africa.

In some countries, however, the law is more explicit. Orders in New

---

[21] This provision took effect by amendment of the law in 1965. Previously action could be taken only against abuses in connection with prices, terms of sale, or tying arrangements.

Zealand are intended to counteract unreasonable increases in prices, costs, or profits, prevention or unreasonable reduction or limitation of competition, and prevention or limitation of supply to consumers. In Israel the ground for action is that but for the monopoly the price level would be lower, or quality or method of production or marketing would be more satisfactory, or the quantity supplied would be greater. In Spain abuses include activities that deliberately seek to destroy competitors by unfair competition; discriminate in a way injurious to third parties; condition purchases on tying arrangements; reduce output, technical development, or investment to the country's disadvantage; or involve allocation or price-fixing. In the United Kingdom the public interest is to be ascertained with attention to all relevant considerations, including specifically the need for efficiency, economy, technical progress, expansion of markets, encouragement of new enterprise, and supply of goods in qualities and quantities appropriate to demand.

Even the more explicit legal standards entrust considerable discretion to those that apply the law. Whether the law is vague or relatively explicit, exercise of such discretion depends either upon appraisal of the relation of the conduct of the large enterprise to accepted principles of fairness and morality or upon appraisal of the current or anticipated effect of that conduct upon economic performance. In the latter type of appraisal the central consideration is not the impact of business conduct upon the vitality of competition but its impact upon the price, quality, and quantity of goods available to the public. Impairment of competition is conceived as a ground for inquiry into the morality and consequences of the anti-competitive behavior, with or without an adverse presumption. Policies differ in the various countries because of a) difference in relative emphasis upon fairness as against performance; b) difference in the extent to which official discretion in using either standard is limited by statutory definition; c) difference in the particular aspects of fairness or performance emphasized in the more explicit statutory standards; and d) difference in the degree of adverse presumption involved.

Application of the Laws

Since discretion is broad, the actual scope and focus of the control of powerful firms can be ascertained only by examining the way the laws have been applied. Information about the application of policy to dominant firms is not available for some of the 17 countries covered by this study.[22] For some of the others, problems concerning dominant firms arise only

---

[22] For Spain and Switzerland, the law is too recent for experience to be available. For France, the same thing is true of the part of the law explicitly concerned with dominance. Belgian law provides for public disclosure of the application of the law only in the case of recalcitrant firms. In Austria and Finland, the statute provides for registration but not for public control. For Israel information is not available to me.

under provisions of law that are generally applicable, whether or not a dominant firm is involved, to restrictions of all kinds or to designated practices; and no special features are evident as to the application of these provisions to dominant firms. Swedish policy in negotiating to remove the harmful effects of restriction and French policy in enforcing prohibitions of refusals to sell and discrimination, for example, appear to be applied to curb particular kinds of conduct, whether concerted or individual and whether involving dominant firms or not.

Dominance as a Significant Fact under General Laws. Curbs upon some specified kinds of restriction have special application to dominant firms, whether or not the relevant legal language is also applicable to restrictions by others. Provisions about coercion have meaning only where there is power to coerce; provisions about tying have meaning only where a product that is tied is not readily available from other sellers. In the countries where such provisions have been adopted, there appears to be no substantial record of their use, presumably because where a law against such practices exists it is seldom challenged.

Where the law contains general curbs upon refusal to sell, discrimination, resale price maintenance, or exaction of excessive prices, special application to dominant firms is also possible but not inevitable. Though none of these practices could have significance in a market that was perfectly competitive, each of them can be undertaken not only by large and powerful firms but also by petty sellers that are partially sheltered from competition by the minor imperfections of actual markets. This fact is evident in the cases: They include instances in which one of several small local wholesalers refused to sell or arbitrarily withheld a customary discount; in which resale price maintenance was undertaken for a branded product that had no special degree of public acceptance; and in which a local craftsman or repair man charged an excessive price. Where the practices in question are subject to generally applicable provisions of law, it is possible to take account of the power of the enterprise in considering the bearing of its conduct upon accepted standards of abuse or of public interest.

Generally applicable rules as to refusal to sell, discrimination, resale price maintenance, and imposition of excessive prices are invoked in some countries with special emphasis upon dominant firms and in some countries without such emphasis. Where this emphasis is absent, the authority requires that the restriction be based upon objective, impartial, and reasonable standards, and that it be consistent with reasonable costs and prices. In Sweden, for example, where two manufacturers of office machines dominated the industry, each was allowed to withhold repair parts from independent repair shops because its own services were adequately available at reasonable prices.[23] Comparable standards are invoked in action against unreasonably high prices. In Norway a legal provision against such prices is applied not only by the national authority against dominant firms but also by local police against sellers of second-hand machinery, repairmen, and other petty traders who take advantage of shortages or of gullible customers.

Where importance is attached to the dominant position of the seller, similar legal standards are supplemented by tests relevant to the effect of that dominance. In Denmark, for example, refusal to sell is forbidden if the buyer does not have adequate access to similar goods. A dominant manufacturer of vacuum cleaners was required to stop requiring that retailers deal in its product exclusively because the requirement prevented retailers from stocking rival products among which their customers might readily choose. A dairy with a local monopoly was required to sell to a grocer because without milk the grocer's competition with a nearby rival would be impaired.

Laws About the Conduct of Dominant Firms. Under laws that authorize specific control of the conduct of dominant enterprises,[24] little control has been actually undertaken. In the Netherlands, only two or three orders have been issued in cases in which the government thought that a dominant position had been used in a way contrary to the general interest. Moreover, the Dutch law as to dominant positions is conceived as relevant to concerted action without formal agreement, to continuance of an agreement after its formal termination, and to a price war among members of a dominant group, as well as to control of the restrictions imposed by powerful enterprises. In a recent proceeding, for example, 35 cigar manufacturers who, under pressure from wholesalers of cigars, had individually refused to sell to certain grocery wholesalers were ordered to resume such sales.

In Germany, market-dominating enterprises are subject to corrective orders if they abuse their market position. To the close of 1961 correction of abuse had been obtained informally in 6 cases, but no case had yet re-

---

[23] Similarly, in France a producer of casseroles was granted permission to maintain resale prices (subject to a requirement that it must permit resellers to grant discounts up to 6 per cent) on the ground that it had reduced the price by from 30 to 35 per cent; and the fact that it furnished more than 83 per cent of the total supply was not regarded as an obstacle to the permission. The decision antedated amendment of the French law to cover dominant firms as well as restrictive agreements, and therefore does not necessarily reflect French policy today.

[24] For Belgium, France, Switzerland, and Spain information is not available because of the secrecy of proceedings or the recency of the law. Information about activities under the law of Israel is not available to me.

sulted in a formal order. The informal cases had been concerned with such matters as exclusion from exhibits by trade associations, other restrictive activities by associations, and abuse by public utilities, rather than with monopoly or oligopoly in free markets. A provision about discrimination is also applicable to dominant enterprises, as well as to associations and to enterprises that exercise legal right to fix prices. It has been invoked moderately often to prevent arbitrary discrimination against particular buyers.

In South Africa, a monopoly of beer resulting from a merger was found acceptable by the authorities, and to the close of 1961 control of dominant enterprise had been undertaken only in the case of motion pictures. In this instance, the Fox group of firms, which imported 75 per cent of all the films released and controlled 43 per cent of all urban cinema seats, undertook, after negotiation, to limit its exhibition contracts with most theaters to twelve months, with uniform dates of expiration, to accept financial guarantees from theaters instead of requiring cash deposits, and to cease setting theater admission fees in the exhibition contracts. Though block-booking and blind selling of films had been subjects of complaint, these practices were not found objectionable.

Under the British Monopolies Act examination of practices deemed to be possibly contrary to the public interest has been undertaken somewhat more often. To August 1965 the activities of powerful enterprises were involved in ten reports by the Monopolies Commission. In three of these reports, concerned with rubber tires, rubber footwear, and metal windows, the Commission saw in the conduct of the dominant firms no significant danger to the public interest that necessitated corrective recommendations. For two of the industries, in which the dominant producer supplied less than 50 percent of the market, the Commission centered its attention upon the effect of restrictions that resulted from agreement. In the third industry, rubber tires, the dominant firm set export prices that were adopted by all exporters, made secret rebates to distributors and dealers, and secretly controlled important distributors and retreaders; but the Commission saw damage to the public interest only in the secrecy of the control of retreaders.

In a fourth report, concerned with chemical fertilizers, the Commission said that the prices charged by a dominant supplier of superphosphates were too high and that elimination of competition on potash by an international cartel was against the public interest. Nevertheless, the Commission recommended only that the dominant producer reduce prices voluntarily and that large buyers of potash develop other foreign sources of supply.

In a report on matches the Commission found that under an integrated monopoly which was controlled by a large foreign firm prices and costs were higher than they would have been under competition and there were obstacles to the development of domestic competitors. It noted that foreign markets were allocated between the British firm and the foreign firm that exercised the control, and that the British firm depended upon the foreign one to conduct research and to furnish basic machinery. Nevertheless, it did not find these facts to be contrary to the public interest. It considered, but disapproved, dissolution of the British monopoly. It recommended instead that the government subject costs and prices to review. The government rejected the recommendation.

In a report on industrial gases, the Commission found that one company had attained 96 per cent of the national supply by acquisitions, exclusive contracts, and use of a fighting company, that prices were excessive and discriminatory, and that profits were excessive. The Commission recommended that fighting companies be used no more, that buyers be allowed to purchase as well as lease equipment, and that a new scale of non-discriminatory prices be established and periodically reviewed by the Board of Trade. The government rejected the idea of controlling the company's prices and profits, but obtained from the company undertakings that the remaining independents would not be absorbed, that selective local price cutting would be stopped, that certain restrictive features of supply contracts would be eliminated, and that plants would be sold to any firm that might wish to buy.

In a report on cigarettes and tobacco, the Commission did not object to resale price maintenance, but recommended that the dominant firm cease granting bonuses for promotion and display by distributors and divest itself of its 42 per cent holding of the stock of the second largest company. The bonus agreements were terminated; but instead of requiring divestiture, the Board of Trade obtained from the dominant firm a formal promise not to interfere in the management of the other company.

In the case of electrical equipment for motor vehicles, the Commission found that each of four firms was dominant in supplying some kinds of equipment; that, in replacement sales of equipment, prices and profits were higher than in sales for use as components of motor vehicles, and that the most powerful of the four firms not only had grown by acquiring competitors but also had practiced selective price cutting as a weapon against its remaining competitors. The Commission recommended that resale price maintenence be terminated, that suppliers publish prices and terms for replacement sales, and that exchange of information about customers, prices, and the trading activities of independent sellers come to an end.

In its last two reports the Commission's recommendation focused on industrial structure as well as market practice. In a report on wallpaper, it found that a market share of more than 70 percent had been attained by means that included acquisition of manufacturers and retailers and exclusive dealing. It recommended, not only that resale price maintenance be terminated and no exclusive dealing arrangements exist without permission, but also that future acquisitions be allowed only when explicitly permitted. In a report on motor fuel it saw value in "solus" arrangements between suppliers of gasoline and retailers, but recommended various changes in the contracts to enable retailers to sell independent lubricants and automobile accessories, and to prevent retailers from being bound to a single supplier for long periods of time. It also recommended that suppliers who furnished more than 10 million gallons of gasoline per year be forbidden to acquire or build more filling stations so long as more than 15 percent of their total gallonage sold at retail was sold by stations they already possessed.

Most of these reports and the subsequent applications of British policy were focused upon the conduct of the dominant enterprises, were concerned with each type of conduct separately, and accepted or rejected lines of conduct on other grounds than their effect in supporting dominant positions. The last two reports included proposals designed to curb further growth of dominance. Divestiture was recommended in one earlier report, but action went no further than to obtain assurance about conduct. Price control rather than economic surgery was usually regarded as the government's ultimate remedy. It is noteworthy, however, that the reports were prepared before amendment of the law in 1965 gave the Board of Trade explicit power to act against mergers and to require divestiture, divorcement, or dissolution.

Special curbs upon the price policies of dominant firms exist in the laws of Denmark. By providing for prior approval of price increases made by anyone that is publicly registered, Danish law subjects to control not only cartel prices but also the prices of single firms that have been required to register because they have a significant influence on prices in any domestic market. This provision has become so important that in the five years beginning in 1955 about 44 per cent of all matters decided by the Danish authority were requests for approval of price increases. Because rising prices have been general since the enactment of the Danish law, the authority's power over the prices charged by dominant firms has been substantial; and since Danish concepts of influence in markets cover influence in markets that are merely local and influence by firms that do not possess a preponderant share of the market, the breadth of the author-

ity's discretionary control has been great. The control has been used to
limit price increases. Danish business argues that it has also prevented
price reductions by arousing fear that a price once reduced cannot be
subsequently increased.

   Laws Directed Against Excessive Power. Concern to exercise surveillance over concentrations of economic power or to curb such concentrations,
rather than merely to control the use of such power, has been evident in only six of the seventeen countries covered by this book. The provisions that express such concern have provided for little control or for
control that remains almost unused. In Spain, statutory provisions require
reports of mergers and related forms of unification but convey to the government no power to prevent or limit the projects that are reported. In
Germany, there is a similar statutory provision; and a special report about
the extent of concentration, which was provided for by Parliamentary resolution, was completed and submitted in 1964. Though South African law
includes provision for dissolution of enterprises as a corrective measure,
no use of this power has yet been made. Similarly, New Zealand has not
yet invoked the provision of its law that permits orders against monopoly.
In 1952, however, a New Zealand law that provides for licensing of motion
picture theaters was applied to deny further licenses to firms that already
had as many as ten theaters. Though until 1965 the law of the United
Kingdom did not explicitly provide that economic concentration could be
limited or reduced, the British government made a few steps in this direction: The Monopolies Commission considered (and rejected) the idea of
dissolving a dominant producer of matches; the government asked for and
obtained a promise that the dominant supplier of industrial gases will not
absorb the remaining independents; the Commission recommended divestiture of the stock of a competitor by the dominant tobacco manufacturer,
though, rejecting the recommendation, the government accepted instead
an assurance that the competitor's management would not be controlled;
and the Commission proposed in recent reports that curbs be placed upon
future acquisitions by the largest producers of paper and by the large integrated gasoline producers.

   In 1965 new legislation authorized the British Board of Trade to refer
to the Monopolies Commission the question whether proposed mergers involving over 30 percent of the supply of a kind of goods or acquisitions of
over £5 million were in the public interest, to delay such mergers pending
the commission report, and to prevent them unless they were found unobjectionable. The same law authorized orders involving divestiture, divorcement, or dissolution.[25] By the end of October, 1965, the Board of Trade

---

[25] Monopolies and Mergers Act, 1965.

had asked the Commission to report upon two mergers. In the first, British Motor Corporation sought to acquire Pressed Steel, a principal supplier of automobile bodies to competing motor manufacturers. In the second, Imperial Tobacco, which produced a brand of potato crisp, sought to acquire Smith's, which supplied more than half of the £50 million of potato crisp consumed annually in Britain.[26]

In February 1966 the Commission was asked to report upon three more proposed mergers. One involved acquisition of an enterprise that caught, processed, and sold fish by a diversified firm that operated trawler fleets and distributed fish. The other two involved a proposal for acquisition of a British dental supply firm by a diversified British firm that produced and distributed dental goods and an alternative proposal that the acquisition be made by an American dental supply firm whose products were distributed by the first British firm. Consummation of the dental mergers was stayed by the Board of Trade pending the report.

Further information about the potato crisp merger is not available to me. Reports about the other three mergers were made by the Commission and published in January, May, and August, 1966.[27]

The automobile body acquisition was not challenged by customers of the acquired company nor by organized labor. The Commission saw in it a) possibilities of increased efficiency through more specialized production of parts of bodies, with assembly elsewhere, and through savings of manpower in planning production; and b) export advantages from BMC's assistance to Pressed Steel, particularly in establishing local production overseas. Moreover, the Commission found some merit in BMC's argument that Pressed Steel might otherwise be acquired by a foreign vehicle manufacturer who would give Pressed Steel's existing customers less consideration than BMC. The possibility that either of Pressed Steel's largest customers might have undertaken to make its own bodies was treated by the Commission as a risk that Pressed Steel might reasonably seek to forestall. The possibility that if Pressed Steel had been acquired by another company BMC might have had to undertake body manufacture was considered a risk of wasteful duplication of national resources. The Commission concluded that, since BMC and Pressed Steel had given assurance that Pressed Steel's other customers would continue to be supplied on fair terms, the merger would not operate against the public interest. At the Commission's request, however, the assurance was reformulated in more explicit terms.

---

26 The Economist, October 23-29, 1965, pp. 413-4.
27 The British Motor Corporation Ltd. and the Pressed Steel Company Ltd., a report on the proposed merger; Ross Group Limited and Associated Fisheries Limited, a report on the proposed merger; The Dental Manufacturing Co. Ltd., or The Dentists' Supply Co. of New York and the Amalgamated Dental Co. Ltd., a report on the proposed mergers.

The fish acquisition resulted in a recommendation by six members of the Commission that the merger be not allowed, with two members dissenting. The majority thought a) that the merged company could significantly influence the price of cod, since it would supply more than half of the amount landed at two ports which received 70 percent of the total national supply; and b) that it might dominate other companies through its controlling position in two associations of owners of fishing vessels and in companies that provided ancillary services. The Commission saw no likelihood that any other group might become large enough to be a counterweight, but instead, anticipated that the merged company's dominance of the distant water trawler fleet (117 vessels in a total of 196) would be enhanced as small owners sold their vessels to it. Since the merged company would distribute at least 14 percent of all fish, nearly twice as much as anyone else, the Commission feared that many customers would have no adequate alternative and might even be deprived of a chance to buy if fish of the merged company were sold through its own outlets. Though the merging companies anticipated that savings of £790,000 pounds would result from the merger, the Commission thought the estimate excessive and concluded that savings probably would be small. It concluded that the merger would contribute nothing toward solving the industry's problem of fragmentation, would eliminate the benefits of competition between two large companies, and would be unlikely to accelerate the rate at which new methods are introduced.

The dissenters thought that since the merged company would control less than one-fifth of all fish, competition would deprive it of power to raise prices excessively, that the merger promised significant financial advantages and might contribute to rationalization, and that if in fact the public interest were impaired by the merger the effect could be counteracted by a recommendation to the Board of Trade that prices be reduced or other appropriate action taken. In view of the industry's dependence upon financial support from the government, such recommendations, it thought, could easily be made effective.

The majority of the Commissioners who signed the report thought that neither of the alternative dental mergers was likely to operate against the public interest. Merger with the American company would not enhance the share of the merged company in domestic trade, though it would place control in American hands. Though merger of the two British companies would give the merged company about one-half of domestic dental goods trade and about one-third of domestic manufacturing capacity, competition from imports would remain strong and the Ministry of Health, a large potential customer as well as a vigilant protector of the public, would be able to exert influence on price and quality. The American merger, intended to preserve the status quo, would be unlikely to increase efficiency soon, though it might do so eventually. The all-British merger might or might not lead to greater efficency.

Internationally, the American merger would be unlikely to shift English production to other countries or to disturb the British firm's role as distributor of the American firm's products in England and elsewhere. It might improve the possibility of exporting British goods to the United States. It would bring in a lump sum of dollars, but subsequently divert to the United States the profits of the British firm in England and elsewhere. The all-British merger might result in loss of the existing contract to distribute goods produced by the American firm, and might also result in export of more goods made in England, the effect on the balance of payments depending upon the relative effect of these possibilities.

One Commissioner, agreeing about the all-British merger, objected to the American merger. He thought that it would result not only in immediate diversion of profits to the United States but also in a long-run failure to develop the full potential of the British overseas outlets as a support for the British industry and probably in failure to increase as fully as possible the size and efficiency of the British manufacturing plants.

Until 1965 Japan was the only one of the seventeen countries in which there were statutory prohibitions designed to prevent the growth of excessive private economic power. Under Japanese law private monopolization is forbidden; holding companies may not operate; a financial company may not hold more than 10 per cent of the stock of any other company without prior approval; mergers must be reported in advance and are forbidden if they involve unfair practices or probably will restrain competition substantially; and where there is probability of a similar anti-competitive effect, no company or person other than a company may acquire or hold stock in a company and no officer or employee of a company may be an officer of another company. These impressive provisions, adopted in terms yet more comprehensive under military occupation, survived amendment of the law by the Japanese in 1953. However, since that time they have had little practical effect except in preventing the reestablishment of holding companies. Cases concerned with monopolization or unreasonable restraint of trade have been undertaken seldom; indeed, none was begun in the period from January 1, 1958 to September 30, 1962. Japan's numerous mergers have included one by which nearly 60 per cent of the national production of dairy products came under a single control; another by which three companies that, before postwar dissolution, had constituted Mitsubishi's heavy industry company were reunited; and a third that completed the reunion of Mitsui's great trading company, which had also been dissolved under military occupation. Nevertheless, no order has been issued against any merger. Proceedings have not been undertaken against the numerous intercorporate stockholdings and the numerous interlocking directorates by which a considerable part of the pattern of pre-war industrial concentration has been reestablished; for the connections are typically conglomerate, and a probability of substantial restraint of competition is not thought to exist in the interconnection of firms that are not in competition with one another. From the amendment of the law in 1953 to the end of September, 1962, only two cases were instituted under the provisions of the law that pertain to concentration of economic power. One of these concerned excessive holding of stock by a financial company; the other an effort to evade the prohibitions applicable to excessive concentrations.

It seems probably that, for some time to come, efforts to control powerful single enterprises will be weaker than efforts to control agreements, and that they will focus upon control of the conduct of the powerful rather than upon attempts to reduce concentrated power or to prevent it from growing. Nevertheless, there are beginnings of the latter type of policy. They are evident in the new British merger law, in the German and Spanish laws about report of mergers, and in the recent German report on concentration, mentioned above. Though the relevant provisions of Japanese law are dormant, they were not discarded by amendment, and are still available if the Japanese government should decide to use them.

Chapter XIII

Appraisal of the National Laws

The ultimate goals of policy toward restrictive business practices in the countries covered by the foregoing chapters are similar. They consist in a) keeping prices low and supplies of goods adequate for the needs of consumers, and promoting improvements in technology and business organization that contribute to these results; and b) preventing private action that impairs business opportunity or access to markets.

Though these goals are similar to the ultimate economic goals of American antitrust policy, they result in policies that are, in many respects, different. Part of the difference is due to the fact that, except in Germany, the policies under discussion are unlike American policy in that they have no political goal of minimizing private concentrations of economic power. Another part, however, is due to the fact that the broadly stated goals, when more closely examined, involve significant differences in exact purposes and priorities. Important among them are the following:

Differences from American Goals

1. The role of competition is conceived differently. Though the laws here under study are all designed to increase competition, most of them seek to do this in the belief that competitive incentives make desirable contributions to good economic performance and hence should be fostered except where there are countervailing considerations. Even where reliance upon competition is strongest, the law creates no more than a rebuttable presumption that anticompetitive restrictions are undesirable. None of the laws rest upon the assumption that underlies the American antitrust laws, that a self-regulating competitive system is the most desirable form of economic organization. To varying degrees, the laws contemplate supposedly desirable private or public impairments of competition.

Of course, one should not presume that the underlying differences between foreign and American policy are as great as the differences in the basic legislation about restrictive business practices. Whereas in the countries here under discussion the limits of reliance upon competition are usually made evident in the restrictive practice laws and the decisions under them, this is not true in the United States. American antitrust laws, as written, appear to be generally applicable; and most of policies that

197

limit their application are set forth in other statutes and in regulations pursuant thereto. Thus there are various statutory exemptions from the antitrust laws, by which the apparently comprehensive sweep of the Sherman and Clayton Acts is substantially reduced—e.g. laws sanctioning agricultural marketing agreements. Business decisions are also controlled by special laws enacted for purposes other than the maintenance of competition, such as conservation of petroleum or protection of automobile dealers from inequitable treatment by automobile manufacturers. The greater reliance upon competition in the United States is evident, however, in the fact that such limitations upon the competitive policy require statutory approval in each instance, that the burden of proof rests in each case upon those who wish to limit competition, and that considerable reluctance to reduce the extent of competitive self-regulation is nearly always evident.

2. Standards of fairness have a different role. In the countries here under discussion, much of what is called an economic basis for policy toward restrictive business practices is actually moral. Applying a concept of a just price, those who apply policy may condemn price-fixing when they consider the resulting prices excessively high, but permit it when they think that the prices that would result from competition would be excessively low. They may require equitable treatment of buyers, not for fear that competition may be impaired by inequity, but because discrimination against particular buyers is not fair. They may appraise practices designed to exclude a firm from a market in the light of the competence and morality of the excluded firm rather than of the competitive desirability of keeping the market itself open to all comers. As was indicated in Chapter II, concepts of abuse that are invoked in such decisions have their roots in moral teachings that antedate the Protestant reformation; and the modern versions of these concepts came to be considered self-evident because they reflected the thinking of culturally homogeneous groups and the stability of the cultural inheritance and the business institutions to which the concepts were relevant.

In the United States, the law of restrictive business practices has a more limited association with a prohibition of unfair practices. The price discrimination law seeks not only to protect competition but also to prevent inequitable impairment of the opportunities of business enterprises; but the law was enacted and is defended on the theory that the equitable provisions are needed to preserve competition. The Federal Trade Commission Act condemns unfair methods of competition and unfair business practices. In the antirust context of this statute, unfairness was initially conceived as activity that might jeopardize the chance for fair competitors to compete; and though amendment has broadened the statute to cover unfairness to consumers, the type of practice subject to the broader concept is typically one that can be envisaged as an impairment of the consumer's ability to distinguish intelligently among competitive offers. Pursuit of equity for its own sake, without regard to its relation to the maintenance of competition, is not a significant part of the American antitrust law.

3. Progress and security have different priorities. In the countries here under discussion, stability rather than change is likely to be taken for granted. Change is often regarded less as a cornucopia of new opportunities than as a source of possibly undesirable threats to the security of established ways of life and established sources of income. There is no counterpart to the American presumptions that the new is probably better than the old, that progress is worth whatever it costs, and that the greatest virtue of an economic system is flexibility in adapting to changing circumstances. Instead, stability and security are important values. The maintenance of existing enterprises and existing ways of doing business is regarded as obviously desirable except where some result that is clearly more desirable is in prospect. Thus policy makers often sympathize with collaborative efforts to assure conformity to well-established business ethics and to protect established business groups against "destructive" competition. However, where a substantial reduction of costs and prices can be foreseen, as in the introduction of chain stores and supermarkets into retail distribution, public policy welcomes the innovation.

Only France has made enhancement of economic productivity a central purpose of its policy. It does so by considering in every case whether or not a restriction enhances productivity, and by giving the answer decisive weight. Elsewhere, enhancement of productivity is not the major purpose of policy but is ground, from time to time, for approval of a restrictive agreement. Neither in France nor elsewhere, however, is impairment of productivity a common ground for disapproving an agreement.

The importance attributed to stability and security in the countries under discussion is, of course, closely related to the importance attributed to fairness. Both reflect homogeneity and absence of dramatic institutional change in the societies in which these attitudes prevail. A people drawn from different cultures and exposed to rapid economic and institutional change is likely to prize ability to adapt to its environment, and is unlikely to develop a compelling moral consensus about its economic behavior. Codes of economic morals are persuasive where they reflect relatively unchanging economic relationships. There is historical reason for American approval of the innovator, without much concern about the impact of his unconventional methods upon his contemporaries; and also historical reason for European approval of economic morality, without much concern about its effect on innovation.

The differences between policy in the countries under discussion and policy in the United States express these differences of opinion as to the function of competition, the importance to be attributed to equitable considerations, and the importance to be attributed to stabiliy and security. But they also reflect important differences in the techniques of public control. With little distrust of concentrated private power, the countries under discussion do not seek to destroy that power but attempt instead to control its exercise. With even less distrust of governmental power, they do this by laws that authorize some governmental authority to exercise broad discretion without much statutory guidance. Distrusting concentrated power, both public and private, the United States endeavors to diffuse private power and thereby to be able to rely on competition with a minimum of government control of business activity. Its policy is expressed in laws that are designed to minimize the administrative discretion of government. Prohibition, exemption, and the substantive content of whatever regulation may be undertaken are for the Congress; powers delegated to administrators are narrowly circumscribed; and interpretation of Congressional enactments is for the courts.

Two differences in the content of policy toward restrictive practices spring directly from these differences in technique. First, exemptions from the general line of public policy can be much more numerous under the foreign laws than under American law. Exemption by statute becomes possible only when those who favor exemption are numerous enough to have political weight and when the case for exemption is strong enough to persuade a legislative body to act. Exemptions can be granted by administrative officials in response to pressures less widespread and after evaluation of arguments that are more nearly equal in persuasiveness. Thus the American techniques foster a policy with fewer non-competitive exceptions than the foreign ones.

Second, under the foreign laws exemptions become a more flexible instrument of action than under American procedures. Exercising administrative discretion, administrators can adapt their decisions and the scope of the resulting exemptions more closely to each new circumstance than would be possible by legislative exemptions. An exemption can be made to approximate, not modification of a statute, but a regulatory activity, in which the content of governmental control is altered to fit varying circumstances. This gain in the relevance of control is likely to be achieved, however, at the cost of a deflection of a public policy by private pressures. The responsible official, protected neither by full publicity nor by explicit statutory standards to which he must conform, may be subjected to pressure from vested interests that, though too weak to move a legislative body, are strong enough to prevail upon him; and so far as this happens, the resulting exemptions and the policy that underlies them may reflect private power.

Comparison with American Policy as to Content

In spite of these differences in the general orientation of policy, the laws of the countries here under discussion cover restrictions generally similar to those covered by American law. They pertain to restrictive horizontal agreements, restrictive vertical agreements, and restrictive behavior by single firms. They are concerned primarily with price-fixing; fixing discounts and terms of sale; resale price maintenance; joint purchase or sale; allocation of goods, markets, or customers; collective control of access to markets; price discrimination; tying; coercion; and refusal to deal with particular enterprises or classes of enterprises. Few of them, however, provide any curbs upon mergers or upon the acquisition or possession of monopoly power. As in the United States, price-fixing receives a major share of attention.

In any effort to appraise the relative impact of these foreign laws and American antitrust law upon a particular type of practice, three important considerations must be borne in mind. The first is the fact that most of the foreign laws are too recent to have become definitive expressions of policy. When this chapter was written, the statutes in which national policies were formulated had been in effect in about two-thirds of the countries for twelve years or less; in about a third, for seven years or less; in two for not quite a year. About half of the laws had been amended since their enactment, mostly for the purpose of strengthening their application or enlarging their scope; and important amendments currently under consideration in two countries were evidence that the main features of policy were still mobile. There was considerable probability that gaps in the statutes might soon be filled and weaknesses might soon be reduced. In most of the countries, parts of the law had not yet been tested by application, and as to other parts gaps or inconsistencies in administrative or judicial interpretations were still evident. The staff employed in administration of the national policy varied from about two hundred persons in some countries to one or two persons with a few part-time assistants in others. The record to date is not necessarily a good indication of the future significance of the statutes.

The second consideration is the fact that the laws in question differ significantly from one another. The degree to which policies and laws differ from those of the United States differs from country to country, with the greatest similarities in Germany and the United Kingdom, and the greatest differences in Sweden, the Netherlands, Denmark and Austria. Comparisons and appraisals appropriate to one country are to some extent invalid for another; and generalizations applied to all of the seventeen countries must be either distressingly vague or distressingly inaccurate in their application to one or more of the countries that they cover.

The third consideration is the fact that in some instances differences in methods of control may obscure what is actually a similar substantive result. For example, a seller who participates in an agreement to allocate territory or customers must, in complying with the agreement, refuse to sell to customers that are not allocated to him. If the law applicable to him forbids refusal to sell, he is unable to do this legally. Thus a prohibition of refusal to sell is the practical equivalent of a prohibition of these types of allocation agreement. In various countries, the curbs upon refusal to sell, though directed primarily at the practices of individual firms, are substantial obstacles to types of restrictive agreements that are not directly precluded by the parts of the national policy that are concerned explicitly with agreements.

For these reasons comparison of the effectiveness of American law and these foreign laws as instruments against restrictive business practices cannot be precise.

Nevertheless, one conclusion emerges clearly—that the foreign laws are not uniformly more permissive toward restriction than the American law. Though various types of restriction are treated more leniently in many foreign countries than in the United States, some types of restriction are treated, in some countries, more severely. Restrictions can be roughly classified, by type, into three groups. As to one, the policy of the countries here under discussion is more permissive than American policy. As to the second, the foreign and American policies are not very different. As to the third, the foreign policies are more repressive than American policy. But because of the many differences from country to country, this crude classification is not an accurate basis for comparison of any single country's policy with that of the United States.

Parts That Are More Permissive. The relatively permissive parts of the foreign policies pertain chiefly to horizontal agreements containing restrictions whose target is persons on the other side of the market—fixation of prices, discounts, or terms of sale, and other restrictions designed to give sellers greater power in their dealings with buyers. Such agreements will be called hereafter exploitative. To varying degrees, the countries here under study permit sellers to act together to reduce competition, but seek to confine such action within bounds set by governmental concepts of fair dealing and by evaluations of the bearing of the concerted restrictions upon the efficiency of economic performance and the quality of service to consumers. The policies that are applied are significantly regulatory rather than competitive. Even in the countries in which prohibitions of horizontal restrictive agreements have a substantial place in public policy, they are typically accompanied by provisions that authorize grant of discretionary exemptions where the authorities believe that concerted restriction would support equitable relationships or improve business performance.

The standards of fairness by which such restrictions may be condemned focus upon distributive justice, with particular emphasis upon just prices. In some countries, prices are appraised by a standard of fair profit, of proper relation to costs, or of relation to prices that are charged elsewhere; and where they are found to be unfair, price agreements are invalidated or changes in prices are required. In other countries, unilateral price-fixing is considered unfair in principle, but may be permitted in particular instances in which it is thought to be useful as a corrective of unduly low prices or as an aid to improvement of economic performance.

Discount agreements are terminated or modified when they are considered discriminatory or otherwise unfair, but are often regarded as useful ways of avoiding unnecessary increases in distributive margins that would be likely to raise prices. Neither as to price agreements nor as to discount agreements is there much evidence of reliance upon competition to put pressure upon prices and costs. Still less is there evidence of desire to make markets self-operative.

There is less difference from American policy in the treatment of agreements about terms of sale other than discounts. Part of what Europeans are likely to approve as means to enhance the "transparency" of markets is permitted in the United States because it is not likely to have restrictive effects,—particularly when buyers have had a voice in formulating the standard terms of sale. In some of the countries under consideration, however, sellers are allowed to establish terms of sale concertedly without taking account of buyers' interests. In such cases, European public policy, unlike American, ignores the restrictive and exploitative effects that can be produced by agreed terms that shift risks or costs from sellers to buyers.

Standards of performance are rarely invoked to condemn concerted exploitative restrictions. Where price-fixing is condemned, attention is seldom centered upon its significance for economic performance. In most of the countries, the idea that restrictions of output, allocations of markets, and similar exploitative restrictions may be impediments to economic performance has had no significant place in policy. In the few cases in which restrictions of the latter types have been curbed, the basis for the action has usually been the indirect impact of these restrictions upon the level of prices.

But standards of performance are used to justify restrictions that might otherwise have been regarded as objectionable. Allocations of types of goods, quotas of sale, allocations of customers, allocations of territorial markets, and joint selling are considered to be often useful in promoting greater efficiency, better service, or more rapid economic progress. Where such benefits can be shown, relevant concerted restrictions are permitted. Such a policy makes "rationalization" by agreement much easier than in the United States, where comparable restrictions can only become lawful so far as their usefulness is sufficiently evident to induce Congress to exempt them from the antitrust laws by statute.

Parts That Are Similar. The parts of the foreign policies that are similar to American policy pertain to collective activity designed to coerce independents or to exclude enterprises from markets or impose discriminatory disadvantages upon them. Among such arrangements are agreements as to boycotts, blacklists, and other types of collective refusals to buy or sell; agreements as to collective exclusive dealing; agreements that establish eligibility requirements for admission to an occupation or that limit the number of members thereof; agreements to withhold from particular classes of buyers discounts that are granted generally to their competitors;[1] and agreements as to rebates upon aggregated volume that include limitations as to the source of the goods that are to be eligible for discount.

In curbing such concerted activities, most of the countries here under discussion have objectives like those of the United States. They seek to preserve business opportunity for new enterprises and to prevent existing enterprises from being excluded from markets or subjected to discrimination. Action against restrictions that are inconsistent with these purposes is usually more vigorous than against exploitative restrictions. But although this part of the policy of the countries resembles American policy in goals and in vigor of execution, it often shows significant difference from American policy in the way it is applied. Instead of prohibiting collective exclusionary and discriminatory activities, several countries control the purposes for which such activities may be undertaken and the grounds upon which any exclusion or discrimination may be imposed. As in the case of price

---

[1] An agreement upon discounts to be granted in uniform amounts, or to be granted in different amounts to non-competing groups of buyers, may be exploitative, but does not necessarily impair the business opportunity of any of the buyers. Discrimination among competing buyers does involve such impairment. Because of the overlapping character of distributive functions, there are borderline situations that are difficult to classify; but in the countries under discussion, public policy has given them little attention.

agreements, fairness rather than freedom is applicable standard. As agreed prices must be fair prices, so agreed exclusions and discriminations must be reasonable in purpose and in method. By this standard, agreements to limit the total number of enterprises in a field of business are condemned. So are agreements to exclude new entrants or to impose arbitrary or discriminatory condition on entry. In these respects the policies under discussion repress as unfair what American policy represses as interference with freedom.

However, unlike the United States, several countries have no objection to private agreements by which persons who cannot meet minimum eligibility requirements as to competence, training, or experience shall be excluded from the trade by their potential competitors. In some countries, minimum requirements as to capital or equipment may also be imposed. To be acceptable, however, such arrangements must meet standards of fairness—establish only objective and non-discriminatory requirements, set these at levels no higher than the national authority thinks reasonable, and be administered impartially. As in the United States in the case of professions such as medicine, public policy does not rely upon elimination of the incompetent by competition, but accepts the usefulness of tests of competence applied by persons already in the field.

Since the exclusionary effect of aggregated rebate arrangements is indirect and less visible than that of eligibility requirements, such arrangements, though also likely to be condemned, are met with less uniformity of policy and less clarity about the conditions under which they may be accepted.

Even less difference from American policy exists in most countries in the treatment of collective refusals to deal and collective agreements for reciprocal exclusive dealing. In most countries, these are contrary to public policy. Two countries are exceptions. Both regard boycotts as permissible means to enforce restrictive agreements provided the agreements themselves serve purposes that the government considers desirable. One of them also does not object to arrangements between trade associations for reciprocal exclusive dealing if each association admits to membership all firms that the government thinks should be admitted and if the substantive programs of the associations contain no restrictions to which the government objects.

Since policy toward exclusions overlaps policy toward discounts, only part of the policies of these countries toward collective discrimination resembles American policy. Arbitrary denial of customary terms to a particular firm or class of firms—e.g. cooperatives, chain stores, or new enterprises —is consistently opposed. But when a large firm benefits from generally applicable volume discounts, policy contains little or nothing analogous to American concern about the possible anticompetitive or inequitable effects of the discount structure. Unsystematic discrimination is likely to be terminated as in the United States; systematic discrimination is not.

The policies that repress collective restrictions upon business opportunity are made more comprehensive and effective by related policies toward restrictions by individual firms. What a firm cannot do individually, it cannot do as a party to an agreement. Curbs upon individual refusal to sell and individual discrimination thus become obstacles to collective boycott, collective exclusive dealing, collective discrimination, and the collective use of eligibility requirements. The impact of such curbs upon collective restraint of business opportunity is probably important enough to offset the weaknesses and gaps in the parts of the policies that are directly concerned with the relevant collective restraints.

Parts that are More Repressive. The parts of the foreign policies that are more repressive than American policy consist chiefly of policies toward individual refusals to sell, vertical price-fixing, and prices charged by powerful single enterprises.

Unlike the United States, nearly two-thirds of the countries covered by this summary undertake to curb refusal to sell. Whereas American law permits sellers to choose their own customers, the countries here under discussion regard withholding goods as an especially dangerous kind of discrimination. The major impact of policies that express this view consists in limiting the right of powerful firms to choose their customers. In four countries the law contemplates orders against refusal to sell only when the refuser is a powerful firm; and in a fifth country, Germany, such orders are applicable only to powerful firms, firms that fix resale prices, cartels, and associations. In most of the other six countries, in which refusals to sell will be forbidden if they are arbitrary, unreasonable or unduly harmful to the rejected buyers, weight is given to the availability of goods from other sources in evaluating harm or unreasonableness; and thus a generally applicable policy against refusals is likely to be invoked most vigorously against powerful firms. The United States lacks a comparable weapon against the practices of large enterprises.

So far as individual refusal to sell is forbidden, the impact of restrictive arrangements that are permissible under other parts of national policy is significantly reduced. Boycotts become illegal; exclusion of new or independent firms from markets becomes almost impossible; arrangements that allocate market areas, customers, or classes of goods become difficult to apply; prescribed channels of distribution cannot be established; other collective restrictions cannot be enforced by withholding goods; and distributors cannot be easily disciplined if they do not maintain prescribed resale prices. The prevalence of curbs upon refusal to sell does much to offset weaknesses in policies toward collective restrictions upon business opportunity and even to reduce the significance of lax policies toward collective exploitative restrictions.

Policy toward resale price maintenance in the countries here under discussion is not, as in the United States, more permissive than policy toward horizontal price-fixing. Where the two types of price-fixing are distinguished, resale price maintenance is subject to repression that is more severe. In about half of the countries under study, collective resale price maintenance is subject either to prohibitions or to regulatory limitations severe enough to make it unattractive. Elsewhere it is treated like horizonal price-fixing, and is more likely to be permitted than in the United States. However, resale price-fixing by individual suppliers, which is permissible under American Federal law[2] if consistent with state law and is thus permitted in about half of the American states, is forbidden or severely repressed in about half of the countries here under study, and is subject to administrative control in one or two other countries.

Policy toward the prices of powerful enterprises in the countries here under discussion consists of regulatory control, not of efforts to terminate the power that enables such enterprises to set their own prices. Since in several of the countries power is conceived more broadly than in the United States, control applicable to powerful firms may extend further than the equivalent American control. Under the Sherman Act, American policy is applied to firms that monopolize or attempt to monopolize a significant part of commerce. In several of the countries covered by this study, policies toward powerful enterprises are applicable not only to monopolies but also to firms that have obtained from their bigness, from the prestige of their products, or from other advantages, a dominant position or a significant influence in their markets. Thus where curbs are applied to prices they may cover oligopolies as well as monopolies.

Unlike the United States, more than one-third of the countries provide for some control of the prices of powerful firms or of firms generally. Norway forbids "unreasonable" prices; Ireland regards unjust enhancement of price as an unfair practice against which rules can be issued; South Africa authorizes orders against acts restrictive of competition that may enhance prices; Germany and the Netherlands conceive excessive prices as abuses

---

[2] Federal statutes permit it if it is lawful in the state in which the resale takes place. In about half the states authorization by state laws is now in effect.

of power against which orders may be issued; and Denmark requires influential firms to obtain prior approval of price increases. Execpt in Denmark and Norway, little use has been made of these powers of control. However, their availability probably influences the price policies of powerful firms.

In spite of recurrent suggestions that "administered prices" should be subjected to some kind of legal control, no comparable authority over the prices of powerful firms is conveyed by American law. Monopolization is unlawful whether or not prices charged by the monopoly are fair. Firms that neither possess nor are seeking monopoly power may charge whatever prices they wish. It is noteworthy, however, that in reecnt years some powerful firms have been summoned before Congressional committees and there subjected to hostile criticism for increasing prices or failing to reduce them, and that informal executive pressure has been occasionally applied to particular powerful firms in an effort to influence their price decisions. The attitudes that underlay such actions were similar to those expressed in the foreign statutes that authorize explicit control.

Effect of the Laws Upon Business Practice

Within the chosen limits of their policies, most of the countries here under discussion have attained significant results during the short period in which their laws have been effective. The impact of the recent statutes has been substantially greater than the meager impact of the American Sherman Act during its first decade. Surveillance over restrictive agreements has resulted in a substantial decrease in the number of agreements, both horizontal and vertical, and appears to have resulted also in significant, though far from uniform, reductions of the restrictiveness of the agreements that remain. There has been a considerable shift from price-fixing to agreements that are limited to control of terms of sale or to exchange of price information. Greater opportunity than before for firms with low costs to charge low prices is usually provided by the price-fixing arrangements that remain. Numerous mandatory schemes that required maintenance of resale prices have been replaced by recommendations about resale prices. Various quota schemes have been modified to increase the opportunity for the abler producers to increase their market shares from time to time. More opportunity has been provided for dissident enterprises to withdraw from restrictive agreements; and the severity of private disciplinary action to enforce agreements has been substantially mitigated. In countries in which particular types of agreements are forbidden unless specifically authorized, authorizations have been few compared with the number of similar agreements previously in force. This has been conspicuously true of horizontal price agreements in Norway and of resale price agreements in all three of the Scandinavian countries.[3]

There is reason to believe that coercive and exclusionary pressures upon independent enterprises have been significantly reduced both by control of restrictive agreements and by surveillance intended to prevent abuses by dominant firms. The impact of the change has been greatest in distribution, in diminishing concerted efforts a) to prevent sale to cooperatives, chain stores, and supermarkets, and b) to prevent suppliers from by-passing intermediate distributors. The laws have supported experiment with new methods of distribution and thus have helped reduce distribution costs.

Whether or not the leeway given by the laws for agreements that supposedly reduce costs and enhance productivity has actually resulted in improvements of economic performance that would not otherwise have taken place is problematical. In particular instances, such as the approval of Dutch programs for allocation of milk routes, agreements that reduced costs have been permitted and made less restrictive than they would have been without government control. In France various features that were thought to enhance efficiency have been added to restrictive arrangements in order to make the schemes acceptable to the government. Exchanges of technical information provided in various agreements have been obviously desirable. The question in all such cases is whether or not, if use of a restrictive agreement to bring about the desirable result had been forbidden, other nonrestrictive ways of doing so would have been devised. The laws do not uniformly require that rationalization agreements contain only restrictions that are indispensible to the purpose. Moreover, when an administrative agency or a court has authority to approve profitable restrictions if it can be convinced that these are necessary to a technically desirable result, the enterprises that desire the restriction have strong incentives to claim that it is necessary, and the authority is unlikely to have adequate access to information and skilled analysis that might support a contrary conclusion. Particularly, the authority is likely to underestimate the dynamic impact of the changes that are cumulatively induced by competition. It cannot readily evaluate the capacity of business enterprises to devise non-restrictive types of collaboration when restrictive ones are forbidden. Similarly, it cannot readily appraise the ability of firms to achieve the beneficial results of restrictive agreements by making, individually, appropriate changes in

---

[3] The evidence supporting these appraisals is greatest in the countries in which registration of agreements was in effect before the present substantive law and in which, consequently, changes in the number and kind of agreements can be ascertained from the registers. This is true in the three Scandanavian countries. In general, official reports and the records of official proceedings support the same conclusions as to other countries.

their size, structure, and conduct. The evidence that rationalization agreements have promoted efficiency is plausible; it is far from conclusive.

There is reason to believe that the surveillance over the level of prices that is a part of restrictive practice legislation in some countries has tended to keep prices down. It is clear, for example, that in particular instances the Danish government has prevented cartels and dominant firms from raising prices, and the Dutch government has prevented an increase of costs from being reflected in a higher increase in prices. It is probable that unused governmental power to limit price increases has had a moderating effect upon private business decisions about prices. What is not clear is the ultimate indirect effect of governmental efforts to hold prices down. Organized Danish business has contended that, because of the necessity of seeking approval for every price increase, business men who might otherwise reduce prices refrain from doing so lest they might subsequently desire to increase them. Moreover, the ultimate effects of repressive control of price increases presumably depend upon the influence of such control upon incentives, allocation of resources, and conservation of scarce goods; and this influence is far from clear in a setting in which private restrictions tend to distort competitive adjustments and public price control then distorts the restrictions.

Should Similar Policies be Adopted Here?

In devising their present policies toward restrictive business practices, most of the countries here under study have examined American experience under the antitrust laws; and some of them have adopted particular features of American policy or procedure. Question arises whether the United States has anything to learn from the parts of policy and procedure in these countries that differ from ours. Does foreign experience suggest the desirability of change in our law, or throw light upon the various proposals for change that are currently advocated in this country?

In considering this question, one must keep in mind the relevant peculiarities of the setting in which American laws are applied. The United States is not a homogeneous country. Its continent-wide expanse gives it sectional differences in climate and resources that are reflected in important sectional differences of economic interest. Its public opinion, shaped by the exploitation of bountiful resources that were recently acquired, has assumed that progress is normal, that the new is likely to be better than the old, and that preservation of opportunity is more important than assurance of security or maintenance of vested interests. Its population sprang from many nations; and accordingly its culture, an eclectic mixture of various traditions, contains relatively little that has the authority of an unchallenged inheritance. Its people are so numerous and so widely diffused that even those who rise to leadership among them are not likely to have personal ties of life-long acquaintance, similarity of background, and continuing intimate contact. These facts have tended to influence the goals of American policy and to perpetuate the distrust of concentrated power that characterized the beginnings of American government. In spite of the various forces that foster a strong central government, these enduring peculiarities have preserved large parts of the original division of government powers and of the consequent emphasis upon judicial processes, explicit laws, due process of law, and curbs upon official discretion. What appears to be desirable and possible to the citizens of a smaller, more homogenous, and less optimistic country may seem neither possible nor desirable to citizens of the United States.

The importance of the differences that have just been mentioned is especially clear in considering the possible usefulness to the United States of procedures similar to those by which most of the foreign laws are applied. No contrast is clearer than that between the relative duration and expense of governmental action about restrictive business practices in the United States and elsewhere. As compared with ours, most foreign proceedings are brief, informal, and inexpensive. Government can act more rapidly; persons affected suffer less cost and delay; and the legal status of conduct becomes clear more quickly. These advantages are derived, however, largely from the breadth of administrative discretion, the narrowness of the safeguards that assure affected persons the right to be heard, and the meagerness of rights of appeal. Where private rights are protected and administrative action is controlled by legal standards and appellate proceedings are fully available, the differences in speed and expense are relatively slight. So long as the United States retains its distrust of official power and its determination to use due process of law as a guarantee of private rights, most of the procedures by which the foreign laws are applied will be unsuited for use here.

Moreover, discretionary exercise of power is inconsistent with the formulation of the clear precedents that are necessary if voluntary compliance is to be a principal means to make public policy effective. Discretionary action is appropriate only where the range of action is so limited as to permit decisions case by case without general rules of conduct. It is not appropriate if restrictions that should be corrected are too numerous to be considered, one by one, by the public authorities.

In the countries here under study, representatives of private interests often have an official part in formulating public policy or in deciding cases. This fact diminishes business resistence to public policy; but it does so by creating major obstacles to the development of policies that the business community is likely to resist. Where the substance of policy consists in the prevention of abusive acts, the partly private authorities and advisory boards appear to work well. Doubtless they have been useful in reconciling business to a novel type of control and in generating an understanding by business men of the publicly significant aspects of private restriction. It is noteworthy, however, that where restriction is repressed rather than merely regulated, little or no use is made of such partly private official bodies. They are not appropriate to a repressive policy like that of the United States.

Procedural Possibilities. In spite of these limitations, three procedural features of the administrtion of the foreign laws deserve consideration for use in the United States.

1. The first of them appears in only a few countries, primarily the United Kingdom, Ireland and South Africa. It consists in examining the problem of restriction on an industry-wide basis, so that the interaction of restrictions by various groups becomes evident and remedies appropriate to the entire industrial setting can be devised.[4] Both the British and the Irish have discovered that this type of procedure, standing alone, can be unduly cumbersome as a means of coping with certain sharply defined and relatively isolated restrictive practices, and so have amended their laws to permit more narrowly focussed action. But in particular instances the industry-wide reports have provided a sense of proportion and have led to comprehensive and coordinated action, beyond what would have been probable in a series of unconnected cases. Industry-wide coordinated investigation and action are possible under American law in three ways. First, legal proceedings can be coordinated by a guiding plan for investigation and action in a given industry, as was done in 1940-41 by the Antitrust Division of the Department of Justice in cases involving restraints upon construction.[5] Second, a rule-making procedure, such as has been recently developed by the Federal Trade Commission, can be used to formulate an industry-wide standard as to the limits of legality for a particular practice.[6] Third, the powers of the Federal Trade Commission to obtain information and prepare economic reports can be used to formulate industry-wide programs of action as a guide for subsequent legal proceedings. But though these possibilities exist they have been used only sporadically. Foreign experience indicates the desirability of using them more consistently.

2. Although the United States should not and will not abandon its emphasis upon due process of law, foreign experience suggests that more flexible means of developing facts for use in legal proceedings might be made

---

[4] In the United Kingdom, this type of procedure was initially used under the Monopolies Act, and still remains available under that act for all restrictions except the agreements that are covered by the subsequent Restrictive Trade Practices Act.

[5] See Corwin D. Edwards, "The New Antitrust Procedure as Illustrated in the Construction Industry," 2 *Public Policy* 321.

[6] See Everette MacIntyre and Paul Rand Dixon, "The Federal Trade Commission after Fifty Years," 24 Federal Bar Journal 377, at 421.

available. American antitrust proceedings have indicated the difficulty of reconciling the need for large amounts of technically complicated information with the requirements of rules of evidence that were developed in ordinary civil or criminal cases. Piece-meal presentation of a complex pattern of facts by testimony and cross-examination is likely to be both expensive and bewildering; and cross-examination in adversary proceedings is often not the best way to evaluate statistics or to appraise differences of opinion among expert witnesses. In several foreign countries, the investigatory process results in a report by the investigator, which is then exposed to criticism by those involved in the case. In the United Kingdom, economic experts in cases that involve restrictive agreements submit written testimony upon which they are subsequently cross-examined. In German proceedings, a witness makes an initial statement without interruption, is subsequently questioned by counsel and by the presiding official, and hears and may object to a summary of his testimony that is made by the presiding official for the official record. Devices such as these deserve examination as possible means by which greater coherence, intelligibility, and possibly brevity can be attained in some antitrust proceedings.

3. Foreign experience also suggests the usefulness of a procedure by which orders that terminate restriction can be developed on a wider basis than a single adversary proceeding. In some countries a corrective order may be applied to the members of a whole industry after an administrative proceeding designed to elicit relevant information and opinion, wtihout allegations of guilt and without separate cases against individual firms. This is true, for example, in formulating trading rules and ministerial orders under Irish law. American legal proceedings have turned upon the question whether or not a law has been violated by particular firms, and where violation was found the result has been a penalty or a corrective order. Under the Sherman and Clayton Acts, decision that the law has been violated has exposed the violator to suit for triple damages by those who suffered from the violation. Though such procedures have great merit and are appropriate in many cases, they have two disadvantages. First, where a decision extends previously accepted interpretations of the law, to characterize the defendant as a law-violator and expose him to punishment or to punitive claims for damages is harsh; and realization of this fact may make the deciding body reluctant to adopt sensible but novel interpretations. Second, where a practice is widespread but, being a violation of the Clayton Act or the Federal Trade Commission Act rather than the Sherman Act, is not subject to punishment, multiple cases against different defendants may be necessary to obtain compliance with the same legal requirement. Alongside existing procedures, therefore, there is need in the American law for a procedure by which a truly

controversial question of interpretation can be settled without a punitive or invidious impact upon those involved in the first proceeding, and by which a legal principle can be applied to groups of similarly placed enterprises that engage in similar conduct without the need to proceed separately against each of them. The Federal Trade Commission's current experiment with rule-making procedures may indicate a way to meet these needs.

Substantive Possibilities. The possibility that the United States could usefully adopt some parts of foreign substantive policy toward restrictive practices deserves discussion as to each of the following matters: a) registration of cartels and dominant firms; b) "conditions" cartels, that is, cartels to fix terms of sale; c) cartels concerned with rationalization; d) resale price maintenance; e) the concept of the dominant firm; f) refusal to sell and discrimination; and g) exploitative pricing by large enterprises. Each of these will be considered below.

A. *Registration.* In several European countries registration of cartels has reduced the number and restrictiveness of cartel agreements and enabled governments to consider the remaining cartels more easily. Registration of dominant firms has been, in some countries, a convenient way of obtaining information about the practices of such firms and of curbing such practices so far as was thought desirable.

The conditions that made cartel registration a deterrent do not exist in the United States as to most kinds of restrictive agreements. Registration requirements were adopted where there was little public information about cartels and where cartel control included possibilities that cartels would be permitted to continue. The deterrent effect of public disclosure was initially substantial, but diminished rapidly as agreements that outraged public opinion were modified and the remaining agreements became familiar. No foreign country has undertaken the useless task of requiring the registration of agreements that were inevitably illegal. As applied to American conditions, foreign examples could suggest registration of agreements only so far as these agreements were possibly lawful, and only on the ground that registration might facilitate survey of the agreements for possible illegality. Since registration is a formidable undertaking in itself, the limited advantage that it might give the antitrust authorities might not be worth the cost.

In three fields, however, this question deserves examination. The first consists of agreements that involve price filing, use of standardized methods of computing an industry's costs, and arrangements by which competitors exchange statistics that are relevant to marketing. Though such arrangements are often innocent, they have been recurrently used to cloak unlawful restraints of trade; and, as in Europe, registration might both deter such misuse and make the authorities aware of it when it occurs.

The second field consists of agreements as to merger, joint venture, and related forms of business concentration. Advance registration of mergers has been urged upon the Congress, thus far without success. It probably would improve the information of the antitrust authorities about the number and nature of such actions; but since the more important mergers are widely discussed, the gain in information would consist chiefly of more knowledge about the less important ones. Registration of corporate acquisitions of stock in other corporations would be more useful, because the facts about such acquisitions are less likely to become available to the government; but the scope of such registration would need to be carefully delimited lest an undigestible mass of detail be demanded. Registration of joint ventures might be an effective way of mobilizing information that is badly needed in order to formulate a more discerning public policy toward such arrangements.

The third field consists of licenses and assignments of patent rights and of the related unpatented information that is colloquially called know-how. As the basis for lawful exercise of monopoly rights, patents are themselves immune from the law against monopoly; and patent licenses share that immunity as means by which the patent is shared and thereby mitigated. Numerous antitrust proceedings have shown, however, that violations of the antitrust laws, and arrangements inconsistent with the policy that underlies both these laws and the patent laws, can be and often are built upon or camouflaged by contractual arrangements about patents. Restrictions can be stretched to cover more than what is patented; invalid patents can be immunized from legal challenge and made the basis of monopoly; control over licenses can be extended for periods much longer than the seventeen-year life of a patent; exchange of licenses and pooling of patents can be used to acquire more market power than the relevant patents convey to their respective owners; allocation of patent rights to different firms can be used to allocate domestic or international markets; powerful holders of many patents can make one-sided arrangements with weak licensees by which the latter are reduced to technological and commercial vassalage. If patent licenses and patent assignments were valid only when recorded with a government agency, the ability of the government to detect and terminate such perversions of the patent system would be substantially enhanced. Suggestions that some such principle be adopted were prominent among the proposals for reform of the patent system that were made immediately after the second World War, while wartime disclosures about abuse of patent rights were fresh in the public mind.

B. *"Conditions" cartels.* Although countries that accept conditions cartels often underestimate the possibilities of severe restriction that such cartels involve, there is truth in the belief that diversity in terms of sale can be so great as to diminish the effectiveness of competition. The characteristic distinction that foreign countries make between cartels that fix terms of sale without fixing prices and cartels that also restrict price competition is not well taken; for American experience has shown that agreements on terms can have substantial price effects. In basing point systems, for example, use of uniform methods of computing terms for delivery to different destinations has repeatedly resulted in comprehensive price fixing. Moreover, the argument for the transparency of markets that foreign countries use to justify conditions cartels can be applied to certain complicated price structures as well. In the steel industry, for example, where the prices of the industry's many products consist of basic prices for certain basic commodities plus numerous extras for various characteristics of a particular product, such as dimension, chemical composition, and method of processing, any significant diversity between sellers in the characteristics of goods to which extras were applied would result in great difficulty in comparing the prices of equivalent transactions. Substantial uniformity in the attributes upon which extras are charged, in the way these extras are classified, and in the amounts of the various extras, fixes, in effect, a considerable part of the price of numerous steel products. Yet without considerable uniformity buyers, sellers, and observers alike might find methods of pricing steel unintelligible.

Thus, where the characteristics of transactions are complex, either as to non-price terms of sale or as to the elements of a price, there may sometimes be need for certain uniformities in the interest of simplicity, and need for simplicity if people are to compete intelligently. But simplicity created by unilateral agreement among sellers involves serious risks that desirable kinds of competition will be prevented or all effective competition avoided. Conditions cartels, as loosely approved and controlled as they are in some foreign countries, could readily result in dangerous restriction rather than in useful simplification.

Existing American policy, which quietly tolerates some arrangements by which elements of price and terms of sale that affect prices are fixed, consists essentially in the use of administrative discretion to refrain from prosecuting what, under legal precedent, may properly be subject to prosecution. This, too, is unsatisfactory. The foreign policies focus upon a problem that has not been solved in American policy, though the foreign solutions of it are not acceptable.

C. *Rationalization cartels.* Foreign experience with rationalization is directly relevant to the question whether or not the United States should similarly authorize certain agreements as beneficial. It is also indirectly relevant to suggestions that are recurrently made by certain American critics of the law of monopolization, that "economic performance" should be the chief or only test of the legality of a monopoly.

Although much that is approved on grounds of rationalization under some foreign laws is of dubious value, or might be accomplished by less restrictive means, or is inadequately circumscribed and safeguarded, or is permitted without adequate concern about possible adverse indirect effects, significant instances remain in which restrictive agreements probably contribute to lower costs and better performance. Under American law, such possibilities can be recognized only by explicit statutory exemptions from the antitrust laws; and such an exemption is impracticable unless the matter is recognized as important and the facts about it are relatively clear. It is probable that one of the social costs of American antitrust policy is failure to achieve some possible economies. It is probable, however, that the net loss to the economy from such failures is small or non-existent; for non-restrictive solutions are often found for business problems when restrictive solutions are known to be unacceptable, and where rationalization is thought to justify restriction there is an inherent danger that excessive and functionless restriction will successfully masquerade as indispensable. If, after allowing for these considerations, there is a net loss of efficiency, it must be considered a necessary cost of American unwillingness to entrust broad discretion to administrative personnel; for programs of rationalization cannot be evaluated, accepted, and policed without exercise of such discretion. So long as the general character of antitrust policy and of American political thinking undergo no fundamental change, rationalization agreements will necessarily be forbidden unless explicitly authorized by Congress.

To give weight to performance tests in cases about monopolization would be even more difficult than to do so in cases about cartels, and the desirability of doing so is even more questionable. Such a policy would raise the foregoing difficulties in greater degree. Approval of a monopoly that was engaged in unconscionable conduct on the ground that its performance, as a whole, was desirable would be no more sensible than to give a good citizen immunity from the requirement that when driving he stop at red lights. An effort to disentangle the desirable and undesirable aspects of a single firm's use of its monopoly power would be a much more formidable task than a similar effort as to the relatively explicit and limited content of a restrictive agreement. It would be possible, if at all, only with complete regulatory control of the enterprise.

D. *Resale price maintenance.* It is noteworthy that various foreign countries treat resale price maintenance as a peculiarly undesirable kind of restrictive practice. Austrian experience supports the view that most firms that desire to maintain resale prices lose interest in doing so under a rule that limits distributors' margins to "reasonable" amounts. German experience indicates that resale price maintenance may be accompanied by a variety of abuses, such as arbitrary territorial price discrimination, sale to consumers by the supplier at prices lower than his distributors are permitted to charge, sale of unbranded goods by the supplier at prices below those he and his distributors charge for identical branded goods, and fixation of resale prices at levels so high that the supplier must try to move excessive inventories by free deals and exceptionally large discounts. Experience in England and Norway has indicated that resale price maintenance by individual suppliers tends to result in prices high enough to support inefficient distribution. Such foreign experiences reenforce the views often expressed in the United States that American law should cease to authorize the exemption of this kind of restriction.

E. *The dominant firm.* Unlike American law, the laws of some foreign countries are so written that the provisions applicable to the practices of large firms cover not only monopolies but also firms that have market power because of their relative bigness or because of the absence of substantial competition between them and other large firms. In other words, these provisions cover oligopolies and cases of parallel non-competitive action. This ambitious formulation of the scope of foreign control over the conduct of large firms is appropriate; for a) in the smaller markets of countries smaller than the United States, oligopolies probably are more prevalent and important than here; b) instances in which oligopolistic concentration has increased with time have been numerous enough, here and elsewhere, to arouse attention; and c) economic thinking, here and abroad, has tended toward a consensus that oligopolies frequently produce results like those of monopolies or restrictive agreements. To conceive the problem of business power in terms of oligopoly was as natural in the 1950's, when the foreign laws were being written, as to conceive it in terms of monopoly had been in 1890, when the Congress passed the Sherman Act.

That American law does not cope adequately with oligopoly is a frequent conclusion by those that study American industrial organization. Efforts to apply the law to oligopoly problems have broadened American legal conceptions of conspiracy, monopoly, and attempt to monopolize, and have resulted in enlargement of the scope of the Clayton Act by amendment. The amendments, however, have been limited to control of price discrimination, intended to afford small firms competitive opportunities more nearly equal to those of large firms, and control of mergers, intended chiefly as an obstacle to further development of oligopolies. The need for further legislation has been repeatedly asserted,[7] and drafts of laws have been repeatedly proposed.[8]

---

[7] See, for example, Irston R. Barnes, "Considerations Concerning Public Policy Toward Administered Prices," in Subcommittees on Antitrust and Monopoly of the Senate Judiciary Committee, *Administered Prices: A Compendium on Public Policy,* Committee print, 88th Congress, 1st Session, pp. 74-82; Alfred E. Kahn, "Public Policies

The foreign laws demonstrate that restrictive manifestation of business power are widely conceived, in other countries as well as here, to be present in fields of business that are not monopolized. They lend support to the suggestion that the United States needs legislation explicitly applicable to dominant firms, more appropriate than can be evolved from strained interpretations of the legal concepts of monopolization and conspiracy. But they afford limited suggestion about the possible content of any such legislation; for they contain little relevant to the acquisition or possession of economic power,[9] and, except as to refusal to sell and price control, which will be discussed below, they have been given only sporadic application to aspects of the conduct of large firms that are not subject to action under the American Clayton Act.

F. *Refusal to sell and discrimination.* In the five countries in which curbs upon refusal to sell by individual suppliers are important parts of legal control, denial of access by buyers to suppliers is regarded as the most significant form of discrimination. Unless the characteristics of the transaction or of the buyers are considered to justify the refusal, government may intervene to require sale where goods have been withheld. It is likely to do so if it thinks that refusal was being used as a means of disciplining customers or as a means of discrimination against unorthodox types of enterprise, or if adequate alternative sources of supply are not available to the would-be buyer. The application of such a policy has involved formidable problems as to appraisal of the characteristics of buyers or of transactions that were alleged to justify refusal and as to ways of reconciling a general right of access to supplies with desirable programs by which particular suppliers try to limit their costs of distribution. Had the governmental authorities not exercised broad discretion with minimum resort to formal

Affecting Market Power," in Ibid, pp. 170-74; Abba P. Lerner, "Seller's Inflation and Administered Depression: An Analysis and a Suggestion for Dealing with Inflationary Depression," in Ibid, pp. 206-212; Gardiner C. Means, "Pricing Power and the Public Interest," in Ibid. pp. 232-39; Edwin G. Nourse, "Government Discipline of Private Economic Power," in Ibid, pp. 260-61.

[8] See, for example, three bills introduced on May 23, 1962, by the Chairman of the Judiciary Committee of the House of Representatives, HR 11870, HR 11871, and HR 11872; a bill introduced by Senator Joheph C. O'Mahoney in 1959, S 215; and a bill proposed by Professor Walter Adams, printed in *Economic Concentration,* Hearings by the Subcommittee on Antitrust and Monopoly of the Senate Judiciary Committee, 88th Congress, 2d Session, pursuant to S. Res. 262, Part 1, pp. 353-78.

[9] The Japanese law and possibly the Spanish law can be used against monopolies; but the relevant parts of Japanese law are scarcely used, and Spanish law is too recent to have provided experience. The German and Spanish laws provide for report of large mergers but convey no power to control them. The Japanese and British laws contemplate control of mergers, but the British law was enacted in 1965 and this part of the Japanese law is not being applied. The British law of 1965 also authorizes orders that require divestiture, divorcement, or dissolution, but no such orders have yet been issued.

tests of legal rights, these problems would have been still more formidable.

It is noteworthy that in most of the foreign countries policy toward refusal to sell is closely coordinated with policy toward discrimination. Indeed, discrimination against individual buyers in prices, discounts, or terms of sale is treated as indirect refusal to sell.

In recognizing the close connection of the two practices, the foreign laws provide policies more self-consistent than American policy. The United States protects buyers vigorously against price discrimination and scarcely at all against refusal to sell. Since the drastic discrimination involved in refusing to supply a customer is much safer for the supplier than the milder discrimination of supplying him on unfavorable terms, suppliers are likely to solve some of their price discrimination problems by such refusals. The foreign experience suggests the desirability of coordinating these two aspects of American policy.

In three of the foreign countries provisions applicable to price discrimination have purposes broader than preventing refusals to sell. In two of these, the purpose is to prevent invidious treatment of particular buyers, but no substantial attempt has been made to amend such discriminations as may inhere in general discount structures that are used by a supplier in all his sales. In the third country, the purpose is to tie a seller's price differentials closely to differences in cost; and therefore functional discounts that do not reflect cost differences are deemed objectionable. The first type of policy is far less ambitious than that of the United States. The second is more ambitious in that, seeking efficiency in distribution, it frowns upon functional price differences even where no direct competitors are injured thereby. If the inept and widely criticized American price discrimination law were to be reconsidered, either in order to coordinate it with policy toward refusal to sell or for other purposes, examination of experience under these policies would be relevant.

G. *Control of the prices of dominant firms.* The experience of several foreign countries is relevant to the suggestion, recurrently made in the United States, that increases in the prices charged by large enterprises should be subjected by law to prior report, public hearing, or some kind of substantive control. In several countries, government possesses the power to intervene correctively when it thinks that a large firm's prices are excessive; and because of that power it can exert substantial influence upon the price policies of such firms by informal means. In Denmark every price increase by a dominant firm must receive explicit prior approval.

To substitute administrative control over the prices of large enterprises for the policy of keeping competition vigorous and prices subject to competitive forces would be a revolutionary change in American public policy.

It would be justified only if large firms were clearly immune from price competition and if structural remedies designed to restore effective competition had failed or had proved unacceptable to the Congress. Through vigorous action against mergers the United States is currently trying to prevent one of the major forms of business concentration; and if it succeeds there is a possibility that the growth of the economy will exceed the growth of large firms and that impairments of price competition associated with large firms will diminish. Thus, even if administrative curbs upon the prices of big enterprises should eventually be found necessary, they are currently premature. If, however, it should become evident that more desirable ways of coping with the power of big business are inadequate, the foreign experience will indicate some of the possibilities and problems associated with governmental corrective and preventative price control.

In summary, an examination of the foreign laws suggests several substantive possibilities that the United States might consider: a) registration of designated types of collective programs for reporting prices or exchanging statistics or using uniform methods of computing costs; b) registration by large corporations of their acquisitions of stock, their mergers, and their joint ventures; c) registration of patent licenses and patent assignments; d) repeal of the laws that permit resale price maintenance; and e) coordination of policy toward discrimination with policy toward refusal to sell. It suggests also the desirability of developing laws additional to those now pertaining to mergers and price discrimination that would be designed to cope explicitly with the problems that arise when firms are so powerful that competition is impaired yet not so powerful that the law against monopolization applies. It brings into focus a question about how transparency of markets can be preserved when prices and terms are complicated, but does not suggest the direction of an appropriate answer. It suggests that procedures under American law might be improved by more resort to industry-wide investigations; by submission of complicated technical evidence in the form of reports subject to critical scrutiny instead of only as testimony subject to cross-examination; and by the further development of the Federal Trade Commission's current experiment with rule-making. Apart from these possibilities, the differences between American and foreign restrictive practice legislation appear to be so closely associated with differences in goals or with differences in political attitudes toward concentrated and private power as to preclude our adoption of even the successful parts of the foreign policies.

Part II
INTERNATIONAL COLLABORATION

Chapter XIV

Projects for International Control
of Restriction

The national laws that have been discussed are concerned primarily with the activities of domestic enterprises in domestic markets. As has been noted in chapters III and IV, they are fragmentary in their application to restrictive arrangements that involve more than one country.

Such arrangements are numerous. The opportunity to make them increases as governments reduce tariffs and similar barriers to international trade, as technology reduces the time and cost of international communication and transport, and as single business enterprises become international in scope.[1]

Restrictive arrangements that have international aspects are of several kinds. They include arrangements in which the participants are nationals of more than one country; arrangements under which, though restrictive activities are confined to a single country, the effect thereof is manifested elsewhere; and arrangements under which restrictive activities are carried on in more than one country.

Since there is now general consensus that foreigners who do business in a country are subject to its laws, the fact that foreigners are participants in a domestic restrictive arrangement does not, in itself, create problems in coping with the arrangement by a national law. Such problems are evident, however, when restrictive activity in one country has effects in others or when the activity takes place in two or more countries. Given the first condition, the country that has an incentive to control the restriction has limited opportunity to do so. Given the second, no country's jurisdiction covers more than a part of the restriction. In either case, control of restriction is likely to be ineffective, and one country's efforts to exert control are likely to be resisted by other countries as interference in their domestic affairs.

American experience under the antitrust laws illustrates these problems. In the cases of natural rubber, potash, and quinine, and in various other

---

[1] See Corwin Edwards, The Internationality of Economic Interests, 111 University of Pennsylvania Law Review 183; Heinrich Kronstein, The Nationality of International Enterprise, in Heinrich Kronstein, Selected Essays, Karlsruhe, 1962, p. 317; Sigmund Timberg, International Combines and National Sovereigns, 95 University of Penn. Law Review 575.

instances, American objections to foreign restrictive arrangements designed to exploit American buyers did not induce foreign governments to take action against the restrictions.[2] American legal action has been repeatedly handicapped or ineffective. In cases involving the asbestos and diamond cartels, American courts lacked jurisdiction over participants, who were not domiciled in the United States.[3] In cases involving international cartels for oil and electric lamps, the American authorities experienced great difficulties, including opposition from foreign governments, in their endeavor to obtain evidence about cartel activities outside the United States;[4] and in both cases they lacked jurisdiction over some of the participants. In the electric lamp case, the court's corrective orders were limited in an effort not to exceed the limits of American judicial authority;[5] and in a case involving an international chemical agreement an important part of the relief thought necessary by an American court was nullified by a British court.[6] Discovery of restrictive arrangements that are intended to affect the United States is made more difficult when American participants keep relevant documents and hold relevant meetings outside the United States.[7] When restrictive action on behalf of American companies is taken by their foreign associates rather than by them directly, there is great difficulty in control by American courts.[8]

Similar problems are evident in other countries. European supplies of potash, for example, are controlled by a government monopoly in France, by a cartel that has been legally authorized in Germany. Producers in these

---

[2] See U.S. v. Deutsches Kalisyndikat Gesellschaft, 31 F.2d 199 (S.D.N.Y. 1929) and U.S. v. 383,340 Ounces of Quinine Derivatives, Admiralty No. 98-242 (S.D.N.Y. 1928.)

[3] U.S. v. Asbestos Corp., Ltd., 34 F.2d 182 (1929); U.S. v. DeBeers Consolidated Mines, Ltd., Commerce Clearing House, 1948-49 Trade Cases, para. 62,248 (1948).

[4] See Kingman Brewster, Jr., Antitrust and American Business Abroad, pp. 46-48, for a well-documented account.

[5] U.S. v. General Electric Co., 115 F. Supp. 835 at 878 (D.N.J. 1953).

[6] See U.S. v. Imperial Chemical Industries, 105 F. Supp. 215 (1952) and British Nylon Spinners v. Imperial Chemical Industries, 2 Eng. L.R. 780.

[7] In antitrust litigation between Zenith and R.C.A., an American court, having jurisdiction over the parties, eventually succeeded in stopping the flight of documents from one foreign country to another to escape discovery. See Edwards, The Internationality of Economic Interests, op. cit., p. 188, footnote 5.

[8] In the case of aluminum, an arrangement that included restraints upon shipments to the United States was developed by an international cartel. In negotiations in Canada to formulate the cartel agreement, one participant was Aluminium, Ltd., a Canadian company controlled by the American stockholders that controlled the Aluminum Company of America, and having as president the brother of the dominant executive of the American company. There was evidence of some discussion of the matter by the brothers while the negotiations were in progress. In a subsequent proceeding, the American courts held that the American company's participation in the cartel agreement had not been established. See U.S. v. Aluminum Company of America, 178 F 2d, 416.

two countries export under an agreement that requires buyers to refrain from selling the products of independent suppliers and to maintain resale prices. They give effect to this agreement through joint sales offices in foreign countries. Their power has been sufficient to induce producers in Spain and Israel to participate in the arrangement, and to create substantial obstacles to Western European buyers who try to buy from East Germany. The largest Irish buyer of potash has tried without success to find reliable independent sources of supply.[9] The British Monopolies Commission has reported that the operations of the international cartel are contrary to the public interest, but, thinking that no action taken in England could make the participants compete, it recommended only that efforts be made to develop alernative sources of supply and that unspecified means be found to strengthen the bargaining power of buyers.[10]

Difficulties in coping with restrictions of international scope have long been evident to those seriously concerned with control of restrictive business practices. For example, a report to the League of Nations in 1930 said:

"But the suppression of abuses that may be committed by cartels or trusts becomes still more difficult in the international sphere, particularly when those responsible do not live in the country where the abuses are committed. If, for instance, an international producers' cartel, enjoying a practical de facto monopoly in certain goods, unreasonably raises its sale prices in a consuming country, buyers living in that country will be faced with the greatest difficulties if they attempt to apply to the courts in the country of origin with a view to obtaining effective protection against the abuses from which they are suffering in their own country.

"The same will be true, if, for instance, a cartel or an industrial trust whose factories are in the countries of production tries to prevent the setting up of new and competing factories in the consuming countries or to ruin already existing factories by the means usually employed, namely, continuous selling below cost price, the cornering of raw materials, the enticing away of technical experts and qualified workmen, etc.

"In most legal systems, there are indeed laws which would enable foreign injured parties to start civil actions on the grounds of unfair competition or even to start a prosecution in the country of residence of those responsible for abuses of this kind. Experience of international law, however, shows that, as regards its practical efficacy, proceedings of this nature are more or less illusory. . . . The judicial authorities of any given state are, in fact, almost solely concerned with protecting the interests of their own nationals or of persons residing within their territory. . . .

---

9 Edwards, *Cartelization in Western Europe*, op. cit., pp. 29-30.
10 Monopolies Commission, Report on the Supply of Chemical Fertilizers, London 1959, paras. 692 and 702.

"But in countries in which the public authorities have the legal power to intervene in the policy as regards selling prices practiced within the national territory, either by a cartel or by a trust proper, they are almost powerless in the case of acts committed outside the national territory.

"When a country is obliged to buy a particular product abroad, it finds itself in an unfavorable position in dealing with an international trust which has succeeded in creating a more or less complete *de facto* monopoly in the product in question. It may be a case of raw materials, foodstuffs or semifinished articles of essential importance to the importing country. Its national industries may be seriously affected by price discrimination. The food supply of its population and even its national defense may be compromised by the policy of the foreign controllers of the products in question. . . .

"States whose internal legislation permits them to intervene directly in the case of abuses committed in their own territories can no longer intervene effectively in the case of abuses committed abroad. In these circumstances, having no direct means of action, states are sometimes induced to resort either to methods connected with commercial and tariff policy or to methods coming within the sphere of their diplomatic foreign policy. Obviously, it is only possible to settle the international problem by methods of this kind in somewhat rare cases. There should therefore be no illusion as to the effectiveness of such expedients."[11]

So long as only a few countries attempted to control international restrictions, while others ignored the problem, the difficulty experienced by the countries that tried to exert control consisted in partial ineffectiveness of national policy and occasional jurisdictional controversy with foreign governments. Now that more countries are trying to control restriction, a further difficulty is becoming apparent—the fact that the uncoordinated repressive policies of the various governments may be inconsistent and burdensome in their application to business activities and business enterprises that have an international scope. An enterprise subject to the reporting requirements of more than one of the countries that register cartels is likely to be confronted with differences as to what restrictions must be reported, what details must be supplied, what reports of changes must be made, what time limits must be observed, and what legal consequences ensue from registration or failure to report. An enterprise that sells in more than one of the countries that curb restrictive practices is likely to be confronted not only with substantial differences in the means by which such practices are investigated, appraised, and controlled, but also with important differences as to the lawfulness of refusal to sell, exclusive dealing, price dis-

---

[11] Henri Decugis, Robert Olds, and Siegfried Tschierschky, *Legal Aspects of Industrial Agreements*, 1930 (hereafter called Decugis), p. 112.

crimination, resale price maintenance, and participation in various kinds of restrictive agreements. To frame an agreement or shape the policies of an enterprise along lines consistent with all of the applicable national laws is increasingly difficult; for the aggregate of what is forbidden under some applicable law is likely to be greater than what is forbidden under any of the statutes, considered separately. Moreover, sometimes, though rarely, practices explicitly authorized or even required under one law may be forbidden under another, and much more frequently, contracts forbidden in one country may be enforceable in the courts of another.

Pre-War International Discussion of Restrictive Practices

Before the second World War, there was little governmental recognition that restrictions international in scope created important public problems. In 1927, an international economic conference under the auspices of the League of Nations resolved that industrial agreements did not "constitute a matter upon which any conclusion of principle need be reached," that such agreements could be either good or bad according to the spirit they expressed, and that the League should study them.[12] Subsequent memoranda under the auspices of the League included a study of the legal aspects of cartels and two memoranda on economic aspects prepared by a group of business executives actively engaged in cartelization.[13] In 1930 the Interparliamen-

---

[12] The conference had before it memoranda on the present position of various industries, including the extent of cartelization in them, and memoranda on various aspects of international cartels and monopolies, which showed great divergence in appraisal. The industries covered by the first group of memoranda were chemicals, cotton, electrical manufacturing, iron and steel, mechanical engineering, potash, shipbuilding, artificial silk, and natural silk. The memoranda concerned with cartelization included the following:

Gustav Cassel—Recent Monopolistic Tendencies in Industry and Trade, Being an Analysis of the Nature and Causes of the Poverty of Nations.
Eugene Grossman—Methods of Economic Rapprochement.
Julius Hirsch—National and International Monopolies from the Point of View of Labour, the Consuming Public, and Rationalization.
Clemens Landers—Review of Legislation on Cartels and Trusts.
David MacGregor—International Cartels.
William Oulid—The Social Effects of International Industrial Agreements; the Protection of Workers and Consumers.
Paul de Rousiers—Cartels and Trusts and Their Development.
Kurt Wiedenfeld—Cartels and Combines.
Report by the Trade Barriers Committee of the International Chamber of Commerce.

[13] The first was Decugis, op. cit. The latter two, by Aloyse Meyer of the steel cartel, M. Marlio of the aluminum cartel, and Sir Harry McGowan of Imperial Chemical Industries, were Review of the Economic Aspects of International Industrial Agreements, and General Report on the Economic Aspect of International Industrial Agreements. Tschierschky also wrote a separate report, Review of the Legal Aspects of Economic Agreements in Germany and Hungary.

tary Union unanimously adopted a resolution that recognized the possibility of harmful effects from cartels and trusts, suggested that such organizations be regulated to avert abuses, and emphasized publicity and nullification of harmful agreements as possible correctives.[14]

But such beginnings of international concern about objectionable restriction were overwhelmed and even reversed by the depression of the 1930's. International interest in cartels now centered upon their possible usefulness to alleviate economic distress.[15] By the spring of 1939, with the sympathy of their respective governments, the Federation of British Industries and the German Reichsgruppe Industrie publicly announced that they had formulated a general plan for price agreements by the industries of the two countries as a step toward cartelization of world trade and for joint requests for help from their governments in coping with competition from countries that refused to join.[16]

Post-War Abortive Proposals for International Collaboration

Sustained efforts toward international cooperation to curb restrictive practices originated in the second World War. Near the beginning of that war, Congressional investigations and antitrust proceedings made the

---

[14] A Danish experimental law for the investigation of price agreements, enacted in 1931, drew its inspiration partly from this resolution.

[15] Such views were expressed, for example, in memoranda by the Economic Committee of the League of Nations on *The Coal Problem*, and *The Timber Problem—Its International Aspects*. They were prominent in the proceedings and reports of the 1930 *Preliminary Conference with a View to Economic Action*, the report of the sub-committee of economic experts to the 1931 *Commission of Enquiry for European Union* and the consideration of this report by the Commission's economic coordination sub-committee, the proceedings of the 1932 *Stresa Conference for the Economic Restoration of Central and Eastern Europe*, the *Draft Annotated Agenta* for the 1934 *London Monetary and Economic Conference*, and the report of the Economic Commission approved by that conference. The only significant international document adverse to cartelization that appears to have been produced during this period was Bertil Ohlin's, *The Courses and Phases of the World Economic Depression*, written under the auspices of the League of Nations.

[16] At the conclusion of a conference in Dusseldorf in March 1939, the two federations issued a joint declaration, which read in part as follows: ". . . 5. The two organizations are agreed that it is desirable that individual industries in both countries should endeavor to arrive at industrial agreements which will eliminate destructive competition, wherever occurring, but prices must be fixed at such a level as not to diminish the buying power of the consumers. 6. The two organizations realize that agreements upon prices or other factors between Germany and Great Britain are only a step, although a most important step, toward a more ordered system of world trade. They would welcome the participation of other nations in such agreements. 7. They are further agreed that the wider the area of such agreements, both as to industries and countries, the more rapidly will international trade be established on a permanently progressive and profitable basis. 8. The two organizations realize that in certain cases the advantages of agreements between the industries of two countries or of a group of countries may be nullified by competition from the industry in

United States government aware that in the inter-war period restrictive agreements among business enterprises had been used by totalitarian states in furtherance of their political objectives. The following summary of the evidence appeared in an article I published in 1953:[17]

"In Germany and Japan, and to a lesser extent in Italy, private business had been brought so far under government control that when great business enterprises participated in international business negotiations they often did so for political objectives as well as for their own business purposes. In non-totalitarian countries, business interests were seldom coordinated with the political interests of governments. When cartel arrangements were made between the business enterprises of the democracies and those of the totalitarian states, the resulting restrictions often served a totalitarian political purpose as well as a monopolistic business purpose. Thus in particular instances, restrictions were imposed upon the productive capacity, technological development, or current production of strategic industries in democratic states without equivalent restrictions in totalitarian states; markets for strategic equipment were allocated in such a way that democratic states were made dependent upon supplies flowing from totalitarian states; a one-way flow of technological information was established from the business enterprises of democratic states to those of totalitarian states, in extreme cases associated with a flow of military secrets; trade was associated with totalitarian political propaganda and used to reward the political friends of totalitarianism or to discipline its political enemies; and properties belonging to the business enterprises of totalitarian states and markets allocated to them were protected from wartime loss by a false cloak of ownership or by a temporary transfer to cartel partners in other countries. Moreover, after war broke out, the continued alliance of business enterprises on both sides of the battle lines with cartel partners in neutral countries created dangerous possibilities of a flow of restricted information to enemy enterprises. As these patterns became clear, there was a tendency to exaggerate them, particularly by attributing to cartelization effects that were inherent in the fact that the larger business enterprises of the totali-

---

some other country that refuses to become a party to the agreement. In such circumstances it may be necessary for the organizations to obtain the help of their governments, and the two organizations agree to collaborate in seeking that help." See British House of Commons, Parliamentary Debates, March 21, 1939, pp. 1108-09.

Interpreting the statement as a declaration that the Federation of British Industries contemplated seeking British government subsidies to help German trade against American, the London Economist commented, "Is there something in the atmosphere of Dusseldorf that causes sensible men to lose their wits?" See The Economist, March 22, 1939, p. 14, Col. 5.

[17] Corwin D. Edwards, Regulation of Monopolistic Cartelization, 14 Ohio State Law Journal 252, at 253-4.

tarian states had overseas branches and conducted overseas trade. Apart from such exaggerations, however, it was evident that various business enterprises in the democracies had failed to see the political implications of cartel arrangements or had acquiesced in them, and that because these enterprises had based their trade policy upon cartelization they could not adapt themselves to the political needs of belligerency without substantial embarrassment."

The Draft I.T.O. Charter. Opinion hostile to international cartels developed rapidly in the United States and, to a lesser extent, in other countries. In 1944 the President wrote to the Secretary of State that "cartel practices which restrict the free flow of goods in foreign commerce will have to be curbed" and that this could be done only through collaborative action by the United Nations.[18] Toward the end of the war the United States took the initiative in suggesting to other friendly countries that post-war trade policy should include international collaboration against restrictive agreements.[19]

The proposal took form in a draft section on restrictive business practices, to be included in a treaty by which an international organization would be created to apply agreed policies toward international trade. As envisaged, the International Trade Organization would have applied policies toward commercial policy, employment, commodity agreements, and restrictive business practices. The proposal about business practices was that member states agree to take appropriate measures "to prevent business practices among commercial enterprises which restrain competition, restrict access to markets or foster monopolistic control in international trade, and which thus have the effect of frustrating the purpose of the Organization to promote expansion of production and trade and the maintenance in all countries of high levels of real income."[20] Member states were also to agree that unless there was proof to the contrary in a specific case the specified effect would be presumed where there were arrangements to fix prices or terms, exclude enterprises from any territorial market or field of business activity, fix quotas of sale or purchase, boycott or discriminate against particular enterprises, limit production, suppress technology or invention, or extend the use of patents, trademarks, or copyrights to matters not properly within the scope thereof. Thus, though recognizing the possibility

---

[18] State Department Release, September 8, 1944.

[19] Department of State, Proposals for Expansion of World Trade and Employment, Developed by a Technical Staff within the government of the United States in preparation for an International Conference on Trade and Employment and presented for Consideration by the Peoples of the World, November, 1945, pp. 4-5.

[20] Department of State, Suggested Charter for an International Trade Organization of the United Nations, September 1946, pp. 25-26.

of exceptions, the proposal would have committed participating countries to the American position that restrictive agreements are typically impediments to economic prosperity. The international organization was to receive and winnow complaints from governments and private interested persons, investigate them, decide whether or not practices had harmful effects, recommend remedial action to member states, and publish reports of its decisions and recommendations and the actions taken.

This formulation aroused widespread opposition among other governments; for most of these governments had never sought to curb equivalent domestic restrictions, and the rest had undertaken domestically no more than the control of certain practices they thought potentially abusive. They were willing to investigate international restrictions and to take action against those that they found harmful, but not to commit themselves to the belief that particular kinds of restriction were inevitably or typically harmful.

After extended negotiation, the representatives of the United States accepted a revised text that became part of the final draft charter prepared in March 1948. Representatives of 53 countries accepted the charter and submitted it to their governments for ratification. In this version participating states were to take action "whenever such practices have harmful effects on the expansion of production or trade and interfere with the achievement of any" of the charter's objectives. The practices that had been specified in the American draft as presumptively harmful were now listed as matters appropriate for investigation when they were used by enterprises possessing effective control of trade among a number of countries. The obligation to act was enlarged, however, to cover not only practices in international trade but also practices affecting it. Procedures were modified so that complaints would be received only if they were made or sponsored by member states.[21]

Anticipating that an International Trade Organization would soon be established, various governments, especially in Europe, began to formulate domestic laws that would provide means of conducting the investigations and applying the correctives to which the Charter would commit them. This preparatory work became one of the bases of the national laws that have been discussed in the first part of this book. However, the International Trade Organization did not materialize. Though the United States had been principal promoter of the project, opposition to the draft charter in the American Congress was so strong that steps to bring about American ratification were first deferred and then abandoned, without major public con-

---

[21] Department of State, Havana Charter for an International Trade Organization, March 24, 1948, pp. 35-38.

troversy.[22] American support having been withdrawn, the other participating countries allowed the project to lapse.

As the prospects for an International Trade Organization waned, projects for international control of cartels were developed elsewhere. They took two forms, projects for regional control in Europe and projects intended to be global. The European projects included one formulated by the Council of Europe, inspired by the Havana Charter, which progressed no further than a tentative draft; and three not directly connected with that charter, which went into effect. Of the latter, the first two—the restrictive practice portions of the European Coal and Steel Community and the European Economic Community—justify extended discussion, and are the topics of subsequent chapters.

The global projects were those developed under the auspices of the United Nations Economic and Social Council (Ecosoc) and later of the General Agreement on Tariffs and Trade (GATT). One led to nothing, the other to nothing effective. They and the project of the Council of Europe will be sketched in this chapter. The restrictive practice provisions of the convention for a European Free Trade Association (EFTA) which are almost as modest as the arrangements developed by the General Agreement on Tariffs and Trade, will also be discussed here.

The Draft Convention of the Council of Europe. In August 1949 the Consultative Assembly of the Council of Europe asked the Council's Committee of Ministers to draft a European convention for control of cartels. In 1950 the Committee decided that such action would be opportune, and in March 1951 a draft convention prepared by the Council's secretariat was submitted to member governments for comment. Though in many respects similar to the relevant provisions of the Havana Charter, this convention included a requirement that restrictive agreements between commercial enterprises within the jurisdiction of two or more of the participating countries be publicly registered. It provided for a commission empowered to receive complaints from private persons as well as governments, to conduct hearings, and to negotiate settlements. It provided that matters which could not be settled by negotiation might be referred to a European Court, which might have power to award damages and impose fines or to make decisions under which participating governments would do so.[23] This plan was con-

---

[22] The charter was not submitted to the Congress until April 1949. Hearings were held on it by the Foreign Affairs Committee of the House of Representatives in the spring of 1950, but no report was issued. In December 1950 the Department of State announced that ratification would not be sought from the new Congress. Presumably this decision reflected belief that such a request would fail.

[23] Council of Europe, Memorandum on the Recommendation of the Consultative Assembly for the Preparation of a European Convention for the Control of International Cartels and Draft Convention Prepared by the Secretariat General, SG/R (51) 15, Nov. 28, 1951, pp. 10–42.

sidered too complicated by some of the participating governments; and in September 1951 Sweden suggested a less ambitious program for registration of agreements and transmission of complaints to the governments concerned.[24] By this time, however, action by the Economic and Social Council of the United Nations had begun; and since several members of the Council of Europe preferred a more comprehensive agreement to a European one, further consideration of a European convention was suspended in 1952 to await the results of the broader undertaking. Subsequently, the Consultative Assembly of the Council of Europe expressed the opinion that the final report by an ad hoc committee established by the United Nations Economic and Social Council seemed "to represent those minimum standards of agreement in this field to which a large number of countries could agree."[25] When consideration of the ad hoc committee's report was abandoned, the Committee of Ministers decided in 1956 to convene a group of experts to consider the advisability of completing the development of a European convention; but in 1958 it deferred doing so and subsequently took no further action.[26]

The Draft for Ecosoc.   In the United Nations Economic and Social Council, efforts to initiate an international program about restrictive agreements began in 1951, shortly after the American Department of State had decided that the Havana Charter could not be ratified. By this time a General Agreement on Tariffs and Trade (known as the GATT) had given effect to an agreement about commercial policy that was roughly equivalent to the commercial policy section of the Havana Charter.[27] A separate agreement equivalent to the restrictive practice provisions of the Charter seemed a logical corollary. At the thirteenth session of the Economic and Social Council, the United States proposed a resolution recommending cooperation to prevent restrictive practices affecting international trade that had harmful effects, and establishing an ad hoc committee to prepare proposals for an international agreement with this purpose. Since the United States and the United Kingdom were in disagreement as to the international body in

---

[24] Council of Europe, Control of International Cartels, Suggestions by the Swedish Delegation, CM/Ad (51) 53, Sept. 20, 1951.

[25] Opinion No. 10, September 23, 1954.

[26] Council of Europe, Consultative Assembly, Eighth Ordinary Session, Supplementary Report to the Seventh Report addressed by the Committee of Ministers to the Consultative Assembly in accordance with Article 19 of the Statute, para. 17, Doc. 543, of Oct. 6, 1956; Tenth Ordinary Session, Ninth Report, para. 11, Doc. 806, of April 18, 1958.

[27] This agreement was formulated by 23 countries in 1947 as a temporary arrangement until the Havana Charter could be completed and ratified. In 1955 it was revised as a permanent agreement and an Organization for Trade Cooperation was created to administer it. See General Agreement on Tariffs and Trade: Basic Instruments and Selected Documents.

which activity about restrictive practices should be located,[28] the resolution did not seek to determine the point, but instead instructed the Secretary-General to solicit views on the matter and to make a subsequent recommendation to the Council. After minor amendment, the resolution was adopted, two countries abstaining and the three Soviet-bloc countries opposing. A committee was established, with representatives from Belgium, Canada, France, India, Mexico, Pakistan, Sweden, the United Kingdom, the United States, and Uruguay.[29]

The committee's report, filed March 30, 1953, was based upon the restrictive practice provisions of the Havana Charter with few changes in substantive content.[30] However, since the administrative organization contemplated by the Charter would not be available, the report included proposals as to appropriate administrative structures and procedures. These contemplated a body representative of the participating countries as the seat of authority, with power to act by majority vote; an executive board chosen by the representative body, diversified but including countries of chief economic importance; an executive secretary to screen complaints, obtain information from members, and perform administrative duties; and a chief advisory officer aided by an advisory staff, to function independently in analyzing and reporting on the facts relevant to each complaint, after giving member countries and private persons opportunity to be heard.[31]

In July 1953, after a brief debate on the report, the Economic and Social Council decided to circulate the report for comment and to resume discussion in 1955.[32] In the intervening time, generally favorable comments were received from France, Pakistan, Norway, Germany, the Consultative Assembly of the Council of Europe, and the International Cooperative

---

[28] The United Kingdom desired to place the work in the GATT, both for the sake of associating it closely with work on commercial policy and for the sake of placing it where the influence of the less developed countries would be minimized. The United States thought the essentially political procedures of the GATT inappropriate, favored judicial forms of action, and desired to use a body as inclusive as possible. For these reasons, it favored a special body within the United Nations.

[29] United Nations Economic & Social Council, Official Records, Thirteenth Session, September 11, 1951-September 13, 1951, pp. 609-646.

[30] Two significant substantive changes were made. One added to the list of practices that were to be subject to investigation the practice of withholding the application of technology with the result of monopolizing an industrial or commercial field. The other exempted from investigation practices that were specifically required by governments in all countries where they existed (while authorizing investigation of practices required by some governments but not by others). It provided for formal comment to governments about required practices that might have harmful effects.

[31] Report of the Ad Hoc Committee on Restrictive Business Practices to the Economic and Social Council, E 2380, E/AC, 37.3, March 30, 1953.

[32] Economic & Social Council, Official Records, Sixteenth Session, July 30-31, 1953, pp. 239-262.

Alliance, generally adverse ones from the Union of South Africa, the International Chamber of Commerce, and the Chamber of Commerce of the United States.[33] The decisive comment, however, came from the United States government. Having proposed the undertaking, the American government, under a new administration, now withdrew its support on the ground that "differences which presently exist in national policies and practices . . . are of such magnitude that the proposed international agreement would be neither satisfactory nor effective in accomplishing its purpose. . . . present emphasis should be given not to international organizational machinery but rather to the more fundamental need of further developing effective national programs to deal with restrictive business practices, and of achieving a greater degree of comparability in the policies and practices of all nations in their approach to the subject."[34]

No delegate at the Economic and Social Council's nineteenth session regarded the project as feasible without American support. The Council reaffirmed its continuing concern over restrictive business practices, urged governments to continue examining them with a view to legislation, recommended that member states continue to send information on the subject to the Secretary-General, and asked him to suggest further consideration of the matter at some later session.[35]

Action under the GATT

Meanwhile, the question of action against restrictive practices was raised in the GATT in the autumn of 1954 by the Scandinavian and German governments. Denmark, Norway, and Sweden suggested that the ad hoc committee's report be used as a basis for a restrictive practice provision in a revised GATT agreement.[36] Germany suggested that contracting parties undertake to prevent restrictive practices that had harmful effects on trade among them, that practices capable of harm be defined as in the ad hoc committee's proposals, but that procedural provisions establish only obligations to consult on such matters upon request and a possibility that the contracting parties might investigate and make recommendations.[37] At the

---

[33] The American National Association of Manufacturers submitted a strong criticism of cartels that included no statement about the proposed agreement.

[34] Economic & Social Council, Restrictive Business Practices, Comments of Governments. . . . E/2612, Add. 2, April 4, 1955, pp. 4-5.

[35] Economic & Social Council, Official Records, Resumed Nineteenth Session, May 23-26, 1955, pp. 91-102, 115-116; and Resolution on Restrictive Business Practices, E/Resolution (XIV) 14, May 26, 1955.

[36] General Agreement on Tariffs & Trade, Review of the General Agreement, Proposals by the Delegations of Denmark, Norway, and Sweden, Restrictive Business Practices, L/283, Nov. 17, 1954.

[37] General Agreement on Tariffs & Trade, Review of the General Agreement, Proposals by the Government of the Federal Republic of Germany, L/261, Oct. 27, 1964.

GATT's ninth session in the winter of 1954-55, consideration of these proposals was deferred because the Economic and Social Council had not yet taken action on the ad hoc committee's report. At the tenth session in the autumn of 1955 discussion was deferred until 1956. Prior to the eleventh session Germany renewed in briefer language its proposal for agreed consultation.[38] and Norway proposed establishment of a working party to recommend whether or not the GATT should undertake control of restrictive practices and if so to what extent and by what provisions.[39] In the eleventh session the United States opposed the Norwegian proposal and reserved its position on the German one. Both proposals were referred to the intersessional committee with instructions to report its recommendations to the twelfth session in 1957. Norway then submitted a new proposal for action, which would have bound governments not only to prevent and abolish on their territory restrictive agreements likely to have harmful effects on trade between the contracting parties but also to prevent dominant firms from taking unfair advantage of their position to the detriment of other contracting parties. It would have established a cartel commission with power to investigate and make findings as to harm; would have obligated contracting parties to act on the findings; and would have provided, in case of failure to act, for report by the Commission to the GATT's executive committee and thereafter by the committee to the GATT's assembly.[40]

At the twelfth session in November 1957, Norway proposed that a working party be established to study the problem in detail. Action along this general line was favored by three Scandinavian countries, five Latin American countries, two Asiatic countries, one African country, and Australia and New Zealand—thirteen in all.[41] Postponement was favored by seven countries (the United States, the United Kingdom, Germany, Canada, Belgium, Turkey, and South Africa.) A compromise suggestion was adopted, under which documents would be assembled and submitted to an intersessional committee, which would decide whether or not to institute a working group. No such group was established; but an analytical report on restrictive practices was prepared and circulated to the delegations.[42] The thirteenth session resumed the discussion and decided to set up a committee of

---

[38] Restrictive Business Practices, Proposal by the Delegation of the Federal Republic of Germany, L/551, Oct. 16, 1956.

[39] Restrictive Business Practices, Proposal by the Delegation of Norway, L/568, October 24, 1956.

[40] Restrictive Business Practices, Proposal by the Norwegian Government, L/653, August 30, 1957.

[41] Apart from Australia and New Zealand, they included Norway, Denmark, Sweden, Brazil, Chile, Cuba, Nicaragua, Uruguay, India, Pakistan, and Rhodesia.

[42] Restrictive Business Practices, Memorandum Submitted to the Contracting Parties for their Thirteenth Session, August, 1958.

experts to make recommendation "as to whether, to what extent if at all, and how" the control of restrictive business practices should be undertaken. Experts from twelve industrially developed countries were placed on the committee.[43]

Unable to agree, the committee submitted majority and minority recommendations in 1959.[44] Both recommendations provided that each contracting party should consult with other contracting parties upon request, and should take such measures as it deemed appropriate if it agreed that harmful effects were present; and that the secretariat should be notified of conclusions agreed upon or of inability to agree. The majority recommended also that a group of experts be designated to study the results of the consultation and after three years recommend a future course of action. The minority desired to give the experts the further task of participating in the examination of practices and making reports thereon when a contracting party so requested.[45]

After considering the recommendations at the seventeenth session, the participating governments discarded both suggestions as to the use of experts, and on November 18, 1960, decided upon the consultation procedure that had been common to both recommendations. The decision was as follows:

"*Recognizing* that business practices which restrict competition in international trade may hamper the expansion of world trade and the economic development in individual countries and thereby frustrate the benefits of tariff reduction and removal of quantitative restrictions or may otherwise interfere with the objectives of the General Agreement on Tariffs and Trade;

"*Recognizing*, further, that international cooperation is needed to deal effectively with harmful restrictive practices in international trade;

"*Desiring* that consultations between governments on these matters should be encouraged;

---

[43] Austria, Canada, Denmark, Germany, France, Japan, the Netherlands, Norway, Sweden, Switzerland, the United Kingdom, the United States. Twenty-one countries were invited to make experts available. The rest did not reply. Few Asiatic, African, or Latin American countries possessed the appropriate types of expertise.

[44] Restrictive Business Practices, Action by the Contracting Parties in Dealing with Restrictive Business Practices in International Trade, Report by the Group of Experts, L/1015, June 30, 1959.

[45] Ibid, pp. 5-7. See also Memorandum by the Government of Norway, L1287, September 12, 1960; Statements submitted by the governments of New Zealand, Sweden, the United States, and the Federal Republic of Germany, L1301, October 13, 1960; Statement submitted by the Japanese government L1333, November 1, 1960. The majority consisted of delegates from Austria, Canada, Germany, Japan, the Netherlands, Switzerland, the United Kingdom, and the United States; the minority of the delegates from Denmark, France, Norway, and Sweden

"*Considering*, however, that in present circumstances it would not be practicable for the Contracting Parties to undertake any form of control of such practices nor to provide for investigations,

"The Contracting Parties

"*Recommend* that at the request of any contracting party a contracting party should enter into consultations on such practices on a bilateral or a multilateral basis as appropriate. The party addressed should accord sympathetic consideration to and should afford adequate opportunity for consultations with the requesting party, with a view to reaching mutually satisfactory conclusions, and if it agrees that such harmful effects are present it should take such measures as it deems appropriate to eliminate these effects.

"And *Decide* that

"(a) If the requesting party and the party addressed are able to reach a mutually satisfactory conclusion, they should jointly advise the secretariat of the nature of the complaint and the conclusions reached;

"(b) If the requesting party and the party addressed are unable to reach a mutually satisfactory conclusion, they should advise the secretariat of the nature of the complaint and the fact that a mutually satisfactory conclusion cannot be reached;

"(c) The secretariat shall convey the information referred to under (a) and (b) to the Contracting Parties."[46]

In the five years since this resolution was adopted, no use has been made of it. None was to be expected; for in three respects ad hoc consultation between governments is seldom, if ever, suited to the problems that are created by restrictive business practices.

1. When harm arises in one country from restrictive business practices carried on in another, neither the facts nor the bad effects associated with them are likely to be clear until investigation has disclosed the scope and character of the restrictions and disentangled the effects thereof from other environmental influences. As was recognized in the Havana Charter, the ad hoc committee's report, the draft proposal of the Council of Europe, and the draft proposal submitted by Norway to the GATT, investigation is a necessary first step in any action about restrictive practices. When a restriction is foreign, the victimized country may suspect, but can seldom prove, who is doing what. At most, it can obtain partial information about international restrictive activities in which enterprises in its own country

---

[46] GATT, Decisions of the Seventeenth Session, L1397, December 5, 1960 (mimeographed), p. 17.

take part. Thus, in the absence of investigative collaboration, a firm factual basis for consultation among governments can seldom be present.

2. Neither does the consultative procedure rest upon any agreement about the way in which harmful effects shall be conceived or the nature of the restrictions that are likely to produce them. The other projects discussed in this chapter set forth categories of restrictive agreement that were to be regarded as subjects for investigation. In the GATT resolution, nothing remains of this listing of practices. The earlier projects, like the GATT resolution, relied upon broad statements of objectives as a basis for appraising harmful effects; but unlike the GATT resolution, they contemplated a series of decisions by continuing international bodies, through which, in time, particular meanings might be developed from general statements and consensus might be attained.

Critics of these earlier projects emphasized the vagueness of the criteria of action they contained; and the ground upon which the United States repudiated the ad hoc committee's report was the diversity in national attitudes and policies. Yet the GATT resolution was vaguer than its predecessors, and contemplated no procedures by which vagueness could be reduced or precedents formulated. Its adoption presumably reflected belief by the United States and other countries that no part of any country's peculiarities of attitude was being compromised or surrendered. Such a negative result, of course, made the resolution harmless by making it almost useless. Action is likely to result from consultation only if, without immediate hope of reciprocal benefit, the government from which action is sought feels so clearly and strongly that the restriction is unconscionable that it is prepared to act. In coping with requests for action, no government is subjected to an obligation to which it can make reference in disregarding domestic pressures from citizens who benefit from the restrictions they inflict on other countries.

3. Moreover, consultation between governments is appropriate only for matters that are individually important enough to justify intergovernmental negotiation. Few restrictive practices are individually of this magnitude. The damage that restrictive arrangements do to international trade, to standards of living, and to technological progress is the cumulative effect of many restrictions, few of which are individually of major importance. Particular restrictions, and especially the important ones, are usually met by counter-restrictions, so that isolated action against a single restriction is likely to seem both futile and unfair. In such a setting, resort to ad hoc consultations necessarily means that few restrictions will be discussed and that fewer still will be corrected.

The virtue of the 1960 resolution consisted merely in the fact that it put the participating countries on record to the effect that restrictive practices can harm international trade and that cooperation among nations is needed to cope with this harm. Since the other projects thus far discussed were not adopted, the resolution contains the most comprehensive commitment to this view that has been thus far formulated. It should not be regarded, however, as an effective nor even as a seriously intended means of establishing that cooperation.

Action in the EFTA

The European Free Trade Association, established late in 1959, was intended as a more loosely organized and more limited alternative to the European Economic Community (E.E.C.). The seven participants are Austria, Denmark, Norway, Portugal, Sweden, Switzerland, and the United Kingdom. As in E.E.C. the members of the Association undertook to reduce by increments the tariffs upon trade among themselves, and to eliminate, for this trade, certain other governmental trade barriers and discriminations. They included in their convention a declaration against concerted business practices that have as "object or result the prevention, restriction, or distortion of competition" within their trade area, so far as these practices "frustrate the benefits" of the reduction or removal of tariffs and quantitative restrictions on trade. Under the convention, a member was authorized to complain to a Council representing all the member states. A majority of the Council was empowered to decide to examine the matter and to set up an examining committee for the purpose. If the Council decided that a benefit of the convention was being frustrated, it was empowered to make recommendations, by majority vote, to a member state; and if the recommendations were not adopted, to authorize, by majority decision, a member to suspend the application of its obligations to the recalcitrant member. In connection with such recommendations or decisions, the Council was authorized to publish a report of the circumstances.[47]

Prior to the end of 1965 no complaints concerning restrictive business practices had been considered by the Council under the EFTA convention. Superficially the available procedure appeared to be stronger than that of the GATT, since recommendations could be made by states that were not immediately involved, and since if these recommendations were disregarded an ultimate sanction was provided. But since the Council and the

---

[47] European Free Trade Association, Text of Convention and Other Documents Approved at Stockholm on 20th November, 1959, Articles 15, 31. Cmnd. 906, Her Majesty's Stationery Office, London.

examining committees that were specified in the convention lacked investigatory powers and the convention did not obligate member states to investigate at the EFTA's request, the basis for knowledge about alleged practices was almost as weak as in the GATT. As in the GATT, too, the convention afforded no basis for agreement about the practices that were suspect, no clear basis for agreement about what was harmful, and no way of considering any restrictive arrangement that was too small to justify intergovernmental negotiation. That a body like the Council, primarily concerned with commercial policy, would decide enough restrictive practice cases to give meaning to the general language of the convention was inherently improbable; and in six years it has actually decided no cases. Moreover, the ultimate remedies provided in the convention—discriminatory tariffs and the like—are restrictions so clearly objectionable in themselves and so unlikely to be appropriate correctives of private restriction that their use was obviously a remote possibility.

The convention provided that no later than the close of 1964 the adequacy of the restrictive practice provisions would be reviewed. Instead of strengthening the plan, the review resulted in a modified procedure that provides no additional means of ascertaining facts or agreeing on policy, but instead reduces the role of the EFTA and relies upon ad hoc bilateral negotiations between interested governments. According to a public announcement late in 1965, a complaint sponsored by a member government is to be discussed informally by that government with the governments in whose territories the parties to the challenged practice are located. If the discussion results in agreement that the practice exists and is incompatible with the treaty, the governments having jurisdiction over the parties will use "administrative means" and, if necessary, legal powers to provide a remedy. In that case the matter will be reported via the EFTA to all member states, but "in general terms," and with care "not to reveal confidential facts." If a matter cannot be thus disposed of, there may be either informal multilateral discussions or formal reference of the complaint to the Council. Meanwhile, a "working party of experts" is to report to the Council whether the legislative and administrative means available to the member states are adequate to an effective program.

Thus, six years after the program began, no use had been made of it, nothing had been done to strengthen it, and doubt that adequate means of action are available had been officially expressed.

Both in the GATT and in the EFTA, the summary treatment provided for restrictive practices, as compared with the careful delimitation of conceptions and formulation of substantive agreements as to commercial policy, were evidence of an intention to do as little about restrictive practices in these organizations as was possible, short of refusal to do anything at all. Under existing arrangements, neither organization is likely to apply a corrective to any restrictive business practice unless restrictions that are both obvious and manifestly outrageous evasions of governmental commercial policy should appear in some industry of major international importance. Though such industries sometimes restrict trade, they are careful to avoid the obviously outrageous.

Chapter XV

The Experience of ECSC

In Europe two international agreements formulated in the 1950's provide arrangements for collaboration in the control of restrictive business practices more ambitious than those of the GATT and the EFTA. They are those that established the European Coal and Steel Community (ECSC) in 1951 and the European Economic Community (EEC) in 1957. In each Community, control of restrictive business practices is only a part of a complex undertaking. In each Community, however, such control expresses a policy established by international agreement and is applied by international means established for the purpose. The work of the two Communities upon restrictive business practices constitutes the only body of experience available to indicate the possibilities and limitations of joint efforts by sovereign states to cope with business restrictions that have international significance.

The two Communities differ substantially in objectives, relation to the constituent national states, administrative characteristics, and policies toward restrictive business practices. The record of each will be examined separately as a basis for subsequent discussion of the problem of international collaborative attack upon such restrictions.

The treaty establishing the European Coal and Steel Community included the first international arrangements to curb cartels, industrial concentration, and restrictive practices. Having been in effect for fifteen years, the treaty has provided the longest sustained experience yet available with international action to control cartels and monopolies.

When the treaty went into effect, coal and steel were excellent examples of a condition that has been common in Europe. Private cartels, government restrictions, and government ownership interacted and reinforced one another. Particularly in Germany, these public and private restrictions had been supplemented between the two world wars by a high degree of horizontal and vertical concentration, not all of which had been removed by the deconcentration policies of the post-war Occupation of Germany.

The coal and steel industries were subject to pervasive public and private control. In Germany the Occupation had recently attempted to decartelize and deconcentrate these industries in the Ruhr. The Ruhr had possessed large steel enterprises (the largest of which produced about nine million tons annually) and vertical integration by large steel and coal producers. Under the Occupation, dissolution had reduced the size of the large firms (to a maximum of two million tons of production) and had broken many, but not all, of the vertical affiliations. In France post-war amalgamations were enlarging the biggest steel companies, coal had been nationalized, and the importation of coal was controlled by a government-sponsored buying monopoly. In Italy more than half of steel production was controlled by a government holding company. In the Netherlands the only important steel company was partly owned by the government, and the largest of five coal producers was a government company. In Belgium three important steel producers had complex financial links with one another and with coal companies. In Luxembourg the largest steel company in Europe was vertically integrated with producers of coal and with steel processors.

Cartelization was prevalent. A powerful international steel cartel had been broken by the war, but several national ones still existed for particular products. For coal, cartels were national. A Belgian joint sales agency fixed prices and established quotas. Two French wholesalers' associations, which were allowed to exclude other wholesalers from membership, had exclusive permission from the government to acquire imported coal for resale; and with government approval, French steel producers bought their coal through a joint buying agency. Sale of coal in south Germany was cartelized. In the Ruhr, the Occupation had recently substituted for the old and powerful cartel six sales syndicates which, for some purposes, were allowed to act through a common central organization.

Restrictions, governmental as well as private, were general. They included tariffs, quantitative restrictions on exports and imports, discriminatory taxes, subsidies, discriminatory transportation rates, and dual pricing. Price control by governments was common, in an effort to mitigate the impact of private restriction and of the post-war shortages.[1]

In this setting, ECSC was intended to improve the performance of the coal and steel industries and to lay a basis for eventual political unification by creating international markets in which the goods could move across the borders of the member states without discrimination. The stated ultimate purposes were to expand the economy, increase employment, and raise standards of living (Article 2). The proximate purposes were to insure regular supplies and equal access to goods and markets, to provide incentives for rational development, to foster trade, and to expand production

---

[1] An excellent summary of these public and private restrictions appears in Wolfgang Renner, *Preispolitik im Gemeinsamen Markt*, doctoral dissertation, University of Tübingen, 1956, duplicated, pages 11-28.

(Article 3). As incompatible with these purposes, four types of public and private restrictions were broadly prohibited: tariffs and quantitative restrictions, discriminations and measures hampering buyers in choosing suppliers, subsidies and special charges, and "restrictive practices tending toward the division or the exploitation of the market" (Article 4). As a central but not sole means to accomplish these purposes with only limited governmental intervention, the treaty provided that the Community should "assure the establishment, the maintenance, and the observance of normal conditions of competition" (Article 5).

In this body of ideas, competition was an instrument of policy. It was to be "normal" and to serve such purposes as expansion, rational organization, adequate employment, and stability. Though restrictive practices were recognized as obstacles to it, they received less attention than the various forms of national public discrimination.

The organization set up by the treaty was given sovereign authority over the field it covered. National states were not only deprived of any share in jurisdiction; they were subjected to the organization's orders if they violated the treaty. The organization consists of a High Authority, the executive body; an Assembly with power to force the High Authority to resign; a Council that must approve some of the more important decisions; and a Court. There is also a Consultative Committee, representative of private interests. The High Authority has broad power to control the management of the coal and steel industries. It can act either to restrict or to expand. It may make grants and loans, review investment plans, allocate products during shortages, establish quotas during crises, fix maximum and minimum prices generally or in export trade, intervene to end discriminations by member states, authorize assistance to enterprises by member states, and authorize schemes of compensation for the purpose of keeping prices down. Its regulatory powers are intended to serve the substantive purposes of the treaty, not merely to maintain competition. Indeed, they include power to restrict competition where competition is thought to be undesirable.

Types of Action about Restrictive Business Practices

The provisions of the treaty that relate to private restrictions are similarly intended to serve the treaty's substantive purposes. They consist of (1) provisions about price publication, discrimination, and other unfair practices generally, set forth in Articles 60 and 63; (2) provisions about restrictive agreements, set forth in Article 65; (3) provisions about mergers and other forms of combination, set forth in Article 66, subsections 1-6; and (4) provisions about abuses by dominant firms, set forth in Article 66, subsection 7. These provisions were written in Washington and adopted as written. Europeans have had some difficulty in reconciling them with European concepts and procedures.[2]

Discrimination and Publication of Prices

Article 60 forbids unfair competitive practices (in particular, temporary or local price reductions for the purpose of acquiring a monopoly) and discriminatory practices by sellers, especially those based on the buyer's nationality. The High Authority is empowered to define the forbidden practices after consulting the Consultative Committee and the Council.

Two further requirements reinforce the prohibitions. First, prices and conditions of sale are to be published, to the extent and in the form prescribed by the High Authority after consulting the Consultative Committee.

Second, use of basing points is presumed, and certain limits are placed upon their use: Methods of price quotation must not have the effect that, when reduced to the equivalent at the basing point, the price is higher than that of the same seller in comparable transactions. Neither may such methods have the effect that this base price equivalent falls below the list price by more than the amount necessary to meet a competitor's delivered price based on another point, or below limits fixed by the High Authority after consulting the Consultative Committee. Such limits upon the right to meet a competitor's prices may be set to avoid disturbances in the market, but, in the absence of abuse, may not be used to prevent enterprises from meeting the prices quoted by enterprises from outside the Community, provided that the High Authority is notified of each action. If the High Authority finds that an abnormal basing point is being used, especially one that evades the foregoing curbs, it is required to make an appropriate recommendation to the offending enterprise. The general concept appears to be that a basing point system will be used (with an apparent presumption that basing points will be near centers of production) and that freight absorption to meet the lower delivered prices derived from quotations from another base will be permitted, except where special rules limit it in order to retard large transfers of business.

It is noteworthy that the treaty grants no right to reduce prices to meet the competition of a competitor whose prices are based upon the same basing point. It is also noteworthy that the right to align one's prices upon those of a competitor is a general one, not dependent upon any showing that the competitor's lower price reduces the opportunity of the align-

---

[2] See statement by Albert Coppé, vice president of the High Authority, in American Bar Association, *Proceedings, Conference on Antitrust and the European Communities*, 1963 (hereafter called ABA Conference Proceedings), p. 239.

ing enterprise to compete in any particular situation.[3] The rules do not indicate any apprehension about the possibility, important in American policy toward restriction, that general adherence to a basing point system may be, in effect and even in intent, the equivalent of a price agreement.

A subsequent interpretation by the High Authority[4] indicated that an enterprise is free to reduce a delivered price by only part of the difference between its price and that of a competitor and is free to adopt basing points other than the point of production. The interpretation did not discuss the difficulties in reconciling use of a basing point other than the mill with the requirement that delivered prices must never produce a base price equivalent higher than the list price.[5] The authorization to meet prices only partially amounts to a sanction for pricing systems in which net yields from different transactions are allowed to differ, but only to the extent that one enterprise refrains from competing price-wise with another for business.[6]

Article 63 seeks to apply to buyers a similar rule against discrimination. However, since in many instances buyers are likely to be enterprises not directly subject to the jurisdiction of the High Authority, it does not contain direct prohibitions. Instead, it authorizes the High Authority to make recommendations to member governments about discriminatory buying practices; to require sellers to impose on their customers or agents obligations to conform to the High Authority's rules; to make sellers responsible for violations of the rules by agents or dealers; and to limit the right of the Community's enterprises to sell to offending buyers. The last three prohibitions contemplate that discrimination may be prevented by vertical control over dealers, enforced through mandatory boycotts.

The general prohibition of unfair practices appears to have resulted in no subsequent action by the High Authority; but the provisions concerned with discrimination, publicity for prices, and basing points have been applied continuously. By April 1956 the High Authority had frequently sent warning letters to enterprises, usually about secret rebates, had insti-

---

[3] In January 1964, the High Authority announced that steel prices could not be aligned upon the prices of steel from state trading countries. (Journal Officiel, hereafter called JO, January 22, 1964, p. 97). It subsequently postponed the effective date of its order until the end of 1965. (JO, December 10, 1964, p. 3602).

[4] Communication Relative aux Modes de Cotation et aux Couts de Transport dans les ventes d'Acier, January 7, 1954; JO, January 13, 1954, pages 224-29.

[5] Compare Ernst-Joachim Mestmacker, "The Prohibition against Discrimination in the European Coal and Steel Community Treaty" in *Cartel and Monopoly in Modern Law,* Karlsruhe, 1961, pages 330-32, and Erich Zimmermann, *Die Preisdiskriminierung nach dem Montanvertrag,* doctoral dissertation, University of Frankfurt, 1959, duplicated, page 277.

[6] For a discussion of the complexities of interpretation that have appeared in decisions, see Renner, *op. cit.,* pages 100-138 and Zimmermann, *op. cit.,* pages 96-348.

tuted 25 proceedings, and had imposed several fines, of which the largest was $16,000.[7] By 1961 systematic checks of compliance were being recurrently made. In 1963 steel companies were temporarily required to inform the High Authority of rebates and special prices that they granted upon "indirect exports"; and in 1964 this requirement was made permanent.[7a] During the year ending January 31, 1964, inspectors made spot checks in more than 100 Belgian collieries and obtained particulars about prices from more than 70 steel firms. Subsequent full investigation of the prices of 18 collieries and some 50 steel firms resulted in 33 disciplinary proceedings—5 about coal and 28 about steel. One steel firm was fined, and eleven steel firms and one colliery admonished. The remaining 20 cases were still in process at the end of the year. The High Authority reported that violations as to coal were "extremely difficult to prove because of the intricacy of the commercial practices, the great variety of products, and the obvious collusion of buyer and seller where a violation occurs." In the case of steel, the High Authority regarded its lack of jurisdiction over distributors and other buyers as a substantial obstacle to enforcement, and hoped to diminish the difficulty by persuading the governments of the member states to make parallel price investigations.[8] In July 1964 the High Authority decided that in the steel industry specified documents must be made available as an aid in verifying prices.[9]

Since the High Authority does not release information about the cases of violation, the firms and practices involved do not become known. A report as to the year 1961, however, indicated that violations included such practices as failure to invoice extra charges for quality, grant of unearned quantity discounts, failure to charge for deferred payments, grant of unpublished trade discounts, and meeting competition by charging less than a competitor's prices. The magnitude of fines was indicated in that report by the fact that in six cases resulting in fines the total fines assessed were $37,500.[10]

That discriminations founded on nationality or applied against particular enterprises are unlawful is so evident that no significant problems have arisen about such matters. Since discrimination is forbidden only for comparable transactions, the rule does not apply to generally available quantity or volume discounts, functional discounts, loyalty discounts, or unique

---

[7] *Fourth General Report,* para. 129.
[7a] JO, December 24, 1963, p. 2977; December 14, 1964, p. 3585.
[8] *Twelfth General Report,* para. 255-261. Since steel companies are important buyers of coal, the High Authority's power to require information from buyers is greater in the case of coal than in the case of steel.
[9] JO, July 28, 1964, p. 1967.
[10] *Tenth General Report,* para. 262-63.

transactions. Thus most discriminations that are covered by the American anti-trust laws are not subject to control. Difficult problems, however, have been involved in territorial price differences and in use of the right to meet competition by aligning a price upon the price of a competitor.

At the outset, much of the Community's coal was sold under zone price arrangements or territorial discounts. To subject this system suddenly to the rules about discrimination probably would have resulted in substantial price increases in some localities and in rapid shifts in production as natural results of inter-area competition. To cushion the impact, the High Authority decided in February 1953 that collieries should not be permitted to reduce prices to meet domestic competition until the following year.[11] By successive extensions of this decision, the prohibition of "alignment" was continued until early 1958. Thus each area was protected against invasion from outside. In 1958 alignment was permitted, subject to restrictions by which collieries, large or small, could not align their prices with those of small competitors, but only with the prices of the joint sales agencies or specified principal producers; and by which products sold at aligned prices could not exceed either 20 per cent of the seller's previous year's tonnage or the amount of competing tonnage sold in the same area in the previous year.[12] Through these restrictions, considerable protection of areas was retained, and the price leadership of the larger enterprises was strengthened.

Sudden application of a basing point system to a product previously sold at zone prices would have created substantial perturbations in the market. The High Authority avoided these by authorizing other forms of price quotation.[13] At the outset, it permitted zone pricing in Germany and Western France[14] and allowed collieries in Lorraine and the Saar to align their prices in south Germany with those of the Ruhr.[15] From time to time the zonal exemptions were changed.[16] The general tendency of these changes was to bring zone prices nearer to those that would have emerged from the general pricing formula; and with the 1958 authorization to align, the zonal exemptions were terminated.

Thus, in the coal industry, the application of rules about alignment and methods of pricing was used to retard the impact of the international competitive market for which the treaty provides, and even the current version of these rules still includes considerable shelter for the high-cost

---

[11] Decision 3-1953; *Second General Report,* para. 55.
[12] *Seventh General Report,* para. 106.
[13] *First General Report,* para. 66.
[14] Decisions 8-1953, 11-1953, 17-1953, and 18-1953.
[15] Decision 16-1953.
[16] *Second General Report,* para. 55; *Third General Report,* para. 96-100; *Fourth General Report,* para. 89-93; *Fifth General Report,* para. 173.

areas. One should bear in mind that this feature of the rules as to competition is not inconsistent with the use of subsidies and publicly-applied restrictions to provide similar shelter, which had been authorized by the High Authority from the beginning, especially for the Belgian coal producers.

Publication of prices and terms, as provided for in the Treaty, was ordered by the High Authority for coal and iron ore in February 1953[17] and for most steel on May 4, 1953.[18] Each order required that all revisions be published at least five days before their effective date. Thus waiting periods were provided that might decrease incentives to reduce prices or might expose the price cutter to pressure from his competitors. The steel order was so drawn as to require direct-buying wholesalers to publish their own prices and terms or observe the applicable prices of their suppliers.

Later orders required publication of prices and terms for those special steels that were comparable[19]—more than 90 per cent of the tonnage and more than 80 per cent of the value of all such steel[20]—and of the amounts (but not the prices) of substandard steel sold.[21]

At first the rule against discrimination was linked to the requirement of publication by forbidding any sale except on the basis of the published prices and terms.[22] By the beginning of 1954, however, this plan seemed unsatisfactory. Modification of published prices and terms to fit unusual transactions is not necessarily discriminatory, provided all comparable transactions are treated similarly. Moreover, publication of every small change in price seemed to the High Authority to be too rigid. It impeded price flexibility and tended toward cartelization.[23] Furthermore, actual steel prices were deviating from published prices; that is, price competition was appearing in secret price concessions. To prevent such deviations seemed to the High Authority impossible, and the usefulness of the published prices as a guide to action was diminishing.[24]

Three orders were issued to meet this situation: One[25] made clear that

---

17 Decision 4-1953. The order was modified in 1963, see JO, December 24, 1963, p. 2975, Decision No. 22-63.

18 Decision 31-1953. The order was modified in 1963; see JO, December 24, 1963; p. 2972, Decision No. 20-63.

19 Decisions 37-1954, and 33-1958. The order was modified in 1963; see JO, December 24, 1963, p. 2973, Decision No. 21-63.

20 *Seventh General Report*, para. 103.

21 Decisions 32-1956 and 33-1956.

22 Decision 30-1953. The order was modified in 1963; see JO, December 24, 1963, p. 2969, Decision No. 19-63.

23 JO, January 11, 1955, page 580.

24 Communication de la Haute Autorité sur l'application de l'Article 60, *JO*, January 13, 1954, pages 221-24.

25 Decision 1-1954.

the test of discrimination was equality of treatment, not conformity to published prices. A second[26] authorized deviation of steel prices from published prices by not more than an average of two and one-half per cent for any class of products in a 60-day period. It also reduced to one day the waiting period before a new publication became effective. A third[27] required reports by steel companies twice per month about the maximum, minimum, and average deviations from the seller's own prices and from any competitor's prices the seller had used for price alignment.

The French and Italian governments appealed these orders. In December 1954 the court set aside the part of the second order that authorized deviations from published prices.[28] It held that the treaty required prior publication of actual prices and terms and that the High Authority's power to fix the extent and form of publication did not permit waiver of this requirement. The purpose of publication, the court found, was not only to discourage discrimination but also to enable buyers to inform themselves about prices and thus help to prevent discrimination, and to enable sellers to know exactly their competitor's prices, which might become standards for alignment. The court affirmed the remainder of the three orders.

By the close of the 1950's, this early decision had become a serious obstacle to the High Authority's action. Deviations from published prices were still being interpreted in practice as discriminatory, in spite of efforts by the High Authority to develop meaningful alternative concepts.[29] Moreover, mandatory publication had tended to restrict rather than foster competition. The obligation to publish prices in advance and conform to them exactly had removed the possibility that any steel company might compete in price except by giving its competitors formal notice, or that it might make any adjustments in its prices or terms unless it regarded the change as worth a new publication. The resulting rigidity of the price structure strengthened tendencies toward price leadership and conscious parallel action in the industry and provided a disciplinary weapon against disregard of any gentlemen's agreements that might develop. The possibilities of avoiding price competition by adherence to a pricing formula were inherent in an industry in which basing point systems, including choice of basing points other than the producer's point of production, had been legally recognized, and formulas about alignment of prices had been publicly prescribed. Indeed, such a system made it probable that all price lists would be coordinated, and that freight absorptions would make all prices

---

26 Decision 2-1954.
27 Decision 3-1954.
28 Decisions in cases No, 154 and 254, *JO*, January 11, 1955, pages 547-75.
29 High Authority Document 851/60f, March 1, 1960.

identical in areas that could be reached by different producers. The obligation to follow the price lists completed the legal support for informal price fixing by formula.[30] What frequently has been a basis for prosecution under the American anti-trust laws had come to be required as a rule of competition in the Community.

In 1963 the rules about publication and discrimination were extended to make clear that they covered sales through sales agencies and other authorized agents.[31] Meanwhile, evasion of these rules had become evident.[32] It consisted in abuse of the right to align prices with competitors and of the right to disregard the rules about discrimination in sales outside the Community. To cope with it, the High Authority modified the rules about alignment to require proof that competition was being actually met, and required that steel companies report cases in which they aligned prices with those of suppliers from outside the community and cases in which they made price concessions upon products indirectly sold for export.[33] Thus the rules about publication and discrimination were further tightened, and their anti-competitive potentialities further extended.

Restrictive Agreements

Article 65 forbids all agreements, decisions by associations, and concerted practices that tend, directly or indirectly, to prevent, restrict, or distort the "normal" operation of competition, and particularly those that tend to fix prices, to restrict production, technical development, or investment, or to allocate markets, products, customers, or sources of supply. The arrangements that are thus forbidden are legally void, and enterprises that form them, comply with them, or enforce them can be fined by the High Authority.

The severity of this prohibition is reduced by interpretations of the phrase "normal" competition. The High Authority has held, for example, that patent agreements do not limit normal competition, and that therefore assignment of exclusive territorial rights in a patent license is not prohibited by the treaty.[34] Conceivably, various other kinds of restriction, accredited

---

[30] Cf. Mestmacker, *op. cit.* Professor Mestmacker says that the obligation to publish prices renders prices as rigid as cartel prices and thus restricts competition.

[31] Decisions No. 19-1963, 20-1963, 21-1963, 22-1963, *JO* No. 187, December 24, 1963, pages 2969-76. See also *Twelfth General Report,* para. 215-18.

[32] Answer by the High Authority to Question No. 101 in the European Parliament, *JO* No. 181, December 11, 1963, pages 2878-9; *Eleventh General Report* para. 335.

[33] Decisions No. 23-1963 and 24-1963, *JO* No. 187, December 24, 1963, pages 2976-7; *Twelfth General Report* para. 219-223. French steel producers filed appeals; see *JO* No. 44, March 13, 1964, page 707. In December 1964 the rule about reporting concessions on indirect sales for export, which originally was temporary, was made permanent. See *JO* No. 209, December 14, 1964, page 3585.

[34] *Fourth General Report,* para. 138.

by other laws, by custom, or by the Community's moral sense, might be regarded as consistent with normal competition.

Moreover, the High Authority has taken the position that agreements are forbidden only where competition is possible, and that competition is not to be expected between enterprises that are under a common control. In 1960, for example, it decided that the principal members of a brown coal sales association were actually controlled by one enterprise and that this enterprise controlled over 87 per cent of the association's production. Because of "the various technical and economic link-ups existing" it considered that no competition between the three independents and the controlled group was possible. On this ground it decided that the brown coal agreement was not calculated to restrict competition within the meaning of Article 65.[35]

The prohibition is made inapplicable in the treaty to two types of agreements, if specified conditions are found. The types are agreements for specialization and agreements for joint buying or selling. Such an agreement *must* be authorized by the High Authority if a) it will contribute to a substantial improvement in production or distribution, is essential to that result, and is not more restrictive than necessary; b) it cannot give power to determine prices or to control or limit the production or sale of a substantial part of the products in question; and c) it cannot protect the parties from effective competition by others. Authorizations may be subject to conditions, may have time limits, and may be renewed, modified, or revoked.

In July 1953 the High Authority announced that all existing cartels that were covered by the provisions of Article 65 would be regarded as forbidden after August 31 of that year unless they were of the types subject to possible exemption and had applied for it by that time.[36] Numerous requests were filed—a total of 114 by the end of January 1965. By that time, in addition, 122 cases had been instituted ex officio by the High Authority. The High Authority had authorized 32 agreements, forbidden six, closed eight cases because the arrangement was liquidated, and found Article 65 inapplicable to 120. Nine cases had been "otherwise handled," with such results as the dropping of cartel projects or the withdrawal of an application.[37] According to the High Authority, these figures do not include "numerous cases" in which enterprises have dropped practices or agreements because of its objections.

Authorization of Agreements: Steel. The major part of the work

---

[35] *Ninth General Report,* para. 274.
[36] Decision 37-1953, *JO,* July 21, 1953, page 153.
[37] Thirteenth General Report, para. 229 and Table 36.

under Article 65 has been considering requests for authorization. Even before the general announcement, an authorization covered joint importation of steel scrap.[38] The High Authority required some revision in the arrangement. Subsequently it required consumers of scrap to participate.[39] The scheme involved not only joint purchase, but also an equalization fund designed to prevent users of imported scrap from incurring higher costs than users that obtained domestic supplies. After the scrap-buying organization had made an exclusive contract with a firm in the United States (Luria Brothers), protests by the American government led the High Authority in 1955 to decide that no exclusive purchasing arrangements would apply to future scrap purchases in the United States, and subsequently, in 1957, to prescribe criteria and procedures for such scrap purchases.[40] An effort by German steel companies to couple purchase of scrap with allocation of the supply was rejected by the High Authority as a restriction beyond that necessary to the constructive purpose.[41] In 1958, after scrap had become more plentiful, the High Authority investigated the joint buying arrangement, and the Council questioned its continuance. The equalization fund came to an end in 1958.[42] On January 8, 1959, the High Authority decided that the joint buying agency could not continue without obtaining new authorization. Apparently this was not obtained.

Few other important cartel problems have arisen about steel under Article 65. At the outset, an iron ore association was liquidated when the High Authority inquired about it.[43] Concerted practices in the scrap market have given recurrent cause for concern. An export cartel was set up by the steel industry soon after the war for the purpose of fixing minimum export prices; and it has tried vainly several times to agree also on export quotas. Since the impact of this body lies outside the Common Market, the High Authority has no general authority over it under Article 65, and has not used its power to fix limits for export prices.

The absence of overt domestic price cartelization in the steel industry is not surprising. As has been said above, the treaty's rules about discrimination and publicity, as interpreted, are sufficient to permit the industry's basing point system to achieve results similar to those of a price cartel.

---

[38] Decision 33-1953, *JO,* June 9, 1953, page 137.

[39] Decision 22-1954; *Second General Report,* para. 83.

[40] Statement by Thorsten N. Kalijarvi, Assistant Secretary of State for Economic Affairs, before the House Select Committee on Small Business, June 21, 1957, Release No. 381, June 21, 1957, Department of State, pages 7, 15-17.

[41] *Fourth General Report,* para. 141.

[42] *Eighth General Report,* para. 78.

[43] *First General Report,* para. 96.

Several specialization agreements for steel have been approved, at first agreements by few firms for minor products. For example, in 1954 two companies were authorized to agree that one would produce a special steel, needed in small amounts, and would sell the other its full requirements.[44] A somewhat more significant agreement, approved in 1961, bound one of the smaller German companies not to make certain flat products and tubes, while another would not make certain sections and pilings. The two were to collaborate in selling merchant bars and to observe specified rules in marketing other products.[45] An agreement for joint sale of about one million tons of steel by Belgian steel producers was authorized in 1956.[46] One or two lesser arrangements for joint sale were made, authorized, and in at least one case, voluntarily abandoned.

In 1965 the High Authority approved an agreement by Dortmund-Hörder, Hoesch, Oberhausen, and Mannesman providing for specialization upon rolled merchant steel and shapes and for allocation of orders to the producers by a joint sales agency. The participants supplied nearly 9 percent of the rolled products and nearly 11 percent of the shapes sold in the Common Market—a total of about 1.7 million tons. Accepting the agreement because it promised substantial operating economies, the High Authority recognized that it might involve significant reductions of competition. Accordingly, the order of approval required the parties to submit periodic reports as to their achievements in rationalization, and reports of the basic resolutions and decisions of the organization formed to carry out the scheme. The latter were not to take effect until the High Authority agreed that they were within the limits of its authorization.[47]

Authorization of Agreements: Coal. The major problems of authorization arose about the joint sales agencies for coal in Germany and Belgium and the related restrictive import arrangements for coal in France. These schemes had been regional or national, and in spite of the High Authority's action to remove barriers to shipments between the states, showed no tendency to become international. Apparently the absence of an effort to cartelize coal internationally was largely due to inherent characteristics of the industry, such as disparity in the levels of cost in different coal regions, the importance of transportation costs, differences in the quality of the product, and the interlocking of coal operations with adjacent operations in steel, electric power, and coal derivatives. Nevertheless, one of the deterrents probably was the fact that an international cartel would have

[44] Decision 31-1954, *JO*, July 6, 1954, page 433.
[45] *Tenth General Report,* para. 274.
[46] Decision 11-1956.
[47] JO, Sept. 2, 1965, pp. 2485-91.

required approval and could have been approved only in the form of a common sales agency.

The High Authority's problem about coal cartels concerned the continuance, reorganization, or dissolution of the national restrictive arrangements. The problem in France centered upon discrimination; that in Belgium and Germany upon the relative claims of the different objectives of the Treaty.

The French restrictions, required or supported by government orders, limited access to coal imports. An association of coal importers (ATIC) had sole legal authority to contract for the importation of coal. Foreign producers and distributors were excluded from sale in the French market, and French distributors and consumers were prevented from direct purchase abroad. ATIC's imports were furnished to an allocation office (ORCIS), from which all steel companies were required to obtain their imported coal, and to distributors licensed by the government to import. Without purchase of stipulated amounts of French coal and membership in one of two importers' associations (GPIR or GPIRT), no distributor could obtain an importer's license; and these organizations determined their own membership. All consumers except ORCIS and four other important ones were required to buy imported coal from a licensed importer.[48]

The French government was soon induced to end the requirement that importers qualify for license by purchasing French coal and the requirement that steel companies use the allocation office, and also to deprive the importers' associations of their rights to exclude members. It stubbornly clung to the other restrictions. In 1956 the High Authority formally found that the exclusive status of ATIC was a violation of the treaty. The French government appealed, withdrew its appeal, and resumed negotiations with the High Authority to formulate a compromise. When these negotiations failed, the High Authority issued a more comprehensive decision in December 1957, condemning the obstacles to direct purchase from foreign sources by French buyers.[49] The French government appealed the decision. The proceedings were stayed early in 1959 by mutual consent while further negotiations were undertaken.[50] Early in 1961 a settlement was reached. The High Authority's decision of December 1957 was rescinded, and the French appeal was withdrawn. Under the amended arrangements, French buyers were required to employ ATIC, under the High Authority's supervision, as their representative in making contracts and paying for coal and transportation in purchases abroad; and French consumers and dealers were

---

[48] *Fourth General Report,* para. 136.
[49] *Sixth General Report,* para. 100.
[50] *Eighth General Report,* para. 96.

required to meet tonnage requirements laid down by French regulations. However, individual consumers and dealers were enabled to buy abroad from foreign producers or dealers. Since ATIC could no longer consolidate the purchases of different buyers, the trading terms of the foreign producers became applicable to French buyers as well as to others. The High Authority reserved its final opinion of the plan until the results were evident, and both the High Authority and the French government reserved their positions on certain related problems.[51]

In Belgium coal was cartelized under a joint sales agency. The sales agency (Cobechar) eliminated from its previous program measures for allocation of production that were considered objectionable by the High Authority. After negotiations had brought about certain further modifications, the High Authority authorized the sales agency in October 1956. The approved plan was applicable only to purchases by large buyers, and covered about seven per cent of Common Market coal.[52] Four important participants withdrew from the plan in 1959-60.

In Germany two joint selling plans were in effect. One, applicable to south Germany, involved joint sale by producers in the Ruhr, the Saar, Lorraine, and the area around Aachen—that is, producers that controlled two-thirds of all coal in the Common Market, and substantially all producers that could supply the south German market. In June 1955 the High Authority indicated that it could not approve such a program.[53] It desired, however, to preserve joint action in transport on the Rhine and joint action in stockpiling in south Germany. For this purpose, it approved a plan by which the sales agency was replaced by a joint buying agency acting on behalf of wholesalers and open to all of them.[54] When renewal of the authorization was requested, the High Authority found that producers had exercised undue influence upon the agency through controlled dealers and through defects in the structure of the organization. It therefore modified the renewal so that only independent distributors were covered and producers' representatives were excluded from meetings. Thus modified, the joint buying agency was authorized, first until 1962, subsequently until the end of 1967.[55]

A more modest form of joint action by producers on the south German

---

[51] *Fifth General Report*, para. 217-18.

[52] *Fourth General Report*, para. 135; *Fifth General Report*, para. 160; Decision 30-1956, October 3, 1956. The authorization was subsequently extended to the end of 1969. See *Eleventh General Report*, para. 343; JO, Feb. 1, 1966, p. 309.

[53] *Fourth General Report*, para. 184.

[54] *Sixth General Report*, para. 97; Decision 19-1957.

[55] *Eight General Report*, para. 35; Decision 31-1959; JO, April 9, 1962, p. 873, Decision No. 3-62.

border was authorized, however, in 1959. A sales agency for Saar coal, formed in accordance with the 1956 treaty in which France and Germany settled their dispute about the Saar, was found by the High Authority to improve production without any of the prohibited restrictive effects.[56]

The most important system for joint sale in the Common Market was that for Ruhr coal, which covered nearly half the coal and coke for the Common Market. The system of sales agencies (known as GEORG) that the Common Market had inherited from the Occupation was regarded as an obstacle to competition. In the *Second General Report* (para. 53), the High Authority said, "The present selling system in the Ruhr precludes any form of effective competition between the enterprises or agencies of that coal-field, the organization of which, in view of the nature and volume of its production, has a predominant influence on the Common Market as a whole." In May 1954 GEORG was told that it could not obtain authorization under the treaty; and the High Authority decided to continue the fixation of maximum prices for coal largely because of the anti-competitive nature of GEORG's activities.[57] The High Authority then refused to approve a substitute plan for two Ruhr sales agencies.[58] After nearly two years of negotiations, during which GEORG continued to function, agreement was reached, and a plan was authorized by the High Authority in February 1956 for a three-year period.[59]

Under this plan three joint sales agencies were established, each with a full assortment of coal and each with from 11 to 16 per cent of the total Ruhr production of coal and coke. Approval was conditioned upon separate membership, control, and management. Nevertheless, the three agencies were permitted to establish a common bureau, and their members were permitted to set up a committee on norms.

The chief functions of the common bureau were to control a reserve stock of coal; to negotiate with large consumers who used more than 50,000 tons per year; to allocate the purchases of these consumers among the sales agencies in such a way as to maintain equity in employment and in the availability of supplies; and to administer schemes of compensatory charges and payments (instituted in 1953) that were said to be designed to offset differences in transportation costs to the principal ports, differences in the net cost of freight absorption, and differences in cost (up to five marks per ton) due to differences in percentage of capacity used. When prices were to be reduced to meet competition from outside the Common Market, the

---

[56] *Eighth General Report*, para. 94; Decision 23-1959.
[57] *Fourth General Report*, para. 160-61.
[58] *Fourth General Report*, para. 133.
[59] Decisions 5-6-7-and 8-1956, *JO*, March 13, 1956.

bureau was to determine the amount of the reduction and the quantities to which the reduced prices were to apply. In times of shortage, the bureau was to adopt rules for allocation of supplies.

The functions of the committee on norms were to adopt rules as to allocation of tonnage among the sales agencies in order to maintain equilibrium in employment; for this purpose to limit local sales, special sales, and consumption by firms affiliated with the producer; and to make rules about the portions of the output that were thus withheld from the sales agencies.

A consultative committee representing mining enterprises, labor, and consumers was a part of the plan.

Provisions for transmission of resolutions to the High Authority, prior approval or power of veto by the High Authority applicable to particular types of action, and reserved general powers of control were intended to assure conformity to the High Authority's policies.

The ambivalence that is evident in this program expressed the High Authority's effort to reconcile conflicting purposes. On May 11, 1955, in foreshadowing the decision, the Vice President of the High Authority had told the Assembly, "The treaty requires, on the one hand, a regime of competition; it requires equally a just allocation of employment; this is a requirement that, by its nature, conflicts with free competition. It was not possible to harmonize these two postulates except by establishing a boundary between sales through autonomous agencies, on the one hand, and sales through a Common Bureau, on the other." The High Authority's *Fifth Annual Report* (para. 3) explained the decision as follows:

"The cardinal fact about the coal mining industry, as we know it in Western Europe, is that once production is interrupted, it is liable to be lost forever. Hence it has been necessary to allow for arrangements for channeling orders and providing financial compensation, to enable enterprises in difficulties as a result of temporary circumstances to carry on. At the same time, it is essential to see that there is a continuous supply of such a fundamental commodity as coal, and consequently to allow arrangements preventing unjustified disparities in the meeting of consumers' requirements.

"The High Authority does not pretend, in this crucial problem of the coal-selling agencies, to have succeeded at the first attempt in bringing about a perfect balance between competition and the requisite degree of equality in supply and in employment. In the Ruhr, the High Authority has insisted on complete separation between three agencies, in place of the old system of centralized selling. At the same time, it is allowing the agencies, should the need arise, to deal with any tightness in the market, or with poor sales, by acting in certain matters through a joint office possessing a large operational reserve central stock: the very big consumers are entitled to obtain their supplies through this body. Alongside the system of selling through the agencies, there are arrangements for supplies to go direct to certain consumer groups, those closely tied up financially with the collieries, and those located within a certain distance who come themselves to fetch their coal."

A part of each of the systems of joint sale authorized in the Ruhr by the High Authority was a set of commercial regulations, uniform for each sales agency. These provided for sale by the collieries to large consumers and qualified wholesalers. They reserved for qualified wholesalers all sales to retailers, to consumers who bought less than 30,000 tons per year, and (for the time being) to large industrial consumers who had bought previously from wholesalers. They defined a qualified wholesaler as one who sold 75,000 tons or more of products from the Common Market (including 40,000 tons within the district to which he was assigned) and 12,500 tons or more of the products of a particular sales agency. They required that the opportunity to qualify be generally available, established transitional provisions to cover the first year, and provided that if, during the first year, 90 per cent of the wholesalers who had previously operated failed to qualify, the standards should be reduced. To prevent the sales agencies from mutually supporting one another, the High Authority rejected a portion of the draft rules that would have denied qualification to wholesalers who bought less than 25,000 tons from the three sales agencies combined. It also disapproved a provision that would have excluded wholesalers from parts of the Common Market where similar standards of qualification were not applied. After appeal by one of the sales agencies, the rejection of the 25,000 ton requirement was sustained by the Court.[60]

Conscious of the principle of the treaty that a buyer should be free to choose his supplier, the High Authority explained these restrictions on distribution as necessary to enable producers to fix a minimum tonnage for direct sale in order to avoid an undue increase in selling costs. The explanation made no distinction between minima fixed by each producer separately and minima fixed by agreement. The same jump across the gap between individual and collective action is evident in further statements by the High Authority that producers must be free to fix discounts and to set objective non-discriminatory criteria for the recognition of wholesalers.[61]

When the transitional year was over, the standards for qualification had proved too high for many wholesalers; accordingly they were reduced to 60,000 tons of Common Market coal, 30,000 tons of coal from the relevant district, and 9,000 tons from the relevant sales agency, with the latter re-

---

[60] *Fifth General Report,* para. 30.
[61] *Fifth General Report,* para. 151.

quirement temporarily waived for wholesaling in the Netherlands.[62] These modifications were set aside by the Court in March 1959 for lack of a sufficient statement of grounds.[63] In 1959 the High Authority again relaxed the standards by eliminating the requirement about tonnage of Common Market coal, reducing the requirement about coal from the relevant district to 20,000 tons, reducing the requirement of coal from a particular sales agency to 6,000 tons, and allowing a wholesaler who qualified in one district to qualify in an adjoining one if he sold only 2,000 tons there. Whether intentionally or not, the language of the decision made these criteria applicable to recognition of wholesalers by particular collieries rather than by sales agencies. Most of this decision was also reversed by the Court as insufficiently reasoned, but the elimination of the requirement about total tonnage from the Common Market was sustained.[64]

The High Authority then made a new effort to define wholesalers that could buy direct.[65] To qualify, the distributor must have sold in the previous year not less than 6,000 tons of coal bought from the sales agency concerned; but when first seeking recognition, an applicant could aggregate his purchases from different sales agencies, and wholesalers in France could be temporarily recognized if they had sold not less than 2,500 tons of three designated types of coal. The previous division of the market into sales areas was abandoned. Early in 1962 the High Authority reported that the change had not produced the predicted upheavals, that the number of recognized wholesalers had increased about 10 per cent, that French wholesalers were now buying Ruhr coal directly, and that overseas wholesalers had obtained "increased scope" from the elimination of the sales areas.[66]

In 1963 a new effort was made by the German sales agencies to prevent sales by wholesalers to large consumers such as the public utilities. Advocates of restriction upon the wholesalers feared that if wholesalers obtained foreign coal and sold it to public utilities, they could exert substantial pressure upon the sales agencies for lower prices. After more ambitious proposals by the German sales agencies had been rejected, the High Authority authorized schemes under which the steel industry and the state-owned railways were to buy direct from the sales agencies, but other consumers who bought more than 30,000 tons per year could buy either direct or from wholesalers.[67]

[62] *Sixth General Report,* para. 95; *Seventh General Report,* para. 112B.

[63] *Eighth General Report,* para. 5.

[64] *Tenth General Report,* para. 40.

[65] Decision 3-1961; *Tenth General Report,* para. 271.

[66] *Tenth General Report,* para. 271; *Eleventh General Report,* para. 306.

[67] The decisions about Germany appear in Decisions No. 17-1963 and 18-1963, *JO,* No. 184, Dec. 16, 1963, pp. 2928-2931; *Twelfth General Report,* para. 234-7. The simple technique of giving large buyers volume discounts has never been used for German

By 1959, when a new decision about the Ruhr sales agencies was nec-essary, their failure to compete with one another had become unmistakable. Identical price increases by the three sales agencies in September 1957 had been noted by the High Authority[68] as an indication that prices were being fixed jointly, and had led to a new requirement that proposed price changes must be communicated to the High Authority four weeks in advance. In February 1959 the High Authority reported that the sales agencies had not developed independent commercial policies, and that the method of sale must be changed so that sales resulted from independent decisions by enterprises, under regulations designed to prevent the reestablishment of a uniform system. It thought sales agencies only consistent wtih this principle if a) some large enterprises sold independently; b) members of a sales agency sold a considerable part of their production outside it; and c) no member of one agency could also participate in other agencies.[69]

The sales agency system was extended for a year, and then for three more months. Two successive applications for authorization of a single sales agency were made and rejected. On June 22, 1960, authorization of the second was finally refused, but with one more extension until the Court could decide an appeal against the refusal.[70]

Under the pressures of a slump in the market for coal, the controversy over Ruhr coal then passed into politics. The European Parliament recom-mended that amendments to the treaty be considered.[71] In November 1960, at the High Authority's suggestion, the Council of Ministers set up a study commission, which received from the German government proposals for the amendment of Article 65.[72] The Commission reported to the Council in March 1961. After the proposed amendment had been discussed and modi-

---

coal, and is not contemplated by sales agencies. Wholesalers' discounts have been reduc-tions in a factory price that was charged in sales to consumers. Large German buyers have had no monetary incentive to buy at the factory.

Similar problems existed in the coal industry in Belgium and France, but apparently involved less controversy. When approval of the Belgian sales agency Cobechar was extended in 1963, the High Authority specified that consumers taking not less than 30,000 tons per year could buy direct from the agency and that wholesale status required sale of at least 2,500 tons for household consumption or 6,000 tons for industrial consumption. (*Eleventh General Report*, para. 343). In France it approved an agree-ment by French wholesalers and retailers about types of customers to be served by each, under which consumers using as much as 240 tons per year might buy from wholesalers if they wished. (JO, No. 169, Nov. 25, 1963, p. 2750).

[68] *Sixth General Report*, para. 96.

[69] *Seventh General Report*, para. 112.

[70] Decision 16-1960, JO, July 23, page 104.

[71] *Ninth General Report*, para. 273, subsection 4; Gerhard Kreyssig, *Révision du Traité Instituant la Communauté Européene du Charbon et de l'Acier*, especially pages 23-24.

[72] *Ninth General Report*, para. 273, subsection 4

fied, the Council approved it by the requisite five-sixths vote and, in accord with Article 95 of the treaty, then asked the Court whether the proposed change violated any of the basic provisions set forth in Articles 2 to 4.[73]

The proposed amendment would have added to Article 65 a provision that where there was a "fundamental and persistent change in marketing conditions," the High Authority had discretion a) to authorize agreements designed to insure adjustment to the new conditions if the agreements were essential to achieve appropriate adjustment objectives and were not more restrictive than necessary for the purpose, and b) to waive the condition that agreements be incapable of determining price, controlling production, or protecting the participants from effective competition, where agreements appropriate to achieve the adjustment objectives were already in existence and were calculated to help avert "serious economic and social disturbances." New power would have been given to the High Authority to control the newly authorized agreements by investigating abuses, making recommendations, fixing prices, terms, and delivery schedules if recommendations were not followed, revoking the authorizations for insufficient results, and enforcing its orders by fines. The Council and the High Authority said in accompanying memoranda that under existing conditions joint buying or selling agreements might be necessary to bring an individual enterprise's plans "into line with the overall adjustment objectives" and "to prevent all-out competition and commercial practices conducted purely with an eye to immediate advantage and commonly at variance with the more permanent elements of competition."

On December 13, 1961, the Court held that the proposed change was not permissible, both because it would confer upon the High Authority power of an undefined scope, some of which was clearly new power, and because the possibilities for agreements restricting competition were so broad as to be incompatible with the prohibition of restrictive practices tending toward division or exploitation of the market, contained in Article 4d of the treaty. The Court then decided the pending appeal against the High Authority's denial of authorization, which had been held in suspense during these proceedings. The High Authority's decision was sustained on May 18, 1962, and thereupon the High Authority ordered that the sales agencies be dissolved by March 31, 1963.[74]

But this decision did not restore independent selling. The High Authority required that a new plan be submitted by the end of December 1962; and by the end of January 1963, reversing its refusal in 1954-55, it had granted a three-year authorization for two sales agencies without joint

---

[73] *Tenth General Report*, para. 265-67.

[74] *Tenth General Report*, para. 268; *Eleventh General Report*, para. 341-42.

activities.[75] Though the Netherlands government filed appeal against these decisions, the appeal was denied.[76]

The decision to give further approval to the sales agency system was made in a setting in which fuel oil had been making inroads on the European coal market. The German coal industry and the German government actively supported restriction for German coal. The French coal industry was monopolized. A sales agency for Belgium had been in existence from the outset, and Belgian coal had been subsidized by other countries in the Community. Although German productivity was higher than that of the French or Belgian mines and was growing more rapidly, the controls in the two other countries hampered the expansion of German sales, and German coal mine employment was declining. In this setting the arguments for preservation of German mining employment and the arguments of German coal mine owners for preservation of their properties attained considerable weight. Although the Ruhr was short of mining labor and was importing miners from other countries, a sociological argument that the older miners could not readily move to other employment reinforced the other pressures. It was argued too that as the largest source of energy the coal industry must be preserved for security reasons. According to responsible estimates, about 80 million tons of coal capacity out of the existing 240 million tons would have been able to survive under unrestricted competition. The objective of the German government, acquiesced in by the High Authority, was to preserve no less than 180 million tons of capacity.

The two new sales agencies were established with separate membership and with some overlapping of territory. Members of each were precluded from joining the other. Formal requirements were imposed to prevent the agencies from exchanging information about their operations, from having common officials, and from otherwise impairing their independence. Approval was limited to a three-year period. The High Authority reserved the right to exercise surveillance over the activities of the agencies and to give its agents access to all relevant documents. A distinguished German economist was designated by the High Authority to exercise this control and to report to it whether or not the desired independence was maintained.

Nevertheless, the hopes of the High Authority were modest. Its intention was to preserve what the Court had called the "minimum of competition that is required by the treaty," and some of its members would have been willing to approve a single sales agency.

---

[75] Decisions 5-1963 and 6-1963, *JO*, April 10, 1963, Colux A 132, April 18, 1963; *Twelth General Report*, para. 230-31.

[76] *JO*, June 19, 1963; JO, Nov. 12, 1964, p. 2897; Thirteenth General Report, para. 19.

In 1965 the High Authority extended its approval of these sales agencies to the end of March 1968. In doing so, it said that they had maintained autonomous organizations, developed their sales somewhat differently, and, in spite of substantially identical prices, shown no power to fix prices, control production, nor prevent outside competition.[77]

The German government was no longer content to rely upon sales agencies for preservation of the Ruhr coal industry. In July, 1963, it enacted a law that required producers of hard coal to join a governmentally supervised rationalization association. The association was authorized to undertake a five-year program involving promotion of mergers, closure of inefficient mines, mechanization, and construction of hard-coal using establishments, and for such purposes to provide loans, grants, and guarantees.[78] The High Authority reserved its opinion about the consistency of the plan with the Treaty.

In September 1963 the German government addressed to the High Authority and the Council of Ministers a proposal for an emergency protocol, to form an integral part of the treaty until the close of 1969. This proposal would have authorized member states to subsidize the coal industry from public funds for the purpose of remedying major disturbances in their economies and of improving the productivity of the industry and its adaptation to changing market conditions. It would have empowered the High Authority to set aside any such scheme upon finding that the required conditions did not exist or that the plan was abusive. In addition, the protocol would have authorized the High Authority, at the request of member states, to establish minimum prices, to limit the power of enterprises to align their prices, and to authorize a member state to impose quantitative restrictions upon coal from other member states if such restrictions were also imposed upon coal from other countries. In subsequent discussions, reluctance to accept national plans that might distort competition was evident, along with a view that national measures could not be opposed as long as there was no general policy about the relation of the various sources of energy (coal, petroleum, and atomic power).[79] No action was taken by the High Authority prior to the end of 1964.

Thirteen years after the institution of the treaty, joint selling was still in effect in the Ruhr; subsidies, quantitative restrictions, and price fixing were being considered; and no serious effort to make Ruhr coal competitive was evident. The preservation of uneconomic parts of an ailing industry had become the overriding objective.

---

[77] JO, December 28, 1965, Decisions No. 17-65 and 18-65.
[78] *Twelfth General Report*, para. 149-54.
[79] *Ibid.*, para. 155-6.

Termination of Unauthorized Agreements. Little information is available about the High Authority's efforts to terminate unauthorized agreements. Mention has been made above of the voluntary liquidation of an iron-ore association after inquiry by the High Authority, of orders forbidding six agreements, and of various agreements or projects for agreements that were terminated while requests for authorization were pending. Three of the arrangements that were forbidden were concerned with iron and steel scrap in Germany and Italy.[80] In 1960 the High Authority decided to keep closer watch upon the possibility of concerted practices in buying steel scrap, and hence decided that certain organizations of scrap consumers must send to the High Authority minutes of meetings, copies of decisions taken, and copies of letters and circulars sent to affiliated enterprises.[81] In 1961 one field check in the scrap market was made by the High Authority's inspectors. In the same year a warning by the High Authority induced dealers in iron and steel products to abandon plans for an agreement on minimum prices and sales quotas in one part of the Common Market.[82]

It appears probable that overt unsanctioned cartel agreements, such as are forbidden by Article 65, have been infrequent, but that informal concert of action has been common. Action against informal cartelization has been difficult because of the surveillance exercised by national governments over the prices of coal and steel and the consequent lack of clear distinction between governmental control and private agreement. In its Sixth General Report the High Authority pointed out (para. 75) that for five years the prices of each national group of steel producers had shown little or no variation and had changed quasi-simultaneously, whereas substantial differences exceeding the costs of transportation had persisted between prices in different countries. It attributed this behavior to "the persistence of traditional links among producers of the same country and of similar links between a country's buyers and sellers," but nevertheless thought that the principal cause was government intervention by pressure upon producers through their associations. It commented that such pressures seemed to be increasing. Nevertheless, it noted that pressure by the French government had kept French steel prices largely competitive and that a government-owned German plant had not followed the German price increases in October 1957. Its comments contained no apparent recognition that the rules of discrimination and the validation of the steel basing point system may have had some part in the continuance of the persistent traditional links.

---

[80] *Sixth General Report,* para. 94; *Fourth General Report,* para. 141.
[81] *Ninth General Report,* para. 278.
[82] *Tenth General Report,* para. 262 and 275.

Concentration

The Treaty provides that prior authorization must be obtained for any transaction that would have, in itself, the direct or indirect effect of bringing about, within the European territories of the Common Market, a concentration of enterprises of which at least one is engaged in production or wholesale distribution of coal or steel. The requirement is applicable to transactions by persons and groups, as well as by single enterprises and groups of enterprises, whether concerning a single product or different products. Thus, it can be applied to conglomerate concentrations. It is applicable to all methods of obtaining control, including not only mergers and stock acquisitions, but also loans, contracts, and acquisitions of assets.[83]

Authorization by the High Authority does not depend upon any finding that the proposed concentration is in the public interest. Whereas there is a presumption against restrictive agreements that can be overcome for certain types of agreements if they are found to be useful, authorization of a concentration is mandatory if the High Authority finds that the project will not produce any of the following specified types of harm: (a) give the interested persons power to determine prices, to control or restrict production or distribution, or to prevent the maintenance of effective competition in a substantial part of the Common Market; (b) give them power to evade the treaty's rules of competition, especially "by establishing an artificially privileged position involving a substantial advantage in access to supplies or markets." In decisions about authorization, the High Authority is required to "take account" of the size of existing enterprises of the same kind, as far as it finds this justified "to avoid or correct the disadvantages resulting from an inequality in the conditions of competition."

The High Authority has power to exempt from the requirement about authorization classes of transactions that in its opinion do not create the types of harm in question. In authorizing a concentration, it may impose conditions. In May 1954 it granted certain blanket exemptions, based partly upon the relative smallness of the enterprises involved, partly upon the extent of competition by others, and partly upon the likelihood that the activities acquired were unrelated to coal and steel.[84] Concentrations of producers uniting less than stated tonnages were exempted if they brought together not more than 30 per cent of the Community's output of any affected product and if at least nine other sources of supply remained. Concentration of distributors was authorized if it did not include producers,

---

[83] See the High Authority's interpretative Order 24, May 6, 1954, *JO*, May 11, 1954, pages 345-46.

[84] Decision 25-1954, *JO*, May 11, 1954, pages 346-47.

bankers, or firms engaged in water transport, and if the activity of the distributors did not exceed a stated monetary maximum. Firms in the coal and steel industries were allowed to unite with outside firms if the latter were not engaged in banking, distribution of the relevant industry products, or, in the case of coal, in water transport, and if their consumption of the relevant industry products did not exceed stated amounts.

The High Authority has also used its power to impose conditions upon concentration as an indirect way of controlling forms of concerted action that are not, in its opinion, subject to control as cartels. In 1963 this policy was described as follows by the responsible staff official:[85]

"High Authority investigations have shown restrictive tie-ups to exist in business practice which do not constitute concentrations within the strict meaning of Article 66, yet which are not exactly cartels within the meaning of Article 65 either: namely, organized cooperation among enterprises holding minority blocks of one another's shares. This is known as "group formation" and the resulting restrictive behavior as "the group effect." Article 66 does not directly apply in such cases, as it makes authorization compulsory only in respect of the acquisition of a controlling interest; nor is it practicable to invoke Article 65 since it is not really possible to assess the restrictive effects of interlockings, treat them as cartels and act accordingly. In dealing with such arrangements, the High Authority has developed a new policy whereby, in granting authorization for concentrations, it aims to contain any potential group effect that exists at the same time, and to insure that the concentration in conjunction with the group effect will not work out to be more restrictive than is permissible."

Unauthorized concentrations are subject to penalties. Failure to seek prior authorization subjects the participants to a fine before authorization is granted. If the concentration is of a kind that cannot be authorized, the High Authority must terminate it by appropriate action. The High Authority may impose daily penalties for failure to obey its orders, may impose fines up to 10 per cent or more of the value of the assets involved, and may, if necessary, suspend the exercise of rights attached to the assets, obtain a judicially-appointed receiver, organize a forced sale of assets, or annul acts and decisions of the directing bodies of enterprises subject to "irregularly established control."

The provision authorizing dissolution is so drawn that it covers concentrations that were not subject to a need for authorization (e.g., concentrations that took place before the effective date of the treaty). Thus the High Authority apparently has a broad power to dissolve what was brought to-

---

[85] Statement by Johannes Petrich, Director for Cartels and Concentrations, in ABA Conference Proceedings, *op. cit.,* pp. 264-65.

gether by merger if the merger was of a kind that would not have been proper for authorization if authorization had been in question. However, the power to dissolve does not apply to enterprises that have acquired dominance by virtue of internal expansion. The power of dissolution could have been used by the High Authority to complete the deconcentration that was in progress under the Occupation when the Community was established, but there was no disposition to use it in that way. Indeed, it has remained wholly unused.

Authorization of Acquisitions and Mergers. To January 31, 1965, the High Authority had disposed of 230 cases concerned with concentration. Of these, 159 originated in application for authorization, 71 in the High Authority's own initiative. Seventy-nine concentrations were authorized; 13 were valid because they antedated the signing of the treaty; 6 were covered by the order of exemption; and 72 were found to be matters to which Article 66 did not apply.

Five cases were "otherwise handled"; apparently applications were withdrawn or projects dropped. No case had yet resulted in refusal of authorization.[86]

One case involved a concentration that required authorization but had been made without applying for it; but whether it was disposed of by fine and approval or by dissolution is not indicated in the reports.

Most of the acquisitions authorized by the High Authority have been vertical.[87] They included acquisitions of steel fabricators by steel companies seeking to safeguard their markets; acquisitions of steel distributors by steel companies; acquisitions of coal companies by German steel companies, through which vertical ties broken by the Occupation were reestablished; and acquisitions of foreign coal companies by French steel companies, through which sources of supply additional to the government monopoly over French coal were obtained. Since at the outset some steel companies controlled their coal supply, a presumption was applied in favor of acquisitions through which others obtained a similar position. Even when the coal resources that were acquired exceeded the acquirer's need for coal, the ac-

---

[86] *Thirteenth General Report,* para. 229 and Table 37.

[87] According to the *Twelfth General Report* paragraph 254, table 34, 64 approved acquisitions fell into the following groups:

steel with steel processing	20	steel with steel	13
steel with coal	8	steel with special steel	4
steel with steel trade	6	coal with coal	5
steel with scrap	3	trade with trade	3
steel with ore	1		
coal with coal trade	1		
Total Vertical	39	Total Horizontal	25

quisition was readily permitted if the surplus coal was marketed. The High Authority assumed that bidding for sources of coal would be sufficient to keep the cost of acquiring these sources at levels suitably related to the cost of coal supplies, current and anticipated, and that therefore vertical acquisition would not distort conditions of competition. If this assumption proved to be wrong, the High Authority's powers to impose allocation in times of shortage and to approve equalization agreements to protect the users of higher-cost imports were available to meet the more obvious difficulties.

It is noteworthy that until recently the High Authority's consideration of proposed consolidations has centered upon formal legal and statistical matters rather than the underlying realities of power. Formal controls that unite enterprises were examined. Informal communities of interest, however strong, were not. Percentages of the market involved in a consolidation have been stated as though each participating enterprise should be measured by the amount of production that it legally controls. Thus, four, five, or seven per cent of Community production has been attributed to major companies (as compared with estimates of 21, 14, and 13 per cent attributed by private observers to groups to which these companies belonged).[88] In a Belgian steel consolidation, the companies united were controlled by two important Belgian financial groups, Société Générale and Lenoit; and by establishing union between these groups, the consolidation may have reduced competition among interest covering three-fourths of Belgian crude steel and one-tenth or more of steel in France and Luxembourg.[89] If the High Authority considered these possibilities, the information that is publicly available does not indicate the fact.

The High Authority has recognized but given little weight to the anti-competitive effect of partial consolidations and joint ventures upon relations between the participating companies. In discussing its authorization of a steel firm, Sidmar, to be established for the production of wide strip and cold-reduced sheets under joint ownership by steel companies in France, Belgium, and Luxembourg, it said that "group control entails concentration as between each of the controlling enterprises and the enterprise controlled, but not necessarily concentration as among the controlling enterprises themselves, since while the controlling enterprises are able jointly to determine the activity of the enterprise controlled, they cannot exercise influence amounting to control over one another, unless either such control— i.e. concentration between the controlling enterprises—already exists in

---

[88] For examples, see Louis Lister, *The European Coal and Steel Community*, pp. 456-65. The Thirteenth General Report, paras. 202-10, does analyze a joint venture in the light of the direct and indirect connections of the parent companies.
[89] *Ibid.*

other ways, or the enterprise jointly controlled is of such importance for the activity of the controlling enterprises that they must be considered concentrated as a result of the group control instituted and of other existing links between them." In the Sidmar case, since Sidmar's products would also be made by its owners, the High Authority thought the joint venture important enough to affect competition between the owners: ". . . in fixing the prices of the enterprise controlled, the controlling enterprises will inevitably take into account their own prices for the same or similar products, and very possible agree all prices (sic)." Yet the venture was approved, subject only to the condition that Sidmar's contemplated line of products must not be enlarged.[90] The case illustrates the type of cartel-like "group effects" mentioned above in the discussion of cartel policy; and the condition imposed is a sample of the limited control that has been imposed upon such effects.

The High Authority appears to have examined each consolidation as a single phenomenon, without concern about the possible cumulative effect of consolidations that are individually of minor importance. In evaluating single concentrations, it has noted both the percentage of national production and the percentage of Community production that would be united, but has tended to stress the latter without discussing the extent to which there is a single Community-wide market for the affected products. However, where several consolidations were formally linked together, the High Authority has considered their relationships.

Good examples of the High Authority's treatment of combinations appear in its decisions in 1961 about acquisitions by a German steel company.[91] August Thyssen Hütte sought authorization to acquire a majority of the stock of Handelsunion, a company that marketed much of the steel plate and sheet produced by another large steel producer, Dortmund-Hörder. Concerned about the possible linkage between Thyssen and Dortmund-Hörder via Handelsunion, the High Authority approved the acquisition of the distributor company only after steps "to obviate the possibility of any restriction of competition" by the Thyssen acquisition. The steps were these: Dortmund-Hörder and Handelsunion entered into a contract guaranteeing delivery and procurement and providing that deliveries would be gradually scaled down "until the percentage of sales through Handelsunion should be no greater than the usual rate for sales by German iron and steel enterprises through independent dealers." Thyssen was made responsible by the High Authority for seeing that the contract was implemented and was required to surrender its minority holding in the Dormund-Hörder sub-

---

90 *Eleventh General Report,* para. 346-9.
91 *Tenth General Report,* para. 277.

sidiary. Thus, by gradually depriving Dortmund-Hörder of the services of an important distributor, the High Authority removed the possibility that Thyssen and Dortmund-Hörder would be allied through that distributor. However, the impairment of Dortmund-Hörder's distributive position was not regarded as a restriction of competition that justified denial of Thyssen's application.

Thyssen also asked authorization to acquire 50 per cent of the stock of Rasselstein, a manufacturer of steel sheets. The other 50 per cent of Rasselstein's stock was held by Otto Wolff, an important distributor that controlled several other steel companies. The High Authority authorized the acquisition provided the existing arrangement, by which Wolff sold all of Rasselstein's output, was continued. In reporting the matter, the High Authority commented that since Rasselstein could only be jointly controlled, the acquisition did not constitute a concentration between Thyssen and Wolff, and that although there was bound to be some restriction of competition between the controlling companies in respect to their other production, their joint share of the sheet market was only about 20 per cent.

The provision in the treaty that the size of comparable enterprises shall be taken into account has been treated by the High Authority as good reason for authorizing horizontal acquisitions that do not set new levels of size. The High Authority has readily authorized horizontal acquisitions by the smaller companies; indeed, such arrangements appear to have been regarded as desirable by the makers of the treaty from the beginning. It has also readily authorized horizontal acquisitions by the larger companies when the resulting concentration did not create a unit larger than the largest one. Thus two of the largest three Belgian steel companies were allowed to form a joint firm that controlled 34 per cent of Belgian crude steel and 4 per cent of the crude steel of the Community but, at two million metric tons, was ranked as sixth or seventh in the Community in steel production.[92]

A test of the limits of this policy was presented in 1958 when Phoenix-Rheinrohr, the third largest steel producer, proposed to unite with August Thyssen Hütte, which ranked about 14th. The joint production of these two companies would have been significantly larger than that of the largest existing steel company. The products of the two companies were, for the most part, complementary, rather than competitive; but since each company was diversified and was an important part of an oligopoly in the pro-

---

[92] *Communauté Européenne du Charbon et de l'Acier,* Assemblée Commune, Exercise 1956-1957, session ordinaire (première partie). Rapport fait au nom de la Commission du Marché Commun sur les concentrations d'enterprises dans la Communauté, par. M. Henri Fayat, Rapporteur, May 1957 (hereafter called Fayat), pages 11, 14, 40.

duction of certain steel products, the united company would have linked numerous oligopoly positions that might be more important collectively than singly. Moreover, each company owned a substantial part of a marketing company that had further links with other companies.

The High Authority decided that it could not authorize the union outright. It then entered into negotiations with the companies in an effort to devise conditions of control over future investments under which it could grant authorization. While these negotiations were in progress in 1960, the request for authorization was withdrawn. It was subsequently resubmitted, however, and in 1963 the merger was approved. The High Authority did not undertake an affirmative control of new investments by the merged company. Instead it required that contracts with Dortmund-Hörder be severed expeditiously and that there be no interlocking directorates between the merged company and other firms in the steel industry.[93] In May 1963 the Netherlands filed an appeal against this decision.

Since the merger between Thyssen and Phoenix-Rheinrohr created an enterprise larger than any existing steel company, it presumably reflected an abandonment of the High Authority's previous theory by which the size of the largest company is the ceiling for concentration by merger.

The control of future investments that was contemplated in the early stage of this case is a controversial use of the High Authority's power to impose conditions. Some persons familiar with the treaty believe that the High Authority may not impose conditions other than those that can be fulfilled prior to the completion of a transaction. Nevertheless, in at least one case the High Authority approved an acquisition with the proviso that all investment programs of the united company above a certain value must be submitted for approval.[94]

In 1957 a committee of the Assembly examined the concentration policy of the High Authority and reported on it publicly. It thought that "undoubtedly, most of the concentrations have had economically sound purposes: to reduce costs through greater unity of production and by specialization in factories under common control; to assure supplies of raw material as well as market outlets; to strength positions in meeting competition within and outside the Common Market; to ward against recessions." It believed that concentration usually contributes to rationalization and stability of production; that security of employment is greater

---

[93] *Ninth General Report,* para. 280, *Twelfth General Report,* para. 240.

[94] Fernand Spaak, "Problems of Competition and Restrictive Trade Practices in the European Coal and Steel Company," in *1960 Institute on Legal Aspects of the European Communities,* Federal Bar Association, Washington, 1960, page 134. Mr. Spaak was at the time Deputy Director of the Division on Agreements and Concentrations.

in large enterprises; and that such enterprises can raise money and engage in research more easily. Thus it saw in concentration possibilities of serving the Community—greater productivity, lower prices, modernization of facilities, improvement of quality. It had more doubts about vertical consolidations than about horizontal ones, for it saw a possibility that a growing part of the coal supply would be held by a group of steel companies, to the detriment of other users of coal. Moreover, it thought that there were limits to the economies of scale and that certain dangers were present: Concentration might impair equal access to sources of production, lead to division or exploitation of markets, fix prices, control or limit production, create monopoly positions, create oligopolies of which each member had a dominant position in a given region or for given products. Hence it thought that the process of concentration should have limits; that concentration for fiscal, political, or personal motives, rather than economic motives, was open to question; and that "giantism" should be denounced.[95] It recommended that a long-run policy be formulated by the High Authority, with a determination of the limits within which concentration is appropriate to the basic purposes of the treaty.

A passage (paragraph 198) included in the High Authority's thirteenth general report in 1965 may be considered as an announcement of such a policy. The purpose in mind was not "to impose a cut-and-dried system of competition," but rather "in the light of developing technology, of new competitive products and the resulting structural changes, and of the teachings of modern economics, to influence the pattern of the Community markets in such a way as to maintain an adequate degree of competition. . . . This has meant over the years that the High Authority has . . . approved larger and larger concentrations," partly in consideration of the size of iron and steel companies in non-community countries. It is recognized, however, that "unfettered concentration" could lead to "para-monopolistic patterns which will ultimately lower the efficiency of the economy despite certain technical advantages." Because it had "taken account of all economic and technical factors in its appraisal of major concentrations" and had "taken the broadest possible view regarding their permitted size," it had used "on an increasing scale" its power "to break financial and personal links, or so to limit them, that restrictions on competition resulting from the concentration cannot extend to other large enterprises or groups of enterprises." It said it would continue to follow this policy.

Thus far the High Authority's control of concentrations seems to have prevented, at most, five consolidations in 15 years. The necessity of applying for approval may have discouraged enterprises from considering types

---

[95] Fayat, *op. cit.*, pages 19-21, 29-31.

of fusion that could not be defended as aids to efficiency or stability, and some firms may have chosen not to combine rather than meet the conditions included in the High Authority's approval.[96]

The High Authority has not regarded the existence or the probability of oligopoly as a good reason for preventing further acquisitions by oligopolists. In the Thyssen-Rheinrohr case, it considered but rejected the idea that cumulation of oligopolistic positions may be a source of excessive power. However, if a time should come at which the High Authority believes that further concentration will jeopardize competition, its power over concentration is available as a weapon against such developments.

Abuse of Dominant Power

In the seventh subsection of Article 66, the treaty empowers the High Authority to make, to any enterprise public or private that possesses a dominant position protecting it from effective competition in a substantial part of the Common Market, any recommendations required to prevent use of that position for purposes contrary to those of the treaty. If the recommendations are not carried out, the High Authority, after consulting the interested government, can fix prices, conditions of sale, and programs of production or delivery for the offending enterprise. These are then mandatory under penalty of fine.

A major function of these provisions, as seen by the drafters of the treaty, was to enable the High Authority to curb the activities of enterprises that had been nationalized or given legal monopoly by national law. Without such provisions there would have been no equivalent to the curbs that competition was expected to place upon the conduct of other enterprises. Moreover, a national government that was unwilling to abandon restrictions formerly embodied in law, and now forbidden by the treaty in that form, might have accomplished its purpose by granting broad discretion to a nationalized enterprise to act in ways capable of producing similar restrictive results. But once the provision had been included in the treaty, its use against government enterprises was not necessary. As in the case of ATIC, both the High Authority and the responsible national government recognized that the enterprise was a creature of the state, and problems were met by interaction between the High Authority and the state.

The power to control abuse by dominant firms is available, of course, for use against private enterprises as well as public ones. It has been occasionally so used. During the treaty's first ten years, the High Authority did not need to correct abuses by formal orders or fines. It addressed rec-

---

[96] An instance of such a decision was mentioned by an official of the High Authority in ABA Conference Proceedings, *op. cit.*, page 275.

ommendations to offending firms, but these were accepted. No comprehensive summary is available to show the kinds of abuse covered by these recommendations nor the types of corrective action recommended. The High Authority's general reports do not discuss particular cases of this kind.

An example, however, is available.[97] On July 11, 1953, the High Authority made a recommendation to the Upper Rhine Coal Union, A.G., which, under agreements with the coal sales agencies, was at that time the sole supplier of the coal of these agencies for consumption in south and southwest Germany. The Union had adopted terms of sale under which it was to sell direct to coal consumers that used 30,000 tons or more of coal yearly. The High Authority regarded these terms as a division of the market between the Union and the distributors, contrary to Article 4 of the Treaty and restrictive of the free choice of supply by users. It recommended that within two weeks the Union abandon practices contrary to Article 4.

It is noteworthy that in 1956 the High Authority authorized terms of sale by the sales agencies of the Ruhr that similarly allocated customers between the sales agencies and the direct-buying wholesalers on the basis of annual consumption. In these later decisions, the benefit from allowing sellers to avoid small direct sales was treated as good reason for limiting the buyer's freedom of choice. Thus the concept of abuse became less ambitious with time, as did the High Authority's attitude toward joint selling.

Appraisal

The effect of the coal and steel treaty in strengthening competition is to be found largely in the abandonment or reduction of governmental measures to keep national markets closed, most of which lie beyond the scope of this essay. Voluntary compliance with the terms of the treaty in this respect and action by the High Authority to bring about further compliance have gone some distance toward the creation of a single international market for steel, and an appreciable but smaller distance in the same direction for coal. Competition has been strengthened by giving consumers access to more sources of supply, enlarging the number of producers that must consider one another's rivalry, exposing regional restrictions to pressure from outside the region, and providing the incentives to expand that appear in a larger market. These effects have been reduced, but not wholly destroyed, by the High Authority's sponsorship of selling syndicates for coal in Belgium and the Ruhr, by the limits placed by regulation upon the power of coal producers to align their prices with the prices of competitors, and by the requirements for adherence to published prices and to pricing formulas.

That the growth of the Common Market has not led to a correspond-

---

[97] *JO,* July 21, 1953, page 154.

ing development of international cartels is a major achievement. In the case of coal, the competitive policy of the treaty has been only one, and probably not the most important one, of the influences against internationalization of the sales agencies. In the case of steel, the pre-war international steel cartel, which applied severe restrictions, has been replaced by something much weaker. By agreement eight national steel federations have agreed that export prices shall be fixed in relation to the exporters' domestic price and the prevailing prices in the market to which the steel is exported. Under this arrangement, according to report, periodic meetings in Brussels by representatives of producers' associations of the Common Market countries formulate recommendations about minimum prices in export markets. However, efforts to reenforce this scheme by an agreement about export quotas have failed. The industry's lack of success in restoring restrictions as severe as those of the pre-war cartel appears to be due to lack of a firm foundation of domestic cartelization in the Common Market countries and in England.[98] Though a basing point system, supported by mandatory adherence to published prices, may be an effective way of avoiding domestic price competition, the reliability of the pricing formula is reduced in the Common Market not only by the uncertainty of some transportation charges, but also by the facts that a) each seller may choose, case by case, whether he will absorb freight to meet a competitive price completely, partly, or not at all, and b) that he may reduce prices to meet competition from foreign sellers who are not participants in the system. Moreover, the choice whether or not to reduce prices in this way must not be influenced by the pressure of boycott, disciplinary cut-throat pricing, or establishment of punitive bases. Price fixing by formula does not readily reach beyond the Common Market and cannot become a basis for allocation of markets, production quotas, and the like, either within the Common Market or outside. The preventative effect of the treaty upon cartelization has been substantial, in spite of the export price agreement for steel, the continuance of traditional links among enterprises in the steel industry, and the weakness of official policy toward regional sales agencies for coal.

The High Authority has accomplished little in limiting concentration, chiefly because it has undertaken little. Its opposition may have been responsible for the abandonment of a few steel mergers. Conditions imposed upon authorizations have occasionally modified the terms of an acquisition or afforded temporary protection for interests likely to be adversely affected, and in at least one case, have imposed control upon future investments. Nevertheless, both vertical and horizontal acquisitions have taken place

---

[98] The steel export agreement is registered under the British Restrictive Trade Practices Act, which became law in 1956. It is thus subjct to invalidation by a court unless the parties can prove that it is advantageous to the public interest.

to substantially the degree proposed by their sponsors. Most of the acquisitions have involved vertical forward or backward integration by steel companies, and the rest have been mostly horizontal unions of steel companies. They have been authorized because the High Authority has regarded the acquisitions as means toward efficiency, stability, and lower prices, with no important risks to competition. This appraisal has been supported not only by analyses of the particular acquisitions, but also by structural comparisons between the steel industry in the Common Market and the steel industries of the United States and England, from which the conclusion has been drawn that concentration is at least as great in England and much greater in the United States.

In the Assembly, however, some apprehension has been evident, lest acquisitions take place without good reason or go too far. If the High Authority should come to believe that these fears are becoming realities, the instruments available to it under the treaty appear to be sufficient for effective action. But such a belief is improbable in the near future. Horizontal absorption of all small steel and coal companies is not likely to arouse the High Authority's objection. Neither is absorption of most of the coal suppliers by the steel companies, unless there is substantial difficulty in obtaining supplies for independent steel producers or for consumers. Horizontal acquisitions in steel that clearly create new levels of bigness may be resisted, but a similar result is likely to be tolerated if it appears slowly, by small increments.

The Treaty's provisions about discrimination and publication of prices are ill formulated and have been made worse by judicial interpretation. They not only sanction but require use of a basing point system. The requirement that prices be published in advance and then observed constitutes a considerable safeguard for informal price understandings in the steel industry. The rule against discrimination establishes a standard of equal treatment of "comparable transactions," regardless of the effect of inequality upon competition or of the importance of it to the disfavored buyer. This rule probably handicaps experiment with price structures; it may even preclude price differences that have a basis in costs. It reaches far beyond what is necessary to prevent discrimination against foreigners or discrimination that may harm competition. Yet, by allowing producers to use basing points other than their own establishments, it sanctions substantial differences unrelated to cost in the prices paid by different buyers and thereby loses the meaning it might otherwise have had as a means of rationalizing industrial location and assuring equal treatment of all.

The right to align prices upon the lower prices of competitors, which mitigates the rules about discrimination and publication, is badly devised. On the one hand, it permits arbitrary discrimination between individual buyers, since an enterprise need not make similar alignments in comparable cases. Arbed, for example, sells most of its steel at aligned prices, and thus usually has a right to sell at any price between its base price and the delivered price from another base, regardless of discrimination. On the other hand, the rule about alignment enhances rigidity in the pricing formula, since a seller has no right to meet the lower price of a competitor who has used the seller's own basing point. The right to align rests upon no requirement that alignment be in good faith or be necessary to retain or obtain business or be undertaken in particular situations rather than by general formula.[99]

It is noteworthy that the High Authority's treatment of rights to align prices has been different for coal and steel, and that in each case the line taken has tended to strengthen some of the industry's traditional ways of avoiding competition. In coal, where a basing point system, including the right of alignment, might have broken the structure of regional joint action, alignment was forbidden and zone pricing readily sanctioned for five years; and the right to align is still substantially limited. In steel, where basing point pricing has been a customary supplement to other overt restrictions, interpenetration of markets, permissible through the right of alignment, helped destroy the effects of previous cartel allocations and quotas, but the rules as to publication, alignment, and discrimination supported the basing point system as a formula that limited price competition.

Though some of the limits of the policy of competition that have been noted above, particularly those pertaining to publication and discrimination, are due to failure of the treaty to apply appropriate distinctions to complex relationships, most of them are due to the fact that the treaty has purposes beyond the enhancement of competition. Stability, continuity of employment, equality of treatment, low prices, improvement of labor conditions, and enhancement of productivity are basic objectives, for which competition is one of the means. Preservation of uneconomic parts of the coal industry has been superimposed as a further objective. Competitive adjustments would be likely to involve instability, shifts of employment opportunity, and drastic curtailment of high cost capacity. Competitors would be likely to take advantage of their varying opportunities to treat their customers unequally. With broad powers to avert such impacts, the High Authority uses these powers to limit competition as it thinks appropriate. Under pressure from interests that desire to see competition limited for other reasons also, it runs the risk of delaying or avoiding competitive adjustments that would contribute to the long-run healthy performance of the Common Market's economy.

---

[99] In 1964 the High Authority forbade steel companies to align their prices on those of steel imported from communist countries. See JO, No. 8, Jan. 22, 1964, p. 97.

Chapter XVI

The Experience of EEC

The European Economic Community (hereafter called EEC) differs from ECSC in structure and scope. Whereas ECSC is limited to coal and steel, EEC covers all branches of economic activity except coal, steel, and atomic energy. Whereas ECSC has sole authority over the field it covers, EEC shares authority with its member states. It uses the same Assembly and the same Court as ECSC and attributes to them the same respective functions. Its power to act, however, is exercised partly by a Council of Ministers that represents the member states and partly by a Commission, conceived as a group of international officials independent of their states of origin.[1] The former makes quasi-legislative decisions. The latter controls administrative action, issues administrative regulations, and makes both executive and quasi-judicial decisions.

Superficially, the Treaty of Rome that established EEC resembles that which established ECSC in the place that it assigns to competition. The ultimate purposes (Article 2) are to promote harmonious economic development, continuous and balanced expansion, increased stability, accelerated increase in standards of living, and closer relations among member states. The means (Article 3) are to establish a customs union, remove obstacles to free movement of persons, services and capital, harmonize certain economic policies and national laws, and establish "a system to ensure that competition is not distorted in the Common Market."

But the role contemplated for competition in the two communities is markedly different. As a project for economic planning to improve the performance of the coal and steel industries, ECSC gives competition a clearly subordinate role. It is concerned with business restrictions chiefly to prevent them from becoming obstacles to official plans. In EEC, however, the function assigned to competition is central. The Commission's first general report[2] said that the aim is not only to suppress obstacles to international trade but also "to establish a system of fair and healthy competition as the

---

[1] Further connection between EEC and ECSC was in prospect in 1964-65-66. Plans to merge the High Authority of ECSC with the Commission of EEC had been worked out and were being negotiated. See Bulletin of the European Economic Community, December 1964, pp. 57-58 and January 1965, p. 58; JO, April 2, 1966; ECSC, Thirteenth General Report, paras. 38-42.

[2] Paragraph 78.

indispensable condition for the achievement of a rational division of economic activities and for ensuring an equitable basis of operations for the productive forces." Similarly, in the Commission's fifth general report,[3] competition is described as "an instrument of guidance" and is said to be "essential to an economy whose characteristic features are free enterprise and the free choice of the place of work and of the method of consumption." Thus the Community has envisaged competition as a regulator of economic activity, an alternative to governmental economic planning.

In the words of a member of EEC's Commission, the treaty "fundamentally relies upon competition to guide the economy of the Community. Two groups of provisions are designed to establish and give substance to a European competitive order. The first seeks to make competition possible in the Community. It includes, first, rules about progressive reduction of tariffs among member states (Articles 12 to 17), quantitative restrictions upon imports and exports (Articles 30 to 37), and establishment of a common external tariff (Articles 18 to 29); second, free movement of workers (Articles 48 to 51), freedom of establishment (Articles 52 to 58), freedom to perform services (Articles 59 to 66), and free movement of capital (Articles 67 to 73); third, coordination of cyclical and monetary policy, designed to maintain general equilibrium among the member states (Articles 103 to 109); fourth, suppression or modification of such state aids (Articles 92 to 94) and taxes (Articles 95 to 99) as distort competition; and fifth, approximation of national laws that result in distortions of competition (Articles 100 to 102).

"While these provisions are designed to create the requisites of effective competition that make competition possible, the second group of provisions seeks to maintain existing competition by regulating the activities that depend upon relations among competitors. . . . It includes, first, European laws against restrictions of competition (Articles 85 to 90), extended by prohibition of discrimination on a basis of nationality (Article 7), and second, a European law about dumping (Article 91)."[4]

In a program thus conceived, measures against private restrictions constitute not only a necessary part of the effort to maintain a competitive economy but also a necessary corollary of the effort to terminate public restrictions. A private restriction may negate the elimination of a public restriction. For example, one purpose of the Rome Treaty is to remove tariffs on goods that pass from one member state to another. A private agreement among enterprises concerned with such goods, by which each enterprise would confine its activities to its own country, would be a private equivalent

---

[3] Paragraph 46.
[4] Hans von der Groeben, Wettbewerbspolitik in der Europäischen Wirtschaftsgemeinschaft, 6 W&W 373 at 374-5. (The translation is mine.)

of a tariff, perhaps more effective than the tariff that had been done away with. Removal of governmental restrictions requires precautions against equivalent private restrictions.

The breadth of conception evident in the quoted summary appears also in EEC's administrative structure. Promotion of competition is treated as a function that includes not only control of cartels and dominant firms but also control of state aid to business and the harmonization of national laws that affect business, including those concerning taxation, industrial property, unfair competition, public contracts, company law, bankruptcy, the characteristics of goods, and the execution of decisions in commercial disputes.[5]

This broad view of competition has evolved because of the differences of economic organization that are evident in the member states. In one state the production and sale of a given type of goods may be carried on by private enterprises united in a restrictive agreement. In another state the same activity may be carried on without agreement by one or two dominant enterprises. In a third state a government monopoly may control the field. For the Community to take action against any one of these forms of organization without equivalent action against the others would be for it to discriminate between the different states. The Community has consistently emphasized the point that its various forms of action should go forward together in close coordination.

Thus a study of the policies of EEC toward cartels and dominant firms covers only a portion of the activities that the Community itself regards as efforts to maintain competition, and conclusions about the effects of policies toward private restriction do not cover the whole field that the Community regards as relevant. This fact should be borne in mind in considering the pages that follow.

The Provisions about Business Restriction

The part of the Community's broad competitive policy that is explicitly concerned with private restrictions is set forth in Articles 85, 86, 87, 88, and 89 of the Rome Treaty and in regulations pursuant thereto. The policies thus expressed are concerned with private restrictive agreements, with restrictive activities and decisions by trade associations, and with uses of economic power by dominant concerns.

Policy Toward Cartels. Article 85, the basic provision concerned with cartels, contains a broad prohibition of restrictive agreements, concerted practices, and decisions by associated enterprises where these agreements are likely to affect trade between the member states and have as their purpose

---

[5] See Seventh General Report on the Activities of the Community (April 1, 1963—March 31, 1964), June 1964, paragraphs 59-95.

or result the prevention, restriction, or distortion of competition within the Common Market. Versions of this provision in the different official languages differ in meaning. The French version means merely *affect;* the German, Italian, and Dutch versions mean *adversely affect.* Thus it is possible to interpret the provision either as one that (subject to its provisions for exemption) forbids all agreements that are likely to reduce competition in international trade or as one that forbids them only where harm to such trade can be shown to be the probable result. In the Bosch case[6] the Advocate-General of the Court (an impartial aide who expresses opinions on points of law) sought to reconcile the two interpretations by arguing that all restraints of competition involve harm to trade. Adopting a view that had been expressed by the German government, he interpreted the provision as one covering restraints of competition that cause "the movement of goods to deviate from its normal and natural course, because an increase of such movement in one direction would result inevitably in an unfavorable influence on movement in the opposite direction." He said that "there is likely to be an unfavorable influence by any restraint on competition whose effects on economic trade between the member States are not totally devoid of importance."[7] The opinion of the Court did not cover the question. In the Gundry case,[8] the Commission adopted the Advocate-General's views.

According to a widely accepted view, the scope of the prohibition in Article 85 grows with time; for as tariffs and governmental restrictions are removed, the possibility of trade among the member states increases, and business restrictions that formerly could have only domestic impact acquire an international impact as well. Thus agreements which were initially permissible may become illegal.

Article 85 contains a list of practices to which particular attention is to be given, but the wording of the treaty makes it clear that even the practices listed are not covered by the prohibition unless they have the appropriate interstate effect. Thus the list merely establishes a certain presumption that the objectionable effects occur in the types of practices listed.

The listed practices are those which

"a) directly or indirectly fix buying or selling prices or any other trading terms,

"b) limit or control production, marketing, technical development, or investments,

"c) effect the sharing of markets or sources of supply,

---

[6] *Common Market Reports,* para. 8003.

[7] *Ibid.,* para. 6539-14.

[8] *JO,* No. 161, October 20, 1964, para. 2549.

"d) apply to trade partners unequal conditions in respect of equivalent transactions, thereby placing them at a competitive disadvantage,

"e) make the conclusion of a contract subject to the acceptance by trade partners of additional goods or services which are not by their nature or by the custom of the trade related to the subject matter of such contract."[9]

Thus the treaty explicitly covers agreements for price fixing, restriction of business activity, allocation of such activity, discrimination, or tying.

The broad prohibition that has just been set forth is limited in the third subsection of Article 85 by an exemption. This exemption is available for any arrangement that "contributes towards improving the production or distribution of goods or promoting technical or economic progress." However, to benefit from the exemption, such arrangements must fulfill three conditions: First, they must reserve to users a "fair share" in the resulting "profit"; second, they must not impose on the enterprises concerned any restrictions not indispensable to the purpose; and third, they must not enable the enterprises to eliminate competition in respect of a substantial portion of the goods. Such arrangements "may be" declared exempt from the prohibition of the first subsection of Article 85.

Policy Toward Dominant Enterprises. An effort is made in the Rome Treaty to apply the same rules to private agreements and to the activities of powerful enterprises. The treaty contains nothing that explicitly challenges the power of enterprises or seeks to prevent them from becoming more powerful. However, it provides that such enterprises are forbidden "to abuse a dominant position in the Common Market or any substantial part thereof."[10] The broad prohibition is also illustrated by a list of particulars. However, the practices mentioned are not mere matters for special attention, but are to be "deemed to be" abuses. Two of them, concerned with discrimination and with tying arrangements, are identical with the corresponding particulars applicable to agreements. The other two consist in "the direct or indirect imposition of unfair buying or selling prices or other unfair trading terms," and "the limitation of production, marketing, or technical development to the prejudice of consumers." The effort to make these particulars correspond to the first two that are applicable to agreements is obvious, though the success of the attempt is doubtful.

The prohibition applicable to dominant enterprises takes effect only "so far as the trade between member states may thereby be affected."

Interaction Between These Policies. It is noteworthy that this pro-

---

[9] The translation is that of OECD in its *Guide to Legislation on Restrictive Business Practices.*

[10] On June 16, 1965, a member of the Commission indicated in a statement to the European Parliament that, as the degree of power approached monopoly, abuse would be more readily found.

hibition is applicable to action by "one or more" enterprises. This seems to mean that where the participants in an agreement are dominant firms, they are covered both by the prohibition of agreements (subject to the exemption) in Article 85 and by the prohibition of abuse of power in Article 86. Differences in the scope of these two articles thus become relevant to the control of agreements.

There are such differences. Unlike Article 85, Article 86 makes no provision for exemption in the case of activities that promote technical or economic progress or improve production or distribution. Activities that have such effects are, of course, not likely to be often considered abusive; yet experience under the national laws suggests that programs for rationalization may include restrictions that are defined as abusive in Article 86. For example, a rationalization program sponsored by a few dominant firms might contemplate price fixing and might be forced by these firms upon certain small rivals or certain distributors. Thus there appears to be a possibility that an agreement might qualify for exemption under Article 85 yet be subject to prohibition under Article 86.

Differences in the definition of particular practices may also contain potential trouble. Whereas Article 85 applies comprehensively to agreements about prices and trading terms, the scope of the corresponding part of Article 86 is obscure. It applies to imposed prices and terms, and thus covers agreements forced upon unwilling parties. This part of Article 86 is concerned with practices that are inequitable. It invites an inquiry into the substance of the trading terms and prices that is not appropriate under Article 85. Thus an imposed agreement among dominant firms about terms or prices might be forbidden under Article 85 but not abusive under Article 86.

Similarly, whereas Article 85 is concerned with limitation or control of production, marketing, development, or investment, Article 86 makes no reference to limitation of investment and prohibits the other types of limitation where they are undertaken "to the prejudice of consumers." Thus Article 86 invites examination of the impact of such restrictive activities beyond what is relevant under Article 85.

If an agreement is made among non-dominant concerns, it is covered only by Article 85 and enjoys the full possibility that its content may be exempt under appropriate circumstances. If it is made among dominant firms, it is subject not only to Article 85 but also to Article 86, which includes no provision for exemption. If the agreement is imposed and the terms (and possibly the prices fixed) in it are inequitable, the resulting violation of Article 86 enjoys no exemption such as might be invoked under Article 85. If the agreement limits production, it escapes the prohibition of Article

86 provided it does not have an adverse effect upon consumers, but does not escape that of Article 85 unless it gives consumers a fair share of its benefits, promotes technical or economic progress, and does not eliminate competition. When dominant enterprises agree to discriminate or to tie goods and services to one another, whatever possibility of exemption such agreements may have under Article 85 is destroyed by the fact that this kind of activity is categorically prohibited under Article 86.

The effect of Article 86 as an instrument against single dominant enterprises is not self-evident. The article clearly prohibits discriminations and tying contracts. It may be capable of use as a means to prevent excessive or otherwise inequitable trading terms or prices. It apparently is an instrument to stop limitation of production or technical development when such limitations are held to be prejudicial to consumers; but it leaves unclear the circumstances under which limitations of this type would not be regarded as involving such prejudice.

Fields not Covered or Subject to Special Treatment. The provisions just described are broadly applicable to the production and distribution of goods and the rendering of service within the Common Market. They do not apply, however, to sales from the Common Market into outside territory nor to activities without influence upon the Common Market's trade that may be carried on outside the Common Market by enterprises domiciled therein. Within the Common Market they do not apply to activities that have no interstate effect.

In the case of agriculture, their application is limited by Article 42 of the treaty to such matters as are specifically determined by the Council of Ministers to be appropriate. Regulation 26, subsequently passed by the Council, provides that the rule against restrictive agreements shall not be applicable to agreements that are an integral part of a national agricultural marketing organization or are necessary to the treaty's agricultural objectives. It provides also that the rule about restrictive agreements shall not apply to agreements by farmers in a single member state about production or sale of agricultural produce or the use of joint facilities, provided such agreements impose no price obligations, unless the Council finds that the effect of them is to eliminate competition or to jeopardize the agricultural objectives. Except in these respects, both Article 85 and Article 86 are made applicable to agriculture, but the Commission retains full competence to rule upon their application.

A special status was given to transportation by Regulation 141.[11] This regulation exempted the restriction of transportation from registration provisions that were applicable under other regulations and provided that

---

[11] JO, November 28, 1962, page 2751.

rules as to competition in transportation were to be developed by June 30, 1964. In accord with this requirement, the Commission proposed to the Council in June 1964 a regulation designed to apply Articles 85 and 86 to transportation after January 1, 1967, subject to a provision conditioning the exemption of existing agreements upon notice of them filed before April 1, 1967. It proposed, however, that the regulation also authorize the Commission to exempt transportation agreements for standardization or interchange of material and equipment, technical cooperation in combined or complementary operation by different types of transport, use of the most expeditious routes, and coordination of time-tables, so far as such agreements do not lead to market-sharing and do not adversely affect the development of trade. The recommendation provided for a further report on competition in transport and on transportation policy, to be made by January 1, 1966, and to this end proposed that the firms and associations in this field be required to report by April 1, 1965 all agreements for fixing rates, regulating supply, or sharing markets.[12] The European Parliament approved the Commission's recommendation in December 1964. Doubts in the Council, however, led it, in December 1965, to extend the temporary exemption of transportation to the end of 1967.[13]

Implementing Regulations

When the treaty had been signed, controversies promptly arose about the meaning and application of Articles 85 and 86. There was argument about whether or not the treaty was a part of the municipal law of the member states. There is now general agreement that it is. There was argument about whether the prohibitions contained in this part of the treaty were directly applicable or only applicable to agreements or practices that had first been found by some proper authority to be violations of the treaty. This question, undecided for a considerable period of time, was settled by a subsequent regulation discussed below. There was uncertainty as to who granted exemptions; and the national cartel authorities assumed that they had this right. There was, of course, uncertainty as to the circumstances under which the substantive provisions of the treaty were to be applied—for example, what constituted an effect upon commerce among member states, and whether or not such arrangements as mergers and patent licenses where covered by the treaty.

Furthermore, the treaty contained no provisions about procedure, no penalty provisions for violation, and no full allocation of authority between the Brussels staff and the national states. These various omissions, it was

---

[12] Supplement No. 7, 1964 to Bulletin of the EEC, pp. 8-12.
[13] Eighth General Report, paragraph 228; Ninth General Report, para. 69 and 219.

clear, were to be remedied by subsequent regulations, such as were authorized in Article 87 of the treaty.

The Council's Regulation 17 was designed to meet many of these needs. After long controversy, it became effective March 13, 1962. It settled major disputes about interpretation, assigned jurisdiction, and set up procedures.

It declares that the prohibitions of Articles 85 and 86 are directly effective without need for prior decision by any official body. In a subsequent legal proceeding,[14] the European Court held this declaration to be crucial: Before March 13, 1962, the court said, only those agreements were invalid that had been held to be so in decisions by authorities of the states or of the EEC. After March 13, 1962, agreements were invalid unless their validity was established provisionally or finally under other parts of the regulation.

Automatic invalidity for forbidden agreements raises questions as to the status of those agreements to which the application of the treaty is uncertain and of those agreements that might qualify for exemption. Regulation 17 seeks to cope with these problems.

It authorizes enterprises and associations to request the Commission to find that Articles 85 and 86 are not applicable to a particular agreement, decision, or practice. After such a request, the Commission is required to publish the essential content of the request and to give opportunity for interested persons to express their views. It can give "negative clearance," that is, make the requested finding. Though such a decision is binding on the Commission, it covers only the facts as stated by the applicant and gives no protection if the statement was incomplete or if the facts change. Moreover, it is not binding on the courts or the national agencies.[15]

Grant of exemption in accord with Article 85 is made a function of the Commission alone, to the exclusion of the national authorities. The Commission can not only grant exemptions but also subject them to conditions, revoke them for cause, and renew them.

Complicated provisions cover procedures for exemptions and, where exemption has been sought, define the status of agreements during the period before the Commission's decision. Member states must receive copies of notifications and requests for exemption and must be consulted through a consultative committee of their responsible officials before a decision is reached.

For purpose of exemption, agreements are divided into classes, according to their effective dates and the likelihood that they significantly affect

---

[14] The Bosch case, Decision Number 13/61, April 6, 1962, JO, May 4, 1962, page 1081.

[15] See Arved Deringer, *The Common Market Competition Rules*, address at Northwestern University School of Law, Oct. 31, 1962 (mimeographed), p. 27.

interstate trade. Certain types of agreements that are considered unlikely to restrict trade among member states are placed in a special category. They are: (a) Those with participants from only one member state, involving neither exports nor imports between member states; (b) those with only two participants, concerned only with prices or terms to be observed by one party in reselling goods acquired from the other; (c) those with only two participants, restricting the right of the acquirer or licensee to use industrial property such as patents, trade-marks, or technical knowledge; (d) those concerned solely with standardization; and (e) those concerned solely with joint technical research in which all parties can use the results.

Parties to agreements of these types may ask the Commission for exemption at any time. If the Commission grants the exemption it may give its decision retroactive effect to the time when the agreement was made. This means that if, contrary to the probabilities, the Commission eventually holds that such an agreement violates the treaty, the agreement will be held invalid from the effective date of the regulation, March 13, 1962, with whatever consequences invalidity may involve. By notifying the Commission of such agreements prior to January 1, 1967,[16] the parties may escape this risk: In denying exemption to an agreement thus notified, the Commission will fix the date of invalidity provided the agreement is then terminated or so changed that the violation ceases. Presumably the Commission will make the decision invalid only for the period subsequent to its decision.

The second class of agreements consists of those, other than the relatively harmless ones already discussed, which were in force on March 13, 1962. Hereafter they will be called old agreements. Old agreements can qualify for exemption only if notice of them was filed with the Commission before November 1, 1962, for multipartite agreements, and before February 1, 1963, for bipartite agreements.[17] Under Regulation 27, the Community originally required that notice of most kinds of agreements include the full text (other than technical matters in licenses), with relevant supplementary information, but under Regulation 153 it subsequently provided a shorter form for two-party exclusive dealing contracts. If the appropriate notice has been given in time, any exemption granted by the Commission may be retroactive to March 13, 1962; and if the Commission denies exemption it may fix the date of invalidity as it chooses, provided the agreement is terminated or appropriately altered. Thus, in practice, the effect of a request for exemption of an old agreement that was suitably notified is likely to be that the agreement remains valid until the date of an adverse decision.

---

[16] The time limit, previously December 31, 1963, was extended for three years by Regulation 118 on November 8, 1963. See *JO*, November 7, 1963, page 2696.

[17] Arrangements by which a single seller enters into a series of two-party agreements of uniform content are interpreted as bipartite.

The third class of agreement consists of those made after March 13, 1962. These will be called new agreements. If not of the types considered relatively harmless, new agreements, though they may also be submitted for exemption, may not be exempted before the date of submission. If the exemption is denied, they were invalid from the beginning. Thus parties to a new agreement can obtain full exemption only by giving notice on or before the effective date of the agreement. They cannot avoid risk if the agreement takes effect before the Commission decides.

Though complicated, the registration requirements express a simple and clear policy: Significant new restrictive agreements are to be reviewed before they go into effect, and permitted only if they are thought to be suited for exemption. Significant old agreements are to be disclosed, and, as a reward for disclosure, are to be provisionally valid until they can be examined under the standards of Article 85. If they are then invalidated, the invalidity is to begin at the time of the decision. Consideration of types of agreement that are not thought likely to be significantly restrictive is to be deferred, except that parties to them who wish to avoid the slight risk of retroactive invalidity may do so by disclosing them. After all old agreements have been examined, no significant restrictive agreement affecting trade between member states can lawfully exist unless it has been authorized by EEC.

The Commission and the authorities of the member states have concurrent jurisdiction to apply the prohibitions of the treaty; but under Regulation 17 a state cannot grant exemption to an agreement. Moreover, when a proceeding for enforcement, exemption, or negative clearance is instituted by the Commission, it supersedes activities by the member states. An application for exemption or for negative clearance does not automatically deprive the states of authority to declare an agreement invalid; it asks the Commission to do so by initiating action in response to it. Prior, to Article 17 an informal arrangement had been developed, by which the Commission was consulted by the states about proceedings of theirs that came under Article 85. Presumably such consultations have continued. Without such informal consultation, a state is unlikely to invoke the prohibitions against restrictive agreements for which exemptions or negative clearances have been sought, lest action by the Commission throw its own proceedings into abeyance.

Action by the Commission is governed by Regulation 17. The Commission can receive complaints both from member states and from private persons and can initiate action ex officio. It can request information, not only from member states but directly from enterprises and associations, and can covert requests to the latter into formal requirements enforceable by fines. It can conduct investigations, examine business documents, and make copies. It must notify the states about complaints, supply important relevant documents to them, furnish them copies of its requests and requirements for information, consult them about investigations to be conducted on their territory, and consult them and a consultative committee composed of technically competent state officials before reaching a decision. It must hear the persons involved and others significantly affected who ask to be heard.[18] The states, in turn, must make investigations at the Commission's request, and supply assistance if an investigation by the Commission is resisted.

If the Commission finds that the provisions of Articles 85 and 86 have been infringed, it may, at its discretion, make recommendations to those concerned, designed to terminate the infringement. It may require such termination by a formal decision, the essential content of which must be published, with due regard for business secrets. It may also impose fines for infringement, running up to one million dollars, or increased to 10 per cent of the previous year's business turnover, as well as penalties running up to $1,000 per day for delay in complying with a decision. However, it cannot impose fines for activities pursuant to a properly notified agreement during the period prior to denial of an exemption. The Commission's decisions can be appealed to the Court of Justice.

In broad outline, then, work upon restrictive business agreements in EEC consists in registering agreements, deciding what agreements are not subject to the treaty, granting exemption to the agreements that qualify, and terminating or amending the others by recommendations or decisions.

The Scope of Reported Restrictions

Though the notification procedures provide substantial incentives to report agreements, many agreements have remained unreported. The foremost Swiss trade association, for example, counselled its members to refrain from reporting, and believes that the advice was widely followed. Numerous enterprises have indicated in private conversations that they chose not to report because they did not want to run the risk that the contents of their agreements might become widely known to government officials and perhaps

---

[18] An implementing regulation as to hearings subsequently issued by the Commission (No. 99/63 of July 25, 1963, JO, August 20, 1963, p. 2268) provides possibility for both written submissions and oral hearings, but states that hearings shall not be public and may consist in hearing participants either in one another's presence or separately. It provides, however, for written record of statements made and for right to assistance from legal counsel and other experts. It stipulates that the Commission can use for decision only material upon which persons subject to the decision have had opportunity to comment, and that prior to a decision in favor of those accused, complainants must be given opportunity to comment.

to others, because they questioned both the legality and the propriety of the reporting procedures, or because of the size of the reporting task. One large American company that did not report estimated that it had 27,000 reportable agreements, of which many would have needed translation into one of the acceptable languages. Some of those who did not report modified their agreements by deleting all provisions which they thought might be subject to the prohibitions of the Rome Treaty. Others chose to rely on the possibility that their agreements would be found lawful or would not be subjected to proceedings. Responsible officials of the European Economic Community and the national states differ widely in their estimates of the proportion of relevant agreements that were reported, the lowest estimate I obtained being 5 per cent, and the highest 50 per cent.

Nevertheless, large numbers of agreements have been reported—a total of about 37,500 by March 31, 1965. Of these 1,034 were multilateral agreements. Of the multilateral agreements 395 involved horizontal restrictions, 259 vertical exclusive dealing, and 380 licensing arrangements for patents or technical knowledge. Of the bilateral agreements, about 81% pertained to exclusive dealing arrangements between individual suppliers and distributors, about 16% to licensing arrangements, and about 3% to other matters.[19]

In March 1965 the Commission's staff was still enaged in analysis and classification of the notifications. No full account of the character of the agreements was available. However, the Commission provided, for a memorandum that I prepared in 1964 for the Department of State, information concerning 493 multipartite agreements that had been reported by the close of 1962.[20]

Of these agreements, 177 included participants from only one country but affected trade between the states of the Community by virtue of their content. An additional 135 involved participants in two countries, and an additional 175, participants in more than two countries. Information about the classification of the other six is not available to me.

The following table indicates the frequency with which different types of restriction occurred in these agreements and the segments of economic life to which the agreements pertained.

The classification of restrictions appearing in these agreements was still broad. Some categories that were imprecise, apparently because of the ambiguity of the reported provisions, overlapped others that had more explicit content. The meaning attributed to the various categories is explained in footnotes attached to the table.

---

[19] *Seventh General Report,* paragraph 65; Eighth General Report, paragraph 56.
[20] Edwards, Cartelization in Western Europe, op cit., pp. 25-26.

RESTRICTIONS IN MULTIPARTITE AGREEMENTS REPORTED TO EEC TO THE CLOSE OF 1962

Restriction	Products							Services				Total restrictions
	Metal	Chemical	Textile	Food	Construction Materials	Paper	Miscellaneous	Insurance	Banking	Department stores and chains	Miscellaneous	
Prices	44	27	14	13	13	16	31	1	8	3	3	173
Discounts	14	2	9	5	2	12	7	—	—	1	1	53
Conditions of sale	28	13	16	8	14	14	21	5	8	3	7	137
Control of production (A)	22	12	4	5	3	—	15	—	—	3	—	64
Control of sale (B)	23	24	3	3	8	7	20	—	—	3	2	93
Allocation of territorial markets	15	5	—	2	5	2	3	—	—	—	1	33
Quotas (C)	23	10	4	5	11	2	20	—	—	—	2	77
Division of sale and purchase (D)	8	17	3	2	14	3	8	—	—	4	1	60
Technical cooperation	25	3	2	4	—	—	5	—	—	1	2	43
"Normalization," joint research, joint publicity, etc.	39	11	12	3	3	10	5	—	—	9	16	118
Export and import	38	23	14	4	10	4	22	2	8	—	—	115
Collective exclusive dealing	35	9	2	1	3	1	6	—	—	—	—	57
Multilateral licensing	101	25	6	7	1	1	11	—	—	3	1	156
Total number of agreements	203	70	37	23	31	24	51	6	8	13	27	493

A. Covers not only limitation of quantity but also all other limitations, such as restrictions on quality, packing, etc. Does not include provisions that contain specific production quotas and obligate participants to observe them.

B. Covers restrictions pertaining to customers, channels of distribution, territory, and amount to be sold, or other limitations on sale. Does not include (1) provisions clearly and solely concerned with allocation of territorial markets; (2) provisions containing specific sales quotas and obligating participants to observe them.

C. Covers provisions, of the kinds excluded from A and B above, that contain explicit quotas for production or sale and obligate participants to produce or sell only their quotas.

D. Covers provisions which attribute to the named firms a role or purchasing organization set up for such

Action About Agreements

Negative Clearance and Exemption. Confronted with thousands of notifications, most of which pertain to bilateral exclusive dealing and bilateral licensing, the Commission has wished to avoid the burden of considering the less important agreements individually and to reduce the period during which the eventual lawfulness of the arrangements will be uncertain. It has made several attempts to do so.

1. In December, 1962, it announced its opinion that two classes of agreements are not subject to prohibition under Article 85. Though without legal effect, these announcements were informal negative clearances. The first[21] said the prohibitions of Article 85 do not apply to contracts by which agents (including exclusive agents) are designated for specific parts of the Common Market. It distinguished agents from independent dealers, primarily on the basis of such criteria as relief from financial risk and lack of power to set prices and terms. It said that exclusive dealing contracts with independent dealers might affect trade between member states and hence must be evaluated case by case.

The second interpretation[22] declared that Article 85 did not prohibit certain restrictions in patent licenses. The restrictions covered were partly those believed to be inherent in a patent right and partly certain accessory restrictions believed to be either harmless to competition or unlikely to affect interstate trade. In giving them clearance, the Commission reserved its attitude toward other patent restrictions, particularly patent pools, cross licenses, and multiple parallel licenses. The restrictions that were given clearance were as follows: (a) Limits upon the scope of the license, as to duration, parts of the national territory covered, or right to assign the license or grant sub-licenses; (b) limits upon activity under the license—field of technical application, amount of product, or type of activity (e.g., manufacture, use, or sale); (c) certain accessory conditions to be observed by the licensee: (1) affixing the patent designation to the product; (2) observing quality; (3) obligation to obtain supplies of products where they are indispensable to the technically faultless exploitation of the patent; (4) obligation to communicate experience or to license improvements on a nonexclusive and reciprocal basis; (d) undertaking by the licensor not to exploit the invention himself nor to license others.

2. The Commission is using applications for negative clearance as a means to establish the boundaries of its policy. In July 1963 it published summaries of two such applications[23] with a press release saying that it

---

[21] JO, December 24, 1962, pages 2921-22.
[22] JO, December 24, 1962, pages 2922-23.
[23] JO, July 4, 1963, page 1853.

was disposed to give clearance and inviting comments. The two cases were intended to become precedents that might make possible the blanket clearance of several hundred similar applications. Objection on the ground that negative clearance is permissible only after specific public notice of the agreements to be cleared was effective in preventing the contemplated blanket action.

One of the applications involved a contract for reciprocal exclusive dealing between Grosfillex, a French producer of plastic kitchen appliances and sanitary articles, and Fillistorf, a Swiss distributor. The manufacturer was obligated not to distribute in Switzerland except exclusively through Fillistorf. Fillistorf was obligated to maintain retail prices, to produce or sell no competing articles, and to refrain from exporting the products. On March 11, 1964, negative clearance was given to the contract.[24] In a subsequent report the Commission mentioned the existence of "numerous similar cases" and commented that the decision in the Grosfillex case makes its views known to others who are parties to such contracts.[25]

The other agreement involved an undertaking by which Nicholas Frères, a French manufacturer of preparations for hair dressing, sold goodwill, trade-marks, a trade name, and know-how to Vitapro, an English enterprise, to be used by the buyer only in certain countries outside the Common Market. Nicholas agreed to refrain from operating in those countries. Negative clearance was granted in August 1964.[26]

During 1964 two more applications for negative clearance were granted. One concerned an agreement by which a Belgian firm became distributor of brakes for the American firm Bendix. The agreement contained neither territorial limitations nor provisions for exclusive dealing.[27] The other involved rules adopted by four Dutch engineering and contracting firms, under which, in contemplation of joint bidding or of allocation of rights to bid, they would report their intention to bid on large contracts for work outside the Common Market. Negative clearance was granted because trade within the Common Market would not be restricted.[28]

At the close of March 1964, the Commission was considering more than 100 further applications for negative clearance.[29] Three of these had been published, with invitations for comment, by the end of the year. Two of

---

[24] JO, April 9, 1964, p. 915.
[25] *Seventh General Report*, paragraph 67.
[26] *JO*, No. 136, August 26, 1964, pages 2287-9, Eighth General Report, paragraph 60.
[27] *JO*, March 13, 1964, page 722 and June 10, 1964, page 1426, Eighth General Report, paragraph 59.
[28] *JO*, March 13, 1964, page 723; October 31, 1964, page 2761, Eighth General Report, paragraph 61.
[29] *Seventh General Report*, paragraph 66.

them concerned contracts by distributors with a French supplier:[30] One of the contracts made a German company the supplier's exclusive distributor in Germany but gave it the right to re-export and to sell goods bought from others. The other made a Belgian firm exclusive distributor in Belgium for the same French firm, but also bound it not to sell competing goods and bound the supplier not to sell directly in Belgium. The requests for comments presumably indicated that the Commission was disposed to grant the applications.

The third application, which involved collective arrangements in the Belgian tile industry, was the aftermath of the first case in which the Commission took action against a forbidden agreement. It will be discussed below in connection with that action.

3. The Commission is giving early attention to applications for exemption of exclusive dealing contracts under the provisions of Article 85. It has sought and obtained formal authority to give blanket exemptions under Article 85. On February 28, 1964, it asked the Council to issue a regulation providing for such action, and indicated its desire to act first with reference to the 31,000 bilateral exclusive dealing agreements registered with it. Comments were obtained from the European Assembly and from the Economic and Social Committee, both of which favored the plan with certain suggested modifications. In March 1965 the Commission was empowered to grant block exemptions to bilateral exclusive dealing arrangements and licensing agreements, to terminate such exemptions when conditions changed, and to withdraw or impose conditions upon the exemptions applicable to particular agreements.[31] Prior public notice and opportunity to be heard are required before a block exemption can be granted. The Commission apparently hopes that a few blanket exemptions can establish, for the time being, the legal status of most exclusive dealing agreements and that many other such agreements will be modified to conform to some one of the patterns that are exempted.[32]

Consideration of exemptions for exclusive dealing began by decisions covering particular agreements. These were regarded as ways of obtaining enough experience to formulate the terms of a general exemption. In a case

---

[30] *JO,* November 7, 1964, page 2860.

[31] Regulation 19-1965. See *JO,* March 6, 1965; Bulletin of the EEC, April 1965, pp. 15-16; and *Eighth General Report,* paragraph 68.

[32] *Seventh General Report,* para. 63; *JO,* May 27, 1964, page 1275; November 30, 1964, page 3320. The Assembly wanted exemption to run for at least five years, and wanted to grant to other agreements than bilateral ones the possibility to qualify for exemption by altering the agreement. The Economic and Social Committee saw no need for a time limit, and agreed with the Assembly about extension of the scheme to multilateral agreements. An English text of the Commission's proposal appears in Supplement No. 4, 1964 to the Bulletin of the EEC., pages 8-11.

of this kind, the parties have assumed, and the Commission finds, that the arrangement involves restrictions that fall under Article 85. The question is whether or not it merits exemption under the relevant standards. By the close of 1965, three exemptions had been granted. These were regarded as part of the process by which the Commission would obtain enough experience to work out the terms of a blanket exemption.

The first covered an agreement by which a Dutch manufacturer of enamelled household utensils (Diepenbrook and Reigers NV) granted to a French firm (Blondel) exclusive rights to sell these products in France. The agreement imposed no restriction upon imports into France by others nor upon re-export from France. The Commission thought that distribution was improved by the agreement and that better availability of the product to French consumers gave them a fair share of the benefits, and saw in the possibility of imports by others a safeguard against unduly high prices. The exemption was granted for an initial period of five years.[33]

The other two exemptions covered similar situations. The second was applicable to an agreement by which a German producer of farm machinery (Hummel) granted to a Belgian firm (Isbecque) sole rights to sell in Belgium, but without restrictions on re-export or on import by others. The facts that Isbecque undertook to demonstrate and service technically complex products, to stock spare parts, and even to arrange for the production of special accessories suited to peculiarities of Belgian soil were regarded as grounds supporting the reasonableness of the arrangement.[34] The third exemption covered two agreements between a French maker of protective footwear (Jallotte) and dealers in Germany (Voss) and Belgium (Vandeputte). The agreements were generally like those previously exempted; but the one with Vandeputte also bound the dealer not to buy or sell goods similar to those made by Jallotte. This two-way exclusiveness was not regarded as objectionable.[35]

The Commission had also invited comment upon a fourth application for exemption involving exclusive dealing between Jacquard Frères and Osvaldo Benaglio,[36] but had not yet disposed of the case.

After these exemptions and a decision (discussed below) in which exclusive dealing was condemned, the Commission thought itself ready to formulate a blanket exemption. Early in 1966 it announced that a draft regulation for bilateral exclusive dealing had been sent to its consultative committee. The draft was published in August.[37]

---

[33] JO August 4, 1965; Bulletin of the EEC, Sept.-Oct., 1965, pp. 16-17.
[34] JO September 23, 1965; Bulletin of the EEC, November 1965, pp. 11-12.
[35] JO January 6, 1966; Bulletin of the EEC, March 1966, pp. 26-7.
[36] JO October 22, 1964, pp. 2606-7.
[37] Bulletin of the EEC, March 1966, p. 27; JO, August 26, 1966, p. 2863.

On the basis of the early cases the Commission included in its ninth general report (paragraph 65) a favorable view of arrangements for exclusive distribution of foreign goods. Such contracts, it thought, reduced difficulties arising from distance, language barriers, and differences of law; enabled producers to adapt themselves more rapidly to foreign market conditions and to supply any needed technical assistance to foreign distributors and users; made the good available to buyers more regularly, rapidly, and easily; facilitated demonstration, service after sale, adaptation of goods to local peculiarities, and maintenance of inventories of spare parts; tended to keep differentials between prices at points of origin and prices in foreign markets appropriate to the additional costs incurred; and might reduce prices by increasing the volume of sale. It considered that exclusive supply by the producer and agreement by him not to compete with the distributor are restrictions necessary to such benefits, but that competition is not excluded thereby so long as the distributor is not given absolute territorial protection and similar goods are available.

Enforcement. The general nature of enforcement activity by the Commission can be pieced together from various passages in speeches, annual reports, and the EEC Bulletin. Cases of violation were informally considered at meetings between the Commission's staff and experts from the member countries as early as 1959. In some instances, working parties were set up for particular cases. By the close of 1963,[38] a total of 33 cases had been examined, of which only four originated in formal complaints. In "a number" of these, the practices in question had been abandoned during the investigation. Among matters that had been examined were agreements involving wall tile, floor tile, metals, and medical supplies. Substantial restrictions that had been examined included (a) refusal by a producer, under pressure from dealers, to supply a trader in another member state; (b) vertical and horizontal cartelization, involving exclusion of the producers of other member states; (c) refusal by a trade journal to publish advertisements by a foreign producer; (d) an agreement that prohibited re-export of imported goods; and (e) two patent licensing arrangements.[39]

At the beginning of August 1963, about 49 proposals to investigate alleged violations had been submitted to the Commission. The Commis-

---

[38] Bulletin of the EEC, Nov., 1963, p. 34.

[39] Bulletin of the EEC, No. 4, 1962, page 34; Fifth General Report, paragraph 48; Fourth General Report, paragraph 50; Hans von der Groeben, *La Politique de la Concurrence dans la Communité Économique Européene*, June 1961, pages 26-27; Herman Schumacher, "The Procedure for Giving Effect to Articles 85 and 86 of the European Economic Community Treaty," in Institute fur Ausländishches und Internationales Wirtschaftsrecht, *Kartelle und Monopole im Modernen Recht*, Frankfurt-am-Main, 1961, pages 363-76.

sion's staff was investigating 22 cases of alleged violation, 20 of which originated in complaints. It was also considering 17 applications for exemption and 12 for negative clearance.[40] Private observers believed that about twelve of the cases involving violation were concerned with the fertilizer industries.

By the end of March 1964, the Commission had received 48 complaints, was investigating 28 of them, and was also investigating one case initiated *ex officio*. These matters and 108 applications for negative clearance or exemption had been consolidated in 39 proceedings. One proceeding had progressed as far as an oral hearing. Most of the proceedings involved manufacturers in more than one member state and were concerned with market-sharing, price agreements, and quota agreements.[41]

A year later, at the end of March, 57 proceedings were under way. They were the outgrowth of 31 complaints, 149 applications for negative clearance or exemption, and one ex-officio action. They covered 164 agreements of which 44 included only firms from a single member state; 47 firms from two member states; 40 firms in a member state and a non-member state; and 33 firms from several member states and/or non-member countries.[42]

The classes of restriction and types of business involved in these agreements are shown in the following table.

When, in considering a complaint or examining an application for exemption or negative clearance, the Commission has come to believe that a restrictive agreement violates the treaty in a way for which exemption is not appropriate, the Commission normally sends to the parties a communication or recommendation summarizing its opinion. By this step it terminates whatever provisional immunity may have been derived from notification of the agreement and exposes the restrictions to the fines provided in the treaty. By January, 1966, eight actions of this kind had been announced.

The first, in July 1963, pertained to an agreement by two Belgian associations of tile dealers with producers of tile in various countries about the distribution of tile in Belgium. At the time of the recommendation, the agreement covered 30 producers in Belgium, the Netherlands, Germany, France, Italy, and England. It provided that tile would be supplied only to approved dealers, who must not be general contractors and must have stated qualifications as to experience, facilities, and volume of business. About 900 dealers had been approved. The participating dealers were obli-

---

[40] *Bulletin* of the EEC, September 1963.
[41] Seventh General Report, paragraphs 65-6.
[42] Eighth General Report, paragraph 57 and Table 6, pp. 66-7.

Restrictive clauses in 164 agreements on which procedure has been initiated
Position on 31 March 1965

Industry	Number of agreements	Exclusive Dealing — With export ban	Exclusive Dealing — With area allocation	Exclusive Dealing — Other (1)	General terms and conditions of delivery and payment	Rebates	Pricing	Market-sharing	Quotas	Purchasing groupings	Sales groupings	Specialization, production control (2)	Technical co-operation	Standards, exchange of information, joint reserarch, advertising	Import-export	Collective exclusive dealing	Tying clauses	Licenses
Chemicals and pharmaceuticals	14	3			2		1	2	7		4		2	1	6	1		8
Fertilizers	28	21	5		2		8	9			18		2	6	15			1
Plastics and rubber	5	3	2		2		2	2			4				5			
Electrical apparatus	27	1	4		2		2					4						12
Precision instruments and optics	10		2	1														2
Non-electrical household apparatus	1																	1
Motor vehicles	3		1															1
Machine tools and other machines	1		2															2
Tools and parts	15				6	1	8	1	7		6	3	3	2	11	3	1	9
Building materials	5	3	1		1		1		3	1	1				1	1		
Beverages	3	1			1													
Textiles	15						2	4						2				1
Services	17							7	5	16			17	17				
Commerce	1																	
Leather and footwear																		
Paper, paperboard, printing and publishing	10				4	1					2			3	5			3
Furniture and toys	1																	
Building	7	1	1				2				7	1		7				1
Total	**164**	33	18	1	20	2	26	25	22	17	42	8	24	38	43	5	1	42
Total restrictive clauses																		

(1) Mutual.
(2) Except quotas.

gated to maintain a stated markup and to buy only from participating suppliers. In addition, the Belgian market was divided into two parts. The agreement was enforceable against the manufacturers by fines and against the dealers by refusal to sell.

Though the facts of the tile case were widely known in Brussels, the official account of the case was brief and relatively uninformative. Without identifying the product, the countries involved, or the scope of the agreement, the Commission described it as one between "a number" of manufacturers and "a considerable number" of customers to trade exclusively with each other, said that admission of further manufacturers was subject to approval by those already parties and that new customers must meet "a number of conditions," and mentioned the means of enforcement. It did not state the content of its recommendation nor the nature of the changes subsequently made by the parties. Thus its announcement had limited value as a basis for development of public opinion about the Commission's policy toward restrictive practices or as a statement from which business enterprises could ascertain the boundaries of permissible concerted action.

After the Commission's recommendation, the parties to the agreement modified it, and applied for negative clearance. In the new version, tile manufacturers agreed with associations of tile buyers and tile dealers that they would sell only to qualified buyers. To be regarded as qualified, a buyer must be regularly engaged in the tile business, maintain a suitable place of business and a stock of tile, be included in the business register of his trade, and, if operating as a tile layer, possess competence in that activity, demonstrated by experience or by evidence of technical training. A committee was to verify qualifications and maintain a list of qualified buyers. Participation was to open to qualified non-members of the association and to any manufacturer who accepted the agreement. Buyers were to be free to buy from any supplier, including non-participants.

Though less restrictive than the previous agreement, this plan resembled the first in its obvious purpose to prevent direct sale of tile by manufacturers to large industrial users and to contractors not regularly engaged in the tile business. Nevertheless, in May 1964, the Commission published a summary of the agreement and invited comment, thereby indicating that it contemplated favorable action. In 1966 it announced that, as a result of comments received, it had undertaken further investigation.[43]

Late in 1964 the Commission announced that it had communicated

---

[43] *JO*, May 13, 1964, page 1169; Ninth General Report, para. 58. The purposes of the Belgian tile program appear to be similar to those of a program undertaken in the 1940's by the North Carolina Tile Contractors' Association. See Corwin D. Edwards, "Legal Requirements that Building Contractors be Licensed," Law and Contemporary Problems, Winter, 1947.

to the participants in a scheme of collective exclusive dealing its view that their agreements were illegal. The announcement identified neither the type of business nor the number of firms involved.[44] From later references to it, however, it appears that the arrangement pertained to building materials and that after the communication the agreement was terminated or modified.[45]

In mid-1965, two similar communications were sent by the Commission to the participants in agreements about sanitary ware and detergents. The sanitary ware agreement involved reciprocal exclusive dealing between manufacturers, importers, and dealers, designed to confine sales in Belgium to Belgian manufacturers, with the result that competition could be almost completely excluded. The detergent agreement involved allocation of national markets between Dutch and Belgian manufacturers and requirements that dealers respect the allocation. After the communications, the agreements were terminated or modified.[46]

In the autumn of 1965 the Commission informed producers and dealers selling sand used in ceramics and in various types of manufacture that it considered two agreements illegal. By the first agreement, four Belgian producers and one German producer had agreed with the only Dutch producer upon quotas for sale in the Netherlands. By the second agreement, four sales agents of these producers were bound, under penalty of fines, to obtain the sand only from the parties to the first agreement and to observe minimum selling prices.[47]

Another communication, issued in November 1965, said that an agreement pertaining to "the rubber and plastics sector" violated the treaty and was not eligible for exemption. By this agreement all manufacturers of the product in one member state established aggregated rebates available only upon dealers' purchases from the participants. The Commission objected to the scheme because it protected the national market against foreign competition.[48]

In the same month, the Commission issued another communication adverse to an agreement among most of the manufacturers and importers

[44] Bulletin of the EEC, December, 1964, pp. 16-17.

[45] Bulletin of the EEC, November, 1965, p. 13.

[46] Bulletin of the EEC, June, 1965, pp. 14-16; November 1965, p. 13; Eighth General Report, paragraphs 64-65.

[47] Bulletin of the EEC, November, 1965, pp. 12-13. According to the New York Times (Sept. 27, 1964, Section 3) and to the periodical European Community (September 21, 1964, p. 16), in September the Commission notified 50 producers of sand and gravel that they would be subject to fines if they continued to agree upon exclusive dealing with users of their product. I have found no formal announcement of such a recommendation. Possibly the stories were inaccurate accounts of the Netherlands sand agreements.

[48] Bulletin of the EEC, January 1966, p. 10.

of pesticides in a member state. This agreement established uniform terms of sale that resulted in identical sale prices and imposed resale prices upon dealers, enforced by collective boycott. Since the Commission had not been notified of the agreement, the communication informed the parties that exemption was ruled out "until such time as the agreement has been notified in conformity with Regulation No. 17."[49]

In a subsequent communication, the Commission condemned a cartel among 53 Belgian, German, and Dutch cement firms. The scheme involved quotas for deliveries of cement and clinker in the Netherlands, uniform selling prices and terms, and an agreement that participants would not build new plants in the territory of other participants without their consent. In March 1966 the participants appealed to the court. The appeal raises question whether or not such communications are subject to the treaty's provisions about appeal.[50]

Only one formal decision declaring an agreement unlawful was published before the close of 1965. Promulgated September 23, 1964, it pertained to a case in which an exclusive dealing arrangement as to tape recorders and phonographic equipment between a German supplier, Grundig, and a French distributor, Consten, had been the subject of a complaint by another French distributor, UNEF.[51] The contract was a particular instance of distributive arrangements used generally by Grundig, in which each dealer was bound not to export the goods he received to the territory of another and not to sell other comparable products. It was reenforced in France by permission for Consten to use one Grundig trademark and to become the owner of another within France. The contract had been reported by Grundig to EEC, and hence was provisionally valid pending a decision about it. UNEF had obtained Grundig products in Germany, brought them to France, undersold Consten, and obtained by 1961 about 10 per cent of the total sales of Grundig recording machines in France. In a suit by Consten against UNEF in a French court, UNEF had contended that Consten's agreement with Grundig was void under Article 85. It had also filed complaint with the Commission. The Paris court of appeal had then suspended the case pending the Commission's decision.

The Commission found that the prices of Grundig products in France were substantially higher than in Germany. For recording machines, the difference, after allowance for tariffs, taxes, and discounts, amounted to

---

[49] *Ibid*, pp. 10-11. Though retroactive exemption is not possible for an agreement not reported to the Commission, a delayed report of it creates the possibility of exemption for the future. The wording of the Commission's announcement implies that this possibility remains available even when the Commission has discovered an unreported agreement and found it contrary to the treaty.

[50] Bulletin of the EEC, March, 1966, p. 26; Ninth General Report, para. 57.

[51] *JO*, No. 161, October 20, 1964, page 2545.

at least 23 per cent, and the difference in the distributors' margin to 53 per cent.

The Commission saw restriction and distortion of competition in the facts that a) French distributors other than Consten could not get Grundig products; b) Grundig was bound not to sell to others than Consten in France; c) Grundig's distributors elsewhere were bound not to export to France; d) Consten was bound not to export. Though it recognized that competition existed between Grundig and other producers, it thought competition among distributors also necessary; for costs of distribution are substantial, and whereas consumers cannot readily appraise price differences among differentiated products, they can easily understand differences upon the same product.

Having held that the agreement came within the prohibition of Article 85, the Commission held that there was no appropriate basis for exemption. Admitting the possibility that exclusive dealing might improve distribution and production, it did not examine this possibility closely because consumers clearly got no share of any such benefit and the restrictions imposed exceeded those that might be relevant to such rationalization. It pointed out that if Consten's prices had been no higher than in other countries there would have been no need to require distributors elsewhere to refrain from exporting to France.

Accordingly, the Commission declared the contract a violation of Article 85 and ordered the participants not to hinder others from acquiring the products anywhere in the Community for resale in France. Grundig and Consten appealed the decision. In July 1966 the Court sustained the Commission's decision on all significant points.[52]

At the end of March 1966, more than 38,000 agreements were before the Commission under notifications that constituted applications for exemption or under requests for negative clearance. In 1,180 instances, such applications or requests had been withdrawn after termination of the agreement or the restrictive features thereof.

During the twelve-month period, the Commission had begun investigation of 109 complaints and 143 matters instituted *ex officio*. It had issued one formal recommendation to 930 firms that violation of the treaty be terminated, and four times had deprived participants in an agreement of the temporary immunity they had obtained from notification by informing them that its preliminary investigation made it believe the agreement illegal and incapable of exemption. In an additional instance it had informed parties to an unregistered agreement that exemption thereof could not be considered until the agreement was properly reported. These five

---

[52] *JO,* Jan. 12, 1965, Jan. 14, 1965, Eighth General Report, paragraph 63; decision of the Court of Justice of the European Communities, July 13, 1966.

communications covered 266 firms. It had given negative clearance three times and had issued ten announcements that it was considering negative clearance or exemption.

In 54 instances investigations, applications for exemption, or requests for clearance had been terminated because relevant restrictions had been abandoned. Among these were eight instances in which questions raised by the Commission resulted in abandonment of joint sale or service (3 times), price fixing (twice), quotas, specialization agreements, agreements not to export, territorial restrictions upon exclusive distributors, and obligations to purchase tied to grants of a patent license (once each). In an unspecified small number of instances, report of previously unreported agreements had brought an *ex officio* investigation to an end by converting the problem into one concerned with the propriety of granting an application for exemption.

At the beginning of April 1966, eighty formal proceedings, involving 225 agreements, were in progress, and an additional 151 agreements were under preliminary investigation. Eighty-one complaints, 47 *ex officio* matters, and 248 applications for exemption or requests for negative clearance were covered by these 376 investigations.[52a]

Though few cases have yet been pushed to a conclusion, the Commission reported in 1965 that certain interpretations of Article 85 had already become clear:[53] The treaty's provisions about agreements are applicable to vertical agreements even if competition is restrained at only one vertical level. If restrictive effects exist within the Common Market, the provisions are applicable even if a participant has its headquarters elsewhere. The restraints of competition covered by the treaty are those that appreciably affect consumers or non-participating enterprises; restraint of the buying freedom of parties to an agreement is not, by itself, to be regarded as restraint of competition. If a restraint changes the conditions under which trade between member states is pursued, this justifies the conclusion that the restraint affects interstate trade. Exclusive distribution agreements between firms in different member states are liable to affect interstate trade. If such agreements give absolute territorial protection, they distort competition, and can be exempted only in special circumstances. Similarly, agreements for use of a trade mark whose chief purpose is to protect the exclusive distributor against imports are efforts to distort competition.

Establishment of Priorities

Confronted with thousands of agreements that differed greatly in importance, the Commission has sought to establish priorities to guide its work. This was a difficult task.

[52a] Ninth General Report, para. 45-48, 55.
[53] Eighth General Report, paragraph 67.

(1) There was need to give prompt attention to complaints, applications for negative clearance, and matters referred to the Commission by the courts of the member countries.

(2) There was good reason to give priority to examination of new agreements in order to prevent additional restrictions from developing and thus destroying the impact of reductions in governmental barriers to trade.

(3) There was good reason to act vigorously against agreements subject to reporting that had not been reported; for such agreements could not be exempted, and action against them would strengthen incentives to report and would discourage secret cartelization.

(4) It was desirable to take action in those instances in which an exemption under Article 85-3 appeared to be unlikely and positive economic results appeared to be possible from remedial action.

(5) There was good reason to undertake test cases that could contribute toward a clearer and more comprehensive interpretation of the treaty and the regulations under it.

(6) There was good reason not to delay unduly the completion of work that had been undertaken before the notification of agreements had given the Commission a relatively full view of its field of action.

The last five of these claims upon the Commission's time and attention could be resolved by internal decisions as to the relative significance of different kinds of work. The first claim, however, represented outside pressures for action by people who regarded particular decisions as important and were not necessarily concerned with problems of over-all priority. These outside claims could not be ignored; for the Commission, like some European governments, can be made defendant in a legal proceeding by an aggrieved person charging it with failure to act.

The significance of the outside claims had been enhanced by a blending of public and private law in the treaty and under Regulation 17. The treaty contains both broad prohibitions and broad provisions for exemption. Agreements that are prohibited are not only subject to corrective action but made invalid, so that they may not be enforced in private suits. Under Regulation 17 the national authorities were deprived of power to grant exemptions, though they retained the power to apply the prohibitions of the treaty in any case in which the Commission had not undertaken consideration of the matter. The effect of this assignment of jurisdiction has been that in a private suit in which the question of the validity of an agreement under the treaty is raised by one of the parties, a national court can hold the agreement invalid but cannot hold it exempt. The logical result is that the national courts, confronted with such issues, suspend the case and refer to Brussels the status of the agreement under the treaty. Seven such cases were pending before the Commission at the beginning of October 1963. Inaction about them would have had the effect of leaving the underlying private suits in limbo.

Applications for negative clearance presented a somewhat similar problem. In such cases the parties to an agreement allege that it falls outside the limits of the Rome Treaty on such grounds as that it does not affect trade between the member states or that it contains none of the relevant restrictions. They ask the Commission to affirm their view. So long as the Commission has not acted, there is a possibility that the interpretation may be later held to be incorrect and that in consequence the agreement, unless granted exemption, may be invalid. This may be a shaky basis upon which to enforce private contractual rights.

In its seventh general report the Commission announced, in accord with decisions taken in July 1963, that it was giving priority to a) complaints that charged violation; b) cases pending before national courts that involved the applicability of Articles 85 or 86; c) agreements that had not been reported; d) new agreements that were reported before their effective date. It also said that priorities were influenced by "the type and gravity of the restriction of competition, its economic importance for the Common Market, an endeavor to spread the cases over the various economic sectors, and the effects of the subsequent decision as a precedent for the interpretation and observance of the rules on competition, and thus for the clarity with which the law can be understood by enterprises."[54]

Apparently the substantive evaluations involved in these priorities will be made on the basis of coordinated investigations of particular segments of the economy, with particular attention to arrangements for allocation of territories, establishment of quotas, and price-fixing in which prices in different countries have been set at different levels. Such studies are expected to provide a basis for appraisal of the importance and prevalence of restrictive practices, and thus to guide the Commission in initiating cases ex officio and in considering complaints and requests for exemption.

The first such general investigation, begun in 1965, was designed to discover why, in spite of large differences in prices in different member states, there was little inter-state trade in margarine.[54a]

Action About Dominant Firms

At the close of 1964 the Commission's work upon concentration was at such an early stage that the scope and character of corrective action was still uncertain. No proceeding concerned with abuse of power by a large

---

[54] Seventh General Report, para. 66.
[54a] Ninth General Report, para. 52.

enterprise had yet been announced, nor had any policy statement sought to interpret the application of Article 86 to abuses of a dominant position. The Commission had indicated in an action program made public in October 1962 that its work under Article 86 would be based upon study of particular branches of industry, with special attention to price movements, and that it would seek to ascertain whether or not the provisions of the treaty were adequate for effective control of abuses.[55]

But the Commission made clear that its concern about powerful enterprises extended beyond control of abuses to cover the entire question of their significance for competition. Though it had repeatedly expressed itself in favor of the trend toward larger business enterprises, which it regarded as appropriate to the enlarged Common Market,[56] it explicitly declared that it could not confine itself to "keeping a strict watch over the conduct of firms now holding dominant positions." The further action that it envisaged had two parts. The first was "to see that concentration having no justification from the standpoint of the economy at large should at least not be artificially encouraged." This involved an effort by the Commission "to secure greater neutrality in respect of competition in company law, tax law, and the law on industrial property." To this end the Commission said that it would soon raise the question with member states and business organizations. The second line of action was to "keep a close watch" on developments by which "new dominant positions come into being," especially "when they result in the stifling or elimination of existing competition."[57] Announcement of this intention presumably foreshadowed first a program of investigation and subsequently either an interpretation of the treaty as adequate to cope with any impairments of competition that were found or else a recommendation that the treaty be appropriately extended.[58]

Policy Studies. As initial steps in developing its program in this field, the Commission sponsored several policy studies. The scope of these studies suggested that the policy to be formulated would be concerned not merely with abusive conduct but more broadly with the relationship between concentration of power and competition and with the implications of this relationship as to need for control of certain types of concentration.

Four studies were undertaken, of which three were to be conducted by private persons. The results of none of them had been announced at the close of 1964.

The first study, entrusted to four professors of law and economics,

---

[55] Aktionsprogram der Gemeinschaft für die zweite Stufe, October 24, 1962, para. 25.
[56] Fourth General Report, para. 84-88; Fifth General Report, para. 92.
[57] Aktionsprogram, *op. cit.*, para. 26.
[58] There is currently widespread belief that Articles 85 and 86 do not apply to mergers and other forms of structural combination. See, for example, Ellis, *op. cit.*, pages 97-105, 110-111.

pertained to the interpretation and application of Article 86, the relation thereof to concentration, and the possibility that powerful enterprises might be required to report certain types of practices and also mergers in which they had a part.

In requesting a report about the interpretation of Article 86, the Commission apparently recognized that such an interpretation raises difficult problems. There is need for working definitions of dominant position and of abuse thereof. As to dominant position, question arises how the lower limits of a dominant position are to be determined, particularly in situations in which only a part of the Common Market is dominated or significant supplies are available from outside the dominated field. Question also arises how domination by a group of enterprises is to be conceived. As to abuse, such questions arise as whether the types of behavior that are listed as abusive in Article 86 are to be deemed so invariably or only presumptively; by what standards other types of abuse are to be identified; how the concept of abuse is related to similar concepts in national laws; whether or not a large firm's use of the advantages it derives from its size is to be considered abusive; what constitutes abuse by a group; and to what extent, if at all, abuse is to be found in "excessive" prices, maintenance of idle capacity, maximization of profits, and impairment of competition.

The Commission's second study, entrusted to a similar group of professors, pertained to a) the effect of cartel policy upon mergers and b) the extent to which Article 85 can be applied to groups other than cartels (such as concerted action by enterprises that are affiliated or bound together in various types of communities of interest).

The third study, entrusted to an institute of comparative law, pertained to the extent of control of mergers by the laws of the member states and the effect of the national policies upon concentration.

The fourth study, undertaken by the Commission's staff, sought to provide statistics relevant to the question whether the mergers currently taking place in the Community tended toward economy in production or toward monopolization.[59]

By June 1965, the Commission's attitude toward powerful enterprises, as expressed in a speech by one of its members to the European Parliament, was as follows:[60]

"For some commodities we can see not only the beginnings of a single European market but even of its development into a world market simply.

---

[59] Seventh General Report, para. 64; speech by J. J. A. Ellis in ABA Conference Proceedings, op. cit., pp. 111-112. The fourth study was mentioned by Mr. Ellis, but not in the report.

[60] Hans von der Groeben, Competition Policy as Part of Economic Policy in the Common Market, address to the European Parliament, June 16, 1965, pp. 12-13, 17-18.

Present economic structures in Europe are in many cases not yet adapted to this twofold reorientation of the world economy. Mergers are consequently to be welcomed where they are economically and technically necessary: where they increase productivity. Such improvements in economic potential strengthen the competitive position and consequently the resilience of amalgamated enterprises on the European and international planes.

"After careful study the Commission has concluded that it is impossible to generalize about the optimum size of firms. It depends on the nature of the product and the production process, on the size of the market and its structure. Nor does technical advance always necessitate increasing the size of firms; the economic optimum can often be achieved by various production processes and by firms of different sizes. But if we think of the firm as an economic and financial unit as well as a production unit, the advantages of a broader financial basis are obvious, especially as regards capital formation and research.

"So it is not a matter of indiscriminate combination; mergers may be desirable or undesirable. The Commission further agrees with industry that mergers should not result from artificial incentives, that obviously the problem is not equally acute in all branches, and that legal or psychological obstacles to economically desirable mergers should be removed.

"The Commission's policy for industrial growth therefore has three main objects. First, it must remove artificial obstacles to mergers that are economically desirable within the Common Market and thus ensure that Common Market firms can compete on world markets. Secondly it must try to eliminate artificial distortions of competition between large firms and medium-size and small firms. Thirdly it must ensure that competition remains effective. . . .

"I have spoken in favour of setting up firms on a European scale and consequently in favour of the great majority of practical cases of merging; I must now say just as definitely that there is a limit. Growth of enterprises: yes. Competition among big firms, if it is workable competition: yes. But monopoly, mergers that prevent competition from functioning and obstruct the freedom of choice and action of consumers, suppliers and buyers: no. To the extent that competition is unable to function, amalgamated firms gain unbridled market power. This can be used in many ways to obtain private business advantages without reducing economic costs or improving performance. Mergers are dubious from the competition policy angle when and in so far as they lead to an excess of market power, and here imports must be taken into account as well as competition within the common market. . . . .

"Article 86 is more important in this context. This prohibits only the abuse of dominant positions in the Common Market. Its application to industrial combines therefore has strict limits. For neither the existence nor the building up of dominant positions is forbidden as such. To what extent the acquisition of other enterprises by an enterprise in a dominant position constitutes abuse of its position within the meaning of Article 86 depends on the market situation in each individual case. But the more an enterprise in a dominant position approaches monopoly by merging with another enterprise and consequently endangers the freedom of action and choice of suppliers, buyers and consumers, the more probability there is that such a merger will constitute an abuse."

The same point of view was expressed in a memorandum by the Commission to member states in December 1965, and in the Commission's ninth general report in 1966.

Action grounded upon this policy prior to May, 1966, was designed to remove the obstacles to the growth of large enterprises, by merger or otherwise. On May 3, the Commission announced that it had submitted to the Council a memorandum as to methods of enabling companies from different member states to form larger units.[61] It said that adaptation to the wider market, to technical development, and to the requirements of modern research "means that many companies must increase in size" and that "amalgamations which increase productivity without impairing workable competition are therefore desirable." To this end it contemplated the possibility of a new intergovernmental agreement for the establishment of "European companies," not subject to the legal systems of the several member states and not having the nationality of a specific state. It proposed that a working party of experts be appointed to make the necessary preparatory studies.

In 1966 the Commission's ninth general report discussed the status of dominant enterprises under the treaty. It defined dominance as the possibility of exerting a substantial and foreseeable influence on the market; said that, since position in the Common Market was the relevant consideration, competition from imports must be considered, but that an enterprise not located within the Common Market might be dominant there; and mentioned price leadership in an oligopoly as an instance of dominance. In discussing abuse of dominant positions, it mentioned not only the types of abuse specified in the treaty, but also price competition designed to drive out weaker firms. Finally, it announced its conclusion that a merger that created a dominant position and thus jeopardized the freedom of action of suppliers, purchasers and users could be treated as an abuse under Article 86.[61a]

---

[61] Press Release, May 3, 1966, Memorandum on the establishment of European companies, IP (66) 47.

[61a] Ninth General Report, para. 70-77.

Action About Patents and Trademarks

Application of the Treaty. Certain important and numerous private agreements—those by which restrictions are imposed in licensing patents and trademarks—have an ambiguous status under the treaty. Whereas Article 85 forbids all agreements that restrict or distort competition in interstate trade unless they are exempted under the provisions of that Article, Article 222 provides that the treaty shall in no way prejudice the property systems of the member states. Property presumably includes patent and trademark rights; and in the member states the laws applicable to patents and trademarks authorize, to varying degrees, restriction in licenses of such property. In some countries a license may forbid the licensee to export.[62] Moreover, when an invention is patented in each member state and exclusive licenses under the six national patents are granted to different licensees, mere enforcement by each licensee of his rights under the relevant national patent can prevent the patent owner and the other five licensees from selling within his national territory. If patent agreements are not to be inconsistent wtih the creation of a Common Market, action to limit their potentially restrictive effects is necessary.

Though there is inherent conflict between national grants of monopoly under patent law and the effort to make trade international within the Common Market, the difficulties are enhanced by the fact that the patent laws of the member states differ so greatly that the differences are believed to be a major source of distortions of competition. Substantial reduction of these differences is thought to be imperative.

The Common Market's effort to cope with patent laws and patent licensing has taken two forms: action by the Commission to define the status of patent agreements under the treaty, and efforts to formulate an inter-governmental agreement about the scope of patent rights.

Thus far the effort at definition has been modest and has consisted in the announcement, mentioned above, that certain types of patent agreements are not subject to the prohibitions of Article 85. Though this announcement is a mere statement of the Commission's opinion, subject to revocation and not binding upon the courts, it provides, in practical effect, immunity under the treaty for certain types of significant restrictions that are common in licenses—exclusive licensing, allocation of lines of activity or of portions of a country to different licensees, restriction of the amount of

---

[62] German patent courts have long held that a license under a German patent may bind the licensee not to export. Until 1962 the German Federal Cartel Office interpreted similarly the exemption for patent licenses of the German cartel law, but then decided that such a restriction is covered, not by the patent exemption, but by the law's provisions about export agreements. See Walter Oppendorf, "Patents, Trademarks, and Know-How," in ABA Conference Proceedings, *op. cit.,* p. 135.

the licensed activity, exclusion of licensed distributors or users from manufacture, exclusion of licensed manufacturers from distribution, provisions binding licensee and licensor to grant reciprocal non-exclusive rights to improvements developed by them, and obligations for the licensee to obtain from the licensor such unpatented supplies as are technically necessary for effective use of the patent. Presumably these types of restriction were selected in the belief that any restrictive effect they may have upon trade is not likely to be international in scope. Though regarded as beyond control under the treaty, they remain subject to any limitation that may be imposed upon them by national law.[63]

The announcement provided no presumptive immunity for concerted restrictions by several patentees under patent pools, cross licensing arrangements, or multiple parallel licensing. Neither did it cover certain types of restriction that are common in licenses by single patentees—for example, price-fixing, obligations not to export nor to operate outside a single national market, non-reciprocal obligations to grant the licensor rights to improvements, obligations to grant such rights exclusively, obligations to grant rights under unrelated patents, obligations to use the licensor's trademark, and obligations to refrain from contesting the validity of the licensed patents. Thus important parts of the relation between the treaty and patent restrictions remain to be determined by later interpretations, decisions in particular cases, or a new intergovernmental agreement.

Development of a Common Market Patent Law. In 1965 the effort to develop an intergovernmental agreement about patent law was well under way. After considering the problem of "harmonizing" national laws, the Commission had decided several years before to draft an international agreement under which a single patent could be granted for the whole of the Common Market. Resistance to abandonment of the national patent laws was so strong that the effort to supersede them was soon abandoned. Instead, the proposal contemplated that applicants for patents would be enabled to obtain a Common Market patent as an alternative to national patents, in the hope that few applicants would seek national patents and the national patent laws would thus wither away. In 1962 a draft Patent Convention based upon this idea was made public[64] and became a subject of sustained controversy. Early in 1964 an ad hoc committee prepared a report on the various principles that might be invoked to meet the major

---

[63] French patent law, for example, provided that an unused patent may be subjected to compulsory non-exclusive licensing.

[64] Comité de Coordination en Matière de Proprieté Industrielle Institué par les États membres et la Commission de la Communité Économique Européene, Avant Projet de Convention relatif a un droit européen des brevets élaboré par le groupe de travail "brevets," 1962.

problems and the probable effects of resort to each. After considering this report in June, the Council asked the Commission for a further report on two points.[65] No agreement had been reached at the close of 1965.

Among the many problems raised by the draft convention, two are particularly significant in their implications for control of restrictive agreements. First, though the convention provides for patents valid throughout the Common Market, it is superimposed upon rather than substituted for the patent systems of the member countries. On the same invention, a patentee may not hold both a Common Market patent and a patent from a member state, but an inventor may choose either kind of patent and may revert to patents from member states if he fails to obtain a Common Market patent. Thus, though the proposal may avoid restrictions arising from disparity of patent laws where these restrictions are objectionable to would-be patentees, it leaves the opportunity for such restrictions open so far as they are favorable to the interests of patentees or are derived from undue leniency in the standards of some of the national laws. A still unresolved controversy exists as to whether nationals of states other than members of the Common Market shall be allowed to obtain patents under the new law. If they are excluded, the national laws will have further impetus, and an element of systematic discrimination will be introduced into the new international system.

Second, the proposed law does not entirely remove the possibility that patents can be used as instruments with which to erect barriers to trade between member states. An important purpose of the Convention is to remove the possibility that counterpart national patents upon the same invention can be used to allocate national territories by licensing or selling the different national patents to different enterprises. Nevertheless, the proposed Common Market patent could be licensed for all or part of the territory to which it applies (Article 29). The patentee could allocate the states of the Common Market to different licensees, and the Commission's interpretation of the bearing of patent law upon Article 85 has not made clear whether or not such allocation of licenses could be challenged as a restraint of trade. The draft Convention provides (Article 20a) that when a patented product has been sold no further right over it is derived from the patent, and (Article 29 sub-section 2) that such a sale shall terminate territorial limitations. But these provisions supply only a partial safeguard. They mean that distributors buying in one country can resell within the territory of another licensee; they do not mean that a licensee can do so. Presumably a French licensee could not sell to a German distributor in a German licensee's territory, though his French distributor could resell in

---

[65] Bulletin of the EEC, April 1964, page 24; August 1964, page 32.

that territory. With this limitation upon export to other countries, reservations of exclusive national markets would often be possible. Producers could integrate vertically, sell through agents, refrain from selling to distributors who export, or otherwise avoid sale to types of distributors who have the desire and the ability to invade another licensee's territory abroad.

Consideration of a Common Market Trademark. Trademark licenses raise problems somewhat similar to patent problems. By sharing the use of a trademark, firms may avoid competition. By allocating use, they may allocate markets. But since national trademark laws differ from patent laws about such matters as the right to import the legally relevant products, the legal protection given to restrictions in the two types of licenses is not everywhere the same. At the close of 1964 the Commission had not published clarifying interpretations about the status of trademark licenses under Article 85. It had begun, however, to formulate an intergovernmental agreement designed to create the possibility of a single Common Market trademark. A draft trademark convention had been prepared by a working party,[66] but had not yet been published.

Apparent Trends

Efforts in EEC to control restrictive activities by international means have involved problems relevant to three matters: a) the relation between private controversies and the treaty's public law; b) the boundary between activities that affect interstate trade and those that do not; c) the substantive scope of the treaty's prohibitions and provisions for exemption.

1. Problems as to the status of private controversies arise necessarily with any significant change in public law, whether the change occurs within a single country or by international treaty. So far as what has been lawful becomes unlawful, private contracts that were valid become invalid; and uncertainties of interpretation of the public law are reflected in uncertainties as to whether or not certain existing contracts are enforceable and whether or not parties who persist in observing them are law-breakers. The magnitude of the difficulties that arise depends upon the extent of the change in public law and the degree of uncertainty about that extent.

In the Common Market the difficulties have been great because the treaty forbids much that was permissible under the laws of the member states, and because the applicability of broad prohibitions, which themselves require interpretation, has been obscured by provisions for exemption that are similarly broad. In such a program it was inevitable that in deciding private controversies the national courts would need to consider whether or not the activities involved in the dispute were forbidden by the treaty, and

---

[66] Bulletin of the EEC, August 1964, pages 31-32.

that the answer to many such questions would remain uncertain until relevant decisions and interpretations had accumulated. There was also a danger that decisions by the various national courts would differ, thus impairing the effort to develop a common policy.

The possibility of substantive divergence in applying the prohibitions is minimized in the treaty by provisions that entrust interpretation to the Court.[67] The possibility of divergence in granting exemptions under Article 85 is minimized in Regulation 17 by establishing the Commission as the sole source of exemptions. The regulation also establishes the supremacy of action by the Commission over action by the authorities of the member states by providing that the national authorities may apply the prohibition of Article 85 so long as the Commission has not undertaken a proceeding to prohibit, exempt, or grant negative clearance.

These precautions, when taken together, have temporarily magnified the difficulties in adjudicating private controversies. Precluded from deciding that an agreement is exempt, national courts are unable to decide controversies in which a party claims that exemption should be granted; litigants can delay decision by making such claims; and there is danger that undecided lawsuits will accumulate while the Court struggles with an excessive load of cases. Moreover, the national cartel authorities, exposed to the possibility that their enforcement activities may be superseded, have an incentive to leave enforcement to the Commission, and thus a similar bottleneck tends to develop as to decisions and interpretations by which the scope of the prohibitions is defined. Since applications for exemption or negative clearance have been filed with the Commission for many thousands of agreements, the difficulties are pervasive.

Nevertheless, the problem will shrink greatly with time. By interpretations that have the effect of blanket negative clearances, by blanket exemptions now that authority to make them has been granted, and by decisions in well-chosen cases, the bearing of the treaty upon most of the less complicated restrictive arrangements is likely to become clear in a relatively short time. As this occurs, the ability of national courts to decide private controversies will be correspondingly enlarged, the burdens that these courts have thrown upon the Common Market Court will decline, the field in which national authorities can safely enforce the treaty's prohibitions will grow, and the Commission will be increasingly able to concentrate upon prohibiting restrictions so broad that single countries cannot cope with them and granting

---

[67] Articles 169-177 authorize appeal to the Court from actions by the Commission, the Council, and the member states; empower courts in the member states to ask the Court to interpret the treaty; and require the courts of last resort in the member states to refer to the Court such questions of interpretation of the treaty as arise in litigation before them.

exemptions in cases too complicated for blanket action. As the law becomes relatively clear, the problem of taking account of it in formulating private agreements and deciding private controversies is likely to shrink to a size comparable to that encountered in the United States in accommodating private contracts to the requirements of the Sherman Act and in keeping state court decisions in private suits consistent with that act.

2. Unlike the problems as to private controversy, the problem as to the boundary between activities that do and do not affect interstate trade is likely to persist and even grow greater. The national markets of the member states are being merged by successive steps in tariff reduction, reduction or elimination of trade barriers contained in assorted national laws, and ventures in the "harmonization" of many kinds of regulatory procedures and standards. As a Common Market progressively replaces the separate national markets, the scope of possibilities for interstate trade increases, and more of what at first had only national effects comes to have international effects also. Moreover, as economic life becomes increasingly interconnected, the scope of interconnected effects is almost certain to grow. Therefore the conception of activities that affect trade among the member states is likely to evolve in a way similar to interpretations of the scope of the commerce clause of the American Constitution, toward inclusion of an increasing part of all economic activity. So far as national and international policies toward cartels and dominant firms remain inconsistent with one another, problems analagous to American problems about the limits of the commerce clause will continue to be significant and international policy probably will cover an increasing part of business activity.

3. Problems as to the substantive scope of prohibitions and exemptions present the greatest difficulties. The underlying national laws and the attitudes expressed in them have afforded little basis for a common policy.

These national laws differ in concept, substance, and procedure. Germany prohibits restrictive agreements, but with numerous exceptions; France seeks to distinguish between good and bad cartels; the Netherlands professes neutrality toward cartelization, and may condemn, modify, or foster particular cartels. Belgium undertakes to prevent abuse of economic power. Italy and Luxembourg have not enacted relevant national laws. In greater detail, Germany prohibits horizontal cartels, subject to numerous types of statutory or discretionary exemption; authorizes prohibition of vertical cartels for cause; permits resale price contracts by individual suppliers; curbs abuses by monopolies through corrective orders; and uses legal proceedings as its means of action. France evaluates cartels and restrictions by dominant firms case by case by administrative procedures under statutory standards, and applies correctives to those it thinks undesirable; but forbids price-fixing, resale price maintenance, refusal to sell, and discrimination. The Netherlands grants unlimited discretion to a cabinet minister to prohibit cartels, revise their agreements, or impose their restrictions upon non-members, as his conception of the public interest suggests; and grants him broad discretion to issue corrective orders against abuses by dominant firms. Belgium uses administrative procedures to issue corrective recommendations to cartels or firms that abuse their economic power. In Germany the national policy is applied through public proceedings and results in published decisions; in France by secret proceedings, summaries of which are eventually published; in the Netherlands by secret proceedings that result in little eventual public disclosure; and in Belgium, in almost complete secrecy.

The most striking feature of the restrictive practice provisions of the treaty and the applicable regulations under it is the fact that, taken as a whole, they constitute a program for the maintenance of competition more ambitious than that of any of the member states. They invoke prohibitions more ambitious than those of the two states that use prohibition domestically. They provide for exemptions narrower in scope and surrounded by greater safeguards than those of the national laws. They entrust less discretion to officials than in the national laws. They provide for more publicity than any of the national laws except that of Germany.

Much of the difference is due to the scope of the activity undertaken. Statutes that invoke vague standards, entrust wide discretion to officials, and provide few procedural safeguards are tolerable only in relatively small and homogeneous states, in which officials are known and trusted and their ideas are familiar. To entrust similar discretion to international officials, of whom a majority come from other states, would not be acceptable. Hence those who framed the treaty and those who have subsequently begun to apply it have needed to define what is prohibited and permitted and, so far as they could not do so clearly, to establish standards and procedures under which it shall be done. Because their problems resemble those of a large diversified country like the United States, their solutions have been nearer to the American solutions than to those used in the member countries.

Moreover, the scope of the effort has tended to make Common Market policy more competitive than the policies of the constituent states. The anticompetitive features of the policies of small states reflect in part the desire of governments to preserve the interests of citizens who have few alternative opportunities. Given the area, population, and diverse resources of the Common Market, opportunities proliferate, and the desire of governments to preserve vested interests diminishes correspondingly. Many interest groups that are strong enough to influence a national state are likely to be too weak to influence the entire Community. Their resistance to a policy that represses their restrictions is weakened by the fact that in the larger market there is considerable chance that this policy serves them by repressing the restrictions of others. Thus Common Market policy toward restrictions tends to be stronger than that of the member states for reasons similar to those that, in the United States, have made Federal antitrust policy more vigorous than state antitrust policy and have induced American business to accept the Federal policy most readily at the times when it was most vigorously and comprehensively applied.

Chapter XVII

Possibilities and Problems of International Collaboration

The Unsolved Problem. Though ECSC has had limited success and EEC has begun with great promise, one cannot yet tell how adequately the Communities will be able to cope with the problem of restrictive business practices that affect trade among their member states. If they do so successfully, however, they may have mitigated, but will not have solved, the broader international problems that were discussed in the opening pages of Chapter XV. International control within the Communities cannot reach restrictions upon imports into the Common Market that are imposed by cartels or monopolies in non-member countries. When restrictive decisions are made and records are kept outside the Communities by a cartel or an international corporate combine that operates within the Common Market, the Communities will encounter difficulties akin to those that have been met by the United States in obtaining information and applying orders. Countries such as the United States that are not members of EEC or ECSC will remain under serious handicap in their efforts to protect their domestic markets from restrictions that are imposed from abroad, whether by firms in other non-member countries or by firms in the Communities that apply restriction only to areas outside the Common Market or only to exports from it.

In some respects success in the Communities' restrictive practice programs is likely to reduce such problems. The field for some kinds of international cartelization and for some kinds of restriction by internationally powerful single enterprises, already substantially narrowed by domestic legislation in twenty-four countries that include all the great industrial ones of the free world, has been further narrowed by strong legislation, international in scope, in the heart of Europe. An EEC system for registering agreements and an ECSC requirement for prior approval of them increase the likelihood that important cartels will be discovered. Community control, in addition to national control in twenty-four countries, diminishes the chance that an important international cartel or combine can engage in significant restrictions without creating impermissible domestic effects in a country in which it operates or in which it has established a safehaven.

321

But Community control has an important gap, like that of the laws of the United States and of others who seek to curb restrictive practices. It does not attempt to prevent restrictions on exports from the Community or restrictions applied by Community firms in non-member countries. The possibility remains open, in the Communities as elsewhere, that firms may restrict their foreign trade provided they are careful to deprive their practices of restrictive impacts within the Common Market. The damage that business in the Communities could thereby inflict upon other countries is greater than before EEC was established, because tendencies toward industrial concentration have developed within EEC and because, for this and other reasons, the Community's firms can maintain a common front in their exports to non-member countries more easily than before. (Coal and steel are exceptions, because in these industries the concentration movement has not restored the degree of concentration that prevailed earlier.) In the Scandinavian countries and in Ireland, lively apprehensions about such potentialities have been expressed, supported by accounts of a few illustrative examples of export cartelization.

A significant and probably representative example of the effect of Community action in limiting restrictions elsewhere, yet leaving opportunity for such restrictions, is supplied by the impact of ECSC upon export activities in steel. By depriving the steel industry of comprehensive cartelization within the Community, ECSC has thwarted the industry's post-war efforts to agree upon export quotas, even though the High Authority's control of restriction does not cover such quotas. Nevertheless, the freedom to restrict that the Common Market's steel companies enjoy in export trade has enabled them to join with British firms and others in an agreement about the level of export prices and to manage this agreement from Brussels.[1] Neither Community law nor British law has prevented this. The international steel cartel is obviously weaker than before the war;[2] but in weaker form, it persists.

National laws and regional collaboration can, at best, alleviate but not remove the difficulty of repressing restrictions that are imposed upon domestic markets by foreign multi-national restrictions of trade. Such curbs can reach only a part of the relevant activity. Therefore there is a continuing reason for governments that desire to curb restriction to explore the possibility of wider international collaboration. The purpose of this chapter is to discuss that possibility.

---

[1] See Corwin D. Edwards, Cartelization in Western Europe, op. cit., p. 27.

[2] For accounts of the international steel cartel as it operated before the second world war, see International Chamber of Commerce, Trade Barriers Committee, Report on International Industrial Ententes, by M. Roger Conte, Paris, 1927, pp. 42-55; International Chamber of Commerce, International Ententes, Paris, 1937, pp. 39-55; Ervin Hexner, International Cartels, Chapel Hill, North Carolina, 1945, pp. 203-216.

The experience of EEC and ECSC throws some light upon the matter. So does the experience of the United States in applying the Federal anti-trust laws throughout a country of continental dimensions, in distinguishing interstate from intrastate commerce, and in relating Federal legislation to that of the states.

The Case for Global Action

The first question relevant to any project for international collaboration is whether it should be global or regional in scope. The proposals in the draft I.T.O. charter and in the report of the ad hoc committee of Ecosoc were global; they contemplated participation from the beginning by as many countries as were willing to take part and subsequent admission of any late-comers. The draft proposal by the Council of Europe contemplated a European regional agreement. The arrangements actually established by EFTA, ECSC, and EEC were set up by groups of seven and six states, respectively, and though more states have become affiliated with EEC, negotiation has fixed in each instance the terms of affiliation.

The case for collaboration on a global scale is strong in two respects. First, in anything less, restrictive relationships between business in the collaborating countries and business in the rest of the world will remain beyond control in respects analogous to those that are now evident as to relationships between EEC or ECSC and non-member countries. The more comprehensive the collaboration, the less important such uncontrolled restrictions are likely to become.

Second, it is to be expected that enlargment of the area covered by curbs upon business restriction will reduce the incentives to restrict. In a small community opportunities and alternatives are few; people cling to what they have; and vested interests can exert substantial influence. As the community grows larger, opportunities expand; parties to a restriction have more to gain from a general removal of restrictions; they therefore are likely to cling to their own restrictions less tenaciously; and those that do so are more likely to find their influence submerged in the cross-currents of opinion and interest of an increasingly complex society.

These inferences are confirmed by the available experience. In the United States, Federal policy has been generally more competitive than that of the states and has expressed itself in stronger legislation, more consistently and vigorously applied. The policies of EEC against restriction are expressed in a law that is substantially stronger than those of the member states; and EEC's initial actions indicate that it probably will use the discretion it enjoys to repress restriction more vigorously than do the authorities of any member state except, perhaps, Germany. In EEC, which covers the whole gamut of trade other than steel and coal, vested interests have been thus far less able to blunt the edge of official policy than in the more narrowly specialized ECSC. Yet even in ECSC the public policy of the Community toward coal and steel has been less favorable to business restriction than that previously applied or currently advocated by the most powerful of the member states.

It is reasonable to assume, therefore, that as control of restriction covers a broader range of industry and a broader geographic area, it will be more ambitiously conceived and more vigorously applied, and will leave fewer significant problems untouched.

The Case for Regional Action

The case for collaboration on a regional scale is also strong. Its focus is the obvious fact that difficulties in collaborating effectually become more formidable as the scale of collaboration grows. Some such difficulties are evident in the experience of the United States and the European Communities. Others would clearly arise if an effort were made to extend collaboration like that of EEC to include countries less contiguous and less homogeneous than EEC's member states. The obstacles to effective collaboration consist in differences among countries in experience, in the nature of the restrictions that must be overcome, and in the methods of overcoming restrictions that are consistent with national institutions and traditions.

Experience. Differences in experience have been sources of difficulty in EEC. Whereas laws to curb restriction had national roots in France, Germany, and the Netherlands, repressive legislation had not existed in Belgium, Italy, and Luxembourg prior to EEC, and in 1965 still did not exist in the latter two countries. Belgium and the Netherlands had experimented during the depression with mandatory cartelization, and Italy and Germany with Fascist or Nazi forms of state control. There has been visible difference in the degree of sophistication and in the preconceptions of the six countries, and of EEC personnel drawn from them, in coping with the restrictive practice problems of the Common Market. But in all six countries there are similar types of business enterprise, constituting parts of similarly oriented industrial economies and having similar incentives to engage in similar types of practices. Under national policies the governments of a majority of the participating countries have had experience with public efforts to modify restrictive business practices; and the rest are at least familiar with the nature and setting of such practices. The impact of inexperience would be much greater in a collaborative effort large enough to include countries at substantially different stages of economic development, with business activity organized in substantially different ways, and with business practices that are also different. Such countries have rarely undertaken domestic control of restriction; and if they should try to collaborate wtih industrial countries in doing so, most of them would not be likely to understand the matters appropriate for control or to know how to undertake the task:

Restrictions to be Overcome. Differences in restrictions that need attention are prevalent even among countries as generally similar as those in EEC and ECSC. Business that is done in one country by an unregulated private firm is done in a second by a regulated one and in a third by a state-owned enterprise. Restrictions applied by a cartel in one country are applied by a monopoly in a second and by national law in a third. The interaction between public and private restrictions and between private restrictions and public regulation of them differs from country to country. So does the degree of competitive advantage afforded to national enterprises over foreign ones by subsidies, trade barrier laws, and other kinds of public intervention. An international program of collaboration must be so formulated that it does not leave untouched the kind of restriction that prevails in one country while repressing a different kind of restriction by which the same restrictive purpose is achieved in another country.

This necessity has been repeatedly recognized. The ITO charter undertook to curb restrictive business practices and restrictive commercial policies simultaneously. The weak restrictive practice policies of GATT and EFTA provide recourse against business restrictions that are inconsistent with the agreements about commercial policy. The restrictive practice provisions of ECSC stand alongside the commercial policy provisions as joint means to achieve the treaty's purposes. EEC has consistently emphasized the need to apply harmoniously all of its means of liberating trade from restrictions both private and public; and, indeed, contemplates the harmonization of national laws to a greater extent than has ever been considered essential for state laws in the United States. In the ITO draft charter and in the proposal by Ecosoc's ad hoc committee, restrictions by private and public commercial enterprises and restrictions by both cartels and powerful single enterprises were to be subject to the same curbs. In ECSC, control of cartels is accompanied by control of mergers and of abuses by dominant firms. EEC's provisions about cartels and dominant firms were obviously designed to be similar; and EEC is sponsoring studies of the interaction of the two.

The broader the area of collaboration, the greater must be the difficulty of applying comparable control to related types of restriction. To do so is hard when the discrepancies in forms of restriction from country to country are confined to a few particular industries or reflect minor differences of organization and policy among countries in which governments seek substantively similar ends by generally similar means. The task is likely to be insuperable when there is a conflict of purposes—when, for example, control of business restrictions is undertaken by countries that deliberately use national power to support their own citizens in economic warfare against citizens of other states. The application of American antitrust policy is simplified by the fact that within the United States people, enterprises, goods, and funds can move freely from state to state. EEC regards similar freedom of movement as the indispensable condition for a Common Market. Nobody has yet seriously proposed or undertaken international collaboration for control of business restrictions in a setting in which tariffs and other forms of public restriction continue to be used as important alternative means to benefit one collaborating state at the expense of another. Such an undertaking would be impracticable. Development of a common policy toward cartels and monopolies is possible, if at all, only within a free trade area or in a setting in which public and private restrictions are reduced to a roughly comparable extent.

Conflict of purpose about the place that private enterprise should occupy in an economy is also a major obstacle to collaboration. Curbs upon cartels and monopolies cannot be simultaneously designed to make business more competitive and to make it an instrument of the state. There is no prospect that international collaboration against cartels and monopolies will be undertaken jointly by communist and capitalist countries. Such collaboration would be handicapped if it were attempted by countries that differ markedly from one another in the degree of their reliance upon state trading, state operation of productive enterprise, or state guidance of the private economy.

Methods of action. Effective collaboration requires agreement about the way that restrictions should be controlled. Such agreement is difficult to reach if the countries involved have different conceptions of the proper functions of officials, courts, and legislative bodies; the nature of due process of law in the protection of private rights; the appropriate uses of corrective and punitive sanctions; the degree of publicity to be given to governmental regulatory activities; the extent of acceptable concentrations of public and private power; and the relative importance of equality, order, opportunity, and well-being. National attitudes toward such matters are expressed in political, legal and economic institutions that evolve through time. At any moment they constitute a cultural matrix that shapes and limits action. Nations in which they differ greatly cannot easily act together. Though the six countries that formed EEC have a common European inheritance expressed in similar legal, political, and economic institutions, the differences in their procedural norms have been obstacles in interpreting and applying their common policy. Similar obstacles would be much greater in any effort at collaboration that included states not dedicated, as are all of the six, to the rule of law and to democratic political processes.

In the light of the difficulties that have been summarized above, international collaboration to control restrictive business practices cannot be global. It cannot succeed if it includes countries that are widely divergent in their legal and political systems or in the place that they give to private enterprise. It cannot succeed if it undertakes a program that is markedly inconsistent with the commercial policies of the participating states. It cannot succeed if the participating states do not have a substantial degree of common experience as to the nature of business enterprises and of business practices. If it includes any substantial number of states that are without experience in domestic control of restrictive business practices, it must be seriously handicapped. Comprehensive collaboration, such as was contemplated by those who drafted the ITO charter and the ad hoc committee's report, is not now practicable.

But the possibilities for collaboration reach beyond the Common Market. The European cultural and institutional inheritance of the states that organized EFTA and EEC is common to them and to the other parts of Europe west of the Iron Curtain. Though not identical, the inheritance of North America is similar. On both sides of the Atlantic, these countries have comparable experience with similar types of economy, comparable mixtures of private and public economic activity, and comparable attitudes toward the role of the market and of private enterprise. Nearly all of them are engaged in similar efforts to reduce governmental barriers to trade. Nearly all of them have had some experience with domestic control of restrictive practices. Though their national differences are numerous and important, they are comparable to those that existed among the Common Market countries when EEC was established.

The field in which further development of international collaboration can be appropriately considered at this time centers in Western Europe and North America. Whatever effort is now made to enlarge the area of collaboration should be concerned with this area. There are, of course, a few countries elsewhere that are, or have prospect of soon becoming, comparable to those of Europe and North America in experience, economic development, and political and legal institutions. Efforts at broader international cooperation about restrictive practices should take account of them, and any project that does not include them should make room for their subsequent inclusion.

The Possible Scope of Regional Action

Four possibilities can be envisaged as to the form of broader cooperation among the countries of Western Europe and North America: a) a comprehensive treaty, which, like the draft ITO charter and the Treaty of Rome, would cover not only restrictive business practices but also related public restrictions and commercial policies and would be applied by an international organization; b) a specialized treaty, which, like that proposed in Ecosoc, would be concerned comprehensively with restrictive business practices but only with them, would be formulated in the light of other international agreements, and would be applied by an international organization; c) a selective treaty, which would be limited to those aspects of restrictive business practices about which there is substantial agreement among developed countries, would be applied by an international organization, and would provide a possibility to enlarge the scope of the commitment as experience brought wider agreement; d) *ad hoc* arrangements, worked out by treaty, executive agreement, or informal means, for cooperation by national authorities concerned with restrictive business practices, without the establishment of any international administrative body.

1. *A Comprehensive Treaty.* When ITO was under discussion, no significant global or regional body existed to perform any important part of its proposed trade-liberalizing functions, and few nations had undertaken domestic control of cartels or monopolies. Now the situation has changed. Liberalization of commercial policy has been undertaken by GATT; and significant beginnings of regional control of cartels and monopolies have been coupled with ambitious programs to liberalize commercial policy in EEC and ECSC. Whatever is done to enlarge the scope of international action about restrictive business practices must be consistent with these activities.

A North Atlantic equivalent of ITO is no longer possible. It would have to be sandwiched between GATT, which is larger, and EEC and EFTA, which are smaller; and it would contain key members of each of these existing bodies. If it limited itself to commercial policy and the control of restrictive business practices, its duplicate activities in the field of commercial policy would be meaningless. If it undertook a more ambitious program, it would be, from the point of view of EEC's member countries, a burdensome duplication of effort.

Neither can a comprehensive treaty be created by modifying GATT. The effort to add significant control of restrictive business practices to GATT was persistent but unsuccessful. The considerations that explain its failure are still valid, and make renewal of the effort undesirable: a) The procedures of GATT, suited to intergovernmental negotiation, are not suited to control of private restrictions. b) The membership of GATT is so broad that an undertaking by it to control restrictive business practices would be handicapped by many of the difficulties discussed above.

There is also no substantial chance that North Atlantic cooperation about restrictive business practices could evolve from an expansion of EEC. The plan of EEC is such that additional countries can become affiliated. Some have done so; and in spite of temporary obstacles, there is a significant possibility that by this means non-Communist Europe may be brought into comprehensive collaboration as to restrictive practice policy and commercial policy. However, the scope and intimacy of collaboration in EEC were planned to provide an economic basis for eventual political federation. The eventual diversity that is envisaged in the national laws and policies of the participating states is less than, from an American point of view, is probably appropriate, even in such a federation. There is no prospect of political unification of North America with Western Europe, nor of such an ambitious economic unification as EEC has undertaken. Affiliation with EEC is therefore an unpromising means to bring about cooperation on a North Atlantic scale as to cartels and monopolies.

The most that seems possible along these lines is either the expansion of EEC to cover more of Europe or the creation, alongside EEC, of other international bodies that include control of restrictive business practices in a comprehensive collaboration. EFTA might develop a more ambitious program of which control of such restrictions was a part; and European countries not now part of EEC or EFTA might join one or the other or form a third international community. To believe that the United States and Canada might undertake a similar comprehensive collaboration strains credulity. But even if three or four such regional bodies covered all of Western Europe and North America, the problems now evident in efforts to curb international business restrictions within the area would not end. They would merely be transformed into problems about the relation of policy in one community to restrictions in another.

2. *A Specialized Treaty.* A North Atlantic treaty limited to comprehensive joint action against international business restrictions would escape most of these difficulties, but probably is not now practicable. The existence of regional programs in EEC and ECSC would not be an insuperable obstacle; a broader program would necessarily take account of them as well as of the programs of the national states.

Two major difficulties, however, would be likely to defeat an effort along these lines. The first is that sweeping international control of cartels and monopolies has been shown by the experience of EEC and ECSC to require significant degrees of international control of some aspects of domestic policy in other fields than antitrust, though not, perhaps, control as extensive and ambitious as EEC is undertaking. Particularly, broad international antitrust action is likely to necessitate significant amounts of international action about state trading, state grants of monopoly, the law of industrial property, and company law.

The second major difficulty is that there are still important differences of opinion between Western Europe and the United States about policy toward restrictive practices. The original differences have diminished as experience with different types of national control has become available. They have diminished further during the development of EEC's restrictive practice program. It has become evident that international action must be, in important respects, more like that of the United States than like previous European national action: The broad discretion entrusted by some national states to their officials will not be entrusted to international bodies; international policy necessarily takes form in prohibitions and exemptions, not in regulatory control; clearly formulated standards that can be invoked to develop intelligible precedents must govern international action; and therefore the character of decisions must be judicial or quasi-judicial rather than administrative. Nevertheless, important differences remain: Western Europe is disposed to permit types of restrictive agreement that are regarded as clearly objectionable in the United States. The United States is disposed to permit refusals to sell by single enterprises that are regarded as objectionable in Western Europe. The United States regards horizontal restrictive agreements as more dangerous than vertical one, whereas most of Western Europe does the opposite. The United States is disposed to prevent excessive concentration by curbing mergers and terminating monopolies, whereas Western Europe is disposed to accept concentrated business and control its behavior. Until differences such as these are substantially reduced, joint action about the whole sweep of international restriction is not possible.

3. *A Selective Treaty.* If a new treaty is to broaden the scope of action about international restriction, therefore, it must be selective. It must not attempt to cover those parts of policy toward restrictive practices as to which there is no consensus, nor those parts that cannot be applied without corollary control of matters other than restrictive business practices. Such a fragmentary treaty might cope with particular kinds of restriction and might afford experience with collaborative action out of which further agreement and further collaboration could grow.

The crucial question in considering an attempt to negotiate such a treaty is whether or not a reasonable degree of agreement can now be attained about any significant and segregable kinds of international restriction. Such agreement is possible in some important fields.

a) Agreement should be possible to take action against concerted efforts to exclude business enterprises from markets. Belief that any qualified enterprise should be free to engage in such fields of business as it chooses to enter is strong in Western Europe, as it is in the United States. Concerted efforts to exclude new enterprises or new types of enterprise are consistently condemned. Though some European countries invoke tests of training, experience, or resources to weed out firms they think are not qualified, this is normally done by public laws that apply modest standards of qualification; and most countries are careful to prevent private groups from applying harsher standards that they think unreasonable. Only two of the countries tolerate punitive boycotts, and they do so only when they approve the underlying purpose. European rules about exclusion are often more severe than those of the United States in that they are applied not only to exclusion by agreement but also to activities by single firms, some of which would be lawful in this country. The difficulty of formulating a rule against exclusionary agreements in North Atlantic trade should be no greater than that of formulating a generally applicable rule within EEC.

b) A limited agreement is probably also possible about the activities of export cartels. Most importing countries encounter instances in which significant parts of the national supply of particular goods are derived from imports controlled by an export cartel operating from other countries. In such instances, the importing country has a direct interest in curbing restrictions by the cartel. However, the importing country cannot reach those who apply the restriction, and the exporting country has no interest in curbing their activities. Since each country exports some goods and imports others, the result is likely to be that each country's interests are hurt where it cannot take corrective action. So long as action is national, such restrictive activities will not be curbed. Yet where economic life is diversified and international trade is important, as in the North Atlantic countries, it is possible, and indeed probable, that the economy of every country would gain more by eliminating cartel restrictions on its imports than it would lose by eliminating such restrictions on its exports. An effort to determine the extent to which this is true would be likely to identify instances numerous and important enough to justify an agreement under which, as in the case of tariffs under the Reciprocal Trade Agreements Act, the participating countries reciprocally terminate particular restrictions by export cartels on a case-by-case basis, to the advantage of all participants.[3]

---

[3] Cf. Corwin D. Edwards, *Cartelization in Western Europe*, op. cit., pp. 92-94.

c) It should also be possible to include in such an agreement provisions designed to reenforce the commercial policy agreements to which the participating countries are parties. The possibility that private barriers to trade may frustrate the benefits of the reduction of public ones is recognized in GATT, EEC, and ECSC. In GATT, however, the consultative procedure established in 1960 is not suited to the problem and has not been used. Those of the contracting parties to GATT that might become participants in a selective agreement about restrictive practices could provide in the new agreement appropriate investigative and corrective procedures, to be available as a substitute for consultation under the GATT when one participant in the new agreement believed that restrictive practices within the territory of another such participant nullified the benefits of GATT.

A selective agreement, initially limited to the kind of subject matter mentioned above, would be a significant achievement. The rule against collective exclusion would strike at the kind of cartel activity in one country that is most likely to injure activities abroad by the enterprises of another. Reciprocal termination of export restrictions on a case-by-case basis could eliminate many of the restrictions most oppressive to importing countries. Corrective action against private restrictions that are inconsistent with the obligations of GATT would impede activities that reduce the benefits expected from existing commitments for liberalization of trade, and would provide experience as to the feasibility of international action against types of restrictive practice not otherwise subject to the selective agreement.

A selective agreement of the scope suggested above would not, like one covering the whole restrictive practice field, necessitate agreement about matters other than restrictive business practices. To stop private concerted exclusion of foreign enterprises does not require governments to agree upon the degree to which their public policies shall permit such enterprises to operate; it merely means that decisions about exclusion of the foreigner must be governmental and thus subject to diplomatic procedures. To negotiate the reciprocal elimination of restrictive practices by designated export cartels need not affect the policies of the participating governments as to business activity in their respective domestic markets; and if instances should appear in which private export restrictions were accompanied by governmental aid to exporters, the connection could be disentangled by negotiation or, failing that, the particular case could be treated as one not suitable for action. To reenforce an agreement on commercial policy by preventing private activities that negate its effects is to bring cartel policy and other aspects of public policy into greater harmony, not to create discrepancies between cartel policy and other policies such as might necessitate further agreement. Unlike some parts of public policy toward cartels and monopolies, these parts could become a basis for agreement among the countries of the North Atlantic without need for further action to prevent significant discriminatory impacts upon the economies of the participating countries.

If such a selective agreement were successful, it might eventually be broadened to cover other types of problems. Among those most appropriate for priority of attention are (a) the problem of the international cartel or international enterprise that operates so widely that no country acting alone can obtain reliable information about its restrictive activities or apply adequate correctives to them; (b) the problem of the safehaven cartel, that is, the cartel that makes and administers its agreements and keeps its records in a country where laws are lax, even though the participants in the cartel do little or no business in that country.[4]

4. *Ad Hoc Collaboration.* International cooperation might be increased in more modest ad hoc ways without waiting for a selective international agreement. An expert committee on cartels, composed of representatives of those countries in the Organization for Economic Cooperation and Development that apply or are considering the application of national policies toward restrictive business practices, has met twice yearly for about ten years as a means of exchanging information and ideas about such policies; and representatives of the two European Communities participate in the work of this committee. The committee is currently sponsoring a study designed to determine to what extent restrictive business practices have harmful effects upon international trade. If the study results in agreement about this matter, much will have been done to provide a basis for concerted policies.

Various forms of administrative collaboration might reduce the difficulties of coping with international restrictions. Some of these measures are possible under existing national laws; some would require new national legislation; and some might require limited intergovernmental agreements. All of them, however, would be means to enable national authorities to act more effectively, without need to invoke internationally agreed substantive law nor to have recourse to an international body. Most obvious among these types of collaboration would be action to make more information available about restrictions that have international significance. Not all countries that require cartels to report make the reports available to the public. EEC does not do so. Few countries require reporting by export cartels, and most such reports are not made public. The reports that are included in national public registers are not systematically studied by officials of other countries

---

[4] *Ibid.,* pp. 94-96.

to determine whether or not they throw light on restrictions elsewhere. If the existing systems of reporting were amplified to cover export restrictions and restrictions in foreign countries, if the national reports were regularly compared, and if the information they contained were made available to other governments, information about international restrictions would be greatly improved. Apart from the varying attitudes of different countries about disclosure of business information, particularly in export trade, an obvious obstacle to such collaboration is the fact that several important countries do not require reporting. Nevertheless, there are unused possibilities of exchanging information among countries that take reporting for granted.

So far as countries can agree that particular kinds of restriction are harmful to international trade or that national sources of information about them are characteristically inadequate, it might be possible for them to agree upon mutual aid in investigating such restrictions. Such an agreement might conceivably provide for (a) repatriation of fugitive documents, after a prime facie showing that records needed in one country's investigation had been transferred to another country to evade scrutiny; (b) elimination of existing statutory or administrative obstacles to compliance with the investigatory requests of foreign governments; (c) exchange of evidence obtained by different governments in investigating related matters; (d) investigation of particular matters at another government's request. Change in national policy or national law would be necessary in some countries in undertaking such an agreement. In the United States, for example, the limitations applicable to information obtained by a grand jury under subpoena preclude disclosure of the resulting information except during legal proceedings that result. In the Netherlands official policy is expressed in a law that forbids enterprises to supply information in response to foreign judicial process without prior government consent, which is frequently withheld. In particular proceedings, the British government has issued orders forbidding similar disclosures in compliance with foreign official demands. As reciprocal needs for information develop, such policies may change, and laws may be altered.

Similarly, something might be done to increase the effectiveness of national corrective orders by consultations among affected governments before one government issues an order that has consequences in the territory of another; and agreement might be sought that, within stated limits, the authorities of one participating country will give recognition to corrective orders issued by the authorities of another.

Cooperation of such kinds is unlikely to be easy. The substantive and procedural problems that must be faced in seeking it are similar to, though less than, those involved in a more ambitious international agreement. In two respects, however, such cooperation may be possible when a more comprehensive agreement is not. First, it can be worked out in bits and pieces, in negotiations with particular governments about particular administrative activities; there is no need to agree simultaneously about everything with everyone. Second, since the establishment of an international agency is not necessary to such cooperation, the problems associated with the interaction of international law and national law or of international authorities with national authorities need not arise. Departures from existing laws and policies would be procedural rather than substantive, and would be less ambitious. Hence they probably are less difficult.

APPENDICES

The Post-War Evolution of the National Laws

Apart from laws under military occupation, laws intended to be temporary, and minor amendments, the postwar legislation outside North America is summarized below.[1] Countries are listed in the order in which the first enduring postwar laws were adopted:

Sweden: 1946, restrictive agreements subjected to registration and to possible investigation. 1953, resale price maintenance and bidding agreements forbidden; restrictive agreements and restrictive activities by dominant firms subjected to registration and to negotiations designed to remove harmful effects. 1956, negotiations extended to cover other kinds of restrictive activities; king given power to fix maximum prices if negotiations fail.

Argentina: 1946, agreements and mergers to establish or maintain monopoly forbidden; monopolistic acts defined to include acts hampering free competition, acts preventing fair competitive prices, acts limiting production, agreements to allocate markets, tying agreements, and resale price maintenance except on trademarked or patented articles.[2]

United Kingdom: 1948, commission established to investigate monopolies and restrictive agreements; government given remedial powers. 1956, restrictive agreements subjected to registration and made void if not proved to be beneficial to the public; collective resale price maintenance forbidden, individual resale price maintenance authorized; 1964 individual resale price maintenance forbidden, with provision for exemptions;[3] 1965, large mergers subjected to control; divestiture, divorcement and dissolution authorized; corrective orders against discrimination authorized.[4]

---

[1] For countries that are members of the Organization for Economic Cooperation and Development, the statutes now in effect are available in English in OECD, Guide to Legislation on Restrictive Business Practices. For other countries, so far as they are not covered in my Trade Regulation Overseas, references to the laws are given at appropriate points.

[2] Act to Provide Heavy Penalties for Acts tending to the Establishment of Monopolies, No. 12906 of December 30, 1946.

[3] Resale Prices Act, 1964.

[4] Monopolies and Mergers Act, 1965.

Denmark: 1949, a commission established to investigate and report (but abolished in 1959). 1955, restrictive agreements and dominant enterprises subjected to registration and to corrective orders; enforcement of resale price agreements forbidden unless specially approved. 1957, permanent status given to a temporary requirement that price increases by registered enterprises must receive advance approval. 1963, power to investigate and to issue corrective orders strengthened; law extended to cover situations in which competition is weak even though monopoly and restrictive agreement are absent.

Austria: 1951, cartels required to obtain approval and be registered. 1958, requirement extended to cover informal agreements that are supported by pressure; conditions for approval tightened. 1962, conditions for approval further tightened; registration of dominant firms required.

France: 1953, refusal to sell, discrimination, and agreements to fix minimum prices forbidden; restrictive agreements that maintain prices or costs forbidden unless they extend markets or foster economic progress. 1963, restrictive activities by dominant firms given a status like that of agreements.

Ireland: 1953, a commission established to formulate fair trading rules and to investigate restrictions; a minister empowered to issue corrective orders. 1958, minister's power enlarged to include the right to set maximum prices to curb restrictions. 1959, refusal to use specified materials or methods subjected to possible investigation.

Japan: 1953, law inherited from military occupation substantially weakened, but private monopolization, concerted restrictions, and unfair practices still forbidden; rationalization agreements, agreements to cope with depression, and approved resale price agreements exempted. 1953-1959, agreements in numerous fields of activity exempted by law.

Norway: 1953, restrictive agreements and dominant enterprises subjected to registration; unreasonable prices or terms forbidden; king empowered to issue corrective orders against harmful restrictions and to regulate many aspects of business. 1957, resale price maintenance, collective or individual, forbidden by royal decree, with provision for exemptions. 1960, king's regulatory power extended by law, and horizontal price fixing forbidden by royal decree, with provision for exemptions.

South Africa: 1955, restrictions, collective or individual, subjected to investigation, negotiation, and corrective ministerial orders; orders may dissolve corporations or associations as well as terminate agreements or practices, may suspend tariffs, and may forbid the continuance of classes of agreements.

Germany: 1957, domestic law replaced laws promulgated by military occupation: Restrictive agreements broadly forbidden, subject to various absolute or discretionary exemptions; individual resale price maintenance permitted, subject to confidential registration; exclusive dealing subjected to possible prohibition but only where it both reduces market competition and unfairly restricts the economic freedom of a participant; permissible restrictions subjected to control of abuse; agreement on fair trading rules authorized, subject to registration; coercion forbidden; discrimination by dominant enterprises, associations, cartels, or firms maintaining resale prices forbidden; certain abusive practices by dominant enterprises subjected to corrective action; larger mergers to be reported. 1965, procedural safeguards applicable to exemption of standardization agreements and specialization agreements reduced; registers of resale price agreements opened to public; prevention of exclusive dealing authorized where either of the specified harmful effects is found; broader concepts of abuse made applicable to resale price maintenance and to the practices of dominant firms.[5]

Netherlands: 1958, confidential report of restrictive agreements required; agreements made subject to orders in council amending or prohibiting classes of them and to ministerial orders amending or annulling individual agreements or making them binding upon nonparticipants; dominant firms subjected to orders correcting abuses; publicity about agreements and about activities of dominant firms made available as a punitive and corrective weapon; 1962, disciplinary action by cartels restricted by order in council; 1964, collective resale price maintenance, resale price maintenance by suppliers of designated types of goods, and third-party enforcement of resale price arrangements forbidden by orders in council.[6]

Finland:[7] 1958, report of restrictive arrangements required when demanded; concerted action in bidding forbidden unless specifically authorized; resale price maintenance subjected to discretionary prohibition. 1964, report of the more substantial types of restrictions made automatically mandatory; resale price requirements forbidden unless specifically authorized; consultation procedure established

---

[5] Law to Amend the Law Against Restraints of Competition, Sept. 15, 1965.

[6] Orders in Council of April 1 and August 31, 1964.

[7] Law for the Control of Restraints of Competition in Trade, No. 47, of January 18, 1957 (effective 1958); Law for the Promotion of Economic Competition, January 3, 1964.

for removal of harmful effects; where consultation fails, reiterated temporary prohibition of restrictions authorized.

New Zealand: 1958, registration of restrictive agreements required; corrective orders against agreements, monopolies, and various business practices authorized, to prevent unreasonable reduction of competition or unreasonable effects on costs, prices, profits, or supply. 1961, requirement of registration repealed; trade association recommendations and activities defined as agreements.

Israel:[8] 1959, registration of restrictive agreements required; such agreements to be submitted for authorization to a board empowered to prohibit them or require their amendment; ministerial orders fixing prices or regulating quality or supply made available to cope with monopolies.

Colombia:[9] 1959, agreements designed to limit production, supply, distribution, or consumption, and practices tending to limit free competition, for the purpose of fixing inequitable prices, nullified and prohibited; exemptions authorized for agreements that aim at stability of important sectors of production; enterprises big enough to fix prices subjected to government supervision; mergers by large enterprises subjected to prior notification and governmental objection; incompatible relationships between offices in large competing enterprises and between industrial and distributing enterprises subjected to control; unfair competition forbidden; failure to observe resale prices set by producers treated as unfair.

Belgium: 1960, abuse of economic power subjected to corrective recommendations and, where necessary, to corrective royal orders, with publicity only for the latter.

Brazil:[10] 1962, abuse of economic power subjected to prohibitory orders reinforced by fines, by temporary governmental administration of recalcitrant enterprises, and by dissolution of enterprises that cannot comply. Abuse includes restrictive agreements, anti-competitive concentration, monopolistic profiteering, reduction of output, attempts to monopolize by manipulating supply or prices, and certain kinds of unfair competition.

Spain:[11] 1963, restrictive agreements and abuse of dominant power broadly forbidden, subject to certain exemptions and to discretionary approval of rules of competition and of agreements that, with benefit

---

[8] Restrictive Trade Practices Law, July 28, 1959.

[9] Disposition Regarding Restrictive Commercial Practices, No. 155, of 1959.

[10] Antitrust Act of September, 1962.

[11] Act to Afford Protection Against Activities that Reduce Competition, July 23, 1963 (effective 1964).

to consumers, improve production or distribution or promote progress; restrictive arrangements and concentration agreements subjected to registration.

Switzerland:[12] 1964, boycotts, blacklists, and collective discriminations forbidden unless compatible with the public interest; safeguards provided for members of cartels as to scope of agreement, withdrawal, disciplinary action by cartels, and access to courts; provision made for investigation of cartels, public report, and judicial modification or annulment of practices that seriously impede competition contrary to the public interest.

Australia:[13] 1965, collusive bidding and tendering forbidden; restrictive agreements subjected to registration and, when a tribunal finds that they reduce competition and are not justified by the public interest, to termination; certain designated practices also subjected to investigation and possible termination.

---

[12] Act Concerning Cartels and Similar Organizations, December 20, 1962, effective 1964.

[13] Trade Practices Act, 1965.

The National Laws in Summary

Of the countries that have enacted post-war legislation, those in Latin America lie outside the scope of this book. The following pages provide a brief summary of the law of each of the seventeen others. For ready reference, the summaries appear in alphabetical order.

Austria. The Austrian cartel law requires registration of agreements that regulate or limit competition. As originally enacted in 1951, it provided that only legally binding agreements were to be registered. In 1958 the requirement was extended to include gentlemen's agreements and price recommendations if economic or social pressure was used to make them effective or if their non-compulsory character was not expressly stated. In 1962 a further amendment required chambers of commerce to register price recommendations they addressed to their members even if the recommendations were explicitly defined as non-binding.

Registration constitutes review in the light of public policy—in other words, cartels may be either disapproved or registered by a Cartel Tribunal. Unregistered agreements are unenforceable at law, and their execution is a punishable offense. Refusal of registration is mandatory if the agreement (a) includes vertical agreements for exclusive selling of the cartelized goods or services; (b) excludes persons desiring to participate in the sale of such goods or services; (c) restricts price or quantity in sale of goods or services similar to those cartelized; (d) restricts the right of a participant to withdraw, with a stated length of prior notice, after a stated period, or to withdraw earlier for reasons such as unreasonable jeopardy to his business; (e) imposes penalties for such withdrawals. A cartel that does not have the prohibited features is registered if the Tribunal considers the agreement justified from the point of view of the national economy. In 1962 an amendment provided that in this appraisal special consideration should be given to the interest of consumers.

By amendments adopted in 1958, resale price agreements can be registered only if, in addition to the foregoing requirements, the margins provided by the resale prices correspond to or are lower than those usually granted and are not excessive. Moreover, the characteristics of commodities covered by such agreements cannot be changed until the Tribunal has satisfied itself that the change involves no deterioration of quality.

Amendments in 1962 reduced the disciplinary powers of cartels by guaranteeing the rights to appeal to the courts against cartel penalties and to insist on judicial proceedings even where a cartel agreement provides for arbitration. If a cartel resorts to punitive concerted refusal to sell, the victims may ask the Tribunal to declare the embargo inoperative or to substitute a "milder penalty."

The Tribunal that considers registration consists of equal numbers of persons representing the chambers of commerce and labor, plus a presiding judge. Its decisions are subject to review by an Appellate Tribunal containing three public officials, two representatives of the chamber of commerce, and two representatives of the chamber of labor. The lower Tribunal is required to consult a Parity Commission consisting of two persons from each of the same two chambers, and when the latter's advice is unanimous the judge is empowered to register the agreement without further ado.

Since this procedure was instituted in 1958, decisions have been characteristically made by agreement between the two chambers, without need for a casting of votes by the public officials. Beneath the apparent agreement is sharp difference of opinion between the chamber of commerce, which supports cartelization, and the chamber of labor, which generally opposes it. Before 1958 the labor representatives were in a minority in the Tribunal and consistently lost their appeals. The Appellate Tribunal held prices reasonable on various grounds—for example, that they were below the costs of the least efficient enterprises, that there was outside competition, or that high domestic prices were necessary to permit export at lower prices. It thought that quota agreements did not affect the interests of anyone other than participants. After 1958 the chamber of labor preferred bargaining to the risk of further similar decisions. Since the chamber of labor had obtained in 1958 both substantive and procedural amendments favorable to its position, the chamber of commerce preferred bargaining to further public controversy.

Beginning in 1957 a part of the control over price cartels was informally exercised by a Price-Wage Commission, consisting of representatives of the two chambers, organized agriculture, and government officials. This Commission was consulted about price increases; and in practice its recommendations were accepted, although they had no legal authority. It was less tolerant of price-raising schemes than the Cartel Tribunal was before the 1958 amendments. In practice, its recommendations pro and con were followed by the Cartel Tribunal.

Use of the registration process has apparently limited the number of cartels and modified their restrictions. By June 1, 1960, only seventy-four cartels had been registered, though only five had been disapproved (all before the close of 1952). For resale price maintenance, agreements had been registered for only six types of commodities.

By amendment of the law in 1962, dominant enterprises were required to register, but for them registration did not involve a process of approval or disapproval. The Parity Commission was empowered to submit to the Cartel Tribunal a report about the economic performance of any such enterprise. A dominant enterprise was defined as one providing more than 50 per cent of the supply to the domestic market if there were more than three domestic producers, or more than 30 per cent if there were fewer.

Belgium. In Belgium, as in the Netherlands, the government obtained power during the depression to require business minorities to observe restrictive agreements; and from early 1947 to mid-1960 it took such action in twelve instances. Three such decisions were in effect in August, 1962: Two, for window glass and molded glass, forbade enlargement of capacity and set limits on the use of existing capacity; the third set limits to private contractual exclusive dealing.

In 1951 the government proposed a bill to curb cartelization, a revised version of which finally became law in 1960. It is applicable both to agreements and to powerful enterprises. It authorizes action against abuse of economic power. Abuses are "practices that distort or restrict the normal play of competition" or interfere with economic freedom or with "the development of production or trade." Economic power is "a dominant influence upon the supply of commodities or of capital to the market or upon the price or quality of a specific commodity or service."

Under this law a Commissioner investigates abuses. Charges by him are considered by a Council for Economic Disputes (the body also concerned with compulsory compliance with cartel restrictions). Where the Council thinks there is abuse, the Minister of Economic Affairs makes oral recommendations to those involved. Failure to accept the recommendations leads first to their reiteration in writing and then, if necessary, to a corrective order by the King. Only in the case of such orders is any publicity to be given to the substance of the offense or of the correction. Violation of royal orders is punishable by fine and imprisonment, with increased penalties for renewed violations. If the original oral recommendation was not accepted, a violation may also result in an order designed to sever the offender's financial and management ties with competing firms.

After enactment of the law, the government moved slowly. Consideration of no case had been completed by August, 1962. In the ensuing year, several cases were informally disposed of by changes in the practices of enterprises that were being investigated.

Denmark. A law enacted in 1955, successor to one of 1937, requires

public registration of restrictive agreements (including those by cooperatives and in the professions) that exert or may be able to exert, nationally
or locally, a substantial influence on prices, production, distribution, or
transportation. Unregistered agreements are invalid. Individual enterprises
with a similar influence must also be registered upon the government's
demand.

The law forbids enforcement of agreements and business practices
that fix resale prices or margins, unless these agreements receive specific
approval. At the close of 1959, fifteen approved resale price agreements
were in effect, of which one was a collective arrangement for the book
trade, the others arrangements by single suppliers.

For other types of agreements and business practices, a Control Authority, consisting of a non-governmental Board and a Director, negotiates
with participants in an effort to terminate rsetrictions that result in unreasonable prices or business conditions, unreasonable restraints upon freedom
of trade, or unreasonable discrimination in trading conditions. Where negotiation fails, the Authority may issue orders that wholly or partly cancel
agreements, decisions, or practices; require alteration in or set maxima
for prices or margins; or require sellers to supply specified buyers on customary terms. Violation of orders is subject to fine or imprisonment and to
forfeit of profits.

Prices may not be increased by organizations on the register until the
increase has been approved by the Control Authority, but since 1960 the
Authority has had power to grant exemption from this requirement. Nearly
half the Authority's decisions concern requests for approval of price increases.

In the four and a half years until the close of 1959, the Board dealt
with 106 cases of restriction, individual and collective. (Separate figures
for agreements are not available.) It settled fifty-five cases by compromise,
made final recommendations in eighteen cases, and issued corrective orders
in thirty-three cases. These cases were concerned chiefly with refusal to sell,
exclusive dealing, discrimination, unreasonable prices, and unreasonable bidding agreements. The first three types of restriction were evaluated chiefly as
to their effect on business opportunity rather than consumer interest. Evaluation of the last two types centered upon unreasonably high prices, and
price control was regarded as an alternative to removal of restrictions. Price
agreements were seldom cancelled outright.

In early 1963 the Cartel Authority was given wide powers to investigate prices and publish the results, to freeze prices during such investigations, and to order invoicing and price-marking. The scope of the act was
broadened to cover the so-called "gray area," in which without cartel re-

striction or monopoly, competition was inactive. All prices were temporarily frozen during part of the year.

Finland. A law enacted in 1964,[1] established a Board for Freedom of Trade assisted by an Office for Freedom of Trade. Arrangements that make reduction or limitation of business activity obligatory or require observance of fixed prices or pricing principles must be reported to the Office, unless the Board grants exemption. Upon request by the Office, other limitations of competition, exclusive rights, and positions so decisive that they reduce competition must also be reported. Relevant further information must be supplied on request. Reports setting forth the nature of the restriction are to be prepared by the Office and, after comment by those supplying the information, to be published with selected accompanying documents.

Two types of restriction are forbidden, except when the Board permits them because they are considered likely to reduce costs or are otherwise regarded as consistent with the public interest. One is requirement that resale prices be maintained; the other is agreement to consult or cooperate before making offers to buy or sell merchandise or perform services in the domestic market. Other types of restriction are deemed harmful if they can cause unreasonable prices or delivery conditions or if, without an acceptable reason, they limit the chance to carry on business or practice a profession. Where harmful effects are thought to be present, consultation to remove them is to be undertaken by the Board, either on request by the Office or on complaint by an affected businessman. For these consultations the Board may require that relevant documents be produced, and may make them public if it chooses; but the consultations are normally to be private. If the harmful effects are not eliminated, the Board must, for important matters, refer the issue to the Council of State; and the latter, at the Board's request, may forbid observance of the restriction for a period of not more than a year, and, if a new consultation fails, may renew the prohibition.

The law is inapplicable to agriculture, fishing, labor markets, exports, purchase for import, competition in foreign markets, and tender of Finnish tonnage in foreign traffic. Special laws apply to banking and insurance.

Under the previous Finnish law, which provided for the reporting of restrictions on request but did not explicitly provide for consultations, an informal consultative process had been used. From the beginning of 1958 to March 1960, about 140 restrictions had been registered; consultation had brought about reduction of restrictions in about 20 percent of the registered agreements; and certain agreements as to electrical products, radios, and television equipment had been cancelled.

---

[1] Law for the Promotion of Economic Competition, Jan. 3, 1964, successor to a law enacted in 1957 and effective in 1958.

France. Four bodies of law affect restrictive agreements: (a) The Napoleonic penal code, as amended in 1926, condemns collective action to raise or lower prices artificially for the purpose of acquiring profit other than that which supply and demand would naturally afford. The provision has been applied by the courts a few times since the war to schemes to withhold supplies from the market or to maintain prices by intimidation. The requisite proof of artificiality and of the abnormal character of the profit desired is hard to develop with the precision requisite for enforcement of a criminal statute; and pre-war precedents reflect great toleration of cartels. Hence this law cannot readily be used as a major instrument to repress price agreements.

(b) A decree issued in 1953 and modified in 1958 prohibits agreements to impose minimum prices or trading margins unless they receive specific exemption. It also forbids any individual trader (and hence any group acting together) from refusing to make normal sales, or discriminating habitually in terms of sale. The Price Law of which it is a part also prohibits tying arrangements. These provisions have been used to eliminate most agreements fixing resale prices. They have been actively applied against refusals to sell and discriminations. They are significant obstacles to use of these devices by cartels as means of coercing recalcitrant enterprises.

(c) Another part of the same decree forbids concerted action with the purpose or effect of interfering with full competition by hindering the reduction of prices or costs or by encouraging artificial price increases, but exempts such action upon proof that it improves or extends markets or ensures further economic progress by rationalization and specialization. Unlike the other provisions of the decree, which are applied by the civil service and the courts, this part of the decree is initially interpreted in recommendations to a Minister by a Commission composed partly of public officials and partly of representatives of private organizations. In practice the Commission's views have been accepted by the responsible Minister with only minor modifications, and thus have been controlling. Ignoring the verbal limits of the statute, the Commission has attempted to evaluate the advantages and disadvantages of each restrictive agreement. It has approved cartels that it considered economically beneficial. When it has thought a cartel objectionable, it has seldom called for immediate termination of the objectionable restrictions. It has sometimes recommended that restrictions be tolerated for substantial periods (up to two years) and has sometimes asked that schemes of "rationalization" be added to the restrictive arrangement in order to qualify the cartel for exemption.

(d) In July, 1963, the decree was further modified to forbid such activities of single dominant enterprises and of groups of enterprises having dominant positions as may impair the normal operation of markets. The exemption as to economic progress and rationalization was made applicable to the amendment, as were the procedural provisions already in effect for concerted action. Thus the Commission was given a role similar to its role in cartel cases.

Delayed and limited publication of facts and actions taken has been an obstacle to public knowledge about the Commission's work. By the end of May, 1963, the Commission had acted upon 38 cases, but published information was available only for the first 20, to the close of 1959. In those 20 cases, the Commission had found 13 violations. In only two cases had it recommended prompt action to correct the violation. In the other cases, it had recommended that time limits be set for compliance (seven cases) or that periods of grace be afforded within which the parties might initiate activity justifying exemption (two cases), or had merely recommended surveillance (two cases).

Germany. The German law, enacted in 1957 after pre-war cartels had been greatly weakened by the partition of Germany and the policy of the Occupation, broadly invalidates and forbids the execution of restrictive agreements that are likely to influence production or market supply and agreements that restrict the freedom of participants to set prices or terms of contracts with others. Horizonal price cartels and vertical arrangements such as collective resale price maintenance are thus made generally illegal. In addition, agreements may be made illegal if they restrain participants in buying from or selling to third parties or in using what is bought, or if they obligate participants to make unrelated purchases. Until 1965 this invalidation was authorized only if the agreements had the double effect of unfairly limiting the freedom of an enterprise and substantially restricting market competition, but by amendment either type of effect now justifies invalidation.[2] In spite of the double requirement, action under this discretionary power during the first four years resulted in two corrective orders and twenty-four cases of voluntary correction without order.

Concerted activity is further curbed in several ways: A trade association may be ordered to admit an enterprise unjustly excluded. Associations are forbidden a) to use coercion for the purpose of forcing others into agreements, uniform action, or merger; b) to induce others to block deliveries or purchases with intent to hurt competitors; c) to use threats or promises to induce others to do what may not be done by contract; and d) to subject others to unfair hindrance or unjustified discriminatory treatment.

Numerous types of agreements are exempted, some absolutely and

---

[2] Law to Amend the Law Against Restraints of Competition, Sept. 15, 1965.

some at the Cartel Authority's discretion. They include (a) agreements on minor terms of sale; (b) standardization agreements;[3] (c) agreements on methods of accounting or specifications in making bids; (d) agreements on discounts; (e) "rationalization" agreements;[4] (f) export agreements; (g) import agreements; (h) resale price agreements by a single producer of identified goods;[5] (i) agreements to adjust capacity to lasting reductions of demand; and (j) agreements to meet exceptional emergencies. Most types of exemption are limited by statutory specification of the circumstances under which they are to be applicable. These limitations have been tightly applied. At the close of 1964, under all of the foregoing provisions for exemptions except that about resale price maintenance, a total of 177 agreements had gone into effect, of which 163 were still effective.[6] Resale price contracts by 1,206 sellers were in effect, as well as resale price recommendations by 820 enterprises.[7]

Special provisions are applicable to six categories of agreements, two of which have pervasive significance: those concerned with unfair competition and those concerned with industrial property (including unpatented technology). For unfair competition, trade associations are authorized to formulate and register corrective rules. For industrial property, agreements are forbidden that extend beyond the protected privilege; but the scope of the protected privilege is stated broadly, and the Cartel Authority can exempt the forbidden restrictions so far as they are not covered by other parts of the statute.

The other four special fields—banking and insurance, transportation, public utilities, and agriculture—are subject to various special types of exemption devised to fit their peculiarities.

---

[3] The 1965 amendments sought to encourage standardization by making agreements for this purpose valid if they were reported and if the report included the comments of a rationalization body. Under the previous law the Cartel Authority was empowered to disapprove such agreements within three months.

[4] The 1965 amendments reduced the safeguards surrounding "specialization" agreements, that is, agreements to allocate products. Previously such agreements were subject to the Cartel Authority's approval, which was to be granted if a) the agreement was likely to raise efficiency or productivity substantially; b) the rationalization effect was adequate in relation to the accompanying restriction, and c) competition in the market was not excluded. Under the amended law, specialization agreements are valid if the Cartel Authority does not object within three months; but objection must be made if the parties have not shown that their purpose is to rationalize and that competition is not eliminated.

[5] Until 1965 resale price agreements were reported but not made public. By amendment of the law the register of them is now public. The same amendment enlarged the concept of abuse of a resale price agreement.

[6] Bericht des Bundeskartellamtes Über Seine Tätigkeit im Jahre 1964 Sowie über Lage und Entwicklung auf seinem Aufgabegebiet, July 16, 1965, Deutsche Bundestag, 4. Wahlperiode, Drucksache IV 3752 (hereafter called Bericht 1964), pp. 72-3.

[7] *Ibid.*, p. 113.

Abuse of exempt agreements may be corrected by the Authority or may result in withdrawal of the exemption. Violations of the prohibitions, and also recommendations by which compliance is evaded, are subject to administrative fines.

Firms that are not exposed to substantial competition (defined as market-dominating enterprises) are subject to orders by which, if they abuse their market position, the abuse may be prohibited and abusive contracts may be invalidated.[8] They are forbidden to engage in unjustified discrimination or to hinder other enterprises unfairly. The provisions about coercion, threats, and inducements that apply to associations also apply to them, and, indeed, to any single enterprise.

Mergers and related forms of consolidation must be reported if thereafter the merged firm exceeds a stated size.[9] But official action on such a report can go no further than to ask for a written statement or to hold an oral hearing.

Numerous proceedings have been concerned with abuses and violations. Corrective action is usually informal. To the close of 1964, more than 340 cases of abuse were corrected, nearly nine-tenths of them informally. Over 1400 cases of violation resulted in informal correction, 166 in administrative fines.[10]

In late 1963 the German Ministry of Economics released a pamphlet setting forth in considerable detail the forms of business agreement that were permissible under the law, and the limitations that must be observed for each. The statement implied that the government was sympathetic to wide use of these possibilities.

The pamphlet listed as permissible (a) joint market research and analysis of business sectors; (b) exchange of business experience and information without agreements or recommendations; (c) joint provision of maintenance, repair, transportation, and storage; (d) joint credit and collection activities; (e) joint non-price advertising; (f) joint buying, provided each participant remained free to buy independently or the arrangement was approved as a rationalization cartel; (g) joint technological research and development that left participants free to apply the results as they individually chose and to do further research individually; (h) joint observ-

---

[8] Until 1965 the power to correct abuse by such firms pertained only to abuse in prices, terms of sale, and tying arrangements. By amendment it now covers all types of abuse.

[9] Until 1965 reports were required for market shares in excess of 20 per cent. Difficulties in ascertaining market shares resulted in an amendment by which reports were required if the merged firm had more than 10,000 employees, more than 500 million marks in sales, or more than 1,000 million marks in assets.

[10] Bericht, 1964, pp. 147-8, 150-1.

ance of standards and types; (i) joint use of productive facilities without either price fixing or agreement to limit output; (j) use of uniform methods of cost calculation, provided that each participant must remain free to refrain from such use, that inclusion of explicit illustrative costs must be avoided, and that, if methods of calculating prices were included, they must be registered; (k) joint business in non-competitive goods and in filling orders too large for one supplier; (l) use of joint sales outlets, sales personnel, and trade-marks, without obligation to abstain from independent selling; (m) joint subsidiaries under independent management, with no restriction except upon the goods to be produced by the subsidiary; (n) specialization agreements, (unless invalidated),[11] and (o) mergers, subject to the duty to notify the Cartel Authority if the merger covered more than 20 per cent of the market.

Ireland. A law enacted in 1953, with minor amendment in 1959, authorizes a Commission, on its own initiative or on a request from business, to formulate and publish rules of fair trading for any kind of goods and any service affecting the supply or distribution of goods. On request by the Minister for Industry and Commerce, the Commission must—and, on its own initiative, may—also investigate conditions of supply and distribution of any kind of goods. These investigations result in reports to the Minister describing the conditions, stating whether they prevent or restrict competition or restrain trade or involve resale price maintenance, giving an opinion as to whether any such interference with competition or trade is unfair or contrary to the public interest, and, if an order is thought desirable, proposing its terms. On the basis of such a report, the Minister has power to issue orders ensuring equitable treatment; prohibiting specified agreements, refusals of supply, preferences, or the imposition of conditions upon supply; and making "such other provision in regard to restrictive practices . . . as he thinks fit." He must furnish the Commission's report to Parliament, must state his reasons if he rejects the Commission's recommendation that an order be issued, and must obtain parliamentary confirmation of any order he issues before it is enforceable as law.

In 1958 the Minister was empowered, in the case of most commodities and services, to set maximum prices if a report from the Commission disclosed excessive prices due to restrictive practices. In 1960 no such action had yet been taken.

In 1959 the 1953 law was extended to authorize investigations at the

---

11 The pamphlet qualified its approval of standardization and specialization agreements by the provisions (then in effect but altered in 1965) concerning the Cartel Authority's invalidation or approval. My summary is modified to take account of the legal changes in 1965.

Minister's request, but not orders, covering refusal by employers or employees to use particular materials or methods. In 1962, no such investigation had yet been requested.

By the close of 1962, the Commission had issued twenty-one sets of fair trading rules and submitted nine reports to the Minister. The Minister had not yet acted upon the latest report. He had accepted, wholly or with minor modification, the Commission's recommendations in seven of the previous eight reports. After one report he had decided to issue no order.

The Commission's rules are not legally binding, but enterprises that observe them need not fear government action; and when rules are not observed, binding orders replace them. In practice, rules and orders have been used to supplement each other. Most of the rules and orders are prohibitory: Their function is to forbid or limit restrictive practices, such as refusal to sell to newcomers or independents, resale price maintenance, or the enforcement of horizontal price agreements. In two instances, however, the Commission has approved individual resale price maintenance; in one, discounts for exclusive dealing. In another instance the Commission itself has prescribed minimum standards for admission to a trade.

Israel. A law enacted in 1959 establishes control over cartels and monopolies. Cartels are broadly defined to include restrictive arrangements, but the definition excludes labor agreements; arrangements among producers or distributors of agricultural products; arrangements as to use of patents, trademarks, and copyrights; arrangements among government-controlled companies; arrangements among affiliated companies; and two-party exclusive dealing. Monopoly means control of a commodity or service to an extent exceeding that designated by the Minister of Trade as monopolistic for the field in question.

Control of cartels and monopolies is entrusted to a controller, a board, and the Minister of Trade and Industry. The controller is a state employee. The board consists of a chairman who is a district court judge and four or more others, of whom at least half are not state employees and at least one represents consumers. The board has the powers of a district court, and its decisions and orders are appealable to the supreme court.

Cartels must be registered with the controller. The register is available to the public except where secrecy has been found advisable by the board to protect the interest of the state or a business secret. The controller has broad powers of investigation which he may use to support recommendations to the board about decisions.

Parties to a cartel must ask the board to decide whether the cartel is permissible, and must abstain from applying the arrangement until the board has decided or until, on the controller's recommendation, the board has granted temporary authorization during the pendency of the case. If the cartel is considered by the board to be contrary to the public interest, all or part of it may be prohibited, absolutely or conditionally and temporarily or permanently. In determining the public interest, the board must hear applicants and opponents and must consider whether or not there is reasonable need for the cartel in order to provide advantages to the public, ensure requisite skill, prevent acts likely to lead to restraint of competition, enable the parties to get fair conditions in dealings with a powerful supplier or customer, enhance efficiency or reduce prices, or protect the existence of a branch of industry. The board's orders are enforceable by contempt proceedings like civil orders of the courts. Conformity to a cartel agreement before the board has decided or contrary to the board's order is punishable by fine and imprisonment.

When the controller thinks that a monopoly exists and that its effect is to keep prices high, or to impair quality or methods of production or marketing, or to reduce supply, he may, with the board's approval, ask the Minister to fix maximum prices or to give orders about quality or methods of production or supply; and the Minister may make such orders. Violation of these orders is also subject to fine and imprisonment.

Persons damaged by violation of the law or of orders under it may recover damages by civil suit.

Japan. A law enacted in 1947 during military occupation, as amended in 1949 during the Occupation and in 1953 after the restoration of Japanese sovereignty, prohibits private monopolization and unreasonable restraint of trade. Private monopolization means business activity, individual or by combination or conspiracy, that excludes or controls the business activity of others. Unreasonable restraint of trade means agreement restrictive of prices, production, technology, products, customers, or suppliers. Each of these definitions is qualified by the language "thereby causing, contrary to the public interest, a substantial restraint of competition in any particular field of trade." The Fair Trade Commission (which administers the law) and the Japanese courts have held that this language, which was placed in the law by amendment in 1953, does not establish a distinction between good and bad cartels nor destroy the weight of precedents in earlier decisions that followed American case law.

Unfair business practices are also forbidden. Such practices are defined as those involving trade at undue prices, undue discrimination against other enterprises, unreasonable inducement or coercion to attract a competitor's customers, imposition of conditions that unjustly restrict the business activity of the other party to a transaction, unwarranted use of a bargaining position, unjust interference with a competitor's transactions with customers, or unjust inducement for an official to act against the interest of his company. The Commission is empowered to designate the particular practices that involve such unfairness. It has done so for thirteen particular industries and has also issued a general list of unfair practices for use where there is no special list. Practices in the latter list, however, are not much more sharply defined than in the statute.

Entrepreneurs and trade associations are forbidden to enter into international agreements that involve unreasonable restraint of trade or unfair business practices. Trade associations are also forbidden to restrict competition substantially, to limit the number of entrepreneurs, to restrict unduly the activities of their members, or to cause unfair practices.

Numerous provisions curb concentration of economic power: Holding companies are prohibited. Financial companies are forbidden to own more than ten per cent of the stock of other companies without obtaining government approval. Where the effect may be substantial restraint of competition, (a) mergers are forbidden; (b) corporations are forbidden to acquire the fixed assets of other companies by purchase or lease or to enter into management contracts or profit-pooling arrangements; (c) both corporations and others are forbidden to acquire or hold the stock of other companies; and (d) corporate officials are forbidden to hold employment in other companies.

The law contains exemptions for natural monopolies, cooperatives, and activities authorized by special laws, including the patent, copyright, and trade-mark laws. It also exempts depression cartels and rationalization cartels. Both types of cartel must be approved by the Commission after a finding that they will not unduly hurt consumers or affected entrepreneurs, are not discriminatory, and provide reasonable opportunity to participate or withdraw. Depression cartels must not exceed what is necessary and must not involve unfair practices; rationalization cartels must not concentrate the production of a particular kind of product in any one entrepreneur.

The law also authorizes resale price maintenance by single suppliers for commodities designated by the Commission; but these commodities must be goods that are in daily use by consumers with readily identifiable uniformity of quality, and must be in free competition with other goods; and the price maintenance must have the producer's approval and must not be "grossly" injurious to consumer interests.

Use of these exemptions has been moderate. By late 1964 eight depression cartels had been approved, but no approval was currently in effect. Fourteen rationalization cartels had been approved. Eleven types of commodity had been designated as suitable for resale price maintenance.

The substantive provisions of the law are reenforced by various reporting requirements, applicable to international agreements, to resale prices fixed upon designated commodities, to the formation, change, or dissolution of trade associations, to concurrent office-holding in corporations one of which has assets of as much as one hundred million yen, to personal stockholdings of more than ten per cent in competing companies, to stockholdings by corporations with assets exceeding one hundred million yen, to holdings of stock by foreign non-financial companies, and to intentions to merge, acquire corporate fixed assets by purchase or lease, enter into management contracts, and enter into profit-pooling arrangements. Though the reports are not publicly registered, they become the basis of recurrent public reports about economic concentration.

The law is applied by a Fair Trade Commission attached to the Prime Minister's office. The Commission investigates, recommends corrective action, issues formal complaints, hears cases, and issues formal decisions and orders. Its orders may be appealed to the Tokyo High Court. Noncompliance with an order is subject to fine. In addition, violation of major provisions of the law is a criminal offense subject to fine or imprisonment. In certain cases that involve patent rights, the relevant patents may be revoked.

The apparent strength and sweep of the law has been greatly reduced, however, by exemptions included in other legislation. By the close of the 1950's, broad exemption existed for export and import trade, medium and small enterprises, transportation, warehousing, insurance, investment trusts, security and commodity exchanges, textiles, manufacture of machinery, coal, liquor, ammonium sulphate, silk reeling and the manufacture of silk yarn, wholesale agricultural markets, retail markets, and various occupations subject to sanitary laws. Some of the exemptions were for specified limited periods, but of course could be extended by further legislation.

During the middle 1950's, while numerous exemptions were being enacted, the law was administered laxly. Parts of it were not applied at all, particularly the provisions about concentration of economic power, and few cases were instituted under other provisions.

After 1958, when an effort to emasculate the law by further amendment was unsuccessful, enforcement became somewhat more active. From 1958 to March, 1964, the Commission disposed of 57 cases, and from April to October, 1964, eight more. In the seventeen years ending in 1964, the Commission decided five cases concerned with private monopolization, 55 with unreasonable restraint of trade, 39 with unfair business practices, and 114 with forbidden activity by trade associations. Recent cases have been concerned almost wholly with the last two types of offense.

The Netherlands. A law that entered into force in 1958, similar to predecessors dating from 1935 and 1941, authorizes the Ministry of Economics to take action ranging from prohibition of cartels to imposition of cartel restrictions upon non-participants. Binding agreements that regulate competition must be reported to the government (and the requirement may be extended to cover unenforceable ones). The Minister is empowered to annul or suspend an agreement or require amendment of it, or, upon request, to require observance of agreements by non-participants. By order in counsel, a whole class of agreements can be prohibited or modified. All important decisions must be preceded by advice from a non-governmental committee. Persons who violate ministerial orders are subject to fine, imprisonment, or suspension of the right to do business.

Secrecy in application of the law is pervasive. The register is confidential. Proceedings under the law and the documents relevant to them, other than summaries of the government's decisions, are confidential. The Ministry's annual report to Parliament must not give identified information about particular enterprises. Even in appellate proceedings, the Minister may withhold documents from parties at interest and from the appellate court. The Minister may, however, publish an agreement that he thinks objectionable, after consulting the advisory committee.

Before the war, the predecessor law was used, though infrequently, to require non-participants to conform to agreements. Since the war, the law has been used only to reduce the restrictiveness of agreements. Expressing neutrality toward concerted restrictions, the government appraises them *ad hoc* in the light of its conception of the general interest. Most cases are settled informally—apparently about 650 out of a total of about 700 from the close of the war to the end of 1957. Agreements are usually modified rather than cancelled. Action has focused chiefly upon two matters, price-fixing and exclusion of enterprises from markets by collective reciprocal exclusive dealing, boycott, and other devices.

In the latter type of case, collective action has been permitted but required to serve reasonable purposes. Minor restrictions have been permitted when considered harmless or based upon acceptable standards of business conduct. Major restrictions have been rejected if, without acceptable reason, they deprived excluded businessmen of opportunity or harmed the public, but have been accepted if they were believed to have desirable economic consequences such as "rationalization." Exclusion of newcomers, cooperatives, chain stores, and the like, has been forbidden, but limitation of the total number of traders has been permitted if not "undue."

In 1962 an order in council prohibited agreements by more than ten enterprises denying independent firms "the right to deal with certain entrepreneurs" or imposing discriminatory terms upon them in such dealings.

It also required that private disciplinary action by cartels comply with various procedural safeguards.

Price-fixing has been considered generally unjustified except to prevent "unduly" severe price competition, which is conceived as competition in which most enterprises sell at or below their costs. But where substantial independent competition exists and schemes do not involve pressure upon independents to conform, price-fixing has been tolerated as harmless. Where price-fixing has been permitted, the government, trying to keep prices reasonable, has required that place be left for "economically justified competition" by establishment of prices no higher than the average costs of the more efficient enterprises.

In 1964 orders in council invalidated all collective resale price provisions; all resale price provisions individually imposed by suppliers of five designated categories of durable goods[12] (unless the resale price did not exceed invoice cost); and all resale price provisions under which private sanctions were imposed or a third party was empowered to detect noncompliance or to institute judicial proceedings. The effect of these orders is to leave valid only individual resale price maintenance for goods other than those specified, and then only if the resale price contracts are enforced, like other contracts, by legal proceedings.

The law also authorizes action against "dominant positions" that conflict with the general interest. The government may publish relevant information or may issue orders (a) requiring that individuals or groups possessing such a position supply designated goods or services for cash to designated persons, at the customary prices and on customary terms; (b) establishing rules that prohibit tying arrangements; (c) establishing other rules as to prices or terms of payment and delivery; or (d) forbidding actions tending to induce designated enterprises to pursue specified practices. These powers have been used occasionally against large enterprises, but more often to curb group restrictions that continued informally after formal arrangements had been terminated.

A special feature of the Dutch law is a provision that prohibits deliberate compliance with decisions of foreign states about regulation of competition unless permission to comply has been obtained from the Dutch Government. Originating in controversy over international aspects of American antitrust proceedings in cases involving petroleum and electric lamps, this provision had been used by the close of 1960 to reject seven out of eleven requests for permission to furnish documents called for by American

---

[12] Radio and television sets, record players, and tape-recorders; electrical refrigerators, toasters, mixers, vacuum-cleaners, washing machines, spin-driers, flat irons, shavers and hair-dryers; cars and station wagons; cameras, flash-light apparatus, cine-cameras, photo-slide and film projectors; records.

official bodies and to limit the scope of the permission that was granted to the other four applicants.

New Zealand. A law enacted in 1958 and amended in 1961 provides for investigation of trade practices by an Examiner, report by him to a Commission, and orders by the latter terminating or modifying practices that, in its opinion, are contrary to the public interest. The Commission's decisions can be appealed to a special judge, whose decisions are final.

The power to issue orders is applicable to eleven specified classes of restrictive agreements, including horizontal agreements on prices, discounts, or terms; vertical collective agreements on prices, discounts, or terms; horizontal agreements to require resale price maintenance; vertical agreements between a single supplier and a purchaser as to resale prices; agreements as to aggregated rebates; agreements to limit output or supply; agreements to allocate markets; agreements to restrict methods of production; and agreements denying particular enterprises or classes of enterprise the opportunity to buy or sell or limiting the number of distributors or sources of supply. In addition, orders are applicable to monopolies, practices that tend to bring about monopoly, refusals to sell, unjustifiable exclusion from a trade association, sale under tying arrangements, payment of excessive royalties or commissions or license fees, and profiteering, black marketing, and hoarding. Practices falling within any of these categories are to be deemed contrary to the public interest if they increase costs, prices, or profits unreasonably, if they limit or prevent the supply of goods to consumers, or if they prevent or unreasonably reduce or limit competition.

The law originally provided for public registration of restrictive agreements, but the provision was inadequately administered and was repealed in 1961.

To February 1966, the Commission had made 21 decisions. In applying the law, it had been concerned chiefly with price agreements, had relied almost wholly upon the provision about unreasonable reduction of competition, and had held that price agreements are inherently unreasonable. Thus it had done much to interpret the discretionary language of the statute as prohibitory. In cases on appeal, the judge at first sustained this general point of view, but invalidated orders if there was a significant amount of non-complance with the restrictive agreement and if the place of the participants was not shown to be important enough in the market to produce an unreasonable effect on competition. Similarly, in the few cases involving refusal to deal, individual or collective, the judge invalidated decisions upon finding that, though the restriction impaired the competitive opportunity of individuals, it did not significantly affect the supply available to the public. In a 1962 case, however, an appellate decision, inconsistent with the reasoning in the other cases, sustained a price fixing arrangement on the ground that its ultimate consequences would be in the public interest.

Norway. The Norwegian law, which took effect at the beginning of 1954, contains provisions about cartels similar to those of pre-war legislation dating from 1926, but also gives the government broad discretionary control over prices, terms of sale, and methods of distribution. In 1957 and 1960, royal decrees, based upon discretionary powers conveyed by the law, superimposed upon the regulatory law two widespread prohibitions.

In the statute, control of prices and control of restrictions are dual means for the purposes of promoting desirable price developments, counteracting unreasonable prices, profits, and terms, and providing safeguards against improper marketing, improper competitive conditions, and restrictive arrangements detrimental to the public interest. Control of prices rests on two basic provisions: One makes it unlawful to agree on unreasonable prices or terms. The other gives the King blanket power to issue reglations about prices, profits, terms, or estimates of cost; to prevent unfair treatment, by control of marketing; and to prescribe conditions for taking specified prices, profits, or discounts. Control of restrictive agreements rests upon provisions that (a) require public registration of restrictive agreements and of associations that regulate prices, profits, cost calculations, terms, production, or distribution; (b) make unregistered agreements invalid and their application punishable; and (c) give the King broad authority to regulate, alter, or annul the restrictions that are registered. Supplementary provisions (a) limit the duration of restrictive agreements, (b) require disclosure of bidding agreements in submitting bids, (c) authorize the government to cancel private penalties and indemnities imposed on violators of restrictive arrangements, (d) empower the government to require that excluded persons be admitted to agreements and associations, and (e) empower it to forbid unreasonable refusal of business connections. A violator of the law or of the orders under it is subject to fine or imprisonment.

Under the policy of this law prior to 1957, cartel prices were attacked because they were too high, not because they were fixed, and corrective action usually took the form of price orders. The power to annul or amend restrictive agreements was used only seven times from 1953 to 1960. Apart from price orders, application of the law consisted chiefly in action against refusal to deal. In the four years, 1954-1957, concerted refusals were prohibited in eighteen cases and permitted in seventeen cases.

Dominant enterprises as well as agreements must be registered. Such enterprises are conceived as (a) those producing or distributing at least one quarter of the national total of a category of goods or services; (b) those subject to the controlling influence of a foreign firm or association that has substantial influence on prices in one or more countries or that is associated with an association possessing such influence; (c) other enterprises engaged in activities so important as to need supervision. Such enterprises, like parties to agreements, are subject to the King's authority to regulate prices, profits, and terms of sale and to regulate registered restrictions.

In 1957 a royal decree prohibited both collective and individual action to maintain fixed resale prices, and also prohibited collective (but not individual) resale price recommendations. Provision was made for exemption in special circumstances. By January, 1959, about 100 collective resale price schemes had been terminated, and nearly 1,000 such schemes by individual suppliers had been either terminated or changed to advisory recommendations. In October, 1961, exemptions were in effect only for books, scrap iron, and methylated alcohol.

In 1960, after the statute had been amended to strengthen the King's power to issue blanket orders against restrictions, a second royal decree prohibited collective horizontal regulation of prices, bids, or discounts, collective horizontal price recommendations, and collective arrangements for price reporting. Exemptions were applied to exports; to producers' organizations in agriculture, forestry, or fisheries; to banking and insurance; and to joint sales organizations. Provision was made for futher exemptions for schemes (a) necessary to desirable rationalization; (b) necessary to afford protection from competition that is unfair or detrimental to the public interest; (c) otherwise in accord with the public interest because of special circumstances. Under this decree, 356 agreements were terminated. Exemption was granted for 204 agreements—thirty-one manufacturing agreements, mostly regarded as means of rationalization; eighty-nine agreements, mostly local, by which groups engaged in baking, candy making, the grocery trade, and other trades agreed on recommended prices within limits set by government price orders; and eighty-four agreements by which coastal water carriers, publishers, and the learned professions were allowed to fix charges by non-enforceable arrangements.

In December, 1961, a further royal decree prohibited business groups from increasing any binding or guiding prices or any guiding resale prices which were in effect. Until August 31, 1962, this decree was supplemented by a provision which, to prevent evasion, forbade revocation of the guiding resale prices that had been issued.

Spain. The Spanish law, enacted in 1963 and effective January 1, 1964, forbids agreements, resolutions, or parallel actions that have the purpose or effect of restriction, suppression, or distortion of competition on the domestic market or a part thereof. Agreements thus forbidden are null and void.

Abuse of dominant power by one or more enterprises to the detriment of the public interest or of the interests of consumers or competitors is also forbidden. Dominance includes not only monopoly but also the presence of two or more firms that do not effectively compete with one another and have no substantial competition from others. Enterprises that by law have a dominant position are subject to the abuse provision. Practices specifically mentioned as abusive include direct or indirect fixation of buying or selling prices or terms; limitation of production, distribution, technical development, or investment to the detriment of the national economy; allocation of markets, fields of operation, or sources of supply; activities intended to destroy competitors by unfair competition; discrimination in the terms of similar transactions whereby the competitive position of participants is impaired; and tying arrangements that cover goods or services that are unrelated in kind or by trade custom.

Exemptions are provided for agriculture. Restrictions under the sanction of law are also exempt. These restrictions include those approved by certain local and special authorities, but such approved restrictions, if already in being, can be set aside or amended by the government after consulting the authorities and the affected private interests, and in the future can only be extended with parliamentary approval.

The Tribunal that applies the new restrictive practice law can approve agreements and collective decisions that contribute to and are essential to the improvement of production or distribution or technical or economic progress and that afford the consumer an appropriate part of the resulting gain. Particular types of arrangements are listed as especially appropriate for approval. They include (a) agreements on standards and types of goods made for the purpose of rationalization; (b) agreements that with due regard to the public interest, adjust supply to demand under conditions when demand is shrinking or there is excess capacity; (c) agreements that foster exports without detriment to domestic trade or violation of international treaties; (d) agreements for import from markets where competition is not free, provided the restrictions are not detrimental to the domestic market; and (e) agreements that promote substantial social and economic development.

The government can also approve rules of competition defining what is permissible under the law when these rules are proposed by business or agricultural syndicates. It can make appropriate changes in these rules.

Parties to forbidden restrictions are subject to private damage suits. They are subject to fines up to 100,000 pesetas. Their gains from their conduct can be confiscated.

The law is applied by three bodies—a tribunal, an executive office, and a policy council. An independent tribunal attached to the Ministry of Trade has power to grant exemptions as specified in the law, to order violators to take specified kinds of action, and to refer cases of violation to the appropriate authorities for proceedings to assess fines or confiscate illegal profits. The tribunal consists of nine members appointed for life on nomination by the Minister of Trade. They must have held responsible positions in the public service or the judiciary. Their decisions must be preceded by a hearing of the interested parties and by consultation with the syndicate to which these parties belong. The decisions can be appealed only on such grounds as violation of law, abuse of official power, or defects of procedure.

An Office for the Protection of Competition, part of the Ministry of Trade, maintains a register of permitted restrictive arrangements and of concentration agreements that involve concentration covering 30 per cent or more of the national market; makes appropriate investigation on complaint or on its own initiative; presents cases to the tribunal; and executes the tribunal's orders in decided cases.

A Council to Protect Competition is also established as part of the Ministry of Trade. It contains representatives of that Ministry and the Ministries of Finance, Public Works, Agriculture, Industry and Labor, plus six representatives of syndicates. It advises on the rules of the syndicates about competition, analyzes the level of competition in branches of industry, proposes legislation to increase competition, proposes investigations by the Office for the Protection of Competition, and advises on decisions under the law.

Sweden. A law enacted in 1953, as extensively amended and supplemented in 1956, prohibits (in the absence of special permission) cooperation in bidding, maintenance of specified minimum resale prices, and specification of advisory resale prices unless the right to charge lower prices is made clear. In the six years 1954-1959, bidding agreements were permitted in four instances. In the same period, collective resale price maintenance was approved in five instances.

All restrictive agreements not subject to these prohibitions must be publicly registered with a Price and Cartel Office at the government's request. The office not only maintains the register, but has authority to investigate prices and competitive conditions and to report on them. A procedure of negotiation is used to remove any harmful effects found in the agreements or in any restraints of competition by individual enterprises. A commissioner reviews complaints, examines the register, conducts investigations, and informally negotiates corrective action in the majority of cases in which he feels that action is needed. He had done so in about 150 instances by early 1958. Where he finds a harmful effect that he cannot remove, he institutes a case before a board composed primarily of representatives of private interests. Corrective action usually takes place before the board finishes considering the case. This occurred in twenty-three of the forty-four cases that had been considered by the board before the close of 1962. If the board decides that a restriction is harmful, it institutes formal negotiations to remove the harm. If the negotiations are not successful, the board is required to report to the King, and the King has power to fix maximum prices. At the close of 1962, nine negotiations had been successfully completed by the board and no report to the King had yet been made. Particular cases had been settled, however, only by compromise after extended negotiation.

The success of informal and formal negotiation has apparently been due to the determination of Swedish business associations to make the law work. When legislation was pending before 1953, these bodies averted a more drastic enactment by "self-sanitation," that is, termination or amendment of the more objectionable agreements. Their representatives on the board apparently use private pressure to obtain acquiescence to the board's decisions, and knowledge of this fact creates willingness to settle matters informally. Their presence on the board, however, tends to limit the board to policies that command broad assent from business.

Restrictive agreements have received diminishing attention in applying the Swedish law. The attention of the Price and Cartel Office has been directed to surveillance over price levels. The attention of the commissioner and the board has been diverted to numerous cases of refusal to sell. Investigations of agreements by the commissioner diminished year by year from 1954 to 1957. Only five such investigations were initiated in the latter year. Of the forty-four cases considered by the board prior to the close of 1962, only fifteen, mostly in the earlier years, had to do with collective action.

Switzerland. The Swiss cartel law, enacted in 1963 and effective February 15, 1964, has a dual purpose: It protects those who desire to compete in their right to do so, and it authorizes intervention by the state against restrictive practices that are seriously contrary to the public interest.

The law is applicable both to agreements that collectively limit market competition and to single or financially linked enterprises or other organizations that dominate or decisively influence a market. The latter are deemed to be cartel-like bodies, and are subject to the same control as cartels. Cartels are generally forbidden to boycott or blacklist independent enterprises or to discriminate against them in prices or conditions of sale when such action tends to impair the opportunity for such enterprises to compete. However, such measures are lawful when they are "justified by preponderant legitimate interests," are compatible with the general interest, and do not restrict free competition excessively in relation to the end contemplated or the method of seeking it. The law lists five illustrative purposes that might justify boycott or discrimination: (a) To protect fair competition and prevent its perversion; (b) to establish reasonable technical and professional requirements in an industry or occupation; (c) to promote an industrial or occupational structure that is desirable in the public interest; (d) to assure the observance of cartel arrangements in foreign markets; and (e) to ensure appropriate resale price maintenance so far as it is necessary to assure quality or service.

An explanatory memorandum by the government has made clear a part of the meaning of four of these categories. The first category not only authorizes refusal to admit to a trade association a violator of the Swiss law about unfair competition, but also permits use of a boycott to enforce cartel policies that are considered reasonable—for example, limits upon the grant of premiums, or rules of price calculation that are thought to assure that costs will be adequately considered, or joint efforts to resist an attempt by a would-be monopolist to take over the market. The second category authorizes boycotts against enterprises that lack reasonable experience or training, but does not authorize the imposition of financial standards of qualification or of requirements designed to exclude newcomers or to limit the total number of enterprises. The third category is intended to permit efforts to prevent excessive concentration or excessively rapid industrial change, yet not to permit maintenance of the *status quo* against desirable progress. The fourth category recognizes a right for Swiss cartels to discipline independent enterprises that jeopardize the effectiveness of their export programs.

When cartel action against an independent exceeds what is permitted, the victim has a right to redress. In that event, the cartel's action may be declared illicit and forbidden by judicial order, damages may be awarded, or the cartel may be required to accept the victim as a member.

To permit more competition, the law also provides certain protections for cartel members. All cartel agreements must be written. New members of a cartel are bound only by those existing cartel agreements that they accept in writing. Members may obtain judicial permission to withdraw from a cartel for adequate reasons and may not, on withdrawal, be subjected to penalties or difficulties. Though a member's compliance with a cartel agreement may be enforced by restrictive means such as boycott or discrimination, such discipline must be reasonable. Arrangements to arbitrate the essential features of cartel agreements must authorize any party to resort to a court rather than to the arbitration tribunal (but this provision does not apply to international agreements to use international arbitration tribunals).

To protect the public interest against harmful restrictions, a Cartel Commission is provided, consisting of economists, lawyers, and representatives of business, labor, and consumers. As initially established, the Commission consisted of four lawyers, two economists, a writer on economics, four persons from consumer organizations, two persons from industry, one person from the trades and crafts, and one person from agriculture. The Commission is expected to advise the government about laws restricting competition, and may be consulted by the courts about questions of principle in cartel cases. It is to investigate cartels, either on its own motion or on request by the Department of Economics, using mandatory powers if necessary; and to render reports that become public unless the Department decides otherwise. After investigating the possible harmful effects of cartels, the Commission is authorized, at the Department's demand, to recommend that cartel arrangements be modified or annulled. On the basis of the Commission's report, the Department may proceed in the Federal Court against a cartel that prevents or seriously hinders competition in a way incompatible with the public interest, particularly to the injury of consumers. The Court may forbid restrictive activities, and may modify or annul cartel agreements.

The United Kingdom. A law enacted in 1948 established a Monopolies Commission to make investigations and submit appraisals and recommendations as to matters referred to it by the Board of Trade. The procedure was applicable both to agreements and to activities by single enterprises provided they covered one-third or more of the domestic supply of a kind of goods or of a kind of domestic processing, or resulted in substantial failure to supply the goods or apply the process. It was also applicable to export trade if one-third or more of a kind of goods domestically produced was involved. Recommendations might result in orders prohibiting the execution of restrictive agreements, or prohibiting refusals to sell, tying arrangements, or discrimination in supplies, orders, or services. Through 1957, twenty reports about arrangements in particular industries were submitted and published, as well as a broad report on collective price discrimination, collective exclusive dealing, and related practices. The latter led to a new statute in 1956, applicable to most kinds of domestic restrictive agreements. The 1948 law ceased to be applicable to these, but was retained in modified form for possible application to the remaining domestic agreements, and to export agreements, widely used business practices, and the activities of powerful firms. To the close of 1965, it had resulted in five reports about the practices of dominant enterprises and in a report about compliance with recommendations in an earlier report.

Under the 1956 law, domestic restrictive agreements concerned with goods (as distinguished from services) must be publicly registered. The registration requirement does not apply to patent and trade-mark agreements, restrictive exchange of unpatented technology, legally approved rationalization schemes, various kinds of vertical agreements between single buyers and sellers, or agreements limited to export or overseas trade. Export agreements, however, must be reported confidentially to the Board of Trade, may be referred to a Monopolies Commission for investigation, and, if reported to be contrary to the public interest, may be the subject of appropriate orders. No report about an export agreement had been made from 1956 until mid-1965.[13]

Registered agreements are subject to a rebuttable presumption that their restrictions are contrary to the public interest. When they are brought before a special court by the Registrar, the restrictions will be invalidated unless the participants show that they are reasonably necessary to furnish one or more benefits specified in the law and that the benefits outweigh the detrimental effects of restriction. The benefits consist of (a) protection of users or their property against physical injury; (b) provision of specific and substantial benefits to users; (c) counteraction of measures by a non-participant designed to prevent competition; (d) negotiation of fair terms with a monopolist or a dominant combination; (e) prevention of serious and persistent adverse effects on the general level of employment in the industrial area; (f) prevention of a substantial reduction in the trade's export business; (g) supplementation of a restriction that is not contrary to the public interest. When an agreement is invalidated, the court can enjoin its continuance; but in practice, has usually accepted instead undertakings that the arrangement will cease.[14]

By August, 1963, the court had decided twenty-six contested cases. It had decided against all restrictions in eighteen instances and against all but a minor one in one instance. In three instances it had accepted major restrictions while setting aside some less important ones; and in four instances it had accepted all restrictions. When major restrictions were approved, the court thought in four instances that costs and prices were held down by the agreement, in one instance that prices were reasonable and buyers were enabled to buy conveniently, and in one instance that export trade was facilitated. By mid-1965 six more contested cases had been decided,

---

[13] Prior to 1956, when reference of matters to the Monopolies Commission was the only means of action available, some of the Commission's reports included matters relevant to such agreements.

[14] Proceedings for contempt of court are available if such an undertaking is not kept. In June, 1965, certain makers of galvanized tanks were fined a total of more than 100,000 pounds in such a proceeding. See the Times, June 22, 1965.

in three of which restrictions were condemned and in three of which substantially all of them were accepted.

Decisions in the contested cases led to abandonment of restrictions in numerous other cases. By June, 1961, the restrictions in more than fifty agreements had been terminated in uncontested judicial proceedings. In the ensuing two years about seventeen more agreements were thus ended. By the end of December, 1964, 1635 agreements had been either revised to eliminate all relevant restrictions or else terminated by the parties. In addition, 75 agreements had expired without renewal.

The law of 1956 also changed the legal status of resale price maintenance. It forbade collective action to require maintenance of resale prices or to enforce resale prices. However, it extended the legal right of a single supplier to enforce resale prices set by him: He could not only obtain an injunction against a distributor who violated a resale price contract with him, but also enforce the terms of this contract against persons who bought from the distributor with knowledge of those terms. By the spring of 1961 one proceeding against collective enforcement had resulted in an undertaking not to recommend a boycott. Several injunctions had been obtained by suppliers against price cutting retailers; but there was some evidence that sellers were reluctant to fix resale prices individually when confronted by competitors who did not do so.

After study of the operation of resale price maintenance by the Board of Trade, a law enacted in 1964 made resale price maintenance unlawful and subjected violators to public and private civil action. The prohibition did not apply to resale price recommendations nor to refusals to sell to persons using relevant goods as loss leaders. The court was authorized to grant exemptions from the prohibition where the detrimental effects of resale price maintenance were outweighed by the need to use it to preserve quality, protect health, preserve necessary services, preserve retail establishments needed by consumers, or avert long-run increase in prices. During the pendency of an application for exemption, the prohibition was inapplicable to the arrangements covered thereby; and thus many such arrangements continued to be provisionally valid.[15]

In 1965 new legislation brought large mergers under control. The Board of Trade was authorized to refer to the Monopolies Commission any merger that involved an acquisition exceeding £5 million or resulted in control of more than 30 per cent of the supply of a particular kind of goods. Orders were authorized by which a merger could be delayed until the Commission completed its report and could be forbidden if the merger was found to be inconsistent with the public interest.

---

[15] See Resale Price Act of 1964 and EMI Records Ltd. v. Morris, LR 5 RP 254.

The same law broadened the application of the Monopolies Act in other ways: The Act was made applicable to services. The power to make corrective orders was extended to authorize orders against price discrimination and other kinds of preference, orders requiring publication of price lists and forbidding deviation from them, orders otherwise regulating prices, and orders requiring divorcement, divestiture, or dissolution.[16]

Union of South Africa. A law enacted in 1955 authorizes the Board of Trade and Industries (the tariff board) to investigate monopolistic conditions when directed to do so by the Minister of Economic Affairs, and to make recommendations to him if it is not satisfied that such a condition is in the public interest. Monopolistic conditions are defined to include agreements, business practices, methods of trading, acts, omissions to act, and situations which, by directly or indirectly restricting competition, have or are calculated to have the effect of restricting output or disposal, limiting facilities for production or distribution, enhancing or maintaining prices, preventing use of the most economical means of production or distribution, preventing or retarding technical improvements or the expansion of markets, preventing or restricting entry by new producers or distributors, or preventing or retarding the adjustment of any branch of trade to changing circumstances. The act does not apply, however, to labor relations, cooperative activities by producers of unprocessed agricultural products, the activities of agricultural marketing boards under applicable laws, or rights under the patent, copyright, and trade-mark laws.

When the Board reports that a monopolistic condition is contrary to the public interest, the Minister may direct the Board to negotiate for the discontinuance of what is detrimental and may then approve the negotiated settlement. Alternatively, he may require the persons involved to terminate their objectionable agreements, practices, methods of trading, or acts. He may also require affirmative actions that he considers necessary, including the dissolution of corporations or unincorporated bodies or severance of connections among enterprises. He may also suspend relevant tariffs. Noncompliance with his orders is subject to fine or imprisonment.

Investigations, reports, and orders may be concerned with classes of agreements, practices, or trading methods. In such a case the Minister may declare such a class to be unlawful, may prohibit its continuance, and may provide for exceptions; but he must obtain approval by parliamentary resolution.

The Minister's decisions can be appealed to a special court and, on questions of law, to the Supreme Court.

In practice, investigations have been concerned not with isolated restric-

---

[16] Monopolies and Mergers Act, 1965.

tions but with whole industries. Only one or two have been undertaken at a time. In making them, the Board has vacillated between two views of the public interest. Its first and fourth reports treated concerted restrictions as objectionable in principle because they reduced competition, impaired business freedom, and thus necessarily reduced efficiency. Its second and third reports, however, accepted the possibility of public benefit from restrictive agreement, and found in the restrictions before it such benefits as avoidance of price wars, preservation of domestic producers, price stability, financial stability, and effective competition in quality and technology.

INDEX

Preface to Index

Since the principal purpose of this book is comparative discussion of types of restriction and ways of coping with them, this index has been focussed accordingly. With commodities indexed in *Trade Regulations Overseas*, from which most of this book's discussion of the operation of the national laws is derived, commodities are not here indexed. Important cases and official bodies indexed in the previous book, are indexed here only for the international communities, which were not covered in that book. The seventeen countries whose laws are analyzed in the first part of this book, each of which is separately discussed in the appendices, are not indexed because a listing of the references to them would be too voluminous to be useful. The other countries mentioned in the text are indexed.

Index